ZAGAT
2020

New York City
Restaurants

New York City
Restaurants

Special 40th Anniversary Edition

Editors
Nell Potter, John Rambow, and Hillary Reinsberg

Coordinator
Katie Cohen

About Zagat

Founded in 1979 in New York City, Zagat is now celebrating its 40th year as a trusted resource for restaurant goers. Since its inception, Zagat has been for diners, by diners.

The reviews in this guide are based on feedback from diners who completed this year's Zagat Survey. The ratings reflect the average scores for each restaurant, while the reviews are written using quotes and sentiments from diners' comments.

In 2018, Zagat was acquired by The Infatuation, an editorially driven restaurant-discovery platform with a presence in cities across the U.S. and London. From an editorial perspective, the brands will continue to operate independent of each other – while The Infatuation's reviews are written by its staff writers, Zagat's reviews will continue to be informed by a community of avid diners. The Zagat team looks forward to preserving, developing, and growing this iconic brand for many years to come.

Acknowledgments

First and foremost, we thank the thousands of people who contributed ratings and reviews – they are the real authors of this guide. We also thank Nina and Tim Zagat, Pam Krauss, Kyle Zolner, Jennifer DePrima, Meg Alcazar, Jess Bender, Erinn Blicher, Simon Butler, Trevor Hagstrom, Melissa Klurman, Diane Mehta, Maggie Rosenberg, Troy Segal, and Mark Sullivan.

Published by
The Infatuation Inc.
424 Broadway 5th Floor
New York, NY 10013
feedback@zagat.com

© 2019 The Infatuation Inc.
ISBN 978-0-578-48361-0
Printed in the United States of America

Zagat is a registered trademark of The Infatuation Inc.

Produced by The Artichoke Group
Composition by Merri Ann Morrell

Foreword
by Danny Meyer

Long before there was anything like an internet search engine, Instagram, or Twitter, there was Tim and Nina Zagat, and the Zagat Survey. Part encyclopedic restaurant guide for consumers and part annual report card for restaurateurs, no source was more broadly informed to answer the question: "Where should we eat tonight?"

New Yorkers trust the Zagat guide because the results don't just come from one critic's perspective, but rather from thousands of meals experienced by local restaurant-goers, who, as we all know, don't hold back.

The day the print guide lands in the Union Square bookstore – usually in October, when the Greenmarket is selling its last tomatoes – has always been one of my favorite days of the year. As soon as we're able to get our hands on the new survey, we voraciously dig into the statistics, trying to ascertain in which categories we've improved or lost ground. We slice and dice and compare the numbers every which way to better understand where we've advanced, and where we still need to double down.

In the early years, my biggest epiphany of all came the first time I noticed that no matter how well Union Square Cafe and Gramercy Tavern were doing in the respective categories of food, decor, and service, they were showing disproportionate success when New Yorkers were asked to name their favorite restaurants for the annual "Most Popular" list. How was it possible there could be a dozen restaurants ahead of us for food, decor, and service, and yet our restaurants were listed near the top when New Yorkers were asked to name their favorites?

That was how I realized we must have been scoring particularly well in a category that's hard to measure, but unmistakable when felt: hospitality. Our ability to serve excellent food with graceful service in a beautiful room – while no doubt essential – did not seem to move the marker on "favorite" as much as the more intangible quality of how our thoughtful staff members were able to make guests feel.

I credit the Zagat Survey with not only fueling my passion for dining out, but also informing a powerful philosophy that I would bring to every subsequent business we've opened. The difference between being "best" and "favorite" almost always comes down to hospitality.

One unsung truth about the history of Zagat – from the early years before there were too many review sites and critical takes to count – is that the brand has been among our industry's staunchest cheerleaders. Zagat first planted the seed for New York Restaurant Week, which provided CPR to our business community when we were facing a near-crippling recession in 1992. And it was largely Zagat that inspired the New York City restaurant industry to start thinking seriously about online reservations in the late '90s (where would we be without those!?).

Zagat doesn't just tell food lovers where to eat; it has also inspired an entire industry to continuously advance our profession and to keep reaching higher in the most competitive city in the world. As we continue to transform the restaurant-going experience, so too will Zagat, and I have no doubt we have a lot to look forward to over the next 40 years.

Danny Meyer

CEO of Union Square Hospitality Group;
Founder of Shake Shack

Contents

ZAGAT
Through the Decades

In the restaurant world, few entities last a decade. Even fewer last several decades. But Zagat has done just that. For 40 years now, Zagat has been publishing restaurant guides that reflect the opinions of the world's most passionate diners.

Over these four decades, New York City's restaurant scene has changed in countless ways. And all those changes – from big openings and closings, to the rise of new celebrity chefs, to cuisines rethought or introduced to the city for the first time – can be tracked through the annual Zagat books.

First and foremost, this book will help you discover restaurants all over New York City – old and new alike. But in honor of this special anniversary we're also taking the opportunity to explore the New York restaurant scene through the lens of 40 years of Zagat Surveys.

1980s

The story of the Zagat Survey in New York City begins in 1979, with Tim and Nina Zagat at a wine tasting dinner, when the topic of the city's restaurant critics – and the group's dissatisfaction with them – became a point of conversation. Tim and Nina were corporate lawyers who had dabbled with the idea of restaurant guides when they lived in Paris some years prior, creating what they called the "Guide des Guides," an aggregation of the scores and notes from several restaurant guides. But here in New York, the idea was different – rather than poll the existing restaurant guides, the Zagats decided to poll restaurant-goers themselves. And so the Zagat Survey was born.

For the first survey, 200 people rated 120 restaurants. Year by year, those numbers doubled. By 1982, the book was published and for sale, and by the mid-'80s, Zagat was a go-to resource for savvy diners across the city.

Those savvy diners were eating at new restaurants both uptown and down. Starting in 1984, NoHo's Indochine drew celebrities from Madonna to Basquiat (even if no one thought the food was that good). In 1985, the Meatpacking District (when it was really still a place where meat was packed) saw the opening of Florent, the legendary 24-hour bistro/diner that was for anyone and everyone. In October of that same year, Union Square Cafe made its debut, while 1986 brought the city Le Bernardin, which has sat high on Zagat's Top Food list for most years since.

1987

Florent

19 | 14 | 14 | $20

69 Gansevoort St.
(bet. Washington & Greenwich Sts.)

A "hot spot"; for "late evening theater" head down to this former coffee shop metamorphized into a trendy French bistro; thanks to good values and an "in" crowd, after 10 PM Florent often resembles "the IRT in rush hour"; for a quieter and more relaxed meal, come early.

1988

Indochine

18 | 18 | 15 | $35

430 Lafayette St. (bet. 4th St. & Astor Pl.)

This upscale Vietnamese attracts celebrities and can be fun, but approach it without illusions – "it's a good place to watch others eat while you wait for your table"; "order only appetizers, they're better than the entrees"; "small portions" lead people to ask "did we eat yet?"

1989

Union Square Cafe

22 | 19 | 20 | $42

21 E 16th St. (bet. Union Square & 5th Ave.)

"Excellent and always improving," this stylish, bustling cafe under the aegis of wunderkind owner Danny Meyer has developed into an "all around delight"; raves go to the "creative American cookery" and "divine wine list"; despite the occasional slip, service is "knowledgeable" and "caring," and the setting is "attractive" and "comfortable"; the arrival of Michael Romano, former head chef of La Caravelle, adds an extra exciting dimension to an already exciting restaurant.

1989

Le Bernardin

27 | 26 | 25 | $69

155 W 51st St. (bet. 6th & 7th Aves.)

This outstanding French seafood specialist, the product of sister-brother team Maguy and Gilbert LeCoze, serves "better fish than you knew existed" in a maximally sumptuous setting; the menu is a veritable "seafood symphony"; desserts are also highly praised; yes, there are a few complaints (sometimes "haughty" service, an overpriced wine list, no non-seafood options), but even doubters concede it's "one of the greats."

1990s

The 1990s in New York City started with a recession and ended in a boom, and the city's restaurant scene reflected that. "Besides offering unmatched quality and breadth, New York has found the keys to the '90s – value," reads the introduction to the 1994 Zagat Survey. That edition saw a 7 percent decline in the cost of a meal, which was attributed to trends like more casual restaurants, more value-driven prix fixe options, and more family-style food, as well as a drop in labor costs because of the recession.

Along with those trends, the decade saw some dips in the overall popularity of high-end, European-style fine-dining standbys. In the 1995 book, Lutèce – which had been Zagat's most popular restaurant from 1983 to 1989, fell to 8th place. By 1999, it had dipped to 30th. The middle of the decade saw the openings of Downtown favorites like Nobu and Blue Ribbon Brasserie, both of which would go on to anchor and build budding restaurant empires.

By 1996, prices began to trend upward, and in the latter half of the decade, new fine-dining favorites – like Daniel (opened '93), Gramercy Tavern (opened '94), and Jean-Georges (opened '97) – began to ascend the Most Popular list ladder. The late-'90s boom also led to a different kind of extravagant establishment: the over-the-top theme restaurant. Those who lived through the 1990s might remember such openings as the supermodel-themed Fashion Cafe (which only made it to '98) or the 33,000-square-foot Martian-inspired Mars 2112 (which somehow lasted until 2012).

1995
Blue Ribbon
22 | 17 | 17 | $33

97 Sullivan St. (bet. Prince & Spring Sts.)

"Deserving of a blue ribbon," this "tiny" SoHo Eclectic is so popular that it's "hard to turn around," besides an "excellent raw bar" there's "deeply satisfying," "creative" "comfort food" that's "priced right" and justifies the inevitable wait; it's one of the few "after-hours" "hot" spots where there's "no attitude," and so good that "other chefs hang out."

1996
Nobu
27 | 25 | 22 | $57

105 Hudson St. (Franklin St.)

The Best New Restaurant of the Year, this "extraordinary" Japanese from LA has NY diners swooning: "outstanding," "a delight," "I died and went to heaven"; with its "chic decor," "celeb-studded" crowd, "sublime sushi," and a menu full of new tastes, it's "a feast for all the senses"; the only problem is getting a dinner reservation.

1997
Daniel
27 | 25 | 25 | $69

Surrey Suite Hotel, 20 E 76th St. (bet. 5th & Madison Aves.)

Many consider Daniel Boulud "NYC's best chef," reporting that his "elegant," "innovative" French food leaves you "floating on air"; though his Upper East Side restaurant has "beautiful" decor, "gracious" service, and serious "people-watching," we still hear quibbles about "cramped" tables and high prices.

1999
Mars 2112
_ | _ | _ | E

1633 Broadway (51st St.)

An Intragalactic answer to Planet Hollywood, this Mars-themed Theater District "global food" newcomer offers a simulation spacecraft ride (BYO Dramamine), rock formation banquettes, a movie screen-sized "Mars window," game room, gift shop, and Martian-costumed staff; given the $14 million price tag to put all this together, let's hope it takes off, otherwise patrons won't be the only ones seeing red.

2000s

After a website launch in 1999, Zagat fully entered the internet era in the early 2000s. By 2003, the survey went completely digital, growing the number of responses and respondents. A 2004 book proudly advertises a Zagat subscription available on a PalmPilot. By 2005, restaurant websites were listed alongside street addresses.

The beginning of the decade, of course, was greatly affected by the September 11 attacks. Zagat played its part in rebuilding the city by rallying around Downtown restaurants. The 2002 Zagat Book had a "Stronger Than Ever" logo on its front cover, and featured a call for diners to support the restaurants of TriBeCa and the Financial District as they reopened.

To get a sense of the mid-decade, it's worth looking to 2004. Shake Shack made its transition from hot dog cart to permanent burger stand in Madison Square Park. That same year, Lutèce finally closed after four decades in business. And the first Momofuku restaurant opened. So did Per Se.

That tells a pretty good story of NYC dining in the 2000s: on the whole, restaurants, particularly those in neighborhoods like the East Village, were becoming more casual, more oriented toward shared plates, and more diverse. But at the same time, the decade brought us the Time Warner Center and its astronomically priced restaurants like Masa.

What else happened in the 2000s? Mayor Bloomberg's smoking ban went into effect, effectively ridding NYC restaurants of cigarettes in one fell swoop. And a lot of restaurants opened in the Meatpacking District, many of which were big and flashy. Remember La Bottega, Matsuri, and Spice Market?

2006
Per Se
28| 27| 28| $201|

Time Warner Ctr., 10 Columbus Circle, 4th Fl. (60th St. at B'way)

Thomas Keller's year-old "shrine to food" has acolytes "swooning" over his French-New American tasting menus, a "parade of culinary wizardry" providing "hours of bliss"; kudos also go to the "seamless," "choreographed" service (No. 1 in this survey) and Adam Tihany's design that's "elegance stripped to its essentials," capped by "stunning" Central Park and Columbus Circle views; sure, the price is a "shocker," but "worth every C-note" for a "temporary pass to heaven"; appropriately, getting a reservation takes "divine intervention."

2006
Masa
27| 23| 25| $356|

Time Warner Ctr., 10 Columbus Circle, 4th Fl. (60th St. at B'way)

Like a "trip to the moon" for "sushi worshipers," this Time Warner Center Japanese (renowned as "NY's most expensive restaurant") is overseen by star chef Masayoshi Takayama, who offers exquisite, "Tokyo"-worthy, kaiseki-style dinners, best taken at the counter "to get the full show"; some find the massive prices hard to swallow (it's a $350 prix fixe before drink, tax, and tip), but most feel it's more than "worth every Benjamin."

2007
Spice Market
22| 26| 19| $57|

403 W 13th St. (9th Ave.)

"Hanging lanterns and diaphanous curtains" play a role in the "spectacular," "exotic," "transporting" decor scheme at Jean-Georges Vongerichten's "spicy hot" SE Asian duplex in the Meatpacking District that serves "elevated" Thai-Malay-Vietnamese street food to a "pretty-people" clientele; portions may be as "skimpy" as the staff's "pajama"-like uniforms, but most agree that the prices, while "not cheap," represent a "relative bargain" for a fab "JGV" venture; N.B. the private rooms downstairs are spicy too.

2008
Momofuku Noodle Bar
24| 13| 16| $27|

163 First Ave. (bet. 10th & 11th Sts.)

David Chang's "addictive" noodle soups and pork buns keep the "hordes" coming to this "affordable" Japanese-inspired East Villager, a "necessary foodie experience" with waits "no matter when you go"; sure, it's "absurdly small" and service can be "harried," but it "couldn't be more delicious."

2010s

In 2011, the Zagat brand was sold to a company some readers may be familiar with: Google. At Google, Zagat further expanded its global digital reach, while continuing to supply readers with the annual Burgundy Bible.

The city's dining scene transformed too, in countless ways. For one, Brooklyn became home to many of the decade's most exciting restaurant openings. That includes neighborhood favorites-turned-destinations like Emily and Olmsted, as well as cutting-edge tasting menu spots like Blanca, which is located in a hidden room behind East Williamsburg pizza spot Roberta's.

The decade also saw a rise in high-end yet trendy Italian restaurants, with examples like Carbone, Lilia, and Charlie Bird. Pricey omakase sushi restaurants also arrived quickly, with openings that included Sushi Nakazawa, Shuko, Sushi Zo, and a lengthy list of others. Meanwhile, restaurants like Cosme, Claro, and Casa Enrique finally made New York City a place to eat some of the country's best Mexican food. New restaurants like Atomix, Atoboy, Oiji, Cote, and several others also made Korean food one of the most exciting cuisines to experience in New York City.

From an industry perspective, the city began its letter-grade health rating system, and a number of restaurant groups experimented with no-tipping policies, some of which were later abandoned. The rise of Instagram and new reservation platforms also changed the dining scene in countless ways.

In 2018, Zagat was acquired by The Infatuation, a restaurant-discovery and review platform founded in New York City 30 years after Zagat but with many of the same values. This guide is the first published under this new ownership. Looking forward, our team is incredibly excited to both carry on and expand the Zagat legacy. Here's to the next 40 years.

2014
Blanca

29 | 21 | 27 | $254

261 Moore St. (Bogart St.)

The "spectacular" fine-dining adjunct of Bushwick darling Roberta's, this "must-try" (if you can get in) New American in spare, "cool" loft digs delivers an "amazing experience" with its lavish tasting menu, offered at a single seating nightly to "only 12 lucky diners"; chef Carlo Mirachi's "exquisite" "morsels" arrive artfully plated on high-end china, appropriate to the $195 prix fixe-only price tag – the few who've tried it say this is "as good as it gets."

2015
Carbone

24 | 22 | 23 | $106

181 Thompson St. (bet. Bleecker & Houston Sts.)

An "homage" to "traditional Italian American cuisine," this "lively" Village "hit" from the Torrisi team turns out "huge portions" of "outstanding" dishes (including a "divine veal parm") for a beyond-"hefty" price; the mood is "Rat Pack," the soundtrack classic "Motown," and the "maroon-tuxedoed waiters" recall the days when "service came first" – no wonder it's "nearly impossible" to get reservations, but "so worth trying."

2016
Sushi Nakazawa

27 | 23 | 27 | $184

23 Commerce St. (bet. Bedford St. & 7th Ave. S)

"Sushi nirvana" awaits at this West Village Japanese "epiphany" from chef Daisuke Nakazawa (a protégé of "famous mentor" Jiro Ono), which "leaves you in awe" with "artfully crafted" omakase meals served by a "polished" team; even though it's "not cheap" (menus start at $120), getting a rezzie is a challenge both in the dining room and overlooking "the action" at the bar.

2016
Cosme

25 | 23 | 23 | $83

35 E 21st St. (bet. B'way & Park Ave. S)

"Renowned" chef Enrique Olvera shows how "mind-blowingly delicious" contemporary Mexican cooking can be at this "much-hyped" Flatiron locale; the "sleek," "cavernous" space reads either "sexy" or "boring" and the bill "adds up quickly," but it's still one of the most "impossible reservations" to get.

About This Survey

This year marks the 40th anniversary of the Zagat brand, and we couldn't think of a better way to honor the brand's history than to revive the print guide. In addition to bringing back the book, we are reverting to the original 30-point rating scale Zagat is best known for.

Restaurants receive not one, but three scores out of 30 points. We understand users have different needs on different occasions, making a variety of factors important to their decisions. By rating restaurants on three key aspects – food, decor, and service – Zagat aims to allow users to easily make a decision based on their individual needs.

Approximately 12,000 diners participated in this year's Zagat Survey, submitting a total of more than 200,000 ratings and reviews. Diners' comments were fact-checked and then combined to create a singular review reflecting overall sentiment about a restaurant. This book contains reviews and ratings for more than 1,400 restaurants across all five of NYC's boroughs. The winners of this year's survey are Le Bernardin (Most Popular and Top Food), Majorelle (Top Decor), and Daniel (Top Service).

Ratings & Symbols

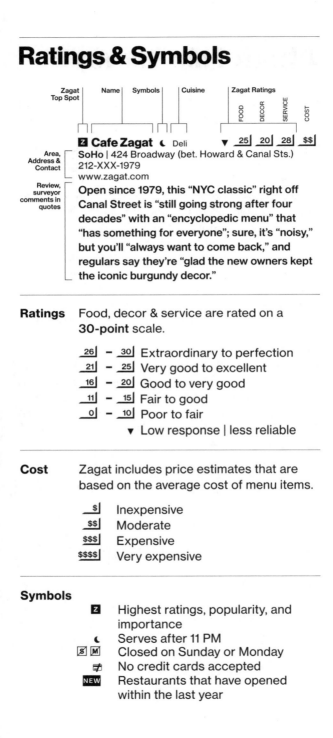

Zagat Top Spot | Name | Symbols | Cuisine | Zagat Ratings

FOOD | DECOR | SERVICE | COST

Z Cafe Zagat ☾ Deli ▼ 25 20 28 $$

Area, Address & Contact
SoHo | 424 Broadway (bet. Howard & Canal Sts.)
212-XXX-1979
www.zagat.com

Review, surveyor comments in quotes
Open since 1979, this "NYC classic" right off Canal Street is "still going strong after four decades" with an "encyclopedic menu" that "has something for everyone"; sure, it's "noisy," but you'll "always want to come back," and regulars say they're "glad the new owners kept the iconic burgundy decor."

Ratings   Food, decor & service are rated on a **30-point** scale.

26 – 30 Extraordinary to perfection
21 – 25 Very good to excellent
16 – 20 Good to very good
11 – 15 Fair to good
0 – 10 Poor to fair
▼ Low response | less reliable

Cost   Zagat includes price estimates that are based on the average cost of menu items.

$ Inexpensive
$$ Moderate
$$$ Expensive
$$$$ Very expensive

Symbols

Z Highest ratings, popularity, and importance
☾ Serves after 11 PM
S M Closed on Sunday or Monday
⌿ No credit cards accepted
NEW Restaurants that have opened within the last year

Key Newcomers

Our editors' picks among this year's arrivals. See full list at page 334.

IMPORTS
Au Cheval
Belcampo
HaSalon
Queensyard
The Zodiac Room

IMPRESSIVE PEDIGREES
Golden Diner
Hudson Yards Grill
Lamalo
Odo
Wayan
Wayla

INSTANT HITS
Crown Shy
Haenyeo
Hanon
Oxalis
Rezdôra
Takeshi

NEIGHBORHOOD STARS
The Fly
Hunky Dory
Jiang Diner
Lokanta
Montesacro Pinseria
Niche
Taladwat
Uluh

REBIRTHS
BLT Prime
Kichin
Pastis

SPINOFFS
Babs
Franks Wine Bar
Kāwi
Maison Yaki
Niche Niche
O:n
Red Hook Tavern
Shabushabu Mayumon

SPLASHY SPACES
The Fulton
Gran Tivoli
TAK Room

Most Popular

Survey takers were asked to name their five overall favorite restaurants. The 50 restaurants named most frequently are listed here in order of popularity.

1. Le Bernardin
2. Gramercy Tavern
3. Peter Luger Steak House
4. Union Square Cafe
5. Daniel
6. Eleven Madison Park
7. Marea
8. Le Coucou
9. Katz's Delicatessen
10. Cafe Boulud
11. Jean-Georges
12. La Grenouille
13. Keens Steakhouse
14. Boulud Sud
15. Balthazar
16. Estiatorio Milos
17. The Modern
18. Brasserie 8 1/2
19. Bouley at Home
20. Del Posto
21. Gabriel Kreuther
22. L'Artusi
23. Via Carota
24. Becco
25. Bar Boulud
26. Felidia
27. The River Café
28. Lincoln Ristorante
29. ABC Kitchen
30. Nougatine at Jean-Georges
31. Grand Central Oyster Bar & Restaurant
32. Lilia
33. 2nd Ave Deli
34. 4 Charles Prime Rib
35. Don Angie
36. Ai Fiori
37. 21 Club
38. Carbone
39. abcV
40. Per Se
41. Smith & Wollensky
42. Vaucluse
43. Aquagrill
44. Cafe Luxembourg
45. I Sodi
46. Loring Place
47. Barney Greengrass
48. Upland
49. Park Avenue
50. Maialino

Top Food

These 40 restaurants received the highest scores for Food rating*

29 Le Bernardin
Daniel
Bouley at Home
Sushi Nakazawa

28 Gabriel Kreuther
Decoy
Lucali
Eleven Madison Park
4 Charles Prime Rib
Via Carota
I Sodi
Hometown Bar-B-Que
Gramercy Tavern
Peter Luger Steak House
Blue Hill
L'Artusi
Jean-Georges
Momofuku Ko
Sushi Yasuda
Adda

Per Se
Don Angie
Tocqueville
Marea
La Grenouille
Cafe Boulud
The Modern
Trattoria L'incontro

27 Scalini Fedeli
Olmsted
Del Posto
Lilia
Oxomoco
Casa Enrique
Porter House Bar and Grill
Le Coucou
Pearl Oyster Bar
Amma
Uncle Boons
Estiatorio Milos

*Excluding restaurants with low voting

TOP FOOD BY CUISINE

American
29 Blanca
28 Atera
Eleven Madison Park
Gramercy Tavern
Blue Hill
Momofuku Ko
The Modern
27 Olmsted
Roberta's
Meadowsweet

Austrian/German
27 Wallsé
Zum Stammtisch

Barbecue
28 Hometown Bar-B-Que
25 Fette Sau
Ducks Eatery

Burger Joint
24 Burger Joint
23 JG Melon
Corner Bistro

Chinese
28 Decoy
26 Birds of a Feather
25 Café China
RedFarm
White Bear
China Blue
Kings County Imperial
88 Lan Zhou
Pacific Palace

Deli
26 Barney Greengrass
Russ & Daughters Cafe
Katz's Delicatessen
24 Mill Basin Deli
Brennan & Carr
Pastrami Queen
Frankel's Delicatessen
2nd Ave Deli

French
29 Le Bernardin
Daniel
Bouley at Home
28 Gabriel Kreuther
L'Atelier de Joël Robuchon
Jean-Georges
Per Se
Tocqueville
La Grenouille
Cafe Boulud

Greek
28 Bahari Estiatorio
27 Estiatorio Milos
26 Avra Madison/Avra Estiatorio
Pylos
25 Kiki's
Taverna Kyclades
Agnant
Kyma
Nerai
Periyali
Telly's Taverna

Indian

__28__ Adda
__27__ Amma
Indian Accent
Tamarind Tribeca
__26__ Rahi
__25__ Junoon

Italian

__28__ Via Carota
I Sodi
L'Artusi
Don Angie
Marea
Trattoria L'incontro
__27__ Scalini Fedeli
Del Posto
Lilia
Convivium Osteria
Al Di La Trattoria
il Buco

Japanese

__29__ Tanoshi Sushi
Sushi Nakazawa
__28__ KazuNori
Shuko
Sushi Yasuda
__27__ O Ya
Masa
Nobu
Torishin
__26__ Sushi of Gari
Sushi Yasaka
Sushi By Bou
Morimoto
Sakagura
Sushi Seki

Korean

__29__ Atomix
Jungsik
__28__ Hangawi
__27__ Atoboy
__26__ Oiji
Cote
Kang Ho Dong
Baekjeong
__25__ Danji
Thursday Kitchen
Her Name is Han

Latin American

__26__ Arepa Lady
__25__ ABC Cocina
__25__ Caracas Arepa Bar
Cabana

Mediterranean

__26__ Boulud Sud
__25__ Taboon
Limani
Ilili
__24__ Little Owl
Gato
Balaboosta
__23__ Shuka
Bustan
Barbounia

Mexican

27 Oxomoco
Casa Enrique
La Contenta
Los Tacos No.1
26 Claro
Cosme
25 Los Mariscos
24 Barrio Chino
Chavela's
Atla
El Parador Cafe

Middle Eastern

27 Miss Ada
Tanoreen
26 Moustache
25 Almayass
Miznon
Naya
24 Yemen Café
Miriam
Nur
Cafe Mogador

Peruvian

26 Llama Inn
23 Pio Pio

Pizza

28 Lucali
27 Juliana's
Prince Street Pizza
Roberta's
26 Manetta's Ristorante
Rubirosa
Emmy Squared
Totonno's Pizzeria
Emmy Squared

Emily
Joe & Pat's
Di Fara Pizza
San Matteo Pizza
Scarr's Pizza
Paulie Gee's

Ramen

26 Okonomi / Yuji Ramen
25 Ippudo
Momosan Ramen
Chuko Ramen
24 Momofuku Noodle Bar
Jin Ramen
Hide-Chan Ramen

Scandinavian

27 Aquavit
26 Agern

Seafood

28 Chef's Table at Brooklyn Fare
27 Astoria Seafood
Pearl Oyster Bar
26 Maison Premiere
The Sea Fire Grill
Aquagrill

Southern

26 Melba's
25 Bobwhite Counter
24 Root & Bone
Queens Comfort
23 Sweet Chick
Jacob's Pickles
Pies 'n' Thighs
Amy Ruth's

Spanish

27 La Vara
Salinas
26 Casa Mono
Txikito
25 Bar Jamon
El Quinto Pino
24 Sevilla
Beso
El Pote Español
El Porrón

Steakhouse

28 4 Charles Prime Rib
Peter Luger
27 Porter House
St. Anselm
Benjamin Steakhouse
Keens Steakhouse
26 Christos Steak House
Wolfgang's
Cote
Wollensky's Grill
Sparks Steak House
Club A Steakhouse

Taiwanese

27 Win Son
23 886
Ho Foods

Thai

27 Uncle Boons
SriPraPhai
26 Pure Thai Cookhouse
Ugly Baby
Ayada Thai
24 Somtum Der
Up Thai

Vegan/Vegetarian

26 Avant Garden
abcV
25 Superiority Burger
24 Nix
Dirt Candy
22 Blossom
Candle Café/
Candle 79

Vietnamese

25 Hanoi House
24 Banh Mi Saigon
Di An Di
23 Indochine
Nha Trang One
Vietnaam
Madame Vo
Bricolage

TOP FOOD BY LOCATION

MANHATTAN
Battery Park City
25 Del Frisco's Grille
23 Gigino
21 Blue Smoke

Chelsea
28 L'Atelier de Joël
   Robuchon
27 Del Posto
   Los Tacos No.1
   Salinas
26 Morimoto
   Sushi Seki
   Txikito
   Da Umberto
   Ayada Thai

Chinatown
25 88 Lan Zhou
24 Peking Duck House
   Wo Hop
   Hwa Yuan Szechuan
23 Oriental Garden
   456 Shanghai Cuisine
   Joe's Shanghai
   Xi'an Famous Foods
   Great NY Noodletown
   Nom Wah Tea Parlor

East 30s
26 Kang Ho Dong
   Baekjeong
25 Her Name is Han

East 40s
28 Sushi Yasuda
27 Benjamin Steakhouse
   Benjamin Prime
26 Avra Estiatorio
   Kurumazushi
   Wolfgang's
   Sakagura
   The Sea Fire Grill
   Wollensky's Grill
   Hatsuhana
   Sparks Steak House
   Agern

East 50s
28 La Grenouille
27 Amma
   Aquavit
26 Wolfgang's
   Valbella
   Felidia
   Club A Steakhouse
25 BLT Steak
   The Grill

East 60s
29 Daniel
27 Majorelle
26 Avra Madison
   Sushi Seki
   Ravagh Persian Grill
   Il Mulino New York
25 JoJo
   Vaucluse
   Tiella

East 70s
29 Tanoshi Sushi
28 Cafe Boulud
26 Sushi of Gari
Caravaggio

East 80s
27 The Simone
26 San Matteo Pizza
Erminia
25 Elio's
Antonucci Cafe
Sistina

East 90s
26 Russ & Daughters
Cafe
Paola's
24 Sfoglia
Table d'Hôte
23 Pascalou
Earl's Beer and
Cheese

East Harlem
28 Mountain Bird
23 Rao's

East Village
28 Momofuku Ko
26 Oiji
Emmy Squared
Joe & Pat's
Tuome
Ravagh Persian Grill
Momofuku Ssäm Bar

Financial District
27 Nobu Downtown
25 The Capital Grille
Delmonico's
24 Morton's
Cipriani Club 55
Kesté Fulton
Manhatta

Flatiron
29 Bouley at Home
28 Eleven Madison Park
Gramercy Tavern
Tocqueville
26 Sushi By Bou
Manzo
Aldea
Cote
Cosme
abcV

Gramercy Park
26 Union Square Cafe
Maialino
Casa Mono
25 Novitá
Bar Jamon

Greenwich Village
28 Blue Hill
Shuko
26 Lupa Osteria Romana
Babbo
Carbone
Il Mulino New York
25 Il Cantinori

Harlem

26 Sottocasa
Melba's
25 Clay
24 Lido

Hudson Square

26 King
24 Café Altro Paradiso
23 Houseman

Little Italy

25 Da Nico Ristorante
24 Il Cortile
Banh Mi Saigon
Nyonya

Lower East Side

28 Spicy Village
Le French Diner
27 Cervo's
La Contenta
26 Russ & Daughters
Cafe
Gaia Italian Cafe
Scarr's Pizza
Wildair
Katz's Delicatessen

Meatpacking District

23 Catch NYC
22 STK Downtown

Morningside Heights

25 Pisticci
24 Jin Ramen

Murray Hill

28 Hangawi
27 O Ya
26 Wolfgang's
25 Café China
Riverpark
Le Parisien Bistrot
Momosan Ramen
Upland

NoHo

27 il Buco
26 Bohemian
BondST
25 il Buco Alimentari

NoLita

27 Uncle Boons
Prince Street Pizza
26 Estela
Rubirosa

NoMad

29 Atomix
28 KazuNori
27 Atoboy

SoHo

27 Le Coucou
Coco Pazzo
26 Raoul's
Aquagrill

South Street Seaport

24 Acqua
10 Corso Como

TriBeCa

29 Jungsik
28 Atera
27 Scalini Fedeli
Tamarind Tribeca
26 Sushi of Gari

Union Square

26 15 East
23 Laut
TsuruTonTan Udon

Washington Heights

23 Malecon

West 30s

28 Chef's Table at
Brooklyn Fare
27 Estiatorio Milos
Keens Steakhouse
26 Ai Fiori

West 40s

28 Gabriel Kreuther
27 Los Tacos No.1
26 Sushi of Gari 46
Sushi By Bou
Wolfgang's
Sushi Seki
Aureole

West 50s

29 Le Bernardin
28 Per Se
Marea
The Modern

27 Porter House
Estiatorio Milos
Indian Accent
Nobu Fifty Seven

West 60s

28 Jean-Georges
27 Nougatine
26 Boulud Sud
25 Lincoln Ristorante
24 Bar Boulud

West 70s

26 Gari Columbus
Sushi Yasaka
25 RedFarm

West 80s

26 Barney Greengrass
24 Elea
Celeste
Jin Ramen
La Mirabelle
Momoya

West 90s

25 Gennaro
24 Awadh
23 Pio Pio
Malecon

West 100s

25 Mama's Too
Sal and Carmine
23 Thai Market
Awash Ethiopian

West Village
29 Sushi Nakazawa
28 Decoy
    4 Charles Prime Rib
    Via Carota
    I Sodi
    L'Artusi
    Don Angie

BROOKLYN
Bath Beach
24 Nyonya

Bay Ridge
27 Tanoreen
26 Elia
25 Gino's

Bedford-Stuyvesant
26 Hart's
25 Ali's Trinidad Roti
    Shop
    Peaches Hot House

Boerum Hill
26 Ki Sushi
    Sottocasa
25 Rucola

Brooklyn Heights
26 Noodle Pudding
25 Henry's End
    Queen

Bushwick
29 Blanca
28 Faro
27 Roberta's

Carroll Gardens
28 Lucali
26 Ugly Baby
25 Frankies 457 Spuntino
    Buttermilk Channel

Clinton Hill
26 The Finch
    Emily
    Locanda Vini & Olii
23 Speedy Romeo

Cobble Hill
27 La Vara
24 Hibino
23 Joya
    Awash Ethiopian

Coney Island
26 Totonno's Pizzeria
23 Grimaldi's

Crown Heights
26 Glady's
25 Barboncino Pizza
24 Chavela's

Ditmas Park
23 Mimi's Hummus
22 The Farm on Adderley

Dumbo
27 Juliana's
26 The River Café
23 Grimaldi's

Fort Greene
27 Miss Ada
25 LaRina Pastificio

22 Habana Outpost
Walter's

Gowanus
26 Claro
25 Baba's Pierogies

Gravesend
25 L&B Spumoni

Greenpoint
27 Oxomoco
26 Chez Ma Tante
Paulie Gee's
25 Bernie's
24 Di An Di
Frankel's Delicatessen

Midwood
26 Di Fara Pizza

Park Slope
27 Convivium Osteria
Al Di La Trattoria
26 Ki Sushi
Sushi Katsuei

Prospect Heights
27 Olmsted
25 Chuko Ramen
23 MeMe's Diner
Sweet Chick
Morgan's Barbecue
James

Red Hook
28 Hometown Bar-B-Que
25 The Good Fork

Sheepshead Bay
24 Brennan & Carr
Randazzo's Clam Bar

Sunset Park
26 East Harbor Seafood
25 Pacific Palace

Williamsburg
28 Peter Luger
Xixa
27 Lilia
St. Anselm
Traif
Win Son
Meadowsweet

BRONX
Arthur Avenue/Belmont
26 Tra Di Noi
Enzo's
25 Roberto's

City Island
24 Artie's
The Original Crab
Shanty

Morris Park
26 Enzo's

QUEENS
Astoria
28 Bahari Estiatorio
Trattoria L'incontro
26 Christos Steak House

Bayside
25 Taverna Kyclades
23 BCD Tofu House

Corona
25 Park Side

Elmhurst
26 Ayada Thai

Flushing
25 White Bear
24 Dumpling Galaxy
23 Joe's Shanghai
Xi'an Famous Foods
Totto Ramen

Forest Hills
24 Nick's Pizza
Alberto
Cabana

Glendale
27 Zum Stammtisch

Howard Beach
25 New Park Pizza

Jackson Heights
26 Arepa Lady
23 Pio Pio

Long Island City
28 Adda
27 Astoria Seafood
Casa Enrique
26 Manetta's Ristorante

Rockaway Park
24 Caracas Arepa Bar

South Ozone Park
26 Don Peppe

Woodside
27 SriPraPhai

STATEN ISLAND
Castleton Corners
26 Joe & Pat's

Dongan Hills
25 Trattoria Romana

Elm Park
25 Denino's Pizzeria

Old Town
26 Bocelli Ristorante

St. George
25 Enoteca Maria
24 Beso

TOP FOOD BY OCCASIONS AND SITUATIONS

BREAKFAST
__28__| Cafe Boulud
__27__| Le Coucou
__26__| Maialino
   Barney Greengrass
   Russ & Daughters
    Cafe
   Buvette
   abcV

BRUNCH
__27__| Olmsted
   Meadowsweet
__26__| Chez Ma Tante
   Estela
   Union Square Cafe

BUSINESS DINING
__29__| Le Bernardin
   Daniel
   Sushi Nakazawa
__28__| Gramercy Tavern
   Jean-Georges
   Marea
   Cafe Boulud

BYO
__29__| Tanoshi
__28__| Lucali
   Spicy Village
__27__| Astoria Seafood
__26__| Di Fara Pizza
   Gaia Italian Cafe

DINING SOLO
__28__| KazuNori
   Spicy Village
   Sushi Azabu
__27__| Torishin

FINE DINING
__29__| Le Bernardin
   Blanca
   Atomix
   Daniel
   Jungsik
   Bouley at Home
   Sushi Nakazawa
   Tempura Matsui
   Kappo Masa

HEALTHY
__28__| Hangawi
__27__| Kajitsu
__26__| abcV
   Avant Garden
   Vatan

LATE NIGHT DINING
__26__| The Commodore
   Sushi Seki
   Katz's Delicatessen
   Kang Ho Dong
    Baekjeong
__25__| Blue Ribbon Brasserie
   Joe's Pizza

OLD NY VIBE

28 4 Charles Prime Rib

Peter Luger Steak
House

27 Keens Steakhouse

26 Raoul's

Barney Greengrass

Katz's Delicatessen

SMALL PLATES

27 La Vara

Atoboy

Salinas

26 Estela

Casa Mono

Txikito

Wildair

The Four Horsemen

VIEWS

28 Per Se

The Modern

26 The River Café

25 Riverpark

24 Maiella

Manhatta

22 Celestine

Gaonnuri

WINE BARS

27 Convivium Osteria

26 Estela

Txikito

Wildair

The Four Horsemen

25 Bar Jamon

Top Decor

These 20 restaurants received the highest scores for Decor rating*

29 Majorelle
Daniel
Le Bernardin
28 La Grenouille
The River Café
Manhatta
Asiate
Eleven Madison Park
Per Se
The Grill

The Polo Bar
Le Coucou
Del Posto
27 Gabriel Kreuther
Buddakan
Jean-Georges
Morimoto
La Mercerie
The Modern
The Leopard at des Artistes

Top Service

These 20 restaurants received the highest scores for Service rating*

29 Daniel
Le Bernardin
Eleven Madison Park
28 Gabriel Kreuther
Sushi Nakazawa
Majorelle
Scalini Fedeli
La Grenouille
Bouley at Home
Gramercy Tavern

Jean-Georges
27 Tocqueville
4 Charles Prime Rib
Per Se
Blue Hill
The Simone
Le Coucou
The Modern
Tamarind Tribeca
Del Posto

*Excluding restaurants with low voting

RESTAURANT DIRECTORY

A La Turka Turkish

21 | 15 | 19 | $$

East 70s | 1417 2nd Ave. (74th St.)
212-744-2424 | alaturkany.com

At this UES standby, "consistent" Turkish meals ("everything tastes fresh and is carefully prepared") are the draw; providing a "different" kind of neighborhood experience, there is also live dance or music a few days a week; diners do warn that the "no-frills" space with "fading" decor can get "noisy" and "crowded," and that service can be "slow."

A Summer Day Cafe American

17 | 19 | 18 | $$

TriBeCa | 109 W Broadway (bet. Duane & Reade Sts.)
646-882-0420 | summerdaynyc.com

"Good avocado toast and salads" and large portions define this TriBeCa standby, which diners say "lives up to its name" with its cocktails (including tempting wine slushies) and a "basic but pleasant menu with healthy choices"; beware falling into the "millennial brunch trap" and you'll be fine; the glass-fronted patio-style room decorated with floral wallpaper and greenery guarantees a "beachy, chill vibe" at other times.

☑ ABC Cocina Latin American

25 | 25 | 22 | $$$

Flatiron | 38 E 19th St. (bet. B'way & Park Ave. S)
212-475-5829 | abchome.com/dine

Jean-Georges Vongerichten's "culinary inventiveness" is on display at this "stylish" Flatiron spot in ABC Carpet & Home, which offers "a superb array of tapas" and other "inspirational" pan-Latin bites in a "visually intriguing atmosphere" that's full of "upbeat energy"; of course, it's "not cheap," and the "loud" digs irk some, but "excellent service" and a "vibrant scene" help even things out – drop-ins can always sample the "amazing cocktails" while "sitting at the bar."

☑ ABC Kitchen American

25 | 24 | 23 | $$$

Flatiron | 35 E 18th St. (bet. B'way & Park Ave. S)
212-475-5829 | abchome.com/dine

There is "such love for vegetables" at Jean-Georges's "Flat-iron institution," which elevates "locavore cooking" to a "haute scale" in a "rustic-chic" environment, with "professional servers who seem to love what they do"; even though it's "a bit loud and overcrowded," and the "bill is large," it's always "worth it in the end" to "come at different times of year and see how the menu changes" with the seasons.

☑ abcV Vegan/Vegetarian

26 | 25 | 23 | $$$

Flatiron | 38 E 19th St. (bet. B'way & Park Ave. S)
212-475-5829 | abchome.com/dine

"Who knew vegetables could be so voluptuous?" ask fans of Jean-Georges Vongerichten's "veggie mecca," which draws even the most "diehard carnivores" for "seasonal," "deliciously prepared," "inventive" dishes in which plants are the "proud stars"; the sleek, "minimalist" space is inside the "Instawor-thy" ABC Carpet & Home, and although service can feel "a bit rushed and busy," it's still "top notch" and "worth visiting."

Abigael's On Broadway American
19 | 15 | 20 | $$$

West 30s | 1407 Broadway (bet. 38th & 39th Sts.)
212-575-1407 | abigaels.com

This bilevel kosher-plex near the theaters in the West 30s serves fusion sushi on one floor and "upscale" glatt steak below; although the service is "friendly" and the prices are "moderate" for the "white tablecloth" interior, it's also a bit "down at the heels," and the "bizarre" or at least eclectic juxtaposition of cuisines can seem confusing; on the other hand, the menu "won't bankrupt" you and works well for groups; N.B. closed Friday and Saturday.

AbuQir Seafood
▼ 28 | 12 | 23 | $$

Astoria | 24-19 Steinway St.
(bet. Astoria Blvd. S & 25th Ave.) | Queens
718-274-3474 | abuqirseafoodqueens.com

"You point to your fish and they make it how you want" at this Astoria storefront, named for an Alexandrian fishing village and famed for the "freshest" and most "fabulously delicious" plates "perfectly matched" with sides of baba ghanoush, "basic" but "delicious" green salad, and rice served by "welcoming" staff; there's no alcohol and few frills, but that doesn't stop fans lining up to experience the "simply amazing" flavors.

Aburiya Kinnosuke Japanese
– | – | – | $$$

East 40s | 213 E 45th St. (bet. 2nd & 3rd Aves.)
aburiyakinnosuke.com

Opened under new management in 2019 after renovations, this well-regarded izakaya in the East 40s has a new focus on top-end Wagyu beef imported from Japan; though best known for the traditional Japanese dishes that emerge from its robata (charcoal grill), there is also a limited menu of sushi and sashimi.

Acme American
19 | 21 | 18 | $$$

NoHo | 9 Great Jones St. (Lafayette St.)
212-203-2121 | acmenyc.com

This "bustling," "fun" spot in NoHo offers "solid" American fare and "relaxed service" and also "comes with a nightclub included in the basement" – with a notoriously tough door most nights; the less party-oriented who come on the early side say it's "good for dining before the Public Theater."

Acqua Restaurant and
24 | 22 | 24 | $$

Wine Bar Italian
South Street Seaport | 21 Peck Slip (Water St.)
212-349-4433 | acquarestaurantnyc.com

Like "dining in someone's home in Southern Italy," this "neighborhood" spot right on South Street Seaport's Peck Slip serves "well-prepared" fare (including "excellent" homemade pastas) and an extensive list of well-chosen wines (the "quartinos especially") in a "comfy setting" of "exposed brickwork" and wooden floors; a "low-key atmosphere," "welcoming" servers, and "reasonable prices" are pluses, too, particularly when coupled with the chance to eat outdoors.

🄩 Adda Indian   28 | 19 | 23 | $$|

Long Island City | 31-31 Thompson Ave.
(bet. 31st St. & Qns. Blvd.) | Queens
718-433-3888 | addanyc.com
Sure, the hype has been "unbelievable," but this "inventive" and
"cozy" LIC Indian with "palpable" energy lives up to it, featuring
a short menu of "rich, flavorsome" dishes with "perfect spice
levels"; "if you manage to squeeze yourself in you will not be
disappointed, say its many boosters: "it's one of the few places
that give you hope that an affordable, uniquely intentioned, and
highly respected food experience can still be had in NYC."

Adrienne's Pizzabar Italian/Pizza   23 | 15 | 17 | $$|

Financial District | 54 Stone St. (Hanover Sq.)
212-248-3838 | adriennespizza.com
Made of "blistered, chewy crust" and "fresh, tasty toppings,"
the "killer pizza" pies (no slices) keep 'em coming to this "low-
key" Italian spot known for its square "Grandma-style" variety
(the classic rounds are available too); "service is pretty spotty,"
especially when it's "crowded at lunchtime," and the interior is
"just okay," but you should go "when you can sit outdoors" on
"charming" Stone Street.

Agern Ⓢ Scandinavian   26 | 21 | 24 | $$$$|

East 40s | Grand Central Terminal, 89 E 42nd St. (Park Ave.)
646-568-4018 | agernrestaurant.com
At this "oasis" amid the "hustle and bustle" of Grand Central
Terminal you'll find the "inventive" Nordic cuisine that you'd
expect from Noma co-founder Claus Meyer, with "unexpected"
twists and "pristine" preparations, in rooms with "somber" and
typically Scandinavian surroundings; the "impeccable service"
and broad list of domestic wine, mead, cider, and non-alcoholic
cocktails all complement meals celebrating American produce
through modern Danish sensibilities.

Agnanti Greek   25 | 15 | 22 | $$|

Astoria | 19-23 Ditmars Blvd. (19th St.) | Queens
718-545-4554 | agnantimeze.com
Like a "small-town taverna" that somehow turned up in Astoria,
this "family favorite" for Greek meze comes with unrushed
service and attracts fair-weather crowds for evening dinners
on the "airy patio"; even if the "cozy" dining room is "spartan at
best" and has gotten downright "shabby" with age, it's worth
squeezing into "tight" tables that have you "packed in like sardines": you'll be rewarded with princely "whole grilled fish."

🄩 Ai Fiori Italian   26 | 26 | 26 | $$$$|

West 30s | 400 5th Ave. #2 (bet. 36th & 37th Sts.)
212-613-0660 | aifiorinyc.com
"Pasta savant" Michael White's "sophisticated spot" for upscale
Italian is inside Midtown's Langham Hotel (a "welcome surprise
in the area"); "sublime sauces," a "beautiful wine list," and
"impeccable service" add up to an experience that "never fails
to please": "always save room for dessert," and be prepared to
leave in a "food swoon."

Aita Italian   22 | 20 | 21 | $$

Clinton Hill | 132 Greene Ave. (Waverly Ave.) | Brooklyn
718-576-3584 | aitatrattoria.com

Aita Trattoria

Crown Heights | 798 Franklin Ave.
(bet. Lincoln Pl. & Eastern P'way) | Brooklyn
917-966-2670

The lasagna and other pastas served at this pair of "magical little corners" are "exceptional," and the rest of the "upscale" Italian fare is "terrific" too; there's a chic vibe in the "small" but "charming" dining room; the bartenders are "friendly," but the service can be "hit or miss"; "getting a table during brunch can be tough," fans say, "but it's worth the wait."

Al Di La Trattoria Italian   27 | 20 | 23 | $$

Park Slope | 248 5th Ave. (Carroll St.) | Brooklyn
718-783-4565 | aldilatrattoria.com

"Can I eat here every day?" ask fans; its "atypical but comforting" dishes have made this Park Slope institution "a revelation" thanks to its "well-edited menu" of homemade northern Italian pastas and hearty meats with "refined and complex flavors" in a "low-key atmosphere"; seating is split between a rustic-chic front room and the cozier wine bar out back, but "eat early or late or wait" – they don't take reservations for groups of five or fewer.

Alberto Italian   24 | 21 | 24 | $$

Forest Hills | 98-31 Metropolitan Ave.
(bet. 69th & 70th Aves.) | Queens
718-268-7860 | albertorestaurant.com

A "neighborhood staple" since 1973, this "dependable," dinner-only Forest Hills establishment serves "above-average Northern Italian," including gnocchi and other homemade pastas; the "homey," fireplace-warmed setting is showing its age a bit, but the "helpful" servers and the "quiet" surroundings are both pluses, making it suitable for "enjoying an evening with friends," whether you're a regular or not.

Aldea Portuguese   26 | 23 | 24 | $$$

Flatiron | 31 W 17th St. (bet. 5th & 6th Aves.)
212-675-7223 | aldearestaurant.com

The plates are "beautiful" and "delicious" at this "welcoming" and "homey" Portuguese spot in Flatiron, where the "creative, yet approachable" dishes are paired with "lively" wines and "seriously good" cocktails served by "knowledgeable" staff; "one always feels at home" in the "intimate," chic room, but sitting at the chef's counter at the back is the "real treat," since it lets you watch the team "meticulously" execute the meals.

Aldo Sohm Wine Bar Ⓢ Wine Bar   22 | 24 | 25 | $$$

West 50s | 151 W 51st St. (bet. 6th & 7th Aves.)
212-554-1143 | aldosohmwinebar.com

"It feels like you're in a rich person's living room" at this "handsome" Midtown wine bar run by the sommelier of nearby Le Bernardin, a "calm," "high-class" escape from the "hustle and bustle" of Midtown that's known for its variety of "top-notch" wines, which are "perfectly" paired with "fun nibbles"; as a handy go-to for a "higher end" lunch, pre- or post-theater bites, or a "luxurious treat," it comes with "first-class" service and a "weighty" check – "please, please take me here on my next date" begs one besotted oenophile.

Ali's Roti Shop Caribbean   25| 12| 19| $|
Wakefield | 4220 White Plains Rd. (E 233rd St.) | Bronx
718-655-2178 | alis-roti-shop.business.site
Ali's Trinidad Roti Shop
Bedford-Stuyvesant | 1267 Fulton St. (bet. Arlington Pl. &
Nostrand Ave.) | Brooklyn | 718-783-0316
Crown Heights | 337 Utica Ave. (bet. President & Carroll Sts.)
Brooklyn | 718-778-7329
Prospect Lefferts Gardens | 825 Flatbush Ave.
(bet. Linden Blvd. & Caton Ave.) | Brooklyn | 718-484-4828
Street food is the draw at these counter-service "fixtures" in Crown Heights, Bed-Stuy, and beyond: they are one of the "few authentic places to get Trinidadian doubles," a "huge, satisfying, and slightly spicy" sandwich of fried bread (bara) that "melds into its filling" of spiced chickpeas; other reasons to get here are standout chicken curry sandwiches.

Allswell American   21| 19| 20| $$|
Williamsburg | 124 Bedford Ave. (N 10th St.) | Brooklyn
347-799-2743 | allswellnyc.com
"On Bedford Avenue, where there's a restaurant every 10 feet," this "tried-and-true" "quintessential Williamsburg" quasi-tavern ("a pub in spirit, but not in layout") "differentiates itself" via "solid" American dishes (burgers, a highly "respectable pickled-vegetables plate," brunch fare, steaks) that change frequently; it "definitely hits the hipster vibe," but "smiley staff make it a pleasant experience."

Alma Mexican   22| 20| 21| $$|
Carroll Gardens | 187 Columbia St.
(Degraw St.) | Brooklyn
718-643-5400 | almarestaurant.com
Go for the "can't be beat" "view of the Manhattan skyline" from the rooftop terrace at this Columbia Street Waterfront hangout, where the "rock-solid" and "consistently high-quality" Mexican dishes pair well with classic cocktails and a long tequila list; the interior of this "neighborhood place" may seem a "bit worn" at this point, but for most it remains a "gem"; N.B. Alma takes reservations, but rooftop tables are first-come, first-serve in spring and summer.

Almayass Middle Eastern   25| 23| 25| $$$|
Flatiron | 24 E 21st St. (bet. B'way & Park Ave. S)
212-473-3100 | almayass.com
There's no need to "travel all the way to the Middle East" when you can get a "happy marriage of Lebanese and Armenian" specialties at the Flatiron branch of this Beirut-based chain; it does the trick for "hummus cravings," and the "elegant," "formal" rooms and "responsive" servers who are "eager to explain and help" make it ideal for a "date night," or for groups who "want to share" some of the lavish spreads.

| | FOOD | DECOR | SERVICE | COST |

Alta Spanish — 23 | 22 | 21 | $$$
Greenwich Village | 64 W 10th St.
(bet. 5th & 6th Aves.)
212-505-7777 | altarestaurant.com
"It always feels festive" at this rustic eatery "in the back of a
Greenwich Village brownstone" that offers "an alluring array of
tapas and small plates" "varied" "enough to satisfy anyone" – it's
"great for double-dating" or "last-minute group dinners"; "service
is personal," if a bit "pushy," and "the noise level can be a bit alta,"
so forget about having a conversation and concentrate on the
Spanish-influenced dishes and downright "dangerous sangria."

Altesi Italian — 23 | 21 | 24 | $$$
East 60s | 26 E 64th St. (bet. 5th & Madison Aves.)
212-759-8900 | altesinyc.com
Altesi Downtown
SoHo | 200 Spring St. (bet. Thompson & Sullivan Sts.)
212-431-1212
"Personalized service" marks these "relaxing" "sleeper,"
"neighborhood spots" known for their "contemporary" Italian
cuisine (including wood-oven pizzas at the SoHo location
and "excellent" house-made pastas both there and at the
brownstone-based UES original), as well as outdoor seating
options; although the interiors are "plain," and the prices can
seem "not-so-good," they are a "pleasant" stopover, especially
after Downtown's happy-hour choices are factored in.

Amali Mediterranean — 22 | 20 | 22 | $$$
East 60s | 115 E 60th St. (Park Ave.)
212-339-8363 | amalinyc.com
"Away from all the chaos" around Bloomingdale's stands this
"pleasant" and "unassuming" UES "neighborhood spot," a Periyali
sibling known for its "simple," locavore Mediterranean dishes,
"interesting wines," and "well-informed" staff; it also "keeps
things interesting" with "an unusual BYOB policy" (no corkage
fee for unique or exceptional bottles – contact them for more
information).

Amaranth ℂ Mediterranean — 21 | 19 | 21 | $$$
East 60s | 21 E 62nd St. # 1 (bet. 5th & Madison Aves.)
212-980-6700 | amaranthrestaurant.com
"Watch the swells go by" from sidewalk seating or "sit next to
them" inside this "sceney" UES bistro, where "well-dressed"
"Madison Avenue types" mingle with a Euro crowd in a "noisy"
space known more for its "people"-spotting than its "fair" but
"consistent" Mediterranean cuisine; the tables probably are
"too close" to each other for the small space, but it still works
for lunch or "dinner after shopping at Barneys or Bloomie's."

Amazing 66 Chinese — 22 | 13 | 19 | $$
Chinatown | 66 Mott St. (bet. Bayard & Canal Sts.)
212-334-0099 | amazing66.com
The food is "tasty" at this Chinatown standby for "quality"
Cantonese fare, with some "inventive twists" (like beef short rib
in pumpkin and sea cucumber over bean curd rolls) available in
the simple, brightly lit setting; the "good value for your money"
makes it a "go-to," particularly for group dinners.

	FOOD	DECOR	SERVICE	COST
American Cut Steakhouse Ⓢ	25	23	25	$$$$

Steakhouse
East 50s | 109 E 56th St. (bet. Park & Madison Aves.)
212-388-5277 | americancutsteakhouse.com
TriBeCa | 363 Greenwich St. (bet. Franklin & Harrison Sts.)
212-226-4736
With "all the swagger of a luxury steakhouse with none of the old stuffiness," these modern interpretations in TriBeCa and Midtown East both feel "classy," with massive tables, "a sleek bar area," and enough space to make them "perfect for a large party"; the steaks are "perfectly cooked," and you "can't go wrong with any cut"; the prices are "expensive," and the decibel levels in the "energetic" rooms are "louder than a heavy metal band."

Z Amma Indian — 27 | 20 | 25 | $$
East 50s | 246 E 51st St. (bet. 2nd & 3rd Aves.)
212-644-8330 | ammanyc.com
At this "upscale" East Midtown destination, the "delicious choices" of North and South Indian dishes are "prepared with care" and include tasting menus "available both for vegetarians and non-veg" diners; the "understated" townhouse space with pale mustard walls is staffed by "courteous" servers, and although it's "a little tight," the "quiet" and "convenient location" lead most to deem this "good stuff."

Ammazzacaffe Italian — 24 | 21 | 22 | $$
Williamsburg | 702 Grand St. (bet. Manhattan & Graham Aves.) | Brooklyn
929-250-2875 | ammazzacaffe.nyc
This Williamsburg "handmade" pasta kitchen does "modern Italian and it does it right," with "nightly specials" made from "seasonal" ingredients, regional dishes not commonly found in New York, and amari-focused cocktails; the "trendy," "intimate" interior and an ideal-for-summer patio, paired with "reasonable" prices and service that won't let you down, make it "perfect for date night," especially since you can sometimes get by without reservations.

Ammos Estiatorio Ⓢ Greek — 23 | 21 | 20 | $$$
East 40s | 52 Vanderbilt Ave. (bet. 44th & 45th Sts.)
212-922-9999 | ammosnewyork.com
Take a "short vacation" from your desk to this Midtown spot well known for business lunches; the "serviceable" whole fish flown in from the Mediterranean and elsewhere gets the "Greek formula" – "fresh" herbs and flavors that always "come through"; power players love the "sociable" aspects of the "inviting," "soaring" dining spaces, although "variable" service can make things take longer than they should.

Amy Ruth's Southern — 23 | 13 | 19 | $$
Harlem | 113 W 116th St. (bet. Lenox & 7th Aves.)
212-280-8779 | amyruths.com
"Stand in line" for sweet tea, "crispy" waffles drenched in syrup, "dream"-worthy "crunchy" fried chicken smothered in gravy, and banana pudding to get a "taste of the South" at this soul food "destination" in Harlem; it's "crowded," exciting, and

"consistent," as well as often "noisy," but the cafeteria decor and "lackadaisical" service are nothing to write home about.

Anassa Taverna Greek   21| 18| 19| $$$|
East 60s | 200 E 60th St. (3rd Ave.)
212-371-5200 | anassataverna.com

A "convenient" spot "after the movies or shopping at Blooming-dale's," this "upbeat" UES spot, a sibling of Avra, delivers "people-watching" opportunities galore, along with a "large menu" of "reliable takes on classic" Mediterranean seafood and other dishes, in a "spacious," "casual" bilevel setting; "deafening" decibel levels, "too much attitude," and "pricey" tabs are turnoffs, but the crowd frequenting this joint keeps it "busy," and "the second floor is less of a scene."

Angelina's Italian   23| 22| 21| $$$|
Tottenville | 399 Ellis St. (Arthur Kill Rd.) | Staten Island
718-227-2900 | angelinasristorante.com

Staten Island's "upscale gem" serves homestyle favorites that make you feel as if you're "eating in Italy," with "creative presentations" of classics served inside a Victorian mansion with "lovely" outdoor seating and "magnificent" waterfront views; although it's "expensive" for the area and service can be "overbearing," it's a "great place to celebrate family special occasions" and play a round of bocce on a summer afternoon.

Antica Pesa Italian   23| 22| 22| $$$|
Williamsburg | 115 Berry St. (bet. 7th & 8th Sts.) | Brooklyn
347-763-2635 | anticapesa.com

"If you can't make it" to the Rome original, come to Williams-burg for the U.S. outpost of this famed trattoria – with "delicate" and "creative" plates, it's a decent option for a "romantic" night out; it's also expensive and "trendy," even for the neighborhood, and its hours (for dinner only) are limited, so "ink it into the calendar" and expect to "wait even with a reservation"; once you sit, though, the staff "go out of their way" to make your time special.

Antonio's Trattoria Italian   24| 18| 24| $$|
Arthur Avenue/Belmont | 2370 Belmont Ave.
(Crescent Ave.) | Bronx
718-733-6630 | antoniostrattoria.com

It's like "going home for dinner" at this Italian stop in the Bronx, where you are served by "accommodating," "attentive" waiters; sure, the decor is "old," but the comfort-food classics (pastas, standout gnocchi, thin-crust pizzas, and grilled meat and fish plates) keep fans coming back, and "much of it's sourced from local purveyors"; pro tip: "share everything family style," because "you're going to want to try it all."

Antonucci Cafe Italian   25| 19| 23| $$$|
East 80s | 170 E 81st St. (bet. Lexington & 3rd Aves.)
212-570-5100 | antonuccicafe81.com

"You want to bathe in the tomato sauce" at this Italian "little charmer" with an "extensive menu"; in its UES dining room, the "ever-present" host and a "staff that greet you as friends" "always make you feel at home"; "call well in advance" for a reservation: the space is tight, but it's "almost charming to be crammed next to the table" beside you.

A.O.C. L'aile ou la Cuisse ⸢ French

21 | 18 | 21 | $$

West Village | 314 Bleecker St. (Grove St.)
212-675-9463 | aocnyc.com

This "super bistro on Bleecker Street" is the "sweet" "neighborhood restaurant that most NYers hope for," with a "classic French" menu "replete with familiar dishes" and a staff that's "welcoming and helpful"; beyond the "small and intimate" interior is a "spacious garden area hidden in the back," which is perfect for leisurely enjoying a variety of "reasonably priced" wines.

⬛ Aquagrill Seafood

26 | 19 | 24 | $$$

SoHo | 210 Spring St. (6th Ave.)
212-274-0505 | aquagrill.com

Ranked "among the best seafood restaurants in NYC" since 1996, especially for "oyster fans," this is a "neighborhood mainstay" where "nothing is overly fussy" (although some say it "could use an update in decor"); there's also "impeccable service" from an "extremely knowledgeable staff," a "pleasant" ambiance, and a "hidden away" location in SoHo; it can get crowded, but it's "worth the wait even without reservations."

⬛ Aquavit ▣ Scandinavian

27 | 25 | 26 | $$$$

East 50s | 65 E 55th St. (bet. Madison & Park Aves.)
212-307-7311 | aquavit.org

Nordic lovers believe they've "died and gone to Sweden" at this "venerable" Midtown "institution," where "creative" tasting menus of "masterfully" presented Scandinavian fare are teamed with a "wide variety" of house-made aquavits in a "relaxed, zen-like" space; sure, "be prepared to shell out major bucks" for the privilege, but if you want "to be transported to another world" among "sublime" servers and "beautiful guests," it's an "above-and-beyond" experience.

⬛ Arepa Lady Latin American

26 | 14 | 21 | $

Jackson Heights | 77-17 37th Ave. (78th St.)
Queens | 917-745-1111

The owner of "this food cart turned restaurant" earned her title "for a reason," and it made her a New York success story that's become "nothing short of iconic": head to Jackson Heights for "four different kinds" of arepas with "glorious amounts of cheese"; the space is "small and "basic," and usually "busy," with "casual" service and a well-priced menu: it's "what eating in New York should always be – simple and fun."

Arepas Cafe Latin American

▼ 24 | 14 | 19 | $$

Astoria | 33-07 36th Ave (bet. 33rd & 34th Sts.)
Queens | 718-937-3835 | arepasny.com
Arepas Grill
Astoria | 21-19 Broadway (bet. 21st & 23rd Sts.) | Queens
718-355-9686

"Soulful" arepas with a "variety of fillings" are the forte of these Astoria Venezuelan restaurants, whose "delicious," "filling" chow pairs up with myriad Latin American beverages, along with "cheap prices"; the original Cafe can be "a tight squeeze," although the Grill offers more space, and the "staff aim to please" at both; P.S. the Cafe does takeout, while the larger one also delivers.

Aretsky's Patroon 🛂 American | 25 | 24 | 25 | $$$$ |

East 40s | 160 E 46th St. (bet. Lexington & 3rd Aves.)
212-883-7373 | aretskyspatroon.com
At this "secret hideaway" of a Midtown steakhouse, seasoned "masters of the universe" treat the "inviting" rooftop "retreat" and "cozy" wood-paneled interiors like their own "private club," without "paying dues" or enduring the "stuffy formalities of similar" places nearby; "butter-knife tender" steak has a "cult" following, but the "variety" of "ever-creative" dishes that go beyond beef are "consistent" and served with "style."

Aria (Italian/Wine Bar | 21 | 21 | 19 | $$ |

West 50s | 369 W 51st St. (9th Ave.)
212-541-9241 | ariawinebar.com
West Village | 117 Perry St. (Greenwich St.)
212-242-4233
An "old faithful" "casual date" night spot, this duo of wine bars with "affordable" pours and "solid" Venetian cicchetti ("Italian tapas") is perfect for a "weeknight catch-up with a friend"; the "romantic spaces" are enhanced by a "cozy" "candlelit feel," "a long list of specials," and an unusually comprehensive menu of "gluten-free choices"; even though it gets "crowded" and the service can be "erratic," the atmosphere is "always festive."

Armani Ristorante Italian | 23 | 25 | 22 | $$$$ |

East 50s | 717 5th Ave. (56th St.)
212-207-1902 | www.armani.com/restaurant
Inside the 5th Avenue Armani boutique, this "upscale" and "sophisticated" "palace" to design serves "delicately prepared" Italian plates; the interior is as "tasteful" and "modernist" as you'd expect, with tiny purple lights framing the windows, and the staff are "attentive," making it a "peaceful respite" from the busy streets outside; there's a "wonderful cocktail lounge" too.

Artichoke Basille's Pizza (Pizza | 22 | 12 | 15 | $ |

East Village | 321 E 14th St. (bet. 1st & 2nd Aves.)
212-228-2004 | artichokepizza.com
With 11 locations throughout the city, this local chain provides "tasty and reliable" "late-night" "drunk walk home" pizza slices "so big and rich you get your money's worth" – especially the "creamy," "salty" signature slice; the lines get long during drinking hours, and the service and interior are basic counter stuff, but even in pizzatown, "there's nothing like it."

Artie's Steak & Seafood Seafood | 24 | 19 | 23 | $$ |

City Island | 394 City Island Ave. (Ditmars St.) | Bronx
718-885-9885 | artiescityisland.com
At this "welcoming" local surf-and-turf on City Island, the seafood is "fresh and plentiful," portions are "huge" ("be prepared to take some home"), and the Italian plates are "reliably good"; true, it's not on the water, but that doesn't matter much to the families and other groups who keep it "crowded," and "lively"/"loud" as a result.

Arturo's (Italian
22 | 18 | 21 | $$

Greenwich Village | 106 W Houston St. (Thompson St.)
212-677-3820 | arturoscoaloven.com

You'll "feel like you stepped back in time" when you walk in this "retro" Italian eatery in Greenwich Village, a "neighborhood staple for years" popular for its "fun, noisy atmosphere," with live jazz and "waiters singing Sinatra"; it serves "terrific," "classic" coal-fired pizza in a "casual, comfy," "not fancy" dining room with "real cred."

Asian Jewels (Chinese
23 | 19 | 17 | $$

Flushing | 13330 39th Ave. (bet. College Point Blvd.
& Janet Pl.) | Queens
718-359-8600 | asianjewelsny.com

"Some of the best dim sum in New York," including "classic" dumplings with "plump shrimp," arrives on traditional rolling carts at this Flushing destination, with an "extensive" menu of Cantonese classics (plus a concise list of raw fish); round tables fill the "cavernous" dining hall, and fans say to "make sure (even if you have to wait longer) that you sit" in the main room – "the carts don't come to the side room and it's just not the same decor-wise."

Asiate American
25 | 28 | 26 | $$$$

West 50s | 80 Columbus Cir., 35th Fl. (B'way)
212-805-8881 | mandarinoriental.com/new-york

Showcasing "killer" views of Central Park, this "stunning" establishment in the Mandarin Oriental teams its "gorgeous decor" with "high-quality" wines, "quietly attentive service," and "artfully prepared and presented" New American cuisine (including "excellent brunch" options); no question, it's "seriously expensive," but it works "if you want to impress" – especially for "corporate entertaining"; P.S. dinner is prix fixe only.

Astoria Seafood ⑤ Ⓜ Seafood
27 | 11 | 15 | $$

Long Island City | 3710 33rd St. (37th Ave.) | Queens
718-392-2680 | astoriaseafoodnyc.com

Like something "out of a movie," this "hectic," "choose your own adventure"–style combination fish market and restaurant serves "knockout" seafood that you "pick out" yourself with plastic bags and then have "prepared the way you want it"; the sides and the "reasonable prices" help counteract the "surly" service, spare decor, and "huge lines," and while it doesn't accept reservations, fin fans are content to go BYOB while "sitting back and enjoying the show."

Atera ⑤ Ⓜ American
28 | 27 | 28 | $$$$

TriBeCa | 77 Worth St. (bet. B'way & Church St.)
212-226-1444 | ateranyc.com

Every bite is a "wonder" at this "exquisite" TriBeCa destination serving tasting menus of "innovative" "high-modernist" New American fare paired with "a wine list that impresses" and "impeccable" service; the "cozy" space has only a dozen-odd seats, and they all face the open kitchen, "where all the magic happens"; while the prices for all this attention are undeniably "steep," most say it's "worth it" for a "memorable," "romantic" evening.

	FOOD	DECOR	SERVICE	COST

Atla Mexican — 24 | 22 | 21 | $$$

NoHo | 372 Lafayette St. (3rd St.)
337-662-3522 | atlanyc.com

This "delicious" NoHo Mexican owned by Cosme's Enrique Olvera and Daniela Soto-Innes dispenses "brilliant fresh flavors" in greenery-filled digs brimming with "fabulous people"; although the often-"squished in" setting can feel "cramped" and "small" portions can turn tabs "pricey" quickly, the "industrial vibe" and "people-watching" potential help make it "fit for a trendy night out" or for brunch – "sidewalk seats are prime real estate for spring and summer," especially when you have one of their house-made aguas frescas or "delicious" cocktails in hand.

Atlantic Grill Seafood — 23 | 21 | 22 | $$$

West 60s | 49 W 64th St. (B'way)
212-787-4663 | atlanticgrill.com

Folks who are "particular about seafood" swear that it's "always top notch" at this "refined spot" near Lincoln Center that's "perfect for pre-performance dinner," with "gracious" servers who always "get you out in a timely manner"; fans say it's "always busy, but worth the wait," with prices that are a "bit on the high end"; most agree that the weekend brunch is a "hidden treat."

Z Atoboy Korean — 27 | 21 | 24 | $$

NoMad | 43 E 28th St. (Park Ave. S)
646-476-7217 | atoboynyc.com

"Stop everything you're doing" and rush over to this "kick-ass" Korean concept in NoMad, whose "riffs" on traditional Korean banchan with "out-of-the-box" small plates take this cuisine "to new places," all while leaving you "very happy" with its "reasonably priced" three-course prix fixe; the "warehouse funky" space may be too "cool" for some, but warm, "relaxed" service compensates for feeling like you're eating in "someone's panic room."

Z Atomix (Ⓢ Ⓜ Korean — 29 | 29 | 29 | $$$$

NoMad | 104 E 30th St. (bet. Lexington & Park Ave. S)
atomixnyc.com

There are "not enough superlatives" to describe the "off-the-chart creativity" presented in this "astonishingly refreshing" chef's counter with a "Korean sensibility," where "mind-blowing combinations" of fresh ingredients and "well thought-out" dishes "stimulate all senses"; waiters consider your dinner a "performance," putting "much thought and care" into the "artistry of service" and presenting you with keepsakes like "beautiful" menu cards and chopsticks at the end of your tasting.

Atrium Dumbo American — 20 | 24 | 23 | $$$

Dumbo | 15 Main St. (bet. Plymouth &
Water Sts.) | Brooklyn
718-858-1095 | atriumdumbo.com

"Greenery covers the walls" of the sleek, industrial, modern interior at this hip "nouvelle" French-accented American bistro set under the Brooklyn Bridge, where sipping something from the comprehensive wine list and savoring "house-baked" bread while gazing at the waterfront are "draws"; the "diverse" menu is "simple and satisfying," with "reasonable prices," and the professional service make the experience a good fit when in the area.

NEW Au Cheval ☾ American   26 | 25 | 24 | $$$

TriBeCa | 33 Cortlandt Alley
(bet. Walker & White Sts.)
917-710-6039 | auchevaldiner.com

"Holy hamburger!" exclaim fans of this "elevated" TriBeCa diner, a branch of the Chicago original with "fantastic takes on classic dishes" (including those "dynamite" patties), along with "on-tap root beer," numerous cocktails, and "an impressive beer list," in a dimly lit space that's "the epitome of cool"; an "energetic" mood and "fast service" temper the "waits," leading most to say "all the hype is true."

Au Za'atar ☾ Middle Eastern   20 | 14 | 18 | $$

East Village | 188 Avenue A (12th St.)
212-254-5660 | auzaatar.com

If you order the "Instagram-worthy" off-the-menu tableside shawarma served at this Lebanese kitchen, you'll have a "kitschy" feast ahead of you; still, the "gorgeous, intensely flavored and colorful vegetable dishes" may be the true star – although service can be "slow," and its interior comes with pretty standard exposed bricks, this East Village hangout is perfect for groups: "you'll leave with a full stomach, smelling like garlic."

Augustine French   23 | 26 | 23 | $$$$

Financial District | 5 Beekman St. (Nassau St.)
212-375-0010 | augustineny.com

The "setting is spectacular" at Keith McNally's "bright" and "inviting" "upscale bistro" in FiDi; inside the Beekman, it brings to "an old hotel new spirit"; unexpected "Austrian dishes" enliven a menu of "classic French dishes done in a contemporary way," and given its "personal, upbeat, and very helpful servers," it's ideal for "romantic date nights" as you'll feel you've been "transported" to Paris or those with generous expense accounts.

Aureole Ⓢ American   26 | 25 | 26 | $$$$

West 40s | 135 W 42nd St. (bet. B'way & 6th Ave.)
212-319-1660 | aureolenewyork.com

"Transport yourself" to Charlie Palmer's "civilized" New American "icon" near Times Square, where "sumptuous" seasonal dishes "packed with flavor" complement an "excellent wine selection" in a "sleek" interior housing a "casual" front section and a "more formal, quiet" rear section serving prix fixe dinner and tasting menus; you may have to "bring your banker along" for payment, but when one considers the "spot-on" service, plus "perfect" pre-theater options, the overall experience "couldn't be much better."

Aurora Italian   23 | 20 | 22 | $$$

SoHo | 510 Broome St. (bet. Thompson St. & W B'way)
212-334-9020 | aurorasoho.com
Williamsburg | 70 Grand St. (Wythe Ave.) | Brooklyn
718-388-5100 | aurorabk.com

It's "impossible to go home hungry" when you enjoy the "fresh and vibrant" fare at these Italian outposts in Williamsburg and SoHo; locals like the "rustic setting," the "friendly staff," and the "family-friendly" vibe, but note that it's also well-suited for "brunch aficionados" and for couples to enjoy a glass of wine on the Brooklyn branch's "outdoor patio full of greenery."

Avant Garden Vegan/Vegetarian
26 | 21 | 24 | $$$

East Village | 130 E 7th St. (Avenue A)
646-922-7948 | avantgardennyc.com

"Beautifully plated," "imaginative, gourmet" plant-based fare is the draw at this "impressive" East Village destination, where the "explosion of delicious flavors" pleases even the "most discriminating vegans" (and it's still tasty even if you aren't); "excellent" servers tend to the "cozy," faux-rustic environs, which some say can feel "tight"; regulars advise sitting at the bar and watching the kitchen in action.

The Aviary NYC American
20 | 27 | 23 | $$$$

West 60s | 80 Columbus Cir. (B'way)
212-805-8800 | aviarynyc.com

You can "bask" in "spectacular" Central Park views from the 35th floor of the Mandarin Oriental Hotel at this upscale cocktail bar, an offshoot of chef Grant Achatz's Chicago original; the "inventive" drinks (some of them like a "crazy science experiment") are poured alongside small plates that include the giant crispy pig skin ("large and in-charge") and other startling but sometimes just so-so creations; it all "adds up to a small fortune" – you have to order from the tasting menu to secure a window seat.

🄩 Avra Estiatorio ◖ Greek
26 | 25 | 24 | $$$

East 40s | 141 E 48th St. (bet. Lexington & 3rd Aves.)
212-759-8550 | avrany.com
Avra Madison
East 60s | 14 E 60th St. (bet. 5th & Madison Aves.)
212-937-0100

"Choose your fish and have it charbroiled" at this pair of "gorgeous, splashy" and "always fresh" grills, where "professional and knowledgeable" servers guide you through a menu of "classic Greek cuisine"; you can either fight the "working-lunch crowd" for "fabulous prix fixe" deals or "bring your corporate card" for "perfectly cooked" seafood dinners on the "outdoor patio" fit for "big parties" and "special occasions."

Awadh Indian
24 | 19 | 22 | $$$

West 90s | 2588 Broadway (98th St.)
646-861-3604 | awadhnyc.com

This UWS spot's "bold" and "tasty" approach to Northern Indian cooking – especially "highly unusual" biryanis and curries both "succulent" and "subtly spiced" and a crispy okra "like no other" – is "a cut above" anything else you'd get in the area – "this is as good as it gets"; the waitstaff make the best of maneuvering around the "snug" space, balancing being "nonintrusive" against being "eager to please."

Awash Ethiopian Ethiopian
23 | 15 | 20 | $$

East Village | 338 E 6th St. (bet. 1st & 2nd Aves.)
212-982-9589 | awashny.com
West 100s | 947 Amsterdam Ave. (bet. 106th & 107th Sts.)
212-961-1416
Cobble Hill | 242 Court St. (bet. Baltic & Kane Sts.) | Brooklyn
718-243-2151

This Ethiopian chainlet encourages a "communal," hands-on approach to eating, so grab hold of "highly seasoned" vegetarian-friendly staples in "complex" sauces that are paired with "spongy," tangy injera bread that gets "addictive" after a few bites; "sparse" spaces spruced up with "huge" paintings and "relaxed" service make you feel "taken care of," even when you're deep into dinner with your friends; cap things off with "strong" black coffee at the end.

Ayada Thai Thai   26 | 13 | 21 | $$ |
Elmhurst | 7708 Woodside Ave.
(bet. 77th & 78th Sts.) | Queens
718-424-0844
Chelsea | 75 9th Ave. (bet. 15th & 16th Sts.)
212-645-9445 | ayadathai.com
"There's no shortage of excellent Thai in" Elmhurst and Woodside, but this option stands apart for its "consistency and good vibes," making it a good choice for "out-of-town guests as well as food-loving locals" – the menu's "well chosen" (the noodle dishes and salads get special praise), it has "no qualms about being spicy when it's needed," and the additional dining room two doors down helps to "relieve the once-long waits"; another sit-down branch is in Chelsea Market.

B & H Dairy Diner   24 | 11 | 20 | $ |
East Village | 127 2nd Ave. (bet. 7th St. & St. Marks Pl.)
212-505-8065 | bandhdairynewyork2.mybistro.online
"A relic of a bygone era," this eighty-something "East Village institution" still delights for "old-school Eastern European diner"/ "coffee shop standards" (and vegetarian options, as it's kosher) "at decent prices" dished by "funny yet efficient" waiters; so "what's not to like?"; well, maybe the "tiny, narrow" digs – basically "a counter and a handful of tables" (please "make them renovate," some plead).

Baar Baar Indian   24 | 24 | 22 | $$$ |
East Village | 13 E 1st St. (bet. Bowery & 2nd Ave.)
212-228-1200 | baarbaarnyc.com
A "fun spot" for small plates of "clubby modern Indian food," with "twists on classics" matched with "divine cocktails" in a "big, over-the-top space"; there's always "attentive" service and a lively scene as people head here before going "for a night on the town" – the energy gets amped up even higher "on weekends, when they have a live band" and it gets much "louder and livelier."

Baba's Pierogies Eastern European   25 | 16 | 22 | $ |
Gowanus | 295 3rd Ave. (Carroll St.) | Brooklyn
718-222-0777 | babasbk.com
This "cute" Polish dumpling house in Brooklyn serves "delicate," "tender," "freshly made" pierogi with "traditional" fillings like sauerkraut, alongside "nouveau" "twists," like crunchy chocolate and mac and cheese; to support a "super-friendly" "family business," or for "comfort-meal" cravings, it's "worth the trip" to Gowanus or a visit to the stripped-down branch in Williamsburg's North 3rd Street Market (credit-card only).

Babbo Italian — 26 | 23 | 24 | $$$$
Greenwich Village | 110 Waverly Pl.
(bet. MacDougal St. & 6th Ave.)
212-777-0303 | babbonyc.com

"The food remains stupendously good" – particularly the "top-notch pasta tasting menu" – at this Italian veteran in the Village; the brownstone setting is "refined but casual" (head for the "more romantic tables upstairs" if you're not into the "cranked up" music), and the service "operates smoothly," even if some diners leave "feeling like part of an assembly line," overall, though, it remains "recommended for a special evening"; N.B. Mario Batali cut his ties with the restaurant in early 2019.

NEW Babs — – | – | – | $$$
Greenwich Village | 72 MacDougal St.
(bet. Houston & Bleecker Sts.)
212-601-298352 | babsync.com

From the team behind nearby Mimi, this Greenwich Village newcomer takes up a small but well-appointed space on Mac-Dougal, designed for enjoying original dishes like scallop crudo topped with trout roe or asparagus with stracciatella, alongside classic cocktails (including highballs served on silver platters) and a curated wine list focused on small producers.

Babu Ji Indian — 24 | 21 | 21 | $$$
Greenwich Village | 22 E 13th St.
(bet. Union Sq. W & 5th Ave.)
212-951-1082 | babuji.nyc

The ever-popular "butter chicken and Colonel Tso's cauliflower are worth the price of admission" at this "bustling high-end Indian" with "really flavorful nouvelle" renditions of classics; "colorful Bollywood films" projected on the wall and "cool Beatles and Maharishi photos" enhance the "hip and attractive" setting, and though some note that many dishes are on the high end and come with inconsistent service, others just "wish it was less popular so we could linger."

Bacchus French — 23 | 19 | 23 | $$
Downtown Brooklyn | 409-411 Atlantic Ave.
(bet. Bond & Nevins Sts.) | Brooklyn
718-852-1572 | bacchusbistro.com

"Well-executed" French bistro fare like "great mussels" and "perfect" fries is what it's about at this "relaxed," "consistent" neighborhood spot in Downtown Brooklyn known for "solid" brunch and a "cute" backyard garden that is a popular venue for baby showers and small weddings; while the menu is "limited," fans agree the service is "attentive" and prices are "reasonable," making it "worth a trip": "A concert at BAM?" "This is your pre- or post-show spot."

Bagatelle (French — 18 | 21 | 17 | $$$$
Meatpacking District | 1 Little W 12th St. (9th Ave.)
212-488-2110 | bagatellenyc.com

"When it's a late Saturday afternoon, the window curtains close, the lights dim and the music turns up," at this "be-seen" scene in Meatpacking; with "bottle service at 3 PM," a "dance party with your eggs" brunch, and "trendy," "clubby" French dinners, it works for "boozy" celebrations (think "massive drinks" with multiple straws) if you're "not afraid of lots of noise" and braving "overpriced" food and "stuck-up" service.

Bahari Estiatorio (Greek   28 | 17 | 24 | $$

Astoria | 31-14 Broadway (32nd St.) | Queens
718-204-8968 | bahariestiatorio.com

It's "worth a trip on the R train any day" to this Astoria "gem," where the "open-window cooking for all to see" is "outstanding" (some of the "best" west of Greece); the "friendly" service makes it "like eating with your extended family" on the long tables; the white tablecloth dining room is "spacious" but "simple" – it's clear diners come for the food, "not the decor."

Balaboosta Mediterranean   24 | 19 | 22 | $$$

West Village | 611 Hudson St. (12th St.)
212-390-1545 | balaboostanyc.com

"So happy it's back," sigh supporters; they missed "the magic of chef Einat Admony" and her "inventive Middle Eastern–Mediterranean cuisine," a "model of consistency"; some call the current rustic-modern decor "a downgrade" from the old digs, but the "caring" staff have returned, too, and so most welcome this "high-energy" "addition to the West Village."

Balade Middle Eastern   23 | 16 | 21 | $$

East Village | 208 1st Ave. (bet. 12th & 13th Sts.)
212-529-6868 | baladerestaurants.com

"If you're a lamb lover" or just craving "fresh" Middle Eastern specialties and "lots of options," stop in for a "down-to-earth" meal served with "friendly vibes" at this neighborhood "favorite" in the East Village; since it can get "cramped and noisy," many opt for "takeout," but either way, the "lunch special cannot be beat," and you "won't feel hurried" when dining in.

Balthazar (French   25 | 25 | 22 | $$$

SoHo | 80 Spring St. (Crosby St.)
212-965-1414 | balthazarny.com

"Much imitated, seldom matched," the SoHo "all-time classic" remains "the bistro against which all bistros are measured," with "every entree well honed," charming environs, some of the "best baked goods in town," and "attentive service" in spite of the "crush of tourists"; should you "check in on this old friend, you'll find nothing has changed" although you may find yourself "wishing it were easier to get a reservation" and struggling to have a conversation once you do get in.

Bamonte's Italian   21 | 18 | 23 | $$

Williamsburg | 32 Withers St.
(bet. Lorimer St. & Union Ave.) | Brooklyn
718-384-8831

"If you like old-style" "back to the '50s" dining, this "classic carb-loaded escape" in Williamsburg brings "the authentic throwback Italian Brooklyn experience," down to "tuxedoed waiters at your beck and call," "red checkered tablecloths," and other "vintage surroundings" that feel like "grandmother's house"; "the food isn't the best you've ever had, but it's all you ever really want: lots of red sauce, lots of butter, lots of red wine."

Banh Mi Saigon 🍴 Vietnamese

24 | 9 | 16 | $

Little Italy | 198 Grand St.
(bet. Mott & Mulberry Sts.)
212-941-1541 | banhmisaigonnyc.com

The Vietnamese sandwiches on "fresh crusty bread" are "the real thing"; "one sandwich will really fill you up" for a price that you "can't beat," and while a noodle dish and cold-case desserts are available, the No. 1 Spicy and the other banh mi get the most love; the bland interior and counter service setup means it's "really not a sit-down place," but there are stools if you must; N.B. cash only.

The Bao Chinese

24 | 16 | 18 | $$

East Village | 13 St. Marks Pl. (bet. 2nd & 3rd Aves.)
212-388-9238 | thebaonewyorkcity.com

Soup dumplings "must not be good" if you don't have to wait "at least 40 minutes" for them, say some mavens, and this "trendy" East Village joint serves multiple "terrific" versions, with the expected wait to match – even the more "creative" versions like "chocolate banana" impress; it's constantly "crowded" here – noisy and "just as lively" as St. Marks Place outside, making it a workable option for groups and those after "value."

☑ Bar Boulud French

24 | 21 | 23 | $$$

West 60s | 1900 Broadway (bet. 63rd & 64th Sts.)
212-595-0303 | barboulud.com

At this "more casual" Boulud bistro, diners say there's a "good selection of well-cooked," "très français" fare (especially the "Bouludified burger"), and believe that the restaurateur "aims to please each and every time"; the "long, narrow," "cavelike" room near Lincoln Center is constantly "crowded" with the "before-concert/opera/ballet set," but some argue that "for the prices, the food isn't exceptional enough," and service can veer between "efficient" and "discombobulated"; in short, its popularity may owe much to the "location and the name."

Bar Centrale American

17 | 21 | 22 | $$$

West 40s | 324 W 46th St. (bet. 8th & 9th Aves.)
212-581-3130 | barcentralenyc.com

"Finding this joint is half the battle," but once you enter this exclusive upstairs "hangout" on Restaurant Row, you'll discover a "small," "retro" space conducive to "extraordinary sightings" of "A-list stars doing a turn on Broadway"; absolutely, most "go for the scene," not for the "limited menu" of American dishes, and it's "hard to get reservations," which are essentially mandatory, although "solicitous" service and "post-show drinking" opportunities make it "worth" the effort.

Bar Jamon 🌙 Spanish

25 | 20 | 22 | $$

Gramercy | 125 E 17th St. (Irving Pl.)
212-253-2773 | casamononyc.com

Much more than just a "waiting spot for Casa Mono," this "quaint," "low-key" tapas bar offers a "pricey" but "striking selection of cheeses, charcuterie, and wine – and they know how to pair them"; the "helpful" servers and Spanish touches add to the experience; it's "often crowded" and has "tight communal seating," so "arrive early if you don't want to stand."

Bar Pitti 🦞 Italian   24 | 16 | 18 | $$

Greenwich Village | 268 6th Ave.
(bet. Bleecker & Houston Sts.)
212-982-3300 | barpitty.com

You could almost "be in Rome" at this trattoria with a "tiny" dining room, where the "specials are written on a chalkboard" (in Italian, of course); the "pastas are fresh," the sauces memorable, and "you'll be waiting a long time for a table on a summer evening," when "their patio is in high demand"; note that sometimes the staff "aren't the friendliest" (it helps to "know them"), they don't take credit cards, and there are no reservations.

Bar Pleiades ◖ American   22 | 25 | 25 | $$$$

East 70s | 20 E 76th St. (Madison Ave.)
212-772-2600 | barpleiades.com

The "single best choice to impress a first date," this "lovely, sophisticated" UES hotel lounge is also the "perfect place for tea or a late-afternoon cocktail with friends"; you'll "feel like a high roller" in the "elegant" main room, especially when you factor in the "free show of designer clothes and Hermès bags at surrounding tables"; there's an "excellent variety of cocktails," and the food, well prepared and mostly "nibbles," is never an afterthought.

Bar Primi Italian   22 | 21 | 20 | $$

East Village | 325 Bowery (2nd St.)
212-220-9100 | barprimi.com

"Not the greatest, but a good place to have in your back pocket," say diners about this "bouncy" East Village joint, an "easy neighborhood spot for classic Italian fare" – primarily "simple pasta dishes done right"; some bristle at "the extremely high noise level" ("upstairs is quieter") and a staff that "needs a tune-up," but on the plus side, "one can usually get a reservation with ease."

Bar Sardine American   23 | 20 | 20 | $$

West Village | 183 W 10th St.
(bet. 7th Ave. S & W 4th St.)
646-360-3705 | barsardinenyc.com

New Yorkers will argue forever about the best burger in the city, but fans say this "bar-centric spot" is definitely in the running; they also like the "laid-back atmosphere," the "sincere service," and the pared-down menu of classics"; it's perfect for "a drink, a date night, or a casual weekday dinner," but as its name implies, it's also "petite," so "don't bring too many people."

Bar Tabac ◖ French   20 | 17 | 19 | $$

Cobble Hill | 128 Smith St. (Dean St.) | Brooklyn
718-923-0918 | bartabacny.com

"Sitting outside with a bottle of rosé and a bucket of mussels is a treat," as is the satisfying burger and fries at this French bistro in Cobble Hill, the sort of place that "every neighborhood should have but doesn't"; the sidewalk tables are perfect "for people-watching," and all in all it's a "place to have fun, not eat seriously" – and one where "always a buzz" also means "always noisy."

Barbetta (Italian

22 | 23 | 23 | $$$

West 40s | 321 W 46th St. (bet. 8th & 9th Aves.)
212-246-9171 | barbettarestaurant.com
This circa-1906 Theater District establishment is known for its
"elegant," "old-world" interior and "beautiful" outdoor courtyard;
"professional" waiters serve traditional Northern Italian plates
(handmade agnolotti, wild mushroom risotto, and a variety of
grilled fish and meats) that can get "pricey," but most still agree
"it's an oldie but a goodie."

Barboncino Pizza (Italian/Pizza

25 | 20 | 20 | $$

Crown Heights | 781 Franklin Ave.
(bet. Lincoln & St. Johns Pls.)
Brooklyn | 718-483-8834 | barboncinopizza.com
Fans say the pizzas don't even have "a right to be" as "overwhelmingly good" as they are at this Crown Heights hangout
known for its Neapolitan pies with "amazing flavors" – especially
the brunch offerings (pancetta, egg, and cheese; pear and
gorgonzola; a Nutella calzone) – all paired with "creative" craft
cocktails with ingredients like matcha and turmeric oil; it's no
wonder the lines can be "long" and the space "crowded," but it
is definitely "delicious" and "fun."

Barbounia Mediterranean

23 | 23 | 21 | $$$

Flatiron | 250 Park Ave. S (20th St.)
212-995-0242 | barbounia.com
"A stalwart in a neighborhood where restaurants come and go,"
this "large yet cozy" Flatiron space with pillars and vaulted ceilings is a "favorite place for a Mediterranean meal" of "creative,
flavorful" mains and small plates (don't skip the hummus),
washed down with "refined, balanced cocktails" and presented
by "knowledgeable waiters"; unfortunately, "it has more deci-
bels than the F train" "when the place is full, which it always is."

Barn Joo Korean

21 | 18 | 18 | $$

Union Square | 35 Union Sq. W
(bet. 16th & 17th Sts.)
646-398-9663 | barnjoo.com
Barn Joo 35
West 30s | 34 W 35th St. (bet. 5th & 6th Aves.)
212-564-4430
Make sure to "go with friends" to these "hip and trendy" spots
"fusing gastropub and Korean cuisine"; you "barbecue your own
meats" in a "club-like" setting, with touches like "greens grown
on the roof" and colorful soju "cocktails"; although it's "hard to
get a server's attention" when it's busy and it's "so loud" that
you can't hear yourself chew, an "unbelievable happy hour" and
scoring free drinks from the "wheel of fun" are incentives.

ⓩ Barney Greengrass Ⓜ Deli

26 | 12 | 18 | $$

West 80s | 541 Amsterdam Ave.
(bet. 86th & 87th Sts.)
212-724-4707 | barneygreengrass.com
"All hail the mighty king of smoked fish," say advocates of this
"throwback" circa-1908 "New York institution," an UWS deli
that's as "old-school as it gets," supplying "flawless" nova, bagels "with a schmear," and other Jewish standards; the "local"

crowd packing the "crowded" digs tolerates the "dated wall-paper" ("you ain't eating there for the decor"), and "cash-only" weekend menus; takeout offers other options, too.

Barrio Chino ⊄ Mexican
24 | 19 | 18 | $$

Lower East Side | 253 Broome St.
(bet. Ludlow & Orchard Sts.)
212-228-6710 | barriochinony.com
This Lower East Side taqueria is widely known for "strong" margaritas that ensure some patrons "never, ever leave sober," but "legit delicious" enchiladas and tacos help make this a go-to beyond their popular happy hour; the "casual" scene remains "bumpin'" after all of these years, although the "tiny, chaotic" space with a "back-room feel" gets understandably claustro-phobic during peak service.

Basso56 Italian
23 | 18 | 23 | $$

West 50s | 234 W 56th St. (bet. B'way & 8th Ave.)
212-265-2610 | basso56.com
"Delightful" service helped win over fans of this "warm," "low-key" Midtown Italian, whose "quality" dishes ("try the homemade pastas"), "solid wine list," and "central location" near Carnegie Hall garner applause, as do the "moderate price points" and "pleasant" "neighborhood" feel (and it's even "spacious" toward the back); P.S. gluten-free options are available, too.

Basta Pasta Italian
23 | 17 | 21 | $$

Flatiron | 37 W 17th St. (bet. 5th & 6th Aves.)
212-366-0888 | bastapastanyc.com
Originating in Tokyo, this "unique fusion of Japanese and Italian cooking" has been a neighborhood favorite since 1990; regulars say that even though it's a bit "cheesy," "just give in" and order the fresh pasta prepared tableside in a hollowed-out wheel of Parmesan; the "unpretentious" attitude and "attentive" service are pluses, and the only big knock is that things sometimes get "cramped."

Bâtard Ⓢ French
26 | 23 | 26 | $$$

TriBeCa | 239 W Broadway (bet. Walker & White Sts.)
212-219-2777 | batardtribeca.com
This "inventive" "French culinary experience" from Drew Nieporent in TriBeCa "offers fine dining without the pretentious-ness" with a customizable prix fixe; you can choose multiple dishes from the same course, for instance, and all come "beautifully plated" and "executed with precision"; the vibe is "sophisticated, yet "understated," with service that's "neither absent nor obtrusive," and the "stylish" decor and fabulous "Burgundy-centric" wine list also win praise.

Bayou Restaurant Ⓜ Cajun/Creole
24 | 22 | 24 | $$

Rosebank | 1072 Bay St.
(bet. Chestnut & St. Marys Aves.) | Staten Island
718-273-4383 | bayounyc.com
"New Orleans comes to Staten Island" at this "small," "quaint" Creole kitchen in Rosebank with a Bourbon Street interior, "strong" drinks, and a "friendly," "knowledgeable" staff to provide genteel service; the food has real Cajun character that

fits this "noisy," lively place – it "feels like being in the French Quarter" – especially on the nights with music; prices are fair for this cuisine that's "unique" on the Island.

Baz Bagel & Restaurant Deli   23 | 20 | 19 | $$

Little Italy | 181 Grand St. (bet. Baxter & Mulberry Sts.)
212-335-0609 | bazbagel.com

Working "to reinvent New York's most famous breakfast bread," this Little Italy hangout sells hand-rolled bagels, flagels (a flattened variation on the classic), and schmears "done right," as well as "Jewish-ish diner classics" (latkes, blintzes, matzo ball soup) alongside sandwiches, salads, and malted shakes – "a perfect mix of modern nostalgia"; "friendly" servers keep things at breakfast and lunch "laid back" amid "neon pastel" decor and "throwback" kitsch accents.

BCD Tofu House Korean   23 | 14 | 17 | $$

West 30s | 5 W 32nd St. (bet. B'way & 5th Ave.)
212-967-1900
Bayside | 220-05 Northern Blvd. (220th St.) | Queens
718-224-8889

Even with "long" lines snaking out the front door, fans love getting into these Korean restaurants in Bayside and West 32nd to "slurp down" "flavorful, hot" soft tofu stew and to down "absolute bonus" fried mackerels and other "unlimited," outstanding banchan; "abrupt" service can be either "patchy" or "rushed," and the humidity inside may have you feeling "hot and stuffy," but you won't mind as much when you leave with "both your belly and wallet full."

The Beatrice Inn ℂ 🅱 Steakhouse   24 | 24 | 23 | $$$

West Village | 285 W 12th St. (bet. W 4th & Hudson Sts.)
212-675-2808 | thebeatriceinn.com

"If you love meat," this "indulgent" former speakeasy in the West Village may be "the place for you," given its "inventive, daring" steakhouse options (including "delicious" dry-aged cuts and other "excellent" updated American dishes), that emerge in "portions fit for Henry VIII"; also notable are the "clubby," fireplace-enhanced digs, "knowledgeable" staff, and the "lively crowd" of "high-rollers" well-"prepared to pay" the prices required here.

Beaubourg French   18 | 20 | 18 | $$$

Battery Park City | 225 Liberty St. (West St.)
212-981-8589 | beaubourgny.com

Ideal for a rosé-fueled "lazy summer weekend," this "gem in the World Financial Center" offers serene "views of the New York Harbor" and is a "fun place all-around"; while the "service is often slow," and the French food is "solid," "not spectacular," the setting is: most find the "drinks and view are worth it," especially if you choose to "sit outside," "order a bottle," and escape.

Beauty & Essex American   22 | 26 | 21 | $$$

Lower East Side | 146 Essex St.
(bet. Rivington & Stanton Sts.)
212-614-0146 | beautyandessex.com

"Once you figure out how to get in" "through a pawnshop," you'll be welcomed into a "hidden" "speakeasy"; the "party scene" of "models and influencers" "who want to go out and photograph their night" is fueled by an "eclectic menu" of "tapas from around the world," and although it's "louder than a frat house," fans say the "swanky service," "luxurious ambiance," and "free champagne" in the ladies' bathroom will "make your friends jealous."

☑ Becco Italian 　　　　　　　22| 19| 21| $$|
West 40s | 355 W 46th St. (bet. 8th & 9th Aves.)
212-397-7597 | becco-nyc.com
"Tutti a tavola a mangiare, indeed," echo fans of this "popular" Theater District "stalwart" on Restaurant Row; it's a "convenient pre-Broadway show" destination for "consistent" Italian "standards," a "bountiful" pasta sampler "bargain," and a "reasonably priced" wine list; sure, the "noisy," "average"-looking digs generally are "crazy-busy" with "a young crowd" of tourists and others, but the "attentive servers make sure you don't miss your curtain," and "your wallet won't be empty."

Beccofino Italian 　　　　　　　　24| 18| 23| $$|
Riverdale | 5704 Mosholu Ave.
(bet. Fieldston Rd. & Spencer Ave.) | Bronx
718-432-2604 | beccofinorestaurant.com
There's nothing "out of the box" and "everything is done just right," like "tender" veal and "perfectly cooked" pasta in "huge portions," at this "cute but modestly" appointed red-checkered-tablecloth neighborhood Italian standby in Riverdale; the "accommodating" staff, "reasonable" prices, and friendly vibes "warm the soul," and for the locals, it's also popular for "takeout."

🆕 Belcampo American /Steakhouse 　　　-| -| -| $$|
West 30s | 20 Hudson Yards
(10th Ave. & 33rd St.)
212-244-4474 | belcampo.com/restaurant
Hudson Yards welcomes the first New York location of this California chain of butcher shops/steakhouses, which raises its own animals, providing a more holistic dining experience and a menu focused on steaks, burgers, and house-made sausage; it delivers a more casual atmosphere and lower bill than other chophouses in the complex, and you can also just get meat to cook at home, or grab a warming cup of bone broth on draft.

Bella Blu Italian/Pizza 　　　　　22| 18| 20| $$$|
East 70s | 967 Lexington Ave. (bet. 70th & 71st Sts.)
212-988-4624 | bellablunyc.com
"Busy," "bustling," "boisterous" – some would add "overwhelmingly loud" – this UES bistro continues to be "wildly popular," with a "loyal following of regulars"; those in the know advise to "arrive early to get a table near the front"; the pasta dishes are memorable, as are the "top-notch pizzas from the brick oven"; the veteran staffers "remember you and how you like your martini."

Ben & Jack's Steakhouse Steakhouse 　25| 21| 24| $$$|
East 40s | 219 E 44th St. (bet. 2nd & 3rd Aves.)
212-682-5678 | benandjackssteakhouse.com
"Go hungry" to this "rock-solid," family-owned East 40s steakhouse in the Even Hotel, a standby for "overflowing plates" of

"consistently excellent" dry-aged meats, along with "fantastic" wines, served by a "courteous" staff that "remembers its customers"; not as lauded are the "expensive" tabs, although the "lovely" setting reduces the sting.

🄰 Benjamin Steakhouse Steakhouse   27 | 23 | 25 | $$$$

East 40s | 52 E 41st St.
(bet. Madison & Park Aves.)
212-297-9177 | benjaminsteakhouse.com
Benjamin Prime
East 40s | 23 E 40th St. (bet. Madison & Park Aves.)
212-338-0818

Carnivores make pilgrimages to this "first-rate" Midtown steakhouse, "a shrine" to "top-notch" meat, particularly "melt-in-your-mouth" steaks and the "to die for" bacon appetizer; combined with a "festive atmosphere" are "incredibly attentive" waiters who "always suggest a winner" on the "extensive" wine list; you can feel the "old-world charm" almost instantly once you step inside the "cool" bilevel dining room, with "sweeping ceilings" and a "functioning" fireplace during the winter.

Benno 🅂 🅼 French   26 | 23 | 27 | $$$$

NoMad | 7 E 27th St.
(bet. 5th & Madison Aves.)
212-451-9557 | bennorestaurant.com

Informed by a "time-tested yet forward-thinking aesthetic," this "exemplary," dinner-only NoMad French-Italian in the Evelyn Hotel showcases "imaginative" cuisine on prix fixe menus in the dining room, along with a "tremendous" group of drinks and "solicitous" service; "pricey" tabs hardly dim the "dramatic but not ostentatious" setting, and diners' ability to "hear each other in conversation" is a big plus; P.S. the bar also has à la carte options.

Benoit New York French   22 | 22 | 22 | $$$

West 50s | 60 W 55th St. (bet. 5th & 6th Aves.)
646-943-7373 | benoitny.com

When you step into this "little gem in the big city," prepare to be "transported" to "a corner of Paris in Midtown" by way of a "classic French bistro" from chef Alain Ducasse that's perfect for a "lovely, elegant meal" in a "warm atmosphere" that "includes French servers" and heaps of "old-school charm"; for quick pre-theater dining, there is a handy "bar area to eat and drink without a reservation."

Bernie's American   25 | 25 | 24 | $$

Greenpoint | 332 Driggs Ave.
(bet. Lorimer St. & Manhattan Ave.) | Brooklyn
347-529-6400 | berniesnyc.com

Like eating in an "Italian diner from the '60s," this retro-by-design corner spot in Greenpoint offers a "limited but fantastic menu" of comfort classics, with touches of "vintage BK," like the "chilled glasses for martinis" served by an "amazing" waitstaff; it's tiny and popular, but "worth the wait" to experience the "chic, cool" interior that you'll "want to hang out in every Saturday night."

Beso Spanish   24 | 23 | 24 | $$

St. George | 11 Schuyler St.
(Richmond Terr.) | Staten Island
718-816-8162 | besonyc.com

You can find "top-quality" Spanish dishes in Staten Island at
this St. George "happy hour" go-to with "attentive" servers,
scrumptious tapas, and sangria, all served in a romantic brick-
walled dining room; it's a popular place, so "bring patience
and your appetite," and since "the only thing tighter than the
seating is the parking," take the ferry if you can – it's right
next door.

Best Pizza (Pizza   25 | 14 | 18 | $

Williamsburg | 33 Havemeyer St.
(bet. 7th & 8th Sts.) | Brooklyn
718-599-2210 | best.piz.za.com

It's "not really a place to sit down," but this Williamsburg shop
has "serious food" and "lives up to its name," with a "perfect
representation of New York–style pizza"; once you smell it, you
"can't walk by without stopping" for a slice – especially "their
white pizza with onion jam" – fans advise avoiding more basic
competitors in the area and going straight here: don't let "loud
music" or the "grungy setting fool you" into missing out.

Beyoglu Middle Eastern   23 | 17 | 19 | $$

East 80s | 1431 3rd Ave. (81st St.)
212-650-0850

At this "neighborhood special" on the UES, you can get "tremendous bang for your buck" with "Turkish delights," including
a meze platter (get either "large to share or small to gorge") and
"freshly baked" bread that's "worth the carbs"; a "noisy" downstairs and "very active" alfresco seating is "high energy," but
the "romantic" second floor has "better acoustics" for intimate
conversations; despite being "always busy," the "cheerful and
efficient" staff "know what they're doing."

Big Wong ⊉ Chinese   22 | 6 | 13 | $

Chinatown | 67 Mott St. (bet. Bayard & Canal Sts.)
212-964-0540 | big-wong.com

The roast meats draw lots of attention at this "oldie but goodie"
in Chinatown that's also known for its duck, "sublime," "comforting" congee, and traditional Cantonese noodle soups; no doubt,
it's a "hole in the wall" with "nonexistent" service, but "oh-so-
good" eats and "cheap" tabs keep the crowds coming.

Z Birds of a Feather Chinese   26 | 22 | 20 | $$

Williamsburg | 191 Grand St.
(bet. Bedford & Driggs Aves.) | Brooklyn
718-969-6800 | birdsofafeatherny.com

The "spicy, spicy" Sichuan plates at this Williamsburg location
(sister to Midtown's Café China and with a similar menu)
appeal to diners seeking "soulful flavors"; the portions are
"hefty," the flavors "complex," and the soup dumplings "bite
back"; a communal table anchors the simple, modern space
with a "super hip" vibe and jibes well with the "boisterous,"
"noisy" crowd.

| | FOOD | DECOR | SERVICE | COST |

BK Jani Ⓜ Indian/Pakistani ▼ 25 | 13 | 18 | $$
Bushwick | 276 Knickerbocker Ave.
(bet. Suydam St. & Willoughby Ave.) | Brooklyn
347-460-5110
"Divine burgers" coexist with "juicy" beef kabobs and lamb
chops at this meat-forward "casual lunch or dinner spot in
Bushwick" with counter service, where subcontinental "influences and spices" ensure "the flavors pack a punch"; as the
handwritten notes affixed to the wall attest, "it's a great little
dive" – just don't be in a huge hurry, as the food can sometimes
take a while to arrive.

Black Ant Mexican 15 | 16 | 16 | $$
East Village | 60 2nd Ave. (bet. 3rd & 4th Sts.)
212-598-0300 | theblackantnyc.com
This "loud and crowded" East Village Mexican with margarita
machines and "club/lounge" vibes keeps crowds coming in for
"creative" dishes seasoned with "creepy crawlers"; although the
spot suits at least some "adventurous eaters," service can lag,
and those famed insect garnishes "don't add much in the flavor
department"; still, the bumping "back patio" keeps the "rowdy"
happy hour–goers and brunching "bottomless-champagne
crowds" jovial enough.

Black Barn American 21 | 23 | 22 | $$$
NoMad | 19 E 26th St. (bet. 5th & Madison Aves.)
212-265-5959 | blackbarnrestaurant.com
This NoMad establishment puts a "unique spin" on New
American cuisine with "farm-to-table" dishes and "interesting"
cocktails in a "cavernous space" appropriate for "after-work
business-meeting drinks"; while the food can sometimes "be
hit or miss" and the service "spotty," its location "near Madison
Square Park" suits the "young crowd" just fine; N.B. the Chelsea
Market outpost merges a café and bar with home decor for sale.

🄩 **Blanca** Ⓢ Ⓜ American 29 | 26 | 29 | $$$$
Bushwick | 261 Moore St. (Bogart St.) | Brooklyn
347-799-2807 | blancanyc.com
Like entering "an alternative universe" through "a wormhole in
the space–time continuum," this "incredible" Bushwick New
American – accessible via "a hidden passageway" connected
to Roberta's – features a "clever," "wildly creative" tasting menu
delivered at a 12-seat, kitchen-facing counter; it's "serious food
with a great sense of humor," and all you have to do is "ignore
the price," although when you consider the "phenomenal service," most can't help but be "carried away."

Blenheim American 21 | 20 | 21 | $$
West Village | 283 W 12th St. (W 4th St.)
212-243-7073 | blenheimhill.com
Using produce from the Catskills farm of the same name, this
"locavore" West Village café serves a "limited," "vegetable-
friendly" American menu in a "relaxed," country-inspired space
conducive to "mellow conversation"; although some call it more
"average" than not, the "corner location" and "postcard-perfect
outdoor seating" fit the bill "for catching up with friends," making it "nice" for brunch.

Blossom Vegan/Vegetarian · · · · · · · · · · · · · · · · · · · 22 | 18 | 21 | $$

Chelsea | 187 9th Ave. (bet. 21st & 22nd Sts.)
212-627-1144 | blossomnyc.com
Blossom on Columbus
West 80s | 507 Columbus Ave. (bet. 84th & 85th Sts.)
212-875-2600

"If you're curious about veganism, start here," say fans of these
hangouts, where the "extensive" menu offers lots of "inventive"
choices (like seitan cordon bleu, jackfruit tacos, Israeli bourekas)
that are also "satisfying": "attentive" servers set a "pleasant"
tone, and while the look on the UWS is a little more "modern"
than the Chelsea original, both are "relaxed" and "casual."

NEW BLT Prime Steakhouse · · · · · · · · · · · · · · · · · · · – | – | – | $$$

East 70s | 1032 Lexington Ave.
(bet. 73rd & 74th Sts.)
212-995-8500 | bltrestaurants.com

This swanky steakhouse chain is back in NYC, where it began,
but this time it's found a new home on the UES; the expansive
bilevel dining room serves a small menu of house-aged steaks
and cheesy popovers alongside updated classic cocktails and
a broad wine list; even though it's not a cheap date, fans of this
family of restaurants are glad it's returned.

BLT Steak Steakhouse · · · · · · · · · · · · · · · · · · · 25 | 22 | 23 | $$$$

East 50s | 106 E 57th St. (bet. Lexington & Park Aves.)
212-752-7470 | bltrestaurants.com

"Not your typical steakhouse," this "high-end" East 50s bastion
of beef "continues to impress" with its "excellent" cuts, "irresistible" signature popovers "served piping hot from the oven," and
portions large "enough to feed an army," as well as the diverse
wines and "friendly" staff; recent renovations ensure the "polished" setting retains its "indulgent" atmosphere that wows the
"business crowd" that spends "big bucks" on lunch and dinner.

Blue Mediterranean · · · · · · · · · · · · · · · · · · · 22 | 23 | 22 | $$

Randall Manor | 1115 Richmond Terr.
(Snug Harbor Rd.) | Staten Island
718-273-7777 | bluerestaurantnyc.com

"Cozy" "outdoor seating and large windows facing the water
amplify" the "well-prepared Mediterranean standards" and seafood dishes at this "romantic," "well-run" site in Staten Island's
Randall Manor; while "the cuisine is good, the atmosphere's
better," especially since "observing the ships along the Kill van
Kull" is pretty cool; overall, most are "satisfied" with this "tranquil dining experience."

Blue Fin Seafood · · · · · · · · · · · · · · · · · · · 22 | 20 | 21 | $$$

West 40s | W Hotel Times Square
1567 Broadway (47th St.)
212-918-1400 | bluefinnyc.com

"A robust selection" of seafood and "glitteringly fresh sushi
and sashimi" makes this "swanky" high-ceilinged dining room
a "solid," if pricey, option for the Times Square area; as a "pre-
theater standby" it gets "crowded and noisy" before 8 PM, so
head upstairs to avoid the "dining factory" feel – those pressed
for time say the "friendly servers" are "quick but not rushed"
and can "get you out on time, with cookies to go."

🆉 Blue Hill American   28 | 25 | 27 | $$$$

Greenwich Village | 75 Washington Pl.
(bet. MacDougal St. & 6th Ave.)
212-539-1776 | bluehillfarm.com

Dan Barber's "O.G. farm-to-table," a Village "temple to fresh food" "before it became trendy," continues to serve "ingenious" locally sourced provisions via modern American prix fixe menus that "emphasize the natural flavors" of the ingredients so much you'll "taste the terroir"; "excellent wines," "top"-quality service, and a "peaceful" interior and garden are also pleasing, and while it's "not for the frugal," most diners confirm it's "a special treat"; P.S. the equally well-regarded Blue Hill at Stone Barns is in Westchester.

Blue Ribbon Brasserie (American   25 | 20 | 24 | $$$

SoHo | 97 Sullivan St. (bet. Prince & Spring Sts.)
212-274-0404 | blueribbonrestaurants.com
Park Slope | 280 5th Ave. (bet. 1st St. & Garfield Pl.) | Brooklyn
718-840-0404

"Still awesome after all these years," these "timeless" eateries serve an "eclectic" American menu of "upscale comfort food" (matzo ball soup, "amazing" fried chicken) to "a cool crowd" that includes other chefs – especially at the original SoHo "mainstay" – "until the wee hours"; while they're "a bit pricey," the "warm service" and "neighborhood atmosphere" ensure "a singularly New York experience."

Blue Ribbon Federal Grill American   21 | 18 | 22 | $$$

Financial District | AKA Hotel, 84 William St.
(bet. Maiden Ln. & Platt St.)
212-337-0404 | blueribbonrestaurants.com

Nearly "hidden away" in the AKA Wall Street hotel, this "quality" Financial District enclave serves "creative" steaks, burgers, and seafood (including caviar) in "businesslike" environs; staff is "engaged," and it's "not too noisy," making it a "solid corporate lunch spot"; N.B. there's breakfast and brunch, too.

Blue Ribbon Sushi (Japanese/Sushi   25 | 20 | 22 | $$$

SoHo | 119 Sullivan St. (bet. Prince & Spring Sts.)
212-343-0404 | blueribbonrestaurants.com

"Superior sushi" is the forte of this "always buzzy" SoHo spot, a raw-fish "mecca" serving its "fabulous" Japanese fare in wood-paneled digs until the early morning; a no-reservations policy means "getting in the door is a challenge," and "high-end prices" can be difficult for some to take, but a staff that "tries hard," plus a large selection of sake and wine make for "a pro operation all around."

Blue Ribbon Sushi Bar &   25 | 20 | 22 | $$$
Grill (Japanese/Sushi

West 50s | 6 Columbus Hotel, 308 W 58th St.
(bet. 8th & 9th Aves.)
212-397-0404 | blueribbonrestaurants.com

Fish "so fresh it's practically swimming on your dish" typifies this West 50s "winner," where there's a "varied menu" of "sumptuous" sushi, combo platters, and other Japanese fare, plus "incredible fried chicken" and a deep sake list, in "cozy"

surroundings within the 6 Columbus Hotel; high noise levels
detract a bit, but it's very convenient to both Lincoln Center and
the Time Warner Center, and its "attentive service" is icing on
the cake.

Blue Ribbon Sushi   25| 22| 23| $$$|
Izakaya ℂ Japanese/Sushi
Lower East Side | 187 Orchard St.
(bet. Houston & Stanton Sts.)
212-466-0404 | blueribbonrestaurants.com

With a brand and "a name that represents quality," this "swanky"
LES establishment supplies "incredibly fresh" raw fish, along
with omakase options and other Japanese provisions in a
"hip" space at the Sixty LES Hotel that "makes you feel like a
character on *Billions*"; "delicious" cocktails, plus numerous sake
and wine choices, mitigate the "costly" bills, and the late hours
also gain plaudits; P.S. "sitting at the sushi bar" comes "highly
recommended."

Blue Smoke Barbecue   21| 19| 21| $$$|
Battery Park City | 255 Vesey St.
(bet. North End Ave. & West St.)
212-889-2005 | bluesmoke.com
Flatiron | 116 E 27th St. (bet. Lexington Ave. & Park Ave. S)
212-447-7733

There's "no smoke and mirrors" at these "surprisingly solid"
chowhouses supplying "Danny Meyer's take on BBQ"; customers "leave full" after downing "stick-to-the-ribs" smoked meats
and sides "with a Southern culinary accent," along with drinks
that "hit the spot"; the "simple," "lively" digs and "reasonable"
prices, plus the Jazz Standard club at the original Flatiron
location (a "bonus"), ensure that 'cue connoisseurs keep these
"standbys" in mind, and some even bring "visiting friends from
Texas" along.

Bluebird London British   16| 23| 17| $$$|
West 50s | 10 Columbus Cir. (W 59th St.)
347-682-2100 | bluebirdlondon.nyc

"Make sure to get a window table," as "magnificent views of
Central Park" from the Time Warner Center are the main attraction at this "hip" London import; although the "Americanized
British food" is "nothing special for the price," and "service is a
bit of a downer," you can still enjoy tea service or make a "special night" out of a "proper beef Wellington" and a gin and tonic.

Boat Basin Cafe American   15| 22| 16| $$|
West 70s | Riverside Park (W 79th St.)
212-496-5542 | boatbasincafe.com

There is "no better place for an NYC sunset" than the "relaxing" patio on the West end of 79th Street, with pink-tinged river
views; service is barely there, the "simple lunches" sometimes
border on the just "edible," and they don't take reservations, but
that doesn't stop the "crowds" that "can't wait for the season
to begin" every summer from lining up to "bask in the sunshine
and watch the boats come and go."

Bobby Van's 🅂 Steakhouse   23 | 20 | 23 | $$$
East 40s | 230 Park Ave. (46th St.)
212-867-5490 | bobbyvans.com
🅂 **East 50s** | 131 E 54th St. (bet. Lexington & Park Aves.)
212-207-8050
🅂 **Financial District** | 25 Broad St. (Exchange Pl.) | 212-344-8463
West 40s | 120 W 45th St. (bet. 6th & 7th Aves.) | 212-575-5623
West 50s | 135 W 50th St. (bet. 6th & 7th Aves.) | 212-957-5050
With "mammoth" steaks so tender they "melt in your mouth,"
this "old-school" steakhouse chain with several locations
in Manhattan is equally well known for its burgers; there's a
"clubby" atmosphere with "lots of hustle and bustle" in the
dining room, a "busy" bar serving "generous" cocktails, and a
"friendly and sincere" staff.

Bobwhite Counter Southern   25 | 15 | 21 | $$
East Village | 94 Avenue C (6th St.)
212-228-2972 | bobwhitecounter.com
You'll "keep coming back" for the Southern soul with a dollop
of "Alphabet City charm" here; the biscuits and chicken rank
among the best north of the Mason-Dixon Line (or at least the
Hudson), at an "affordable guilty pleasure" price; "be prepared
to wait," and expect "friendly" service in a "super-casual"
atmosphere that's bustling and best "for brunch," "quick dinner"
fill-ups, and for excellent happy hour specials.

Bocca Italian   23 | 19 | 23 | $$
Flatiron | 39 E 19th St. #1 (bet. B'way & Park Ave. S)
212-387-1200 | boccanyc.com
Diners perk up when describing the "delicious" pasta cacio e
pepe that's prepared with a flourish next to your table at this Flatiron "go-to" for Italian fare, which was renovated in early 2019;
the rest of the "always-changing" menu gets high marks as well,
as does the "personable and excellent" service from the staff
and an owner who is "always recognizing and greeting you."

Bocelli Ristorante Italian   26 | 23 | 24 | $$$
Old Town | 1250 Hylan Blvd.
(Parkinson Ave.) | Staten Island
718-420-6150 | bocellirest.com
"Delish" "Grandma's cooking"-style Italian dishes shine at this
"solid" Old Town Staten Island standby, popular for "special occasions," that showcases its fare in a "nostalgic" bilevel interior
outfitted with a "curved staircase," Tuscan-style murals, and
white-tablecloth settings; that might be a somewhat "dated"
look to some, but the professional staff keep things humming.

Bodega Negra ☾ Mexican   21 | 24 | 20 | $$$
Chelsea | Dream Downtown, 355 W 16th St.
(bet. 8th & 9th Aves.)
212-229-2336 | bodeganegranyc.com
Fueled by "alcohol flowing freely," the "atmosphere is sexy" and
perfect for "pretty-people-watching" at this "lively," "clubby"
Chelsea site, which is true to its name and "dark" ("be careful
not to trip"); the tacos and the rest of the Mexican food, though
"tasty," feels "overpriced," but "if you're looking for a great pregame and money is not a concern, this will do the trick."

Bodrum Mediterranean   20 15 20 $$

West 80s | 584 Amsterdam Ave. (bet. 88th & 89th Sts.)
212-799-2806 | bodrumnyc.com
"The Mediterranean meets Istanbul" at this "dependable" UWS
joint, which furnishes a "solid menu" (including meze and brick-
oven pizzas) at "fair" prices; while some note that its food is
"dependable but not inspiring," its "tiny" space is on the "bare-
bones" side, and the "crowds" make it "a little noisy," "pleasant
service" and a "neighborhood feel" ensure it's "a frequent haunt
for locals"; P.S. outdoor seating in good weather is "a delight."

Bogota Latin Bistro Latin American   21 18 20 $$

Park Slope | 141 5th Ave. (St. Johns Pl.) | Brooklyn
718-230-3805 | bogotabistro.com
"Come for the drinks and empanadas" and for the Colombian
food in "huge portions"; the pan-Latin Park Slope standby
"within walking distance of Barclays Center" is "high energy,"
with its "bustling space," indoor and out, well suited for kids or
groups; the "good vibes" also mean things may get "noisy and a
bit chaotic."

Bohemian Japanese   26 25 26 $$$

NoHo | 57 Great Jones St. (bet. Bowery & Lafayette St.)
unlisted | playearth.jp/eng/bohemian_ny
"Good luck entering here," chuckle insiders who've discovered
this NoHo Japanese with a "password premise" that's part of an
international chain and has a butcher shop as its cover; a refer-
ral from a previous diner (or at least light vetting) is required
for reservations; if you get in, you'll enjoy a "unique" experience
of "eclectic," "tasteful bites," "quality cocktails," a "serene,"
loungey atmosphere, and "speakeasy-type vibes"; "gracious"
service and non-bohemian prices round everything out.

BondST ◖ Japanese/Sushi   26 22 22 $$$$

NoHo | 6 Bond St. (bet. B'way & Lafayette St.)
212-777-2500 | bondstrestaurant.com
For a "cool space" and "consistently" excellent Japanese fusion,
visit this "elegant but aging" NoHo sushi club, where the old
townhouse it's built in is still bumping, the bartenders are still
"charming," and the tuna tarts are still "to die for"; partiers say
that while it's tasty, all that "food is really a foil for" the "downstairs lounge" where you'll feel "like an A-lister"; either way, fans
feel it's "worth the splurge" – "lychee martini, anyone?"

Boqueria Spanish   23 19 20 $$

East 70s | 1460 2nd Ave. (76th St.)
212-343-2227 | boqueriarestaurant.com
Flatiron | 53 W 19th St. (bet. 5th & 6th Aves.) | 212-255-4160
SoHo | 171 Spring St. (bet. B'way & Thompson St.)
212-343-4255
West 40s | 260 W 40th St. (bet. 7th & 8th Aves.)
212-255-6047
Serving "reliable" tapas (it's "a go-to place" for them), along
with "wonderful wines" and "huge pitchers of sangria," this
"bit of Barcelona in New York" has a "boisterous and festive
atmosphere" that makes it right "for noisy celebration, but not
an intimate dinner"; the chain's service is "friendly and eager to

please," although the "space is a little cramped" and "you can't leave without knocking over someone's water glass."

Boucherie **(** French
20 | 22 | 19 | $$$

Gramercy | 225 Park Ave. S (bet. 18th & 19th Sts.)
212-353-0200 | boucherie.nyc
(West Village | 99 7th Ave. S (bet. Grove & Barrow Sts.)
212-837-1616

Expect "satisfying versions of the usual suspects" at these "classic" and "approachable" French bistros near Union Square and the West Village; they are known for their steaks, broad wine selection, "impressive" desserts, and an appealing brunch; dark-wood furnishings, leather furniture, "spindly chairs," and bistro tables set the "full Left-Bank brasserie drag" look in the dining area, while "accommodating" servers keep things "welcoming."

Z Bouley at Home Ⓢ French
29 | 25 | 28 | $$$$

Flatiron | 31 W 21st St. (bet. 5th & 6th Aves.)
212-255-5828 | davidbouley.com

"A home away from home," sigh smitten diners over David Bouley's "fabulous" Flatiron venue, which "offers two distinct dining experiences": one where you "interact with the chefs," sitting at cooktop tables in "space-age kitchen" surroundings, and another, "more traditional" service in "a mash-up of an elegant living room and hippie loft"; either way, you feast on "thrilling," "health-focused" French dishes that "wring extra flavor out of each ingredient," engineered by "well-trained staff" who are "knowledgeable and passionate about their work."

Boulton & Watt **(** Gastropub
18 | 18 | 18 | $$

East Village | 5 Avenue A (1st St.)
646-490-6004 | boultonandwattnyc.com

This "Americanized gastropub" – complete with "big open windows," steampunk decor, pickleback shots, and a "top-notch burger" (lots of apps and salads too) – is not the best "if you're in a rush," but it's an "easy" "corner joint" that attracts a "young crowd"; "hang out with friends and have a casual drink . . . or three" or end a spree of East Village "bar-hopping" with "late-night bites" until last call.

Z Boulud Sud Mediterranean
26 | 24 | 25 | $$$

West 60s | 20 W 64th St. (bet. B'way & CPW)
212-595-1313 | bouludsud.com

There are "not many UWS places of this caliber, but they always perform" at this "consistently creative oasis" at Lincoln Center, where there's an "inventive," "easy-breezy menu" of "snazzy riffs on pan-Mediterranean" creations; while it may feel like you're eating "inside a ship," the "unusually thoughtful and accommodating service" is ready to "get you out in time for the curtain"; it's "not a cheap date," but fans of the grapefruit givré say the elaborate icy "dessert alone is worth" the price of admission.

Bowery Meat Company Steakhouse
24 | 23 | 23 | $$$

East Village | 9 E 1st St. (Bowery)
212-460-5255 | bowerymeatcompany.com

How swell to have a "solid steakhouse not in Midtown or Downtown" say those mightily "impressed" by this East Villager, from the "excellent apps" and "juicy, tender" mains to the "cool vibes" of its glossy wooded, midcentury modern decor to the near-"warm and professional service" (the chef "brings out a tray of raw meat and you choose your cut"); in short, if you're a beefeater, "go, go, go."

⚡ Brasserie 8½ French   24 | 25 | 25 | $$$

West 50s | 9 W 57th St. (bet. 5th & 6th Aves.)
212-829-0812 | brasserie812.com
Diners "love the Hollywood entrance" to this "underground" Midtown French brasserie, where they descend a "dramatic" spiral staircase to a "chic," "spacious" interior highlighted by "fine art" and a "sound level conducive to conversation"; add in the "lovely" edibles – including a "wonderful" Sunday brunch (among other "value" menu options), "lively bar scene" and "gracious" service, plus "convenience" to Carnegie Hall and City Center – and you've got an experience that "leaves your soul better off."

Brasserie Ruhlmann French   19 | 21 | 19 | $$$

West 50s | 45 Rockefeller Plaza
(bet. 50th & 51st Sts.)
212-974-2020 | brasserieruhlmann.com
It's "more about decor than food" at this red-velvet-and-mahogany "monument to Art Deco" named after the famed 1920s designer/avatar of the era; the French dishes are "acceptable but decidedly secondary," as is the service ("slow"); it's also all "a bit overpriced – but then again, you are in Rockefeller Center," and "when the weather is nice," you can "sit outside and watch the beautiful people go by."

Brennan & Carr ⓒ Deli   24 | 14 | 20 | $$

Sheepshead Bay | 3432 Nostrand Ave.
(Avenue U) | Brooklyn
718-769-1254 | brennanandcarrbrooklyn3.mybistro.online
Regulars of this circa-1930 Sheepshead Bay sandwich joint advise "throwing decorum to the wind" and ordering the "melt-in-your-mouth" roast beef sandwich double-dipped – "eat this baby with a knife and fork" for an "unforgettable" experience; servers clad in butcher coats work a wood-paneled space that "hasn't changed in forever" – it's a real "throwback" that "can't be beat for old Brooklyn nostalgia."

The Breslin ⓒ British/Gastropub   22 | 20 | 18 | $$$

NoMad | Ace Hotel, 16 W 29th St.
(bet. B'way & 5th Ave.)
212-679-1939 | thebreslin.com
A visit to this all-day option in the Ace Hotel proves that there's still lots of life left in "British classics," with a spotlight on a "to-die-for" lamb burger and other "innovative, yet old-school" plates out of a "carnivore's dream": blood sausage, gamey terrines, and a whole roasted suckling pig for larger groups; the service runs hot and cold, and some find it "cramped and noisy," but most agree it's "the place to go" when you want to eat "hearty."

	FOOD	DECOR	SERVICE	COST

Brick Lane Curry House Indian | 22 | 15 | 19 | $$ |

East Village | 99 2nd Ave. (6th St.)
212-979-8787 | bricklanecurryhouse.com

"If you like spice" and are ready for the challenge, try the infamous face-melting phaal; those with more moderate tastes will find a menu full of "comfort" curries with a British accent that remind Londoners "of home"; even if the "tired" digs and mediocre service don't wow, the food remains "a cut above" most competitors in the environs of Sixth Street, and the "moderate prices" just sweeten the deal.

Bricolage Vietnamese | 23 | 20 | 21 | $$ |

Park Slope | 162 5th Ave. (Degraw St.) | Brooklyn
718-230-1835 | bricolage.nyc

An "inventive menu" (including decent vegan and vegetarian options) makes this "supercool" Vietnamese gastropub a reliable bet along Park Slope's restaurant row, with standout dishes (the obsessed "dream of their ribs") and cocktails that attract a varied crowd of "adventurous eaters" who appreciate the "relaxed" warm-brick setting and "lovely patio" – it's got "laid-back California style."

Brioso Italian/Pizza | 24 | 22 | 23 | $$$ |

New Dorp | 174 New Dorp Ln. (9th St.) | Staten Island
718-667-1700 | newyork.briosorestaurants.com

You can "smell the pizza" as soon as you walk into this New Dorp, Staten Island, trattoria that's centered around a rustic brick oven; in a "neighborhood where Italian cooking is taken seriously," it's known for "high quality," "reasonable" prices, and an overall "elegant experience" with "professional service" – and in spite of it getting "noisy" at times, regulars keep coming back.

Brooklyn Cider House Ⓜ Gastropub | 18 | 23 | 23 | $$ |

Bushwick | 1100 Flushing Ave. (Varick Ave.) | Brooklyn
347-295-0308 | brooklynciderhouse.com

At this industrial-chic warehouse (with "cool" murals) in Bushwick, the New American dishes "complement" the "amazing" selection of ciders, "not the other way around"; diners like both the service and the tour, but what they really bask in is the fun of catching the cider served straight from the barrel, the real "not-to-be-missed" attraction here, especially for groups – "what a blast."

Brooklyn Crab Seafood | 19 | 22 | 18 | $$ |

Red Hook | 24 Reed St.
(bet. Conover & Van Brunt Sts.) | Brooklyn
718-643-2722 | brooklyncrab.com

"Put your aprons on and take out that mallet" for "steamed Maryland crab" at this "funky seafood shack" in Red Hook, an experience difficult to find elsewhere in NYC; the signature dish is solid, but "it's all about the seaside vibe and the view of the harbor"; fans advise bringing "ten of your closest friends for a fun and interactive meal" and then heading upstairs for sunsets and a panorama of the bay.

Brooklyn Farmacy & Soda Fountain American

22 | 26 | 21 | $$

Carroll Gardens | 513 Henry St.
(Sackett St.) | Brooklyn
718-522-6260 | brooklynfarmacyandsodafountain.com

An "old-fashioned malt shop" in Carroll Gardens offers "a wonderful retro experience," from the vintage 1920s apothecary cabinets to the penny tile floors and marble counter at which to indulge in "phenomenal and decadent" treats, from "giant ice-cream sundaes" to "terrific egg creams," and just about any milkshake and float combo you can dream up, along with sandwiches, breakfast items, and a rotating selection of pies.

Brunetti Italian/Pizza

24 | 15 | 22 | $$

West Village | 626 Hudson St.
(bet. Horatio & Jane Sts.)
212-255-5699 | brunettipizza.com

"This is pizza to savor!" say fans of this West Village spot "that feels like Italy"; the wood-fired pies are celebrated for their "crunchy, chewy thin crust," and the addition of small plates and salads make this equally "great for a casual date night or a large group"; sidewalk seating is "prime people-watching" – and "don't forget about the hidden garden in the back."

Bryant Park Grill American

20 | 23 | 20 | $$$

West 40s | 25 W 40th St. (bet. 5th & 6th Aves.)
212-840-6500 | bryantparkgrillnyc.com

"Perfect location – if only the food and service were better," sums up sentiments about this "festive" "fairyland" behind the New York Public Library; the American fare actually is "pretty decent" (if "a little pricey"), and the staff "friendly" enough; "but you're really here for the views of Bryant Park," whether on the "classy" umbrella-covered stone terrace in summer, the heated tent in winter, or the interior, "an impressive tribute to midcentury modern design and maple."

Bubby's American

21 | 17 | 19 | $$

Meatpacking District | 73 Gansevoort St.
(bet. Greenwich & Washington Sts.)
212-219-0666 | bubbys.com
TriBeCa | 120 Hudson St. (Moore St.) | 212-219-0666

At this "brunch mecca," the breakfast served "all hours of the day" includes "indulgent biscuits" and "fluffy and flavorful" pancakes; the "top-notch comfort food" at these two "no-frills but absolutely delicious" spots, the original in TriBeCa and the other in Meatpacking, also includes "heavenly fried chicken" and "apple pie like Mama used to make"; "quirky" as well as "family-friendly," it's often "packed," so "be prepared to wait."

Buddakan ☾ Pan-Asian

25 | 27 | 22 | $$$$

Chelsea | 75 9th Ave. (bet. 15th & 16th Sts.)
212-989-6699 | buddakannyc.com

"Still hot after all these years," this "temple to Pan-Asian dining" "seems always packed" with patrons reveling in the "absolutely gorgeous" "theatrical" atmosphere and a "varied menu" presented by "knowledgeable servers"; although "waiting for your table can be annoying" ("they run behind on reservations"), the faithful still "love coming here for group dinners and special occasions"; if the "noisy" scene isn't your thing, "the many smaller rooms" are more "intimate."

Bukhara Grill Indian · 21 | 16 | 18 | $$

East 40s | 217 E 49th St. (bet. 2nd & 3rd Aves.)
212-888-2839 | bukharany.com

"An exceptional lunch buffet" – with sixteen-odd regional specialties from India's Northwest served seven days a week – helps elevate this East 40s site near the UN "above the average Indian" venue; some prefer to get takeout, though, as the "waiters tend to hover" amid the stone-finished walls and paisley-patterned banquettes.

Bunker Vietnamese · 22 | 15 | 20 | $$

Bushwick | 99 Scott Ave.
(bet. Meserole & Randolph Sts.) | Brooklyn
718-386-4282 | bunkernyc.com

"Tightly hidden behind" a bunkerish exterior in Bushwick, this "casual bar/lounge/restaurant" is "not easy to find, but once you do, you'll be happy" with the Vietnamese vittles whose "home-cooked" "flavors burst in your mouth"; adorned with colorful flags and paper lanterns, the interior is "funky," and the "friendly staff" send out "good vibes."

Bunna Cafe Ethiopian · ▼ 26 | 22 | 21 | $$

Bushwick | 1084 Flushing Ave. (Porter Ave.) | Brooklyn
347-295-2227 | bunnaethiopia.net

This vegan Ethiopian spot is a "beacon of light" in Bushwick, with a "coffee ceremony" that helps keep North Brooklyn wired; combos like the aptly named "Feast" make it possible to try "everything on the menu," so it's the perfect place for sharing; to-go orders emerge in pizza boxes lined with injera (Ethiopian flatbread), and dishes tend to "highlight the veggies and skip the fillers," further enhancing the value.

Burger & Barrel American · 21 | 17 | 18 | $$

SoHo | 25 W Houston St. (bet. Greene & Mercer Sts.)
212-334-7320 | burgerandbarrel.com

Stop here on your way to the Angelika or post-screening for its famed burger, although the varied menu checks a lot more boxes, with salads, pastas, and chicken lollipops and additional bar-food classics; the "low-key, low-light" vibe, with wood and brick paneling in a modern "semicasual" space, makes it "good for date night."

Burger & Lobster American · 19 | 16 | 18 | $$

Flatiron | 39 W 19th St. (bet. 5th & 6th Aves.)
646-833-7532 | burgerandlobster.com
West 40s | 132 W 43rd St. (bet. 6th Ave. & B'way)
917-565-9044

"You know exactly what you're getting when you walk in the door," say diners about these "not-too-fancy" and sometimes "touristy" Flatiron and West 40s spots, part of a London-spawned chain with a "basic," "purposely limited" American menu of "solid" burgers and lobsters (steamed, grilled, and on rolls); "accommodating" (though sometimes slow) servers, an "energetic feel," and "humongous" digs fit for "big groups" and after-work gatherings are additional draws.

Burger Joint ◖ Burger Joint　　24 | 14 | 15 | $$
West 50s | Parker New York Hotel, 119 W 56th St.
(bet. 6th & 7th Aves.)
212-708-7414 | burgerjointny.com
Sunset Park | Industry City, 220 36th St.
(bet. Gowanus Exp. & 2nd Ave.) | Brooklyn | 718-801-8393
"The secret's been long out" about the "thick, juicy" patties
and "scrumptious fast-food-style" fries served here, but the
delicious bites still bring "tears of joy" to the hungry masses;
you'll have to be okay with dining "on top of the trash can" if you
can't land a seat in the "graffiti-covered" branch at the "posh"
Parker Hotel – it's "often packed with tourists" – but the "funky"
Industry City location remains under the radar.

Burke & Wills ◖ American/Australian　　20 | 20 | 21 | $$
West 70s | 226 W 79th St. (B'way)
646-823-9251 | burkeandwillsny.com
"Hoppin'-good" kangaroo burgers bring mates together at this
"low-key" UWS "hangout," named for a major 19th-century ex-
pedition; the "surprisingly fine" Australian and American dishes,
service, and "conversation"-ready atmosphere are the "perfect
recipe for a first date"; happy-hour options, a "lovely" weekend
brunch, and the chance to "enjoy a pre-dinner cocktail" in the
"dimly lit" upstairs speakeasy, Manhattan Cricket Club, get most
patrons stoked.

Bustan Ⓜ Mediterranean　　23 | 19 | 21 | $$
West 80s | 487 Amsterdam Ave. (bet. 83rd & 84th Sts.)
212-595-5050 | bustannyc.com
This Mediterranean/Middle Eastern spot "with a strong Israeli
accent" makes it "hard to decide" what to order with "surprisingly creative" selections, although generous dips are "a meal in
itself," and the "outstanding" homemade pita is hard to forget;
Upper West Siders can't help but succumb to "happy" vibes and
the "colorful, fun" interior, although the garden is "nice" and a
good escape when it gets too "bustling" during dinner.

Butcher Bar Barbecue　　23 | 17 | 21 | $$
Astoria | 37-10 30th Ave.
(bet. 37th & 38th Sts.) | Queens
718-606-8140 | butcherbar.com
The "juicy," "tender" burnt ends are the "absolute star of the
show" – "be careful, they sell out quickly" – at this Astoria BBQ
joint also known for "mouthwatering" ribs, plus burgers, sandwiches, and platters, as well as creative cocktails; the friendly
interior is decorated with a lot of dark wood, subway-tile walls,
and red accents, and the "cute outside space in the back is nice
on a summer day."

The Butcher's　　19 | 21 | 18 | $$
Daughter Vegan/Vegetarian
NoLita | 19 Kenmare St. (Elizabeth St.)
212-219-3434 | thebutchersdaughter.com
West Village | 581 Hudson St. (Bank St.) | 917-388-2132
Williamsburg | 271 Metropolitan Ave. (Driggs Ave.) | Brooklyn
347-763-1421
"Trendy" "Instagrammable" dining – think bleached wood and
hanging plants paired with avocado toast, açai bowls, and

"incredible" shakes – is on offer at these "sceney" vegetarian cafés with dishes "in good portions"; there's typically a wait to snag a spot, and the communal tables can feel "cramped," but its fans agree it's "worth" a visit – "a really solid job."

Butter American

22 | 22 | 22 | $$$$

West 40s | 70 W 45th St. (bet. 5th & 6th Aves.)
212-253-2828 | butterrestaurant.com

This "tony and tasty option" in the Theater District serves American cuisine with an "inventive" spin, creative cocktails, and desserts "worth saving room for"; "cozy booths," "well-spaced" tables, and "low noise levels" all make the "chic" "subterranean" space with "soaring ceilings" a comfortable dining space with plenty of room for groups, although some reviewers miss the original Downtown location's atmosphere.

Buttermilk Channel American

25 | 20 | 22 | $$

Carroll Gardens | 524 Court St.
(Huntington St.) | Brooklyn
718-852-8490 | buttermilkchannelnyc.com

Fans say the fried chicken is "to die for" at this "true comfort-food establishment" in Carroll Gardens; it's also known for its "loud," "packed" weekend brunches (be prepared for a "long" wait) and has a "convivial," family-friendly rep; the space can get pretty "crowded," but seats at the bar or on the patio during warmer months provide some respite from the action at what's become a "solid neighborhood joint."

Buvette ℂ French

26 | 23 | 21 | $$$

West Village | 42 Grove St.
(bet. Bedford & Bleecker Sts.)
212-255-3590 | ilovebuvette.com

"As close to the City of Light as you will get in Manhattan," this "delightful" West Village bistro whips up "fantastic" (albeit petite) French plates in a "casual" space that's "cute as a button" (and "small as a thimble"); the "tight quarters" translate to "crowds," and a no-reservations policy can spur "waits," yet "fair prices" and generally "friendly" servers keep its many fans coming back – as one reviewer puts it, "j'adore Buvette."

Cabana ℂ Latin American

24 | 19 | 21 | $$

Forest Hills | 107-10 70th Rd.
(bet. Austin St. & Queens Blvd.) | Queens
718-263-3600 | cabanarestaurant.com

Delivering "a . . . menu full of flavorful items," this "lively" Latin spot on Forest Hills' "restaurant row" supplies "excellent" "home cooking," plus "amazing mojitos" and other tropical drinks in a "bright," "casual" setting; though "you might want to introduce yourselves" to your neighbors, as you're almost "sitting on top of them," the "friendly staff" and "celebratory" vibe get that "mini-vacay" feeling going; N.B. no reservations.

Cacio e Pepe Italian

21 | 16 | 20 | $$

East Village | 182 2nd Ave. (bet. 11th & 12th Sts.)
212-505-5931 | cacioepepe.com

At this "unpretentious" trattoria, you can choose between a "quaint, small, and dimly lit" dining room and an "attractive garden space in the back"; a "reliable" spot in the neighborhood, it's named for the chef's "signature dish" of pasta with pecorino and pepper, but everything on the menu is "well prepared"; the prices are "not too over the top," and there's a "good selection of reasonable wines."

Café Altro Paradiso Italian   24 | 22 | 22 | $$$

Hudson Square | 234 Spring St. (6th Ave.)
646-952-0828 | altroparadiso.com

"Simple" yet "stunning tastes" typify this "super-buzzy" Hudson Square Italian café with "excellent" dishes, "creative cocktails," and a "deep" wine list in a "bright," "sexy," "upscale" space marked by "soaring ceilings"; with so many "interesting people" around you (including the "after-work" crowd), it's easy to ignore the "pricey" tabs, and the "decent" service and an appealing brunch help make this "a perfect post-SoHo-stroll spot."

🄯 Cafe Boulud French   28 | 25 | 26 | $$$$

East 70s | 20 E 76th St. (bet. 5th & Madison Aves.)
212-772-2600 | cafeboulud.com

Culinary "magic" abounds at Daniel Boulud's "civilized" East 70s "classic," which offers "first-rate" French dishes, a "wonderful wine list," and "impeccable service" in a "posh" interior sparking "easy conversation"; of course, "your wallet will be lighter" after dining here, but the chance to "watch the UES movers and shakers come and go" helps make it "a pleasure"; N.B. "the lunch prix fixe is a bargain."

Café China Chinese   25 | 19 | 20 | $$

Murray Hill | 13 E 37th St. (bet. 5th & Madison Aves.)
212-213-2810 | cafechinanyc.com

This Murray Hill mainstay is "the place to go for spicy Chinese" "if you don't want to take a hike to Downtown or Queens," serving "distinctive" classic dishes ("by all means, have the mapo tofu!") amid an interior that evokes 1930s Shanghai; there's "always" a line, so prepare to wait, but service is "friendly" and "accommodating"; P.S. no reservations for groups under eight people.

Cafe Clover American   19 | 22 | 19 | $$$

West Village | 10 Downing St. (6th Ave.)
212-675-4350 | cafeclovernyc.com

"Green gals" and guys groove to the "foresty" ingredients employed by this "reliable" West Village café, where a "creative crowd" digs the "scene" while consuming "light," "all-right" veggie-oriented locavore dishes – including at brunch – and seasonal drinks in a "chic" space; the staff doesn't quite compare, and it gets "noisy," but if you want to "please your friend who does yoga," this "serves its purpose"; P.S. there are "al fresco" options on "sunshiny" days, too.

Cafe Cluny French   22 | 22 | 22 | $$

West Village | 284 W 12th St. (W 4th St.)
212-255-6900 | cafecluny.com

A "lovely corner spot" with a "bustling brunch scene" that locals count themselves "lucky to have stumbled upon," this "quintessential West Village bistro" feels "like you're dining in someone's townhouse," with a menu that mixes "French favorites" (omelets are "eggy, fluffy perfection") and "culinary flights of fancy"; fans recommend reservations, but stress that "the wait is never long for a table."

Cafe D'Alsace French

| | 22 | 19 | 21 | $$ |

East 80s | 1695 2nd Ave. (88th St.)
212-722-5133 | cafedalsace.com

At this "Alsatian haven" on the UES, the "unusual" and "not very heart-friendly" French fare includes a "masterpiece" duck à l'orange and choucroute that's "to die for"; in fact, this "throwback brasserie" feels "more French than Paris," especially when the "funky," "close quarters" are filled with an "upbeat" neighborhood crowd; waiters treat you "like family," and a dedicated beer sommelier "separates this from the ordinary."

Cafe Fiorello ◖ Italian/Pizza

| | 22 | 19 | 21 | $$$ |

West 60s | 1900 B'way (63rd St.)
212-595-5330 | cafefiorello.com

Right "across from Lincoln Center" stands this Italian "fixture," a "convenient" "hangout" serving "hearty" "standards" (including "simple" pizzas and "appealing" antipasti) "fast" enough to be "in time for the show," despite the fact that it's "always crowded"; the "energetic (read: noisy)" atmosphere may also be the right "backdrop to critique the soprano" post-opera while "people-watching" inside and out; the "dated," art-enhanced digs and "tight seating" garner less applause.

Cafe Gitane ◖ French

| | 22 | 18 | 19 | $$ |

NoLita | 242 Mott St. (Prince St.)
212-334-9552 | cafegitanenyc.com
Dumbo | 70 Hudson Ave. (Water St.) | Brooklyn

This place didn't invent avocado toast, but it's long been known for its superlative version: "hipsters now mix with tourists" at the umbrella-shaded tables out front or in the "low-key" dining room; the couscous and the other dishes on the Moroccan-French menu of "fancy food" are "tasty" and "inventive," and the "people-watching is prime" at this "unpretentious" "NoLita classic," where "everyone seems famous."

Café Habana Cuban

| | 22 | 17 | 17 | $$ |

NoLita | 17 Prince St. (bet. Mott & Elizabeth Sts.)
212-625-2001 | cafehabana.com
Habana To Go
NoLita | 229 Elizabeth St. (Prince St.) | 212-625-2002
Habana Outpost ⌤
Fort Greene | 757 Fulton St. (Portland Ave.) | Brooklyn
718-858-9500

Fans agree that although the Cuban sandwich here is "epic," it's also "an extraordinary place for Mexican" food, serving the "best homemade tacos," "delicious frozen drinks," and "cold beers"; although blessedly "fun" and "energetic," the "NoLita space is small, so it's hard to get a table right away"; in contrast, the Brooklyn Outpost has a "large outdoor area that's usually bumping with music and people on nice weekends."

Café Henri French
20 **16** **20** **$$**

Long Island City | 1010 50th Ave.
(Vernon Blvd.) | Queens
718-729-5794 | henrinyc.com

"Casual and comfortable," this "cute little" LIC bistro has a "limited menu" of "classic dishes" "with French flair" (it's especially "great for crêpes"); it gets "super-busy on weekends around brunch time," causing the service to "slow," but chilled-out patrons advise to just "grab a café au lait and relax" among the chandeliers and the brown-red walls.

Cafe Luluc 🗗 French
22 **16** **18** **$$**

Cobble Hill | 214 Smith St.
(bet. Baltic & Butler Sts.) | Brooklyn
718-625-3815

"Pancakes (fried in butter)" are "consistently" appealing at this "cash-only bistro that offers a taste of France" along with cheerful red banquettes, wicker seating, and a pretty garden built around a tree out back; Cobble Hill locals flock here at brunch and lunch for meals that are "inexpensive for the quality" and for the chance to "go with friends and linger."

❷ Cafe Luxembourg French
22 **20** **22** **$$$**

West 70s | 200 W 70th St.
(bet. Amsterdam & West End Aves.)
212-873-7411 | cafeluxembourg.com

An UWS "mainstay" since 1983 whose "longevity speaks for itself," this "popular" brasserie offers "straightforward French classics" and "well-chosen" wines in a "small," "chic" space so drenched with "European charm" that you'll "swear you're in the Sixth Arrondissement"; "locals" mix with an "older," "pre–Lincoln Center crowd" – plus a "celebrity" or two – in "buzzy" surroundings while ignoring the "claustrophobic" seating and "noise"-amplifying acoustics.

Cafe Mogador Middle Eastern
24 **19** **21** **$$**

East Village | 101 Saint Marks Pl.
(bet. Avenue A & 1st Ave.)
212-677-2226 | cafemogador.com
Williamsburg | 133 Wythe Ave.
(bet. 7th & 8th Sts.) | Brooklyn | 718-486-9222

"Traditional," "well-prepared" Moroccan cuisine is on offer at these "popular" East Village and Williamsburg "old reliables," where "comforting" North African and "hearty" Middle Eastern dishes complement the requisite drinks in "casual" digs; the "cramped settings" and "interminable waits" aren't ideal, but "pleasant" service, "outdoor seating," and "reasonable prices" check all the boxes for a "Sunday brunch after a night of cocktails"; P.S. there's an indoor garden at the Brooklyn location.

Cafeteria ☾ American
18 **17** **17** **$$**

Chelsea | 119 7th Ave. (17th St.)
212-414-1717 | cafeteriagroup.com

"Still trendy" and therefore "usually a bit cramped and crowded," this "neighborhood hangout" is also open 24/7, with "quite the late-night scene," "from people in formal attire to models in skimpy outfits to drag queens"; fans say the "comfy"

modern diner fare ("from healthy to stoner's delights") makes
it a go-to place for breakfast and brunch/lunch; "al fresco sidewalk seating garners ample people-watching."

Campagnola Italian 23 | 20 | 23 | $$$

East 70s | 1382 1st Ave. (74th St.)
212-861-1102 | campagnola-nyc.com
When it comes to "fancy people"-watching, this "old-world" UES
"institution" still delivers, with "well-prepared" Italian dishes,
"quality drinks," and "excellent" service boosting the "lively" surroundings, which get even livelier when someone gets behind
the piano ("you never know who will get up and entertain");
some say only "frequent" customers receive "A+ treatment,"
and "prices do run high," but if you "go with a regular," you're
bound to have a "lovely" time.

Candle Cafe Vegan/Vegetarian 22 | 17 | 21 | $$$

East 70s | 1307 3rd Ave. (bet. 74th & 75th Sts.)
212-472-0970 | candlecafe.com
Candle 79
East 70s | 154 E 79th St. (bet. Lexington & 3rd Aves.)
212-537-7179
"Tasty and innovative," whether you are vegan or not, is the
feeling diners have as they sink into greens and "well-prepared"
proteins from an evolving menu concocted by a kitchen that
"never stops trying to improve"; although Candle 79 can seem
a little "stodgy" to some who like the more casual approach of
the others, they all are appreciated for providing "surprisingly
luscious" plant-based meals.

The Capital Grille Steakhouse 25 | 24 | 25 | $$$$

East 40s | 155 E 42nd St.
(bet. Lexington & 3rd Aves.)
212-953-2000 | thecapitalgrille.com
Financial District | 120 Broadway (Pine St.)
212-374-1811
West 50s | 120 W 51st St. (bet. 6th & 7th Aves.)
212-246-0154
This "favorite chain" of steakhouses is perfect for "upscale networking": "each location stands out" with a unique design, but
they all appeal to the "business lunch crowd" by offering "handsome interiors," "private room options," and "steaks cooked
just the way you" ordered; although you might want a "company
credit card" to handle the prices, "getting in is no problem," and
you'll "keep going back for the service."

Caracas Arepa Bar Latin American 24 | 15 | 20 | $$

East Village | 91 E 7th St. (1st Ave.)
212-228-5062 | caracasarepabar.com
Williamsburg | 291 Grand St.
(bet. Roebling & Havemeyer Sts.)
Brooklyn | 718-218-6050
Rockaway Park | 106-01 Shore Front Pkwy
(Beach 106th St.) | Queens | 718-474-1709
"Fantastic cheap eats" based around "all handmade," "chewy,
dense, and filling" arepas that are perfect for a "quick and
ready to devour" "casual weeknight dinner"; although fans do

enjoy the "friendly" "laid-back vibes at this mini-chain, they also say "you come here for the food" and "stay for the green sauce," not the "tight quarters."

Caravaggio Italian · 26 | 25 | 25 | $$$$

East 70s | 23 E 74th St. (bet. 5th & Madison Aves.)
212-288-1004 | caravaggioristorante.com
"Every course is more delicious than the last" at this "spot for proper pasta," a "reminder of what the UES can be"; the kitchen is "not breaking any culinary barriers," but every dish is "beautifully crafted" and the wine list is "extensive"; with "funky" art on the walls, the "sophisticated and chic" dining room is that rare thing, "quiet enough to carry on a conversation," with "nicely spaced" tables; just prep for "sticker shock" when you get the bill.

◪ Carbone Italian · 26 | 24 | 25 | $$$$

Greenwich Village | 181 Thompson St.
(bet. Bleecker & Houston Sts.)
212-254-3000 | carbonenewyork.com
From the Rat Pack soundtrack to the tuxedo-sporting staff, "everything is entertainment" at this "slick" Greenwich Villager that made an "old-school Italian red sauce joint" "new-school trendy"; it's "one of the hardest tables in the city to get," thanks to "impossible-to-keep-to-a-diet portions" of "superb" pastas, a "charming" chandeliered interior, and those "attentive servers"; the tabs cause even the "big-budget-minded" to blanch, but most maintain it's "worth every penny": "eating here makes you feel like a boss."

The Carlyle Restaurant French · 24 | 26 | 25 | $$$$

East 70s | 35 E 76th St. (Madison Ave.)
212-744-1600 | thecarlyle.com
A "New York City classic," this eternal favorite provides an "old-fashioned but delightful dinner experience" – it's "elegant" and "relaxed," with food from a "limited but satisfying menu" of American and Continental classics and "excellent" service "to match"; the "gorgeous room" is also a "see-and-be-seen" destination, so more jaded commenters suggest "listening carefully for evidence of insider trading, extramarital affairs, and the next preschool admissions bribery scandal."

Carmine's Italian Restaurant Italian · 21 | 17 | 19 | $$

West 40s | 200 W 44th St. (bet. 7th & 8th Aves.)
212-221-3800 | carminesnyc.com
West 90s | 2450 Broadway (bet. 90th & 91st Sts.)
212-362-2200
This perpetually "jam-packed" pair on the UWS and in Times Square is "a destination for locals and tourists alike (more tourists at the West 44th St. location)"; they all gather for "enormous platters" of "varied but basic" "old-school red-sauce Italian" dishes "served family-style" by "brash" staffers; skeptics sniff it's "time to cut back on the size and increase quality – more is not better here," but the "circus" scene works well for groups, who raise their glasses to "gluttony glorified!"

Casa Apicii ⑤ Ⓜ Italian
21 | 24 | 21 | $$$

Greenwich Village | 62 W 9th St. (6th Ave.)
212-353-8400 | casaapicii.com

"Set in a beautiful, peaceful townhouse" with "majestic" tall ceilings and a "fireplace," this is the perfect "date night spot" in the heart of Greenwich Village; serving pasta and other "modern" Italian dishes with an "attentive staff" and "a vast wine list," it's "definitely good" food, but "you're coming for the ambiance," and maybe a "perfect nightcap" at the hidden amaro-focused "library bar upstairs."

Ⓩ Casa Enrique Mexican
27 | 20 | 24 | $$

Long Island City | 5-48 49th Ave.
(bet. 5th St. & Vernon Blvd.) | Queens
347-448-6040 | henrinyc.com/casa-enrique

At this "unique" Mexican "standout," well "worth the schlep" to LIC, "stellar" dishes with "unusual flavor profiles" – plus "killer margaritas," myriad tequilas, and other drinks – are on offer; sadly, the "simple, all-white" interior is "a bit lacking," and "crowds" of "hipsters" make it "hard to get a table," although the "warm staff," "upbeat" vibe, and "relatively affordable prices" put things in perspective.

Casa Lever Italian
23 | 25 | 24 | $$$

East 50s | 390 Park Ave. (53rd St.)
212-888-2700 | casalever.com

Entering this Midtowner in the Lever House is "like stepping into a power-lunch movie set from another era" – say, the "chic 1960s," given the art that makes it feel like an "Andy Warhol museum" – its "refined furnishings" are "filled with the banking and corporate crowd"; the staff are "exceptionally knowledgeable about the wines" and the many "interesting choices" on the Milanese-oriented menu, while a "vibrant" patio scene "provides leverage" to the "expense-account-heavy" tabs.

Casa Mono ❰ Spanish
26 | 19 | 22 | $$$

Gramercy | 52 Irving Pl. (17th St.)
212-253-2773 | casamononyc.com

Tapas fans are in "snack heaven" at this "intimate" Spanish option, which turns out "inventive," "delish" small plates, along with "fantastic wines," in a "cozy" (read: "closet"-size) Gramercy Park space staffed by "pro" servers; just "cram" yourself in, "be prepared to know your neighbor," and prep for a "hefty" bill – it's a "small price to pay for such a wonderful meal," especially if you "sit at the bar for the show."

Cascabel Taqueria Mexican
17 | 15 | 17 | $$

East 80s | 1556 2nd Ave. (81st St.)
212-717-7800 | nyctacos.com
West 100s | 2799 Broadway (108th St.)
212-665-1500

"More for the Columbia University crowd" and their crosstown equivalents than anyone else, these "energetic" and "busy" UES and UWS taquerias sell lots of "upscale tacos," with a "wide range of protein options" (along with gluten-free choices), plus margs and other drinks; they're "not fancy" – the interiors have a lucha libre thing going on – and the service can be "disappointing," but "decent prices" and "boozy brunch" selections ensure they work for groups or "for a quick meal."

Casellula (Wine Bar
24 | 19 | 21 | $$

West 50s | 401 W 52nd St. (bet. 9th & 10th Aves.)
212-247-8137 | casellulahk.com

The cheese comes first at this Hell's Kitchen wine bar, with more than forty varieties to fill out your board; it's perfect for a "romantic" date, and the "pleasant," "knowledgeable" servers and a "decent" wine list enhance the "quaint," "cozy" "hometown" feel; that said, because it's "always crowded" and you'll probably have to wait for a seat, you quickly remember that you're still in Midtown.

Catch NYC (Seafood
23 | 23 | 19 | $$$

Meatpacking District | 21 9th Ave. (bet. Little W 12th & 13th Sts.)
212-392-5978 | catchrestaurants.com

This "swanky" "see and be seen" restaurant/bar "in the heart of the Meatpacking District" is "better than you'd think" – it "actually delivers"; "get a rooftop table" to enjoy the "panoramic views" along with the "freshest, briniest oysters" and "inventive" seafood dishes and "killer cocktails," but keep in mind that the "buzzing" atmosphere also means that the noise can reach "rock-concert decibel levels," and that servers "get lost for extended periods of time among the crowds."

Caviar Russe French
26 | 26 | 26 | $$$$

East 50s | 538 Madison Ave. (bet. 54th & 55th Sts.)
212-980-5908 | caviarrusse.com

A "little jewel box" on the second floor of a commercial building on Madison Avenue, this "exquisite" and "romantic" dining room is the "place for caviar"; the experience is "decadent" and the prices predictably "expensive," but "life is too short to miss indulgences such as this," especially when you factor in its distinction as "one of the very, very few restaurants in NYC where you can have a quiet conversation."

Cebu Bar & Bistro American
18 | 19 | 19 | $$

Bay Ridge | 8801 3rd Ave. (88th St.) | Brooklyn
718-492-5095 | cebubrooklyn.com

This Bay Ridge hangout is a "fun spot" for a "late-night cocktail" or classic American eats, including a "killer" tomahawk steak as well as burgers and salads plus eggs Benedict for weekend brunch; it can get "super busy" and "loud" here (it sometimes "seems like one big bar"), but servers are "attentive," and in the summer there's sidewalk seating to escape some of the noise.

Cecconi's Italian/Pizza
20 | 26 | 19 | $$$

Dumbo | 55 Water St. (Brooklyn Bridge Park) | Brooklyn
718-650-3900 | cecconisdumbo.com

For sunset-tinted dinners outside with a "view of the bridge" overhead that's "second to none," it's worth heading to this Dumbo branch of an international chain of Italian eateries to lounge and drink; many say the best options are appetizers and handmade pasta – the wood-fired pizzas are "overpriced" and don't feel "memorable" compared to other Brooklyn options, and the service requires "patience," but the scene and scenery are "spot on."

Celeste ✍ Italian/Pizza   24| 13| 20| $$|
West 80s | 502 Amsterdam Ave.
(bet. 84th & 85th Sts.)
212-874-4559 | celestenewyork.com
Just the place to "take your Italian mother," this "cash-only" UWS "staple" serves "exceptional" wood-oven pizzas, house-made pastas, and other "simple but comforting" fare at "ridiculously low prices" to the "hungry patrons" who "cram" the "teeny tables"; some bemoan the "noisy," "bare-bones" setting and hot-and-cold service, but it seems to suit the "neighbor-hood crowd" just fine; P.S. you can get reservations, but go "early or late, or you'll be waiting on the sidewalk."

Celestine Mediterranean   22| 24| 21| $$$|
Dumbo | 1 John St. (John St. Park) | Brooklyn
718-522-5356 | celestinebk.com
At this "neighborhood place" for wood-grilled Mediterranean and "creative" brunch, the "pricey" food isn't "mind-blowing," but it's fresh, "light," and generally "satisfying"; what does make it a "destination" are the skyline and Manhattan Bridge views; the competent service and "casual," "modern," "candlelit" set-ting also help clinch its role as a superb "date spot."

Cervo's Seafood   27| 24| 24| $$$|
Lower East Side | 43 Canal St.
(bet. Ludlow & Orchard Sts.)
212-226-2545 | cervosnyc.com
"Imaginative" yet "approachable" seafood drives this LES "charmer" offering "home-style" Spanish- and Portuguese-inspired dishes (the crispy "shrimp heads are the bomb"), in a "lovely" space that feels like "being in someone's kitchen"; the "energetic" mood and "gracious service" also help win over the many fans of this "low-key," intimate space, where "they really care about serving you a great meal"; P.S. "sit at the bar" to watch the culinary action.

Cesca Italian   22| 20| 21| $$$|
West 70s | 164 W 75th St. (Amsterdam Ave.)
212-787-6300 | cescany.com
This "neighborhood warhorse" on the UWS is "still holding its own for well-prepared Italian food" "in an airy, well-lit room" that includes a "lively" "tap room for casual snacks" ("get a table in the back for a more relaxed atmosphere"); on the downside, "service can be a little disjointed," and watch out "if you are go-ing before a show at the Beacon Theater" – it will be "crowded" and "too noisy."

Chadwick's American   24| 21| 24| $$|
Bay Ridge | 8822 3rd Ave. (89th St.) | Brooklyn
718-833-9855 | chadwicksbrooklyn.com
"It's no surprise" that this steakhouse on Bay Ridge's restau-rant row is "still going strong," given its "excellent" steaks,

"to-die-for" beef Wellington special, pork chops, other classic plates, all paired with solid drinks (the bartenders "don't skimp") and served by "friendly," "professional" staff; the "traditional" dining room has white tablecloths and works well for families and big groups.

Charlie Bird American/Italian
25 | 23 | 23 | $$$

SoHo | 5 King St. (6th Ave.)
212-235-7133 | charliebirdnyc.com

There's "quite the happening vibe" at this "sexy" SoHo hot spot, where "'90s hip-hop" is the soundtrack for "exciting" Italian-infused American dishes drawn from a "not-too-fancy menu" – "don't miss the pasta course"; in addition, an "impressive" small-producer wine list, "upscale-casual," "unfussy" digs with boombox prints on the walls, outdoor seating in summer, and a "pleasant staff" all help serve the right amount of "chill."

Charlie Palmer at The Knick American
23 | 23 | 23 | $$$

West 40s | 6 Times Square
(bet. B'way & 42nd St.)
212-204-4983 | charliepalmer.com

"Elegant with a capital E" sums up the experience at this eatery, from the "contemporary" decor to the "awesome view of Times Square"; "somewhat hidden" in a "spacious and quiet" room on the second floor of the Knickerbocker Hotel, it's that rare New York spot that's "great for conversation," and although the "extensive and innovative" menu is "a bit pricey," the "pre-theater prix fixe is an especially good deal."

Chavela's Mexican
24 | 23 | 23 | $$

Crown Heights | 736 Franklin Ave.
(Sterling Pl.) | Brooklyn
718-622-3100 | chavelasnyc.com

"High-quality" eats recalling "home-cooked meals made by your abuela" exemplify this "festive" Crown Heights "corner joint," which serves familiar options like tacos and enchiladas as well as some Mexican "deep cuts," plus "fab margaritas" and other drinks in a "hip" space frequented by "a crowd ready to party"; "reasonable" prices and happy-hour "bargains" help make it "worth the trek" – "other places are nicer," observes one fan, but few are as "unpretentiously outstanding" as this.

Chef's Table at Brooklyn Fare S M Seafood
28 | 25 | 28 | $$$$

West 30s | 431 W 37th St. (bet. 9th & 10th Aves.)
718-243-0050 | brooklynfare.com

The "highest level" of seasonal ingredients spark the "imagination" of a chef at this "special" spot "in the back of a grocery store" in Midtown West; diners savor "maddeningly delicious" seafood-focused Japanese-French fusion dishes at an oval communal counter that lets them witness the kitchen's "terrific" "military precision"; the price tag is steep (upward of $400), but most say it's "worth every penny," at least if "you're looking to celebrate"; the staff are "warm" and "unpretentious."

Chefs Club ⑤ American
25 | 24 | 24 | $$$$

NoLita | 275 Mulberry St. (Jersey St.)
212-941-1100 | chefsclub.com
It's "always a roll of the dice" here, where the menu reflects the skills of a rotating roster of guest chefs, but fans say the food almost always comes out "inventive and outstanding" and the service is "impeccable"; take their advice and "be sure to be seated at the counter" so you can gaze into the open kitchen, "where the magic happens"; it's also "noisy," so it's "not the place to have a conversation or propose."

Cherry Point Ⓜ American
22 | 20 | 21 | $$

Greenpoint | 664 Manhattan Ave.
(bet. Nassau & Norman Aves.) | Brooklyn
718-389-3828 | cherrypointnyc.com
This "refined, modern" "neighborhood bistro" in Greenpoint brings "laid-back" "Brooklyn vibes," a menu that mixes "modern English cookery" with American farm to table, and house-made charcuterie; the passable service and basic design don't make it a "must-go," but it's a pleasant spot for small plates, natural wine, or a "solid brunch" – "don't sleep on the sticky toffee pudding for dessert."

Chez Ma Tante American
26 | 20 | 23 | $$$

Greenpoint | 90 Calyer St. (bet. Franklin &
West Sts.) | Brooklyn
718-389-3606 | chezmatantenyc.com
It's "worth crossing an ocean" for "out-of-this-world," "fluffy, crisp-around-the-edges" pancakes, but you only have to cross the river to get brunch at Greenpoint's "neighborhood restaurant of your dreams"; the rest of the menu is full of delectable, internationally informed "soul food" served by a "no-nonsense" "professional" crew in a "modest" space with "modern," "minimal decor"; the "insider vibe" makes you feel like you've discovered a "service industry staple."

Chez Moi ☾ French
22 | 18 | 22 | $$

Brooklyn Heights | 135 Atlantic Ave.
(bet. Henry & Clinton Sts.)
Brooklyn | 347-227-8337 | chezmoiny.com
Head to this Brooklyn Heights bistro for "solid" interpretations of traditional French plates (like crispy frog legs, steak frites, mussels, seared duck breast) alongside "excellent" signature cocktails; the servers are "friendly," and the "intimate" space feels "chill" and "relaxed," keeping "neighborhood regulars" happy; after dinner, the party can continue downstairs in Le Boudoir, a Marie Antoinette–themed speakeasy.

Chimichurri Grill Steakhouse/Argentinean
24 | 15 | 22 | $$$

West 40s | 609 9th Ave. (bet. 43rd & 44th Sts.)
212-586-8655 | chimichurrigrill.com
A "dependable and delicious Argentinian steakhouse" with the "sweetest service in town," this "temple to excellent beef" gets the nod from those headed to a Broadway show, especially with its "affordable" prices; the meat is "flavorful and always cooked

perfectly," and the "eponymous sauce is always on the table"; the decor is "minimal" and "rustic," but it's also "pleasant" and "romantic," making it a "wonderful place for celebrations, political discussions, and business lunches."

China Blue Chinese   25 | 22 | 19 | $$$
TriBeCa | 135 Watts St. (Washington St.)
212-431-0111 | chinabluenewyork.com
"On a quiet TriBeCa street," this "upscale" Chinese eatery regales customers with "a robust menu" of "delish" Shanghainese specialties, plus a wide range of drinks; the "big," "high-ceilinged space" is good for groups, and there's a fair amount of seating outside; it's too bad the service doesn't quite match the "elevated" fare, although the prices certainly do.

Cho Dang Gol Korean   24 | 14 | 18 | $$
West 30s | 55 W 35th St. (bet. 5th & 6th Aves.)
212-695-8222 | chodanggolnyc.com
The silky tofu is made fresh every morning at this "healthy," "homestyle," "value-oriented" Korean favorite known for "traditional" spicy stews and its broad selection of banchan (complimentary side dishes) that make it a respectable alternative to the more BBQ-focused places closer to West 32nd; it's a simple place with plain decor, and there's "usually a wait," as they often "don't take reservations for small groups," but "efficient" service keeps the line moving.

Chola Indian   22 | 15 | 19 | $$
East 50s | 232 E 58th St. (bet. 2nd & 3rd Aves.)
212-688-4619 | cholany.com
"On a block with several Indian restaurants," this "mainstay" on the UES stands out for "fragrant and spicy" curries inspired by the southern coasts of the subcontinent, while also including favorites from the north; the weathered, "upscale" setting and "friendly" service aren't as distinguished as the bold flavors, but the prices are "reasonable," and the popular "value lunch buffet" has numerous options that make it "one of the great deals in NYC."

Christos Steak House Steakhouse   26 | 19 | 24 | $$$
Astoria | 4108 23rd Ave. (41st St.) | Queens
718-777-8400 | christossteakhouse.com
"Meat lovers" gladly make the trip for this "old-school" Astoria steakhouse, known for "top-notch" aged cuts plus sides and "a wide-ranging array of appetizers," all "augmented by delicious Greek touches" as well as professional service; the "Manhattan prices" and merely "comfortable" digs notwithstanding, the spot gets a "thumbs-up" overall, and valet parking is "a plus"; P.S. you can feast at the bar, too.

Chuko Ramen Japanese/Ramen   25 | 18 | 19 | $$
Prospect Heights | 565 Vanderbilt Ave.
(Dean St.) | Brooklyn
347-425-9570 | chukobk.com
"There's depth in the broth" in the signature offering at this "solid" Prospect Heights noodle house, and diehard regulars

swear that the "soul-healing" noodles ("this must be what they serve in heaven") are "hands down" best in Brooklyn; "the egg on top adds an extra layer of deliciousness and umami effect," advise fans, who also like the "build-your-own bowl!" and vegetarian options and the "sleek, modern space."

Churrascaria Plataforma Latin American   22| 19| 22| $$$|
West 40s | 316 W 49th St. (bet. 8th & 9th Aves.)
212-245-0505 | plataformaonline.com
"Be careful not to fill up on the delicious" salad bar, because this Brazilian-style barbecue joint near the Theater District is a "meat blizzard," where a single price allows you to eat until you tell them to stop; "considering the size of the place" and the "big groups" that fill it, the service is decent, and diners who "keep their head in the game" will be highly rewarded.

Cipriani Italian   24| 24| 23| $$$$|
Ⓢ **Cipriani Club 55**
Financial District | 53 Wall St. (William St.)
212-699-4096 | cipriani.com
Harry Cipriani
East 50s | 781 5th Ave. (bet. 59th & 60th Sts.)
212-753-5566
Cipriani Dolce ☾
East 40s | Grand Central Terminal, 89 E 42nd St.
(bet. Park & Vanderbilt Aves.) | 212-973-0999
Cipriani Downtown
SoHo | 376 W Broadway (bet. Spring & Broome Sts.)
212-343-0999
Giuseppe Cipriani of Harry's Bar in Venice invented the bellini, so you'll want to begin with the peaches-and-prosecco classic; these "clubby, gossipy, and exciting" restaurants have what "could be the best people-watching in NYC," drawing both celebrities and "well-heeled and fabulously dressed" regulars; the "old-style" service and "amazing" food "turn a meal into an event" – "like walking onto a Broadway stage" and being the star – but "expect to pay big, big bucks."

City Island Lobster House ☾ Seafood   21| 15| 19| $$|
City Island | 691 Bridge St.
(City Island Ave.) | Bronx
718-885-1459 | cilobsterhouse.com
Seafood "adventures" await at this "boisterous" City Island spot known for its "enormous" portions, lobster "deals," and "relaxing views" of the Sound from an outdoor terrace; some landlubbers point out it's "nothing fancy" ("don't dress up – please"), "noise levels" can be "disconcerting," and things get a bit "chaotic," but those after a "summertime outing" "won't go away hungry"; P.S. getting here is a lot easier "if you have a car."

The Clam Seafood   23| 19| 22| $$$|
West Village | 420 Hudson St. (St. Lukes Pl.)
212-242-7420 | theclamnyc.com
As you'd expect, the namesake bivalves are "fresh as can be," but all the seafood on the "small," "seasonal" menu" at

this "cozy" spot on a "sunny corner" is "inventive" and "well executed," and there's a "nice wine list to match"; although it's often "relaxed" and "comfortable" here, when it's crowded the noise level "can be painfully cacophonic."

Claro Mexican
26 | 20 | 23 | $$$

Gowanus | 284 3rd Ave.
(bet. Carroll & President Sts.)
Brooklyn | 347-721-3126 | clarobk.com

From a "compact storefront in Gowanus," this Mexican hangout serves an "upscale" menu of "modern twists" on classic Oaxacan eats (including "serious" moles) alongside a long list of "amazing" mezcal; the rustic-chic space is "hip" enough, but it's "really about the backyard" in warmer months. P.S. "bring your paycheck," as the dishes add up.

Claudette French
21 | 22 | 21 | $$$

Greenwich Village | 24 5th Ave. (9th St.)
212-868-2424 | claudettenyc.com

"North African and French styles meet" at this Greenwich Village spot, where a "whitewashed Mediterranean feel" and "welcoming staff" create "a warm atmosphere"; there's some nice outdoor seating, but "if it's at all busy, the noise level is unacceptable," and others feel that the food on the "limited menu" "won't blow you away, but the vibe is "impressive."

Clay Ⓜ American
25 | 24 | 24 | $$$

Harlem | 553 Manhattan Ave. (123rd St.)
212-729-1850 | claynyc.com

Step "away from the overwhelming buzz of" 125th Street before sitting down at this "special-occasion" spot for brunch or for a dinner of "handmade" pastas and other "exuberantly flavorful," "creative," "locally sourced" Italian dishes that "you will be dreaming about"; it has "unobtrusive" service, a "knowledgeable" sommelier, and a "trendy" atmosphere that feels "more like Downtown" – "reserve well ahead of time."

Clinton St. Baking
25 | 16 | 19 | $$

Company American/British
Lower East Side | 4 Clinton St.
(bet. Houston & Stanton Sts.)
646-602-6263 | clintonstreetbaking.com

"Happiness is a long wait" for the popular brunch at this LES bakery/café, known for its "show-stopping" pancakes, especially the blueberry – although "every morsel" of its American menu is "excellent"; the decor is just "a little nicer than a diner," but its "efficient" service and "reasonable prices" make the grade; N.B. "go in the evening" to sample "breakfast for dinner" and other chow while sidestepping the "maddening" "crowds" at peak times.

The Clocktower American/British
23 | 26 | 23 | $$$

Flatiron | Edition Hotel, 5 Madison Ave. (24th St.)
212-413-4300 | theclocktowernyc.com

You take the spiral staircase up to "another world" at this Flatiron spot, which serves "pub-style" food with American twists and modern presentations; inside the Edition Hotel, it has memorable Madison Square Park views, and while some find it "overpriced" and "club-like," the service keeps up, and the "beautiful," dimly lit, cozy setting makes you wish it was "the study in your home"; go ahead, play a "game of nine-ball" in the pool room at the end of your meal.

Club A Steakhouse Steakhouse   26 | 23 | 25 | $$$

East 50s | 240 E 58th St. (bet. 2nd & 3rd Aves.)
212-688-4190 | clubasteakhouse.com
This rare "low-key," "family-owned" steakhouse in Midtown East is best for perfectly charred "porterhouse to share," served on "sizzling platters" with plenty of "generous sides"; it's also known for "gracious," "committed" service that "falls all over itself trying to please," and the "cozy," "romantic," plush-jewelry-box decor and soft "jazz music" set an "intimate" mood perfect for when you want to actually "hear your dining companion."

Coco Pazzo Italian   27 | 24 | 26 | $$

SoHo | 160 Prince St. (Thompson St.)
917-261-6318 | cocopazzonyc.com
"He's back!," pasta lovers exclaim as they step inside the "protean" chef Pino Luongo's "more relaxed," "inviting" iteration of his megahit from the '90s, cooking "thoughtful, stimulating" Italian food "served like nonna" does, for diners "who know what it tastes like"; it's basically a "raucous" dinner party catering to a "very New York SoHo crowd," but elements like the "fabulous" wine shots win over first-timers.

Cocoron ⌿ Japanese   25 | 13 | 18 | $$

Lower East Side Ⓜ | 16 Delancey St. (Allen St.)
212-477-1212 | cocoronandgoemon.com
NoLita | 37 Kenmare St. (Elizabeth St.)
212-966-0800
"The whole world raves about ramen when they should be" "getting into soba," pairing them with "to-die-for" dipping sauce, say fans of these NoLita and LES favorites; with "many different vegan options," the "extensive" and "hilarious" menu also "notes how each ingredient and dish is somehow good for you"; while the "service and decor are nothing special," diners say "you'll be coming back for a bowl of buckwheat noodles sooner than you might think"; N.B. there's no takeout, and it's cash only.

Colonie American   24 | 23 | 22 | $$$

Brooklyn Heights | 127 Atlantic Ave.
(bet. Clinton & Henry Sts.) | Brooklyn
718-855-7500 | colonienyc.com
"Local ingredients" reign at this "lively" Brooklyn Heights modern American, where the "inventive" and frequently changing dishes (including "fresh vegetables that taste like they were picked that morning") share the spotlight with "well-thought-out" cocktails in a "cute" space featuring a greenery-enhanced wall and a kitchen counter where you can "watch the chefs in action"; "friendly" service and a "hip" vibe complete the picture, but keep in mind that "there are often lines, particularly at brunch."

The Commodore ℂ American   26 | 15 | 13 | $

Williamsburg | 366 Metropolitan Ave.
(Havemeyer St.) | Brooklyn
718-218-7632

"Don't expect white tablecloths" at this "sticky" bar – the look is more "disheveled" bowling alley, with "slow" to "nonexistent" order-at-the-bar service to match; that said, its party-hearty vibes, "late-night" hours, "throwback" "tiki-party" cocktails, and, most important, the "killer" fried chicken, are the powerful lures that keep Williamsburg "consuming 2,000-calorie" meals "in the dark" corners of what amounts to a quintessential faux-dive.

Community Food & Juice American   22 | 16 | 20 | $$

Morningside Heights | 2893 Broadway
(bet. 112th & 113th Sts.)
212-665-2800 | communityrestaurant.com

Columbia and Barnard students put on their best "ripped jeans" and "crowd" this "healthy-ish" Morningside Heights farm-to-table eatery when their parents are in town, particularly for breakfast and the "no-reservations" brunch, when stacks of "terrific" blueberry pancakes fly out of the kitchen at record speed; "pretty high" noise levels and tables "smack next to each other" aren't ideal, but "friendly, fast" waiters and outdoor seating make it "well worth" dealing with those small flaws.

Congee Village Chinese   21 | 14 | 15 | $$

Lower East Side | 100 Allen St.
(bet. Broome & Delancey Sts.)
212-941-1818 | congeevillageny.com
Flushing | 36-36 Prince St. (37th Ave.) | Queens
718-888-9799

Aside from the "creamy" namesake dish, this "popular refuge" for Cantonese "cheap eats" delivers via "warming," filling meals, both "stalwarts" and newer offerings that let you "experiment with new tastes"; the decor is "dated" and everything inside is a bit "worn at the corners," but rarely does that stop crowds from jamming into the "chaotic" space for its "dependable" fare.

Contra Ⓢ Ⓜ American   25 | 20 | 23 | $$$

Lower East Side | 138 Orchard St.
(bet. Delancey & Rivington Sts.)
212-466-4633 | contranyc.com

Serving prix fixe menus that amount to "accessible" tasting tours through seasonal food combinations and flavor profiles, this experimental American produces results that are "amazingly unique, every single time"; "attempts at creativity" don't just end on the plate, since the chefs and staff also make the most out of their "tight," "contemporary" LES space and accommodate many dietary restrictions to make their dinner a "special" one for (almost) everyone.

Convivium Osteria Italian   27 | 24 | 25 | $$$

Park Slope | 68 5th Ave.
(bet. Bergen St. & St. Marks Ave.) | Brooklyn
718-857-1833 | conviviumosteria.com

On offer in this aptly named Park Sloper are "unusual and delicious" Mediterranean dishes with "traditional and creative" preparations that take you "from Cinque Terre to Costa del Sol"; the "kickass pastas" and "cozy, romantic" farmhouse-rustic setting attract cheerful regulars and revelers, everyone pulled in by a "convivial staff" and a dark "to-die-for" wine cellar that feels medieval.

Cookshop American

`22| 19| 21| $$$`

Chelsea | 156 10th Ave. (20th St.)
212-924-4440 | cookshopny.com

Those after "a High Line break" or just a little "relaxation" after a midday "gallery hop" head to this "consistent" Chelsea spot for "inventive," "locally sourced" American eats (they're "famous for their brunch") and "excellent cocktails"; it's a "pretty" space with alfresco tables, weather permitting; sure, this is "not the place for a quiet conversation," but factor in the "genial" servers, "cool vibe," and "trendy" crowd, and you've got a "satisfactory" option "for all types of eaters."

Coppelia (Cuban

`22| 14| 19| $$`

Chelsea | 207 W 14th St. (bet. 7th & 8th Aves.)
212-858-5001 | ilovecoppelia.com

Open around the clock, this diner "has healthy food for the friend who wants a kale salad, and everything else for people who came to eat Cuban food" (the cubano sandwiches and plantains always get high marks); there's a "funky atmosphere" and a "cool crowd," but the "noise level becomes overwhelming once people begin to drink" at the bar, so "don't expect to carry on a conversation above the din"; it's a real "scene."

Corkbuzz (Wine Bar

`21| 20| 24| $$$`

Chelsea | Chelsea Market, 75 9th Ave.
(bet. 15th & 16th Sts.)
646-237-4847 | corkbuzz.com
Greenwich Village | 13 E 13th St.
(bet. 5th Ave. & University Pl.)
646-873-6071

At these "sleek" wine bars in Chelsea Market and the Village, there's a "huge selection" ("lots of wine by the glass") and "knowledgeable and friendly" sommeliers who work hard to make sure you "love what you're drinking": their pairings are on point, although the food – "think cheese boards and charcuterie" and other "light bites" – "takes a backseat to the wine."

Corner Bistro (Burger Joint

`23| 14| 16| $`

West Village | 331 W 4th St. (Jane St.)
212-242-9502 | cornerbistrony.com
Long Island City | 47-18 Vernon Blvd.
(47th Rd.) | Queens
718-606-6500

Consistently ranked "one of the best burger joints in the city," this "casual" "institution" serves them neatly ("no fuss, no muss"), with the "perfect ratio of meat to bun" – the "extra crispy" fries and "cold beer in a mug" also get high marks; locals love that it's "divey" but "not too divey"; the jukebox and "friendly yet quirky bartenders" are also pluses, and "inexpensive" prices make it "the best deal in the West Village."

Z Cosme Mexican 26 | 24 | 23 | $$$$

Flatiron | 35 E 21st St. (bet. B'way & Park Ave. S)
212-913-9659 | cosmenyc.com

In an "atmosphere that drips with cool elegance," "servers patiently give descriptions" to guide you through the "highly inventive" dishes, made from "hyper-seasonal ingredients"; add in "interesting cocktails" and you have what some see as the "most elevated Mexican dining experience in New York City": "go for a special occasion," "order as much as you can afford," and save room for the "outstanding desserts."

Z Cote Korean/Steakhouse 26 | 24 | 24 | $$$$

Flatiron | 16 W 22nd St. (bet. 5th & 6th Aves.)
212-401-7986 | cotenyc.com

"Attention, all carnivores": this "upscale" Flatiron Korean BBQ "redefines what constitutes a steakhouse," serving American "brontosaurus-size," "top-quality cuts" "grilled tableside" "by attentive servers" who "almost feed you each bite"; while "beautiful," the "dark" "modern interior" has some acoustical problems ("dear God, it's loud"), but most say this "doesn't distract" from what can often be "an amazing experience all around."

Cotenna ◖ Italian 24 | 21 | 20 | $$

West Village | 21 Bedford St. (Downing St.)
646-861-0175 | cotenna.com

Tiny and "tasty," this "intimate" small-plates Italian wine bar is "affordable" and "reliable" and "perfect for a casual" West Village dinner; pasta is "fresh, well prepared, and delicious" and the prix fixe lunch pasta and wine combo is a "phenomenal" deal; some call the space "cozy" and "romantic," others say "cramped" and "tight," but either way there's limited seating, so make a reservation or come off-hours to skip a wait.

Court Square Diner ◖ Diner 19 | 16 | 21 | $

Long Island City | 45-30 23rd St.
(Jackson Ave.) | Queens
718-392-1222 | courtsquarediner.com

Now, "this is what I want in a diner," declare fans: an "encyclopedic menu" served "at all hours" "at a good price, with good service," and "plenty of seating" amid "train-car: architecture"; small wonder "all of Long Island City goes" "with skyscrapers looming over it now, there should be a children's book written about the classic little Queens" holdout that's "been around forever" (since 1946, actually).

Covina Mediterranean 22 | 20 | 21 | $$$

Murray Hill | Park South Hotel, 127 E 27th St.
(bet. Lexington Ave. & Park Ave. S)
212-204-0225 | covinanyc.com

Part of the Park South Hotel, this "under-the-radar spot serves personal-size pizzas" and wood-fired grilled mains on its "uncontroversial Mediterranean menu" – "no fancy surprises here!"; "decent prices," "cute decor," and an "efficient staff" mean it's "always a safe bet for a bite to eat or cocktails" if you are in the Murray Hill area.

Cowgirl SeaHorse American/Mexican   19 | 19 | 19 | $$

South Street Seaport | 259 Front St. (Dover St.)
212-608-7873 | cowgirlseahorse.com

At the South Street Seaport, this "funky" "dive" comes with edge, a "sense of humor," "Sunday drag lunches," and "kitschy decor" – a stuffed blue marlin hangs on the wall; "go for the party, stay for the party," say fans, many of them locals, and although the food (lots of fried options) "isn't bad," it's "not the main attraction" – the "affordable prices" and friendly atmosphere are what make this a "solid choice for drinking and dining."

Craft American   25 | 23 | 24 | $$$$

Flatiron | 43 E 19th St. (bet. B'way & Park Ave S)
212-780-0880 | craftrestaurant.com

Celebrity chef Tom Colicchio "knows his stuff," say fans of the TV-tested "master's" Flatiron "perennial," a "dependable" New American "standby" for "sophisticated" seasonal fare that's "prepared for sharing," plus an "exhaustive" wine list – all delivered by a "smooth," "hospitable" staff; the "modern" space offers "plenty of table room," too, and if prices seem a little too "upmarket," at least it's "not too noisy" to discuss it here.

Crave Fishbar Seafood   23 | 18 | 21 | $$$

East 50s | 945 2nd Ave. (bet. 50th & 51st Sts.)
646-895-9585 | cravefishbar.com
West 80s | 428 Amsterdam Ave. (bet. 80th & 81st Sts.)
646-494-2750

The "outstanding" nightly dollar oyster happy hour is the main attraction at these "lively" nautical themed spots, where mussel Mondays are also a "favorite" and "fresh" seafood is the name of the game; the "nice" waitstaff keep the vibe "friendly" and the cocktails coming amid the "noisy" crowd ("don't go with people you want to talk to").

Crispo 🆂 Italian   25 | 21 | 21 | $$

West Village | 240 W 14th St. (bet. 7th & 8th Aves.)
212-229-1818 | crisporestaurant.com

At this "cozy and comfortable neighborhood place" with a lighthearted vibe, the "consistently excellent and interesting Italian food" comes in "generous" portions, while the wine list is "reasonably priced"; in the "bustling" dining room the noise level can be "deafening," so try to snag a table in the "rustic" back room or the "inviting" patio; service is "pleasant" but "can be slow when it's busy."

NEW Crown Shy American   ▼ 27 | 22 | 26 | $$$$

Financial District | 70 Pine St.
(bet. Pearl & Willliam Sts.)
212-517-1932 | crownshy.nyc

"Outstanding" churro-shaped gruyère fritters, an impressive drinks list crafted by publicans who "truly know their alcohol," and "spectacular," daring desserts are just a few highlights inside this "must-try" New American FiDi showstopper; despite its high-roller location in a landmarked building, the "beautiful" Art Deco dining room feels "adult without being stuffy," with mellow touches like an open-air kitchen and neutral colors.

Cull & Pistol Oyster Bar Seafood

24 | 15 | 21 | $$$

Chelsea | Chelsea Market, 75 9th Ave.
(bet. 15th & 16th Sts.)
646-568-1223 | lobsterplace.com

"After fighting your way through the Chelsea Market crowds," reward yourself with a visit to this "simple" and narrow spot with "marvelous seafood options"; "fresh" is the word that comes up most often, whether it's about the oysters and clams at the raw bar or the grilled fish that tastes like it just "leapt into the frying pan"; the staff is "so knowledgeable" about the menu and are happy to share what they know.

Da Andrea Italian

24 | 17 | 23 | $$

Greenwich Village | 35 W 13th St.
(bet. 5th & 6th Aves.)
212-367-1979 | daandreanyc.com

The staff "always welcome you with a smile" at this "neighbor-hood trattoria" for "old-world Italian fare" and a "well-matched wine list" at "prices that won't tear a hole in your pocket"; the pasta tastes "just like Mama made it," exemplifying "Bolognese cooking at its best"; the "quarters are very close," so "go early to avoid the crowds," and note that they don't take reservations for fewer than four people, which is good for walk-ins.

Da Nico Ristorante Italian/Pizza

25 | 20 | 24 | $$

Little Italy | 164 Mulberry St.
(bet. Broome & Grand Sts.)
212-343-1212 | danicoristorante.com

This Little Italy "standout" with a menu full of New York comforts like saucy pizza and zeppoles "made to order" is so good that "they do not need to beg you to enter," as some competitors do; the "quaint" interior has "tight quarters" for the "big-size plates of food," but the "outdoor garden" provides a "terrific experience," and the service is "friendly" and "atten-tive," whether you're a curious tourist or one of the "regulars."

Da Noi Italian

24 | 20 | 25 | $$$

Travis-Chelsea | 4358 Victory Blvd.
(Crabbs Ln.) | Staten Island
718-982-5040 | danoinyc.com

"Why travel into 'The City'?" ask fans of this Staten Island desti-nation for Italian cuisine – it's hard to go wrong "no matter what you order," and its "large menu" is known for "tasty" classics like antipasti, pasta, fish, and meat plates; family-run and with an "excellent" staff in place, the bilevel dining room here makes a "solid" option for lunch and dinner.

Da Tommaso Italian

21 | 16 | 20 | $$

West 50s | 903 8th Ave. (bet. 53rd & 54th Sts.)
212-265-1890 | datommasonewyork.com

"Classic red-sauce Italian" fare reigns at this Midtown "throw-back," a well-"established" local spot for "civilized," "enjoyable" meals at relatively "reasonable" prices; sure, it may all feel a bit "tired," but the "old-world" servers "know how to get you in and out if you're going to the theater," and the "window tables" provide "people-watching" opportunities aplenty, making for a "pleasant" time overall.

Da Umberto Italian   26 | 21 | 25 | $$$

Chelsea | 107 W 17th St. (bet. 6th & 7th Aves.)
212-989-0303 | daumbertonyc.com

Stepping inside this longtime favorite for "classic Northern Italian food" is like "going to Italy while sitting in New York"; it's been open since 1987 and "in a bit of a time warp," but the "spectacularly delicious" food, "luxurious" setting, and "exquisite" service "only gets better year after year" – the "fabulous" lighting makes "everyone look like a star," but in fact it's also still a bit of a "celebrity hangout," partly due to its "understated entrance."

Z Daniel ⑤ French   29 | 29 | 29 | $$$$

East 60s | 60 E 65th St. (bet. Madison & Park Aves.)
212-288-0033 | danielnyc.com

"In a class of its own," "culinary genius" Daniel Boulud's "transcendent" UES flagship delivers "consummate elegance" via its "marvelous" New French cuisine (offered through main-room prix fixe menus) and "excellent" wines – all provided in an "enchanting" space by a "world-class" staff who helped earn it this year's Top Service rating, as well as high placements in Food, Decor, and Popularity; naturally, this jackets-required "gourmet paradise" draws the "expense-account crowd" ("bring two credit cards"), and it remains a "wonderful place to celebrate a meaningful event"; the bar has à la carte options, too.

Danji Korean   25 | 18 | 21 | $$$

West 50s | 346 W 52nd St. (bet. 8th & 9th Aves.)
212-586-2880 | danjinyc.com

"Inventive twists" make this modern Korean spot, which serves "creative," artfully plated dishes, a popular pre-theater destination; opt for the tasting menu to sample the full scope of the "fabulous" "non-traditional" menu; "attentive" service makes up for "tight quarters" where most seating is at communal tables; "it's easy to see why this is packed on a regular basis."

Dante NYC ℂ Italian   21 | 23 | 20 | $$$

Greenwich Village | 79-81 MacDougal St.
(bet. Bleecker & Houston Sts.)
212-982-5275 | dante-nyc.com

This "quintessential Greenwich Village bar, and perhaps a quintessential New York bar" is your destination for "some of the best cocktails in the city" (especially something from the "comprehensive Negroni list"); open in various forms (and with various ownership) since 1915, it remains "fresh" and entertaining, so "make a reservation or risk a wait"; the "drinks are better than the food," so "get a drink (or two) at the bar and catch up with friends."

Darbar Indian
22 16 20 $$

East 40s | 152 E 46th St. (bet. Lexington & 3rd Aves.)
212-681-4500 | darbarny.com

Darbar Grill

East 50s | 157 E 55th St. (bet. Lexington & 3rd Aves.)
212-751-4600 | darbargrillnyc.com

"Ah, the delight" of an "above-the-ordinary" North Indian lunch buffet, "UN staffers" and others sigh as they dig into "top-of-the-line" butter chicken and "knockout" house-made naan; the interior "needs updating," but both Midtown East locations are also "quiet" detours before commuting home from Grand Central nearby.

Davelle Japanese
24 19 23 $$$

Lower East Side | 102 Suffolk St.
(bet. Delancey & Rivington Sts.)
646-771-7855 | davellenewyork.com

This "tiny" LES all-day Japanese café starts the day with a unique menu of both savory and sweet toasts – the cinnamon sugar option is "particularly life affirming" – alongside Kyoto-style cold brews and other specialty coffee drinks that are "worth" their premium, then continues with plates like uni spaghetti ("heaven"), various curries, and fried chicken; the minimalist setting feels like a "getaway" from the rest of the city.

David's Brisket House Deli
▼ 26 7 17 $$

Bedford-Stuyvesant | 533 Nostrand Ave.
(Herkimer Pl.) | Brooklyn
718-789-1155 | davidsbriskethouseanddelibrooklyn
.taverndesigner.site

"Sensational Jewish-style pastrami, brisket, and corned beef, made by Yemeni Muslims" is stuffed into sandwiches in "overwhelming amounts" at this "well-priced" and -loved Bed-Stuy mainstay; true, the "decor's worn – but you come for the food," anyway, which includes breakfast options in the morning.

Dawat Haute Indian Cuisine Indian
24 20 23 $$$

East 50s | 210 E 58th St. (bet. 2nd & 3rd Aves.)
212-355-7555 | dawatny.com

"High-quality, sumptuous meals" draw fans to this "reliable" Midtown East "standby," which got many of its recipes directly from cookbook author Madhur Jaffrey; North Indian and other less common regional classics – "delicious" curries, "tender and juicy" tandooris, and elevated versions of Mumbai street food – make it a decent "choice for experiencing the cuisine in Midtown," while its "attentive" service and "pleasant" interior help solidify its place as an "old-time favorite."

db Bistro Moderne French
25 22 24 $$$

West 40s | 55 W 44th St. (6th Ave.)
212-391-2400 | dbbistro.com/nyc

Pre-matinee lunch is the draw and the "prix fixe is a steal" at Daniel Boulud's Theater District staple, with "French-variant dishes and always a bargain wine"; even if you stuff yourself with the "legendary foie gras–stuffed burger," don't skip the "wildly imaginative" desserts; regulars note the "dark-wood-paneled decor straight out of the 1950s," and call the service "friendly but not overbearing."

☑ **Decoy** Chinese   28 | 19 | 25 | $$$

West Village | 529½ Hudson St., downstairs
(bet. Charles & 10th Sts.)
212-691-9700 | decoynyc.com

They've "mastered the art" of Peking duck with "crispy lacquered skin" at this trendy spot underneath sister restaurant RedFarm in the West Village; the fowl comes in "so many ways" in "ample portions," with "attentive service" and cocktails shaken by "knowledgeable bartenders"; if you don't mind that it's "hard to get a reservation" and don't get "claustrophobia" sitting at "communal seating" in a "dimly lit basement," you'll find the food "well worth the hassle."

Dee's Ⓜ Italian/Pizza   23 | 18 | 21 | $$

Forest Hills | 107-23 Metropolitan Ave.
(74th Ave.) | Queens
888-488-3337 | deesnyc.com

Families and others head to this "reliable" Forest Hills Med-Italian, calling it a local find for its "huge selection" of "old-fashioned red-sauce" staples (including specials and "flavorful" brick-oven pizzas) and proximity to the nearby movie theater, though not as much for its "big," "busy," "noisy" space; on the positive side, prices are "reasonable," the patio's a nice addition, the menu covers a lot of bases, and it's convenient for lunch or dinner.

Del Frisco's Grille Steakhouse   25 | 23 | 24 | $$$

Battery Park City | 250 Vesey St.
(North End Ave. & West Side Highway)
212-786-0760 | delfriscosgrille.com
Del Frisco's Double Eagle Steak House
West 40s | 1221 6th Ave. (bet. 48 & 49th Sts.)
212-575-5129
West 50s | 50 Rockefeller Plaza (51st St.)
212-767-0371

"In a city of great (and not-so-great) steakhouses," this "upscale" chain holds its own; whether they're looking for a "power lunch or drinks after work," fans gravitate toward the "outstanding" steaks and other meaty meals (there are plenty of lighter choices, including seafood); on the other hand, the prices are "hard to justify" and the noise is like "an airport runway – a very busy runway."

☑ **Del Posto** Italian   27 | 28 | 27 | $$$$

Chelsea | 85 10th Ave. (bet. 15th & 16th Sts.)
212-497-8090 | delposto.com

Serving "grand luxe below Chelsea's High Line," this "cavernous" but "impressive" dining room has many fans who say it "never disappoints," with "magnificent" service that's "grand enough for royals"; the "outstanding" modern Italian fare served via prix fixe and tasting menus also help make it "more than a meal – an experience," and the wine list is "formidable," but "be prepared to spend the big bucks" for all this "pageantry."

Delmonico's ⑤ Steakhouse ⎯ 25| 24| 24| $$$$|
Financial District | 56 Beaver St. (William St.)
212-509-1144 | delmonicoskitchen.com
Delmonico's Kitchen ⑤
West 30s | 207 W 36th St. (bet. 7th & 8th Aves.)
212-695-5220

"You can feel the history" at this "legendary" FiDi steakhouse
and its "terrific" contemporary outpost near Penn Station,
where "the wealth of the nation" gathers for "exceptional" cuts,
plus baked Alaska, lobster Newburg (originated here), and other
classics, in "attractive" surroundings overseen by "professional"
servers; true, the "ridiculous prices" bring all this "nostalgia"
back to earth, but if you want to "reminisce about long-ago"
meals among assorted "titans of industry," keep it "on your
bucket list."

Denino's Pizzeria Italian/Pizza ⎯ 25| 15| 21| $$|
Elm Park | 524 Port Richmond Ave.
(bet. Hooker Pl. & Walker St.) | Staten Island
718-442-9401 | deninossi.com
Greenwich Village | 93 MacDougal St. (Bleecker St.)
646-838-6987

Staten Island's "legendary" pizzeria is still "always crowded,"
with fans lining up for "thin," "charred crust" clam pies, and fried
calamari; believers don't mind the "little-league trophy party" it
all just makes it feel more like that "same place Grandfather ate
at as a young man," and while the Greenwich Village location
has "little discernible drop-off," the original is worth "paying the
Verrazzano-Narrows Bridge toll."

Desnuda ⓒ Seafood ▼ 26| 22| 26| $$$|
East Village | 122 E 7th St. (Avenue A)
212-254-3515 | desnudawbk.com
Williamsburg | 221 S 1st St. (Roebling St.) | Brooklyn
718-387-0563

"Wow, they have awesome dishes" at these "quaint" neighborhood wine and cocktail bars in Williamsburg and the East
Village, where, as the name implies, the emphasis is on raw or
minimally cooked food, including South American small plates
like "interesting" ceviches and "unforgettable" smoked oysters;
overall it has a "dark and moody" look that suits "date night" or
those seeking a "unique food experience."

Dhaba ⓒ Indian ⎯ 23| 14| 17| $$|
Murray Hill | 108 Lexington Ave.
(bet. 27th & 28th Sts.)
212-679-1284 | dhabany.com
Named for the roadside restaurants common in Pakistan and
North India, this "casual," "consistently good" choice in Curry
Hill turns out "well-done versions" of dishes popular in the
Punjab and beyond; along with providing "lots of options," it's
also a "great value," especially the daily lunch buffets; despite
the "vibrantly" striped walls, the "ambiance isn't great" – it "gets
incredibly noisy" and "service is brusque" – but for a "quick"
meal, "you're taken care of here."

Di An Di Ⓜ Vietnamese   24| 26| 22| $$|
Greenpoint | 68 Greenpoint Ave.
(bet. Franklin & West Sts.)
718-576-3914 | diandi.nyc
The atmosphere is "picture-perfect" at this "bright, modern,"
"flower-festooned" "tropical paradise" in Greenpoint, and
since it can often be "hard to get a reservation," diners wait in
line alongside "little red stools" to experience the energy and
"super-friendly" service, and to feast on "enticing," "creative
Vietnamese fusion" dishes as well as classics typically composed of "simple combinations" and "tons of fresh herbs" – as
the name says, let's go eat.

Di Fara Pizza Pizza   26| 7| 12| $|
Midwood | 1424 Ave. J (15th St.) | Brooklyn
718-258-1367 | difarapizzany.com
"A New York landmark," this "classic neighborhood pizza joint"
is "as good as it gets in Brooklyn," with the owner still sometimes on hand to assemble the pie "right in front of your eyes"
at a "glacially slow" pace in a "small and spartan" room; service
is "terse" and the "long wait" can seem endless, but it's "worth
the hassles" for a taste of New York that "can't be re-created
when it's gone"; "may Dom live forever."

Dim Sum Go Go Chinese   21| 11| 17| $$|
Chinatown | 5 E Broadway
(bet. Catherine St. & Chatham Sq.)
212-732-0797 | dimsumgogonyc.com
"Decent dim sum" that you "order off a menu" instead of grabbing from carts differentiates this "unusual" spot that's a stone's
throw from "the hustle and bustle of central Chinatown"; it
serves a "wide variety" of "reliable" ("if not exciting") choices,
including some vegetarian options, in "nothing-fancy" digs that
are often "crowded"; although the service leaves a lot to be
desired, soothing tabs make it ripe for "sharing" with friends.

Dimes American   22| 20| 17| $$|
Lower East Side | 49 Canal St. (Orchard St.)
212-925-1300 | dimesnyc.com
"California vibes" keep patrons dreaming at this "trendy,"
"eclectic" LES American, where the "healthy-enough menu" of
"tasty" toasts, bowls, and salads reels in the "people-watchers";
maybe the "eccentric," "modernist" interior is "not worth the In-
sta-fame it has received in the past," and the service sometimes
leaves much to be desired, but wallet-friendly prices and all-day
meal options still do for an attractive clubhouse Downtown.

Diner ◖ American   25| 23| 24| $$$|
Williamsburg | 85 Broadway (Berry St.) | Brooklyn
718-486-3077 | dinernyc.com
"Quintessentially Williamsburg," this "tiny," "old-timey-looking"
"old guard" of the local "food renaissance" is anything but a
diner, although it is housed in an actual 1920s dining car; the
"seasonal" American eats are "exciting and locally sourced,
always," and are explained by the "waiters, who write out the
menu for you on the spot and explain the dishes of the day";

"it's the burger that's the mainstay, and rightfully so" at this "adorable" place.

Dinosaur Bar-B-Que Barbecue 22 | 16 | 18 | $$
Morningside Heights | 700 W 125th St. (12th Ave.)
212-694-1777 | dinosaurbarbque.com
Gowanus | 604 Union St. (4th Ave.) | Brooklyn
347-429-7030
"Unpretentious" Southern dishes on "massive plates" high-light "barbecue at its best," including "Fred Flintstone–style," "fall-off-the-bone" ribs and "delightfully greasy" sides; "get there early," since the "family-friendly" Syracuse chain is "often crowded"; the large space, "high on the fun factor," feels like "a Western ski town," with well-worn wooden seating and antique lighting fixtures.

Dirt Candy M Vegan/Vegetarian 24 | 21 | 25 | $$$
Lower East Side | 86 Allen St. (Broome St.)
212-228-7732 | dirtcandynyc.com
They do "magic with veggies" at this "innovative" LES vegetar-ian, a "gold standard" for "whimsical," "incredibly flavorful" fare (presented via tasting menus at dinner) "that even a carnivore would like," plus "delish," produce-enhanced drinks; "thought-ful" service, "quirky" digs, and bills with a service charge included help even out the "upscale" prix fixe pricing, and it's easy to eat vegan and gluten-free here; P.S. à la carte apps are available at the bar.

Dirty French French 24 | 24 | 21 | $$$
Lower East Side | The Ludlow, 180 Ludlow St.
(bet. Houston & Stanton Sts.)
212-254-3000 | dirtyfrench.com
"Ultra-cool" reigns supreme at this "sultry" LES hangout from the Carbone team, where the "scene" set in the Ludlow Hotel complements "inventive," "elevated" French classics with global touches, along with a "solid wine list"; the charms of this "lovely," "playful" – OK, "noisy" – brasserie overshadow the just-decent service (and "pricey" tabs), and most feel it "checks all of their boxes" once they do get in (reservations can be "impos-sible" at peak times).

Docks Oyster Bar Seafood 22 | 20 | 21 | $$$
East 40s | 633 3rd Ave. (40th St.)
212-986-8080 | docksoysterbar.com
Whether it's for live jazz brunch, a "business lunch" "at the bar," or meeting up with the "after-work crowd" for happy hour, this "solid and dependable" "neighborhood mainstay" for seafood "near Grand Central" offers "fresh fish at reasonable prices," raw bar fare and "gigantic martinis" served by staff who remain "helpful and attentive," even when it gets "crowded" and "noisy."

Dominick's ⊄ Italian 24 | 13 | 21 | $$
Arthur Avenue/Belmont | 2335 Arthur Ave.
(bet. 184th & 187th Sts.) | Bronx
718-733-2807
Open since 1962, this is the "quintessential Arthur Avenue experience," with dishes served "family style," and "communal

seating" in "cafeteria" surroundings; "ask for recommendations" and "turn yourself over to the waiter" – it's so "old school" and quirky that there are "shared tables," "no menu," "no desserts," "no reservations," "no credit cards," no website, and no fish on Sundays, but those are the sort of charms that keep it "loud and crowded," with "long waits."

Domodomo Japanese/Sushi   24 | 21 | 22 | $$$
Greenwich Village | 138 W Houston St.
(bet. MacDougal & Sullivan Sts.)
646-707-0301 | domodomonyc.com
"Hand rolls are the focus" of this "standout" Village Japanese, noted for its "signature" nori rolls, along with its "grand assort-ment" of "sophisticated" sushi options offered à la carte and on omakase and other set menus; "cool" digs, a "sceney" vibe, and a professional staff add oomph, and it's "reasonably priced relative to other high-end" raw-fish specialists; N.B. sibling joint Rawbar, a walk-in-only oyster house with happy-hour dishes, is next door.

Z Don Angie Italian   28 | 24 | 25 | $$$
West Village | 103 Greenwich Ave. (W 12th St.)
212-889-8884 | donangie.com
Turning out "one memorable dish after another," this "startlingly original" West Village "hot spot" elicits "wows" for its "intricate," "playful" Italian American dishes (including "epic" lasagna), "awesome cocktails," and "caring" staff; it may be "nearly impossible to score a reservation" for the "cozy" space, since "expensive" tabs don't deter the crowds, and neither do the "trendy" atmosphere and "killer location."

Don Antonio Italian/Pizza   25 | 14 | 21 | $$
West 50s | 309 W 50th St.
(bet. 8th & 9th Aves.)
646-719-1043 | donantoniorestaurant.com
Straight from Naples, this West 50s venture from a legendary old-world pizzaiolo offers "many choices" of "outstanding" "designer" wood-fired pies (featuring the signature flash-fried crust Montanara); it's also "as close as you can get to Italy" before seeing a Broadway show; "rushed" service from a "na-tive Italian" staff gets you "in and out" fast, which is welcome, as the "cramped" and often "noisy" interior reminiscent of an airport lounge is "best not discussed."

Don Peppe M ♫ Italian   26 | 12 | 20 | $$
South Ozone Park | 135-58 Lefferts Blvd.
(154th Ave.) | Queens
718-845-7587
"Everyone but you is family, but the food is great," say diners of this clubby "time warp" of a place, although it's "worth the drive" out to nearly JFK (at least once) to soak up the "Sunday dinner" vibe, with the "unbelievable abundanza" of old-style Southern Italian ("best linguini in clam sauce around," "baked clams to die for") all served in large portions for the table; it's cash only, and they don't accept reservations.

Donovan's Burger Joint   22 | 20 | 22 | $$
Bayside | 214-16 41st Ave. (Bell Blvd.) | Queens
718-423-5353 | donovansny.com
Donovan's Pub C
Woodside | 57-24 Roosevelt Ave. (58th St.) | Queens
718-429-9339

The impressive pub food ("classic juicy bar burgers," "some of
the best in the city") is the main draw at these Woodside and
Bayside "neighborhood gems," where the kitchen's open late,
the boisterous atmosphere can get "a little noisy," and a "busy
bar scene" makes it "good for a quick pint or two"; locals head
here for the "attentive wait staff," the "cozy" dining room with its
"romantic nooks," and the tab that "doesn't break the bank."

Dons Bogam C Korean   24 | 16 | 20 | $$
Murray Hill | 17 E 32nd St. (bet. 5th & Madison Aves.)
212-683-2200 |

"Slightly more upscale Korean BBQ" is the draw at this option
slightly off the Koreatown strip; with traditional cook-it-yourself
meals on low tables, it's "fun for groups" and serves other classics like bibimbap and dumplings that are paired with "creative"
condiments; the interior is relatively "hip" and dramatic, also
making it a memorable spot for out-of-towners; P.S. lunch specials stand out and are "easy on the wallet."

Ducks Eatery Barbecue   25 | 16 | 21 | $$
East Village | 351 E 12th St. (1st Ave.)
212-432-3825 | duckseatery.com

The "eclectic," meat-centric menu at this East Village joint
showcases "rustic food" that's "perfect for keto dieters," but
the kitchen also "knows how to treat vegetables subtly" and
when to apply "smoke and fermentation" – its knowledgeable
staff can explain these processes; even with seats that are
"uncomfortable" and contained in a "small," "funky" space, it's
"well worth enduring" for "bold" flavors.

Dumpling Galaxy Chinese   24 | 14 | 17 | $$
Flushing | Arcadia Mall, 42-35 Main St.
(Franklin Ave.) | Queens
718-461-0808 | dumplinggalaxynyc.com

True to its name, "an encyclopedia of dumplings, every one
exemplary," in "varieties you can't find elsewhere" is the draw
at this Chinese Flushing favorite ("some of the other dishes are
quite good, too"); true, service is minimal, and "you're eating
in" a "huge room carved out of" the Arcadia Mall, "but who
cares?" – "it's the cooks that count."

The Dutch American   21 | 20 | 20 | $$$
SoHo | 131 Sullivan St. (Prince St.)
212-677-6200 | thedutchnyc.com

"Boisterous" and "lively," with an "open kitchen," "vibrant
bar," and, most important, "large windows" for SoHo "people-
watching," this neighborhood "staple" delivers Southern-
accented American comfort food from brunch to supper, with
their beloved hot fried chicken and an oyster-lined raw bar;
even through "uneven service" and "noisy" crowds, it remains
"solid," especially for brunch and "big group" dinners.

E.A.T. American   21 | 13 | 16 | $$$
East 80s | 1064 Madison Ave. (bet. 80th & 81st Sts.)
212-772-0022 | elizabar.com
It may be "the most expensive diner in the world," but the
museum-adjacent location, fresh "bread basket," and "well-
prepared" "creative" deli classics are all part of "living the high
life" on the UES; although it can feel "crowded" and "cold," and
the service doesn't match the prices, noshers still say this Eli
Zabar classic has "soups, breads, sandwiches, and salads that
are all outstanding."

Earl's Beer and Cheese American   23 | 15 | 21 | $$
East 90s | 1259 Park Ave. (bet. 97th & 98th Sts.)
212-289-1581 | earlsny.com
Throwing off "hipster hunter" vibes, this divey "little slice of
Midwestern heaven hidden on the UES" isn't playing games with
its name: though grilled sandwiches, tacos, salads, pretzels and
other "elevated bar fare" round out the menu, the beer cheese
is a must: it's "everyone's go-to to accompany" the frequently
rotating list of craft beers served in a "low-key," "friendly" room
that's often a "tight fit"; still, it's "worth it to try to get a seat."

East Harbor Seafood Palace Chinese   26 | 17 | 18 | $$
Sunset Park | 714 65th St. (bet. 7th & 8th Aves.) | Brooklyn
718-765-0098 | eastharborseafoodpalace.us
"Be prepared to battle it out with other cart hogs" (the waiters
roll them by quickly) at this "super-huge" Sunset Park dim sum
"heaven," known for dishing up a "wide" variety of classic and
less-common Cantonese plates – "fresh and snappy shrimp
items are a specialty"; despite the "large" banquet hall space,
weekend waits can be "long" and tables get combined, so get
ready to "make new friends."

The East Pole Kitchen & Bar American   21 | 19 | 20 | $$$
East 60s | 133 E 65th St.
(bet. Lexington & Park Aves.)
212-249-2222 | theeastpolenyc.com
Possibly the "closest thing to a Downtown dining experience in
Bloomingdale's-land," this "buzzy" UES American serves "decent" seasonal dishes with "fresh" and "bright" ingredients, including a "reliable brunch"; maybe the "pricey" fare "isn't going
to blow you away," and the "intimate" space can feel "cramped"
and get "overwhelmingly loud," but it's a "pleasant" spot "for a
lighter meal with friends," and there's a "lively bar scene."

Eastfield's American   19 | 17 | 19 | $$$
East 70s | 1479 York Ave. (78th St.)
646-964-4918 | eastfieldsnyc.com
"If you want to feel downtown when you're uptown," try this
"popular neighborhood destination" on the UES; you can "cover
all the B's" in one fell swoop, with "satisfying burgers and beers"
(it's a "no-brainer for bar food") and a "nice brunch"; fans love
the "cozy setting," although some say it "feels a little cramped"
and that the "deafening" noise levels make them think twice.

	FOOD	DECOR	SERVICE	COST

Egg American — 22 | 16 | 19 | $$

Williamsburg | 109 N 3rd St.
(bet. Berry St. & Wythe Ave.) | Brooklyn
718-302-5151 | eggrestaurant.com

"A great way to start the day" – even if your day starts after noon – is with this "busy breakfast place" in Williamsburg that serves eggs until 5 PM in a variety of "all-American" ways, along with "solid Southern-inspired" dishes, including biscuits and gravy; the whitewashed surroundings and service are "simple" but "pleasant."

Egg Shop American — 19 | 16 | 16 | $$

NoLita | 151 Elizabeth St. (Kenmare St.)
646-666-0810 | eggshopnyc.com
Williamsburg | 138 N 8th St. (bet. Bedford Ave. & Berry St.) | Brooklyn | 646-787-7502

A "solid spot to get rid of a hangover or meet a large group," this "lively" NoLita spot is known for "creative riffs on classics" for breakfast and lunch; the egg sandwiches and the rest of the "very egg-centric menu" is "impressive," but the "space is packed and hard to move around in" and the "wait is often long," so you should "definitely show up early if you want to eat in peace"; a second "eggcellent" location is in Williamsburg.

886 (M Taiwanese — 23 | 19 | 21 | $$

East Village | 26 St. Marks Pl. (bet. 2nd & 3rd Aves.)
646-882-0231 | eighteightsix.com

"Unique" twists" on Taiwanese classics come "quickly," hitting the table once they're ready, at this "experimental" kitchen on St. Marks in the East Village; and although the space is "small" and they "don't serve hard liquor," it's "worth the wait": "if you struggle with committing to just one dish," bring as big a group as you can fit in to share "generous" servings that will not "break the bank."

88 Lan Zhou Handmade ∌ — 25 | 8 | 13 | $

Noodles Chinese
Chinatown | 40 Bowery (bet. Canal & Bayard Sts.)
646-683-0939 | lam-zhou-handmade-noodle.com

Noodles and dumplings are the main event here, "with variations on how they're prepared" at this "bare-bones," cash-only Chinatown stop for "easy-on-the-wallet" prices; service can be a little iffy, but you're coming for the "deliciously prepared" food, "not the frills," and "you will leave extremely full"; P.S. 88 sells its dumplings frozen to-go: they are "magical."

Eisenberg's Sandwich Shop Deli — 21 | 11 | 18 | $

Flatiron | 174 5th Ave. (22nd St.)
646-675-5096 | eisenbergsnyc.com

"Time warps" don't get much more "classic" than this 1929 Flatiron lunch counter, which slings "solid," "well-priced" deli fare (reubens, tuna melts) that customers "knock back with egg creams" and other fountain drinks while sitting on stools beside other locals; "scruffy" digs, "rushed" service, and crowds are part of the "nostalgic" "experience," so if you're seeking a "quick bite" with "lots of history," this is your jam; P.S. takeout and delivery available, too.

| | FOOD | DECOR | SERVICE | COST |

El Parador Cafe Ⓢ Mexican 24 | 19 | 22 | $$$
Murray Hill | 325 E 34th St.
(bet. 1st & 2nd Aves.)
212-679-6812 | elparadorcafe.com
"A mainstay" since 1959 "in an ever-changing neighborhood,"
this "classic" Murray Hill Mexican "keeps the tradition going"
with "flavorful" fare (including vegetarian options), "superb margaritas," and "accommodating" service; while the "old-world"
interior isn't much, it's "possible to have a conversation" in this
"quiet" space – just "as things used to be."

El Porrón Spanish 24 | 19 | 20 | $$
East 60s | 1123 1st Ave. (bet. 61st & 62nd Sts.)
212-207-8349 | elporronnyc.com
Named for the failsafe Catalonian wine decanters used on the
premises, this family-run East 60s bar serves "superb" sangria
by the pitcher, "out-of-this-world paella," and saucy Spanish tapas (in little warm crocks with bread to "soak up all the
goodness"); the "casual," "lively" setting, "moderate" prices, and
"courteous" service make it a neighborhood go-to, especially
when happy hour's in effect.

El Pote Español Ⓢ Spanish 24 | 15 | 22 | $$
Murray Hill | 718 2nd Ave. (bet. 38th & 39th Sts.)
212-889-6680 | elpote.com
"Who needs new" when you have this "charming," "old style,"
"neighborhood place" in Murray Hill, which since 1977 has been
delivering "awesome" paella and other "traditional" Spanish eats,
plus sangria, to both regulars and newbies by way of an "attentive" staff; relatively "thrifty prices" make overlooking the simple
interior easy, and "weekday bargains at lunch" make its case
even stronger.

El Quinto Pino Spanish 25 | 19 | 22 | $$
Chelsea | 401 W 24th St. (bet. 9th & 10th Aves.)
212-206-6900 | elquintopinonyc.com
The "tiny kitchen" here "delivers big tastes" and "wrote the
book on tapas," in NYC with "so many delicious options from
different parts of Spain"; the food and wine selection is "unique
and extraordinary," and that goes double for the "must-have"
signature dish, a sea urchin panini; the "cozy" dining room and
"sweet" bar "make it feel as if you're at the home of a really
good chef," and the staff "couldn't be friendlier."

El Toro Blanco Mexican 16 | 15 | 17 | $$
West Village | 257 6th Ave.
(bet. Bedford & Downing Sts.)
212-645-0193 | eltoroblanconyc.com
At this "Cinco de Mayo" hot spot in the West Village, there's a
"happy," casual staff and "lively," downright loud interior; on
offer are "plentiful" portions of "creative Mexican" (including
popular tacos) and "killer margaritas," and while the food "does
not stand out as exceptional" and verges on "too expensive for
what it is," the party scene and sunny "patio tables" make up
for it.

| | FOOD | DECOR | SERVICE | COST |

El Vez Mexican
Battery Park City | 259 Vesey St.
(bet. North End Ave. & West St.)
212-233-2500 | elveznyc.com

20 | 21 | 21 | $$

If you're after a "Mexican place with some great guac" and a "lively bar scene" in the "'burbs' of Battery Park," look no further; there are plenty of "cozy nooks to dine in" at this "cavernous" branch of a Philly favorite, and even more room on the outdoor patio, with a "direct view of the glittering Freedom Tower"; it's a natural for groups and kids, who will feel "taken care of at all times," and it's also useful for take-out burrito cravings.

Elea Greek
West 80s | 217 W 85th St. (B'way)
212-369-9800 | eleanyc.com

24 | 23 | 23 | $$$

"Like a sunny café on a Greek island," this "spacious," "light"-filled bilevel space on the UWS has "attentive" waitstaff who serve "classic" Hellenic specialties with "elevated" "flourishes," along with an "excellent wine list"; it's "a little pricey," and since it's "always hopping" ("reservations are a must"), "the noise level can make conversation challenging" – but if you "go early" and avoid "rush hour," things get a lot more "civilized."

Elephant & Castle ◖ American
West Village | 68 Greenwich Ave.
(bet. W 11th St. & 7th Ave. S)
212-243-1400 | elephantandcastle.com

20 | 17 | 20 | $$

"Everything else on the block has been replaced" except this "favorite" "still chugging along" in the West Village; it remains a "nice spot for a quiet meal" (especially brunch) and is known for its burgers, omelets, crepes, and other "consistent and good" dishes that are "pure comfort"; it keeps its "most loyal following" because the "prices are low" and the "quality is high," although the "decor hasn't changed in the many years it's been open" and "space is nonexistent."

❷ Eleven Madison Park American
Flatiron | 11 Madison Ave. (24th St.)
212-889-0905 | elevenmadisonpark.com

28 | 28 | 29 | $$$$

"How could anything surpass this?" ask admirers of Daniel Humm's "magical" Madison Park New American, a "gold standard" for dining, with "stupendous" tasting menus ("your taste buds will be lavished with treat after treat") and a "breathtaking wine list" in a "soaring space"; the "unparalleled" service will leave you "feeling like a VIP," and while taking a "second mortgage may be necessary" to pay the bill, most feel this "once-in-a-lifetime" experience is "worth every penny."

Eli's Table American
East 80s | 1413 3rd Ave. (80th St.)
212-717-9798 | elizabar.com

22 | 15 | 19 | $$$

"The freshest ingredients" enliven the seasonal American menu at this "convenient" UES standby, where the "well-prepared" meals are deemed "up to Eli Zabar's standard" and complemented by an "unparalleled" wine list; true, service can be "spotty" and it can get "crowded and noisy," but most agree it's a "dependable" choice that's "particularly good for brunch."

Elia Ⓜ Greek 26 | 21 | 21 | $$$

Bay Ridge | 8611 3rd Ave. (bet. 86th &
87th Sts.) | Brooklyn
718-748-9891 | eliarestaurant.com

"You can't go wrong" at this "dependable," family-run restaurant in Bay Ridge, named for the olive; many of its fans say the Mediterranean dishes here are "vibrantly colorful" and some of the better Greek food in NYC, with "delish" spreads, fresh fish, and "outstanding" lamb options; the subtle lighting and white tablecloth interior is "intimate" and "pleasant," and while some find it "a little pricey," especially for the area, most agree it's "worth it."

Elias Corner ◖ ⇶ Seafood 25 | 10 | 18 | $$

Astoria | 24-02 31st St. (24th Ave.) | Queens
718-932-1510 | elias-corner.business.site

This "chaotic," cash-only neighborhood destination simply swims with "quite large" portions of "excellent" grilled fish "without any frills" and "all kinds" of Greek specialties ("you can cut the octopus with a butter knife"); the patriarch's legacy lives on with his family "manning the nets," and they insist you put your trust in their "capable hands," especially since there are "no menus" to peruse; the interior is "sparse" at best, but outdoor patios open things up in summer.

Elio's ◖ Italian 25 | 18 | 21 | $$$

East 80s | 1621 2nd Ave. (bet. 84th & 85th Sts.)
212-772-2242

The "delectable Italian dishes are revered" at this "upscale" UES "classic"; the "noisy" room's tight tables, "packed every night of the week," will have you "crammed" next to a "well-heeled" old-school clientele and celebrities delighting in daily specials and the secret menu's bone-in chicken parm; it's "pricey" and they don't give you much attention "unless you're a regular," but the food makes becoming one a worthy goal.

Emilio's Ballato Italian 25 | 18 | 22 | $$$

NoLita | 55 E Houston St. (Mott St.)
212-274-8881 | ballatos.4-food.com

"Looks just like it did when it opened" in the 1950s, and that's on purpose," say observers of this "old-school Italian" in NoLita, with "delish linguine and clams and chicken or veal parm," "house-made tomato sauce" ("Emilio is always there") and "tasty pastas"; it's a hub for celebrities and regulars, making it hard for mere mortals to get in without braving a line – there are no reservations.

Emily American/Pizza 26 | 19 | 21 | $$

West Village | 35 Downing St. (Bedford St.)
917-935-6434 | pizzalovesemily.com
Clinton Hill | 919 Fulton St.
(bet. Clinton & Waverly Aves.) | Brooklyn
347-844-9588

"Game-changing" is what people say about the pies available at these "indulgent" West Village and Clinton Hill pizzerias; the "phenomenal," "crispy"-crust pizzas (plus "amazing" but not always available burgers) "will make you forget about whatever diet you're trying to be on"; no wonder these "small" spots with "knowledgeable" servers are "perpetually packed."

Emmy Squared American/Pizza   26| 19| 21| $$|
Williamsburg | 364 Grand St. (Marcy Ave.) | Brooklyn
718-360-4535 | emmysquared.com
East Village | 83 1st Ave. (5th St.)
917-463-3737
"Sister restaurants to favorite Emily," this "casual but cool" Williamsburg–East Village duo offer a "welcome addition to the thin-crust-saturated NYC pizza scene" via its deeply "delicious" Detroit-style square pies with "creative topping combinations"; however, the "juiciest burger" and other sandwiches "are absolutely awesome" as well, and since it's "so hard to decide" what to get, reviewers recommend you "go with a group so you can try all of it."

Empanada Mama ◖ Latin American   23| 13| 16| $$|
Lower East Side | 95 Allen St.
(bet. Broome & Delancey Sts.)
212-673-0300 | empmamanyc.com
West 50s | 765 9th Ave. (51st St.)
212-698-9008
The variety of empanadas seems "endless" at these fast-food-style Latin hangouts, which serve "new- and old-school" options like mac and cheese or "the Viagra" (filled with seafood stew), alongside ground beef and jerk chicken versions, plus a full menu of arepas, tapas, and sandwiches; service can be "slow" (for both dining in and takeout), but the food is always "tasty," especially for "late night drunchies"; P.S. the West 50s location is open 24/7.

Empellón ⑤ Mexican   22| 20| 21| $$$|
East 50s | 510 Madison Ave. (53rd St.)
212-858-9365 | empellon.com
A bit more uptight (or perhaps "sophisticated") "than the rest of the Empellón empire," this still-"lively" spot delights with "inventive, eclectic Mexican" – like pastrami tacos and avocado ice cream – "that looks like art" and is presented by "casual but good" servers; it all goes down in a "festive" "if somewhat noisy room," so "go in the off-hours" (in Midtown, that can be as early as 8 PM).

Empellón Taqueria Mexican   23| 19| 19| $$|
West Village | 230 W 4th St. (10th St.)
212-367-0999 | empellon.com
This isn't "your usual chips-and-salsa place," "but who needs that when you can have brussels sprouts tacos?"; this West Village favorite is a destination for "fantastic Mexican-inflected dishes" (including an "interesting mix of salsas" made from cashews and other unexpected ingredients) and a "breathtaking variety of tequilas and mezcals"; the bar is "very much a scene for millennials," or at least those ready for its "noisy and almost frantic" vibe.

| | FOOD | DECOR | SERVICE | COST |

Empire Diner American   20 | 20 | 20 | $$
Chelsea | 210 10th Ave. (22nd St.)
212-335-2277 | empire-diner.com
A Chelsea classic that reopened in 2017, this "real chrome diner"
has "charming 1950s decor" while also being "reinvented with
elevated food and cocktails"; from brunch to dinner, the "modern
takes on American classics" help make it a "go-to," and while it
may be "hard to decide what to order," the " friendly staff" can
help you narrow it down; it might not be anything groundbreak-
ing, but locals and gallery hoppers are "glad it's back."

EN Japanese Brasserie Japanese   24 | 25 | 23 | $$$
West Village | 435 Hudson St. (Leroy St.)
212-647-9196 | enjb.com
Although you might be intimidated by the "large, almost overwhelming menu" – "let your server guide you" through all the
choices – you can't go wrong with any of the "delicious small
plates that celebrate the season": the tasting menu with sake
pairings is "truly spectacular," and the "beautiful" dining room
with "high ceilings" is "upscale" and "engaging to the eye."

Enoteca Maria Ⓜ 🍴 Italian   25 | 18 | 24 | $$
St. George | 27 Hyatt St. (Central Ave.) | Staten Island
718-447-2777 | enotecamaria.com
You'll get the "the nonna experience" with a rotating cast of
women cooking here from cultures around the world, reflecting
the "diverse" Staten Island neighborhood of St. George; the "intimate" lobby opens to the kitchen and "allows you to watch the
chefs at work" preparing their own dishes alongside a steady
menu of "generously" portioned Italian classics; the unique experience is worth the limited hours (it's closed Monday through
Wednesday) and having to pay cash.

Enzo's Italian   26 | 20 | 23 | $$
Arthur Avenue/Belmont | 2339 Arthur Ave.
(bet. 183rd & 187th Sts.) Bronx
718-733-4455 | enzosbronxrestaurant.com
Enzo's Of Williamsbridge Road
Morris Park | 1998 Williamsbridge Rd. (Neill Ave.) | Bronx
718-409-3828
"It's like time stood still" at these separately owned "pieces
of the old Bronx" in Arthur Avenue/Belmont and Morris Park,
where "plentiful" portions of "outstanding" "red-sauce" Italian
dishes lead to calls of "buon gusto"; meanwhile, "moderate
prices" and an "attentive" staff mean that "once you step in the
door, you're instant family."

Epistrophy ☾ Italian   17 | 19 | 18 | $$
NoLita | 200 Mott St. (bet. Kenmare & Spring Sts.)
212-966-0904 | epistrophynyc.com
You may have seen "cute brunch" snaps of its exposed brick
interior "all over your Instagram feed," but you should experience this "healthy," "friendly" NoLita café in person: it's best
for "catching up with a friend," first date, or mingling among the
"European crowd," who enjoy espresso, aperitifs, and "small
plates" of Sardinian-inspired dishes with a "lighter vibe" at an
easygoing price – plenty of vegan options, too.

	FOOD	DECOR	SERVICE	COST

Erawan Thai Cuisine Thai   21 19 20 $$
Bayside | 42-31 Bell Blvd. (bet. 42nd & 43rd Aves.)
Queens | 718-428-2112 | erawanthaibayside.com
This Thai kitchen has been on Bayside's Bell Boulevard for "many years with good reason"; aiming for modern interpretations of classics, it has a "friendly" staff, "good-value" lunch special, and hefty portions that all help make regulars of diners; there is also local delivery and a children's menu, making it a natural for families.

Erminia Italian   26 24 26 $$$
East 80s | 250 E 83rd St. (bet. 2nd & 3rd Aves.)
212-879-4284 | erminiarestaurant.com
"Tucked in among endless residential high-rises," the interior at this UES trattoria "exudes romance" and "transports you straight to Italy" for "real-deal" Roman cuisine and "old-time class"; the "welcoming" staff and "intimate" "candlelit" "Valentine's Day"–ready ambiance make this a prized date-night ticket, and it remains a "throwback to days gone by when one could just dine, talk, and enjoy" food that recalls "Grandma's home cooking."

Esme American   23 20 21 $$
Greenpoint | 999 Manhattan Ave. (Huron St.) | Brooklyn
718-383-0999 | esmebk.com
With "fresh" bistro fare and European touches like "mussels with Pernod" alongside "incredible Negronis," this little Greenpoint brunch and date-night escape has a "thoughtful" menu with memorable salads, "reliable" service, a "lot of heart," and a backyard perfect for a "quiet getaway"; the stark, modern interior may have a predictable Brooklyn feel, but the food won't let you down.

Estela American   26 21 24 $$$
NoLita | 47 E Houston St. (bet. Mott & Mulberry Sts.)
212-219-7693 | estelanyc.com
The "impeccably seasoned and beautifully presented" shared plates here are "innovative without being overly complicated"; diners "can't stop thinking about the mussels escabeche on toast," they "dream about the lamb ribs" and the burrata, and believe the panna cotta "insane"; it's all part of the buzzy, "sexy, and effortless" impression this NoLita American exudes via an organized staff and attentive sommelier.

Z Estiatorio Milos Greek   27 25 24 $$$$
West 50s | 125 W 55th St. (bet. 6th & 7th Aves.)
212-245-7400 | estiatoriomilos.com
NEW West 30s | 20 Hudson Yards, 5th Fl. (10th Ave. & 33rd St.)
"Fish doesn't get any better" than the "sophisticated yet simply prepared" and delicately grilled versions of "anything from the sea" at this "special-occasion destination"; it remains in "the elite of Greek food" in New York, and a "civilized oasis in Midtown" (there's a new Hudson Yards outpost, too); from the "open and airy" setting to the "professional service" and "excellent wine list," "you pay for the best"; pick out your fish from the "display on ice," "just don't pick up the bill."

Ethos Gallery 51 Greek

East 50s | 905 1st Ave. (51st St.)
212-888-4060 | ethosrestaurants.com

"Opa!" echoes around this "light and bright" Mediterranean in the East 50s whenever dishes like "fresh, fresh, fresh" fish that "looks back atcha" and "consistently fine" (and complimentary) desserts hit the table; some "don't even realize" they're still in Midtown East, inside a room decorated to look like "a trip to the Greek seashore," and it all "feels like family," especially during birthday celebrations, when "everyone claps" ("it's fun the first time" but can be a bit much).

Excellent Dumpling House Chinese

Chelsea | 165 W 23rd St. (bet. 6th & 7th Aves.)
212-989-8885 | excellentdumpling.com

"The name says it all," according to fans of this Chinatown exile, now in Chelsea: "the dumplings are indeed excellent," and they're also "inexpensive," especially if you go for the "reasonable lunch specials" on weekdays; the surroundings are "super-casual," but you're there for "reliable quality and awe-some flavors."

Extra Fancy ◖ American

Williamsburg | 302 Metropolitan Ave.
(Roebling St.) | Brooklyn
347-422-0939 | extrafancybklyn.com

"A bro-y, albeit fun place to get drinks after work, after the after-party," or even during the day (thanks to the "huge" partially covered patio) sums up this Williamsburg hangout that boasts "nice bartenders" and a selection of raw seafood; the rest of the American menu is "not memorable," but "the kitchen is open late" – besides, "anything for an excuse to sit outside at a picnic table."

Extra Virgin Mediterranean

West Village | 259 W 4th St. (Perry St.)
212-691-9359 | extravirginrestaurant.com

It's "all about the prime sidewalk seating" at this "tried-and-true" West Village café, where the "excellent people-watching" pos-sibilities via "warm-weather" outdoor tables make it "popular" with folks in their "20s and 30s"; it's "a madhouse during brunch," which is a showcase for the "decent drinks," although the "reasonably priced," just-"OK" Mediterranean on offer – along with a "small," "dated" space and service that can be "lacking" – keep it from being a must-go.

Famous Sammy's Roumanian

Steakhouse Steakhouse

Lower East Side | 157 Chrystie St.
(bet. Delancey & Rivington Sts.)
212-673-0330 | sammysromanian.com

"Every night is a bar mitzvah" in this LES basement where every-thing comes "loaded with schmaltz," from the bottles on the tables to "the kibitizing musical entertainers"; the food consists of "steaks the size of frisbees" and "heavy" Jewish specialties, washed down with ice block–enclosed "libations poured like in ancient Rome" by "sassy" staffers; "be prepared for crowds, a hectic scene," and "to pay for all that vodka you don't remember drinking."

The Farm on Adderley American
22 | 17 | 21 | $$

Ditmas Park | 1108 Cortelyou Rd.
(bet. Stratford & Westminster Rds.) | Brooklyn
718-287-3101 | thefarmonadderley.com

The "offerings reflect the seasons" at this "charming," "family-friendly" Ditmas Park "mainstay" where the "creative" farm-to-table New American meals are "consistently good" and "fresh," especially at a brunch many call "excellent"; the backyard patio is especially appealing during warmer months, but just beware of "spotty" service.

Faro Italian
28 | 23 | 25 | $$

Bushwick | 436 Jefferson St.
(bet. St. Nicholas & Wyckoff Aves.)
Brooklyn | 718-381-8201 | farobk.com

"Beyond words" is how fans describe this Bushwick establishment serving "to-die-for" seasonal Italian cuisine: there's "unforgettable" house-made bread and butter and "inventive" pastas, paired with an "expansive" wine list – just be sure to "order the carbs, otherwise you might end up feeling like you played yourself"; service is "on point" in the industrial space decorated with white walls, concrete floors, and rustic wood furniture.

The Fat Radish American
20 | 22 | 21 | $$

Lower East Side | 17 Orchard St.
(bet. Canal & Hester Sts.)
212-300-4053 | thefatradish.com/new-york

A "well-decorated" cross-pollination of "farm chic" and "gastropub," this "self-contained little universe" looks (and acts) "more mature" than its LES neighbors; "carnivores and vegans" can both agree that the menu with lots of small plates finds a happy medium between "light and satisfying," and nobody can complain about the samples of the "lowly, underrated" radishes served at every table.

Fausto Italian
23 | 20 | 23 | $$$

Park Slope | 348 Flatbush Ave.
(bet. Sterling & St. Johns Pl.) | Brooklyn
917-909-1427 | faustobrooklyn.com

The "pastas are handmade" and "they nail it on flavors" at this "solid and familiar" Grand Army Plaza spot, which uses wood-fired ovens for many of its dishes, including a "knockout chicken"; the "cocktails are utterly slurpable," especially in the backyard, and it all feels "warm and welcoming," whether you "want to celebrate or unwind" in its "1960s Italian dreamscape" of a room, done in "artistic" midcentury modern.

Fedora American
23 | 22 | 22 | $$$

West Village | 239 W 4th St.
(bet. Charles & W 10th Sts.)
646-449-9336 | fedoranyc.com

A few steps below street level, this "intimate and cozy basement" with a "speakeasy vibe" feels "like you're in a friend's living room – a friend who can really cook"; although some reminisce about the "cheap and cheerful" version that sat here for decades (the original neon sign still hangs outside), many prefer Gabriel Stulman's "painfully hip reincarnation"; the bar is "always busy and energetic," making this the "ideal West Village date spot."

Felice Italian   20| 19| 19| $$|
Financial District | 15 Gold St. (Platt St.)
212-785-5950 | www.felicenyc.com
Felice 64
East 60s | 1166 1st Ave. (64th St.) | 212-593-2223
Felice 83
East 80s | 1593 1st Ave. (83rd St.) | 212-249-4080
"The menu can please everyone" at these "reliable" Italian spots presenting "consistent" pastas and other classics alongside a deep wine list; it's all served by "accommodating" staff, and the "classy" enough interiors lend themselves well to a date night or a hangout with friends; the FiDi location inside the Gild Hall hotel is handy for lunch, and the outdoor seating at the UES locations are summer favorites.

◼ Felidia Italian   26| 23| 25| $$$$|
East 50s | 243 E 58th St. (bet. 2nd & 3rd Aves.)
212-758-1479 | felidia-nyc.com
The "crown jewel" in Lidia Bastianich's empire since 1981, this "quintessential" Northern Italian restaurant in an "elegant town-house" in Midtown has "withstood the test of time" by remaining fresh and innovative"; its "amazing homemade pasta" and "superb wines" are served by a staff that is "attentive without being intrusive," and "if you're lucky, Lidia stops by the table to greet you."

NEW Feroce Italian   –| –| –| $$$|
Chelsea | 105 W 28th St. (bet. 6th & 7th Aves.)
212-888-1092
Chelsea's Moxy Hotel hosts a collaboration between Francessco Panella of Antica Pesa and the Tao Group, serving modern Italian-flavored dishes like grilled swordfish and veal chops, often sourced from small producers and with classic touches like tableside preparations and an after-dinner grappa cart; set as it is in a grand interior with a greenhouse patio, the stage is set for high-energy dining and large groups.

Ferris American   25| 20| 23| $$$|
NoMad | 44 W 29th St. (bet. 6th Ave. & B'way)
212-213-4420 | ferrisnyc.com
"They nailed it" when they created this "special" NoMad New American beneath the MADE hotel, where "exciting," "creative" seasonal dishes are served by an "engaging" staff in a "hip," woody space featuring an open kitchen and chef's-counter seating; the "tiny" room may "feel cramped," and it's also "tricky to find," but it's "just off the beaten path enough to make it seem a little exclusive," as the somewhat high prices and "small portions" also emphasize.

Fette Sau Barbecue   25 | 16 | 18 | $$

Williamsburg | 354 Metropolitan Ave.
(bet. Havemeyer & Roebling Sts.) | Brooklyn
718-963-3404 | fettesaubbq.com

For "barbecue worth the schlep," with smoked meats and an "excellent" selection of cocktails and microbrews, head to this old auto-body repair shop in Williamsburg; the waits "can be long" for the "lunch-line" service, but the indoor/outdoor "communal seating" is high energy, and the "glossy pork and charred ribs" served on butcher paper are a good fit for the "casual, laid-back" beer-garden surroundings.

Fiaschetteria Pistoia Italian   26 | 22 | 23 | $$

East Village | 647 E 11th St. (Avenue C)
212-777-3355 | fiaschetteriapistoia.com
West Village | 114 Christopher St.
(bet. Bedford & Bleecker Sts.)
646-609-2911

"As 'real Italian' feeling as anywhere" in New York, say those enamored of this "rustic Tuscan trattoria" with outposts in the East and West Villages; "most of the servers speak Italian fluently," say regulars, "which adds to the experience"; the pastas are "expertly prepared," the "approachable" wine list is a "crate of empty bottles," and the "convivial atmosphere is perfect for a date or casual dinner with friends."

15 East Japanese/Sushi   26 | 22 | 24 | $$$$

Union Square | 15 E 15th St.
(bet. Union Sq. W & 5th Ave.)
212-647-0015 | 15eastrestaurant.com

This "temple for raw fish" near Union Square offers a "fantastic omakase" that takes you on a "culinary journey" in a "zen setting"; along for the ride is a team of "helpful servers," including "sake sommeliers" to assist you in discovering "exclusive bottles" to pair with your food; it "costs as much as NYU tuition," but it's "worth it for a special evening" of sushi that "goes way beyond typical."

Fig & Olive Mediterranean   22 | 21 | 21 | $$$

East 50s | 10 E 52nd St.
(bet. 5th & Madison Aves.)
212-319-2002 | figandolive.com
East 60s | 808 Lexington Ave. (bet. 62nd & 63rd Sts.)
212-207-4555
Meatpacking District | 420 W 13th St. (bet. 9th Ave.
& Washington St.) | 212-924-1200

After a "shopping spree at Bloomingdale's," "grab a glass of wine and some apps" at the Lex branch of this small chain; its "Mediterranean-style" small plates are "beautifully prepared" with "interesting flavor combinations," and the wine list is "surprisingly good," although the "tables are practically on top of each other," and during the lunch rush the noise level can be "unbearable"; the Meatpacking branch is "larger," and they all share the same "vibrant" mood.

The Finch American
26 | 24 | 25 | $$$

Clinton Hill | 212 Greene Ave.
(bet. Cambridge Pl. & Grand Ave.) | Brooklyn
718-218-4444 | thefinchnyc.com

"They get it right" at this "mellow" Clinton Hill standout from a Gramercy Tavern vet, who puts a "a creative twist on old standards" with "exciting," seasonal fare while also offering "fantastic wines and other tipples" at both tables and the marble-topped bar; a "welcoming staff" and a "neighborhood vibe" compensate for the "small" interior.

Firenze Italian
22 | 20 | 22 | $$$

East 80s | 1555 2nd Ave. (81st St.)
212-861-9368 | firenzeny.com

This Tuscan-meets-UES trattoria, open since 1981, remains "dependable" and "reliable," catering to its "adult" audience with home-cooked pastas and parmigiana dishes that are filling and "pleasant enough"; textbook "old-school" romanticism defines the dining room – "lighted" menus in dim lighting, white tablecloths, peace and "quiet" – and "warm, welcoming" staff members only add to the convivial feelings, as does the outdoor patio.

Fish Seafood
23 | 14 | 19 | $$

West Village | 280 Bleecker St. (Jones St.)
212-727-2879 | fishrestaurant.nyc

"Swim among the sharks and minnows" at this "seafood dive," where schools of locals stop by for "big fish, little fish" and "casual" oyster specials during happy hour; the Village "staple" doesn't waste time on "puffery" or pretension, but that also means you'll need to be OK with cramped tables that can leave you "squirming" during peak hours and "peanut shells" scattered beneath your feet.

Fish Cheeks Thai
23 | 18 | 20 | $$$

NoHo | 55 Bond St. (bet. Lafayette St. & Bowery)
212-677-2223 | fishcheeksnyc.com

"There do not appear to be" any actual fish cheeks on the menu, but there's "nothing boring" either at this "inventive" shack highlighting Thailand's seafood and "excellent" curries, with spice levels that'll have you inhaling "rice like it's water"; the "colorful, homey," plant-filled space might seem "too trendy" for some, but the upbeat scene wins diners over pretty easily.

5 Burro Cafe ⊄ Mexican
23 | 16 | 19 | $$

Forest Hills | 72-05 Austin St. (72nd Ave.) | Queens
718-544-2984 | 5burrocafe.com

"Numbing" frozen margaritas and other "strong drinks" exemplify this "neighborhood" Forest Hills spot where such libations pair up with "tasty" Tex-Mex and Mexican dishes in a "small" (borderline "claustrophobic") and "funky" space that "looks like a college dive bar" and has an "ear-popping noise-level" to match; but the "happening bar scene" filled with "lots of under-30 singles on dates or hanging out" implies that "it's all about being there and having fun."

Five Leaves ◖ American ◖ 22 | 19 | 17 | $$

Greenpoint | 18 Bedford Ave. (Lorimer St.) | Brooklyn
718-383-5345 | fiveleavesny.com

"Vinyl plays in the background" of this Greenpoint brunch and lazy-afternoon cocktail staple right off McCarren Park, a "real scene" that has stayed cool after all these years; the wait can be "endless" at peak times ("tell a patient friend to go"), and service is "decent" at best, but it's become an institution and "a little piece of Australia" on the north side of Brooklyn; get the "fantastic" house-special burger.

Flex Mussels Seafood 24 | 18 | 21 | $$

East 80s | 174 E 82nd St. (bet. Lex. & 3rd Aves.)
212-717-7772 | flexmussels.com
West Village | 154 W 13th St. (bet. 6th & 7th Aves.)
212-229-0222

"Elbow-to-elbow crowds" and tight seating don't keep fans from heading to the West Village or the UES for "consistent" seafood: the 23 "crave-worthy sauces" create "sloppy, delicious fun in every pot of mussels" (it's "perfect for a moules frites fix" too); if you're overwhelmed, ask the knowledgeable servers to help you choose, and remember to leave room: "the donuts cinch the meal."

Flor De Mayo Chinese/Latin American 22 | 10 | 19 | $$

West 80s | 484 Amsterdam Ave. (bet. 83rd & 84th Sts.)
212-787-3388 | flordemayo.com
West 100s | 2651 Broadway (bet. 100th & 101st Sts.)
212-663-5520

This UWS landmark offers mix-and-match "Latin food at reasonable prices" and a "down-to-earth Cuban-Chinese kitchen," a winning combo for longtime regulars who return for the "out-of-control good" Peruvian rotisserie chicken; it's good to "stick with the basics" at this "no-nonsense joint," which can sometimes resemble a "mob scene" despite "friendly service."

Flora Bar Ⓜ American/Seafood 24 | 22 | 22 | $$$

East 70s | Met Breuer, 945 Madison Ave. (bet. 74th & 75th Sts.)
646-558-5383 | florabarnyc.com

This "delightful spot" in the basement of the Met Breuer is one of the "coolest" locations on the UES; there's a "super interesting" wine list and an "exciting, adventurous" though "somewhat limited" menu that emphasizes seafood; many dishes "add ingredients that you wouldn't expect together, and it works"; the interior "is not quite as upscale as the food," so in warm weather consider sitting in the garden.

NEW The Fly American – | – | – | $$$

Bedford-Stuyvesant | 549 Classon Ave.
(Fulton St.) | Brooklyn
347-405-5300

From the people behind Hart's, just down the block, this combination wine bar, cocktail den, and chicken shack is located in a hip corner of Bed-Stuy; the New York-raised roasted birds are organic and free range, and come with a small menu of sides – a highly curated approach that matches the list of natural wines and well-priced cocktails.

Follia Italian/Pizza

21 | 18 | 21 | $$

Gramercy | 179 3rd Ave. (bet. 16th & 17th Sts.)
212-477-4100 | follianyc.com

A "beacon of hope in an otherwise lackluster area for restaurants," this "upscale yet affordable" neighborhood spot is perfect for everyone from couples on a date to families; the wood-oven pizzas are "fast and fresh," the "pastas are always done al dente," and the "sauces, particularly the wild boar ragu," are memorable, as is the impressive wine list.

Fonda Mexican

22 | 18 | 20 | $$

East Village | 40 Avenue B (3rd St.)
212-677-4096 | fondarestaurant.com
Chelsea | 189 9th Ave. (bet. 21st & 22nd Sts.)
917-525-5252
Park Slope | 434 7th Ave. (bet. 14th & 15th Sts.) | Brooklyn
718-369-3144

"Always packed and sometimes a little bit rushed," and with a young crowd often installed "two deep at the bar," these spots for "legit" Mexican and "excellent margaritas" will only suit those who can "withstand the roar of the crowd"; fans say dishes like the enchiladas are "super traditional and satisfying," while others recommend the "boozy brunch" and happy hours; additional "upscale" but still "funky" locations are in Park Slope and the East Village.

Foragers Table American

22 | 17 | 20 | $$$

Chelsea | 300 W 22nd St. (8th Ave.)
212-243-8888 | foragersmarket.com

"Tucked in the back of the fancy Forager's Market" in Chelsea, this "lovely" farm-to-table restaurant "proves to be a surprisingly good dining experience," especially at brunch; the kitchen "takes its mandate seriously" and serves "fresh, scrumptious main dishes" from a "limited" menu that uses ingredients grown on plots upstate; with all the retail going on, it can get "crowded and loud," but you'll appreciate the "reasonable prices."

Fornino Pizza

23 | 17 | 18 | $$

Brooklyn Heights | Brooklyn Bridge Park Pier 6
(Joralemon St.) | Brooklyn
718-422-1107 | fornino.com
Greenpoint | 849 Manhattan Ave.
(bet. Milton & Noble Sts.) | Brooklyn
718-389-5300

A "wonderful variety" of "terrific" wood-oven pizzas are the force behind these "fairly priced" Greenpoint and Brooklyn Heights pie purveyors, which also carry other "solid" Italian specialties; the interiors are so-so, but then there's the outdoor seating at both locations – the Pier 6 site, open in season only, has rooftop "views of the East River and the Manhattan skyline," and luckily the quality of the food means "it's no sacrifice to eat there."

44 & X ᒪ American

22 | 21 | 23 | $$

West 40s | 622 10th Ave. (44th St.)
212-977-1170 | 44andx.com

This "amiable" "oasis in bustling" Hell's Kitchen is a "fabulous find" for pre- or post-theater dining; the "solid" "homey" American menu offers a "fresh take on comfort food," and brunch, featuring whimsically named cocktails like the Ethel Mermosa and Bette Mitzer, is especially popular; the "warm welcome" and outdoor seating in warm weather make this a "tried and true" neighborhood "mainstay."

🔲 4 Charles Prime Rib ☾ Steakhouse   28 | 27 | 27 | $$$

West Village | 4 Charles St. (Greenwich Ave.)
212-561-5992 | nycprimerib.com

"Rock-star" steaks – including the namesake prime rib – take center stage at this "indulgent, over-the-top," dinner-only West Village "den" in which diners go to town on the aforementioned meats, plus "flavorful" burgers, while downing "excellent" cocktails in a dimly lit room with wood walls that resembles a "Prohibition-era movie" set, "spot-on" service augments the allure (it's "nearly impossible to snag a reservation").

456 Shanghai Cuisine   Chinese   23 | 13 | 17 | $

Chinatown | 69 Mott St. A (bet. Canal & Bayard Sts.)
212-964-0003 | 456shanghai.com

It's "wonderful" – "A++" for soup dumplings," say fans of this Chinatown favorite for "consistent" Shanghainese fare, as well as a popular Peking duck; it gets "busy" and "crowded" inside, but "fast" turnover and non-posh pricing cements its position as a "legit" option in the neighborhood – "good for bringing your out-of-town friends."

The Four Horsemen   Wine Bar   26 | 23 | 25 | $$$

Williamsburg | 295 Grand St.
(bet. Roebling & Havemeyer Sts.) | Brooklyn
718-599-4900 | fourhorsemenbk.com

"Trust the staff," "you will be in good hands" at this "bumpin'" Williamsburg spot, where they're "well educated" on the intricacies of the natural wine list and which of the "creative" small plates to pair with your glass; "it's hard to reserve," "crowded," and "loud," but worth it once you're in its "casual, comforting" confines.

Fragole Restaurant   Italian   26 | 17 | 24 | $$

Carroll Gardens | 394 Court St.
(bet. Carroll St. & 1st Pl.) | Brooklyn
718-522-7133 | fragolenyc.com

"Everything is delicious" and homemade at this "lively" Italian neighborhood spot in Carroll Gardens, best known for its pastas created with "fresh" ingredients and served by "friendly" waiters; the brick-walled space feels rustic and is pretty "tiny," but there is outdoor seating in season, plus "you can make reservations, and you should."

Frank ☾ 🍴 Italian   26 | 20 | 21 | $$

East Village | 88 2nd Ave. (bet. 5th & 6th Sts.)
212-420-0202 | frankrestaurant.com

At this "quintessential East Village restaurant" (sister spot to Lil' Frankies and Supper), "the attention they pay to detail isn't for elegance, it's for taste"; you'll get "unpretentious" Italian food dished up by "friendly" servers who make you "feel at home"; the somewhat "wacky" space has high "energy and buzz," but it can be "tight" and "noisy": try to snag a "covetable" outdoor seat in the summer; P.S. cash only.

Frankel's Delicatessen   Deli

24 | 19 | 20 | $

Greenpoint | 631 Manhattan Ave.
(bet. Bedford & Nassau Aves.)
718-389-2302 | frankelsdelicatessen.com

"Your Jewish delicatessen prayers are answered" at this "lovely neighborhood" noshery near McCarren Park, a source for "tasty" bagel sandwiches stuffed with smoked fish, plus options like latkes and a "perfect pastrami, egg, and cheese," and all offered at "reasonable" prices (and no aggravation); the "small" space has just "a few tables," so "carrying out or eating quickly" is often a better option, as is delivery.

Frankie & Johnnie's Steakhouse   Steakhouse

22 | 18 | 21 | $$$

West 30s | 32 W 37th St. (bet. 5th & 6th Aves.)
212-947-8940 | frankieandjohnnies.com
Ⓢ West 40s | 320 W 46th St. (bet. 8th & 9th Aves.)
212-997-9494

This "consistent and reliable" carnivorous palace with two locations in Midtown makes "steak lovers" and "obvious regulars" salivate over "well-executed" meat cuts and portions "big enough to share"; "even after being updated," the "Damon Runyon-esque" chophouse still feels "right out of the '20s and '30s," with an interior that looks like it hasn't "changed in years."

Frankies 457 Spuntino   Italian

25 | 20 | 23 | $$

Carroll Gardens | 457 Court St.
(bet. 4th Pl. & Luquer St.) | Brooklyn
718-403-0033 | frankiesspuntino.com

The Carroll Gardens flagship of the two Queens-raised chefs named Frank brought Italian American food "up to date" years before bright, ingredient-driven cuisine became popular; it's a "neighborhood joint" with a "delectable" limited menu – the "homestyle" dishes are "prepared with care" – but are tastiest when enjoyed in the "pretty garden" rather than the tiny front room, packed with "large and fun-loving crowds"; P.S. the wine bar next door features an "interesting rotation" of pours.

Frankies 570   Italian

23 | 18 | 20 | $$$

West Village | 570 Hudson St. (11th St.)
212-924-0818 | frankiesspuntino.com

Second-generation Italian Americans, who also own Frankies 457 in Carroll Gardens, are behind the "honest," "affordable" red-sauce dishes here, as well as "fantastic" gnocchi and focaccia; with "low ceilings and hard surfaces," the "cavernous" interior makes it "hard to hear" even conversations happening in front of you, but that rarely deters "relaxed" diners from having "nice, long-drawn" meals.

NEW Franks Wine Bar   Wine Bar

– | – | – | $$

Carroll Gardens | 465 Court St (Luquer St.) | Brooklyn
718-254-0327 | frankswinebar.com

From the dynamic pair of Franks behind the Frankies restaurants comes this Carroll Gardens wine bar with globetrotting small dishes – everything from salt cod croquettes to farro arancini – as well as the full menu from Frankies Spuntino, and an ever-rotating list of twenty-five wines by the glass, with hundreds more on an encyclopedic bottle list that maintains several vintages from outstanding producers; the bar takes no reservations, but the original next door does.

Fraunces Tavern ✦ Gastropub   19 | 24 | 20 | $$

Financial District | 54 Pearl St. (Broad St.)
212-968-1776 | frauncestavern.com
"George Washington bade farewell to his officers" at this "ancient tourist spot" full of "fantastic" "hidden nooks and crannies" in FiDi, "and they're still serving his favorite sticky toffee pudding"; we cannot tell a lie – the "service is less than stellar" and "pub-type food dependable" at best, "but ye olde charm is undeniable," especially after sampling the "outstanding whiskey selection."

Freds American   22 | 20 | 21 | $$$

East 60s | 660 Madison Ave., 9th Fl. (61st St.)
212-833-2200 | www.barneys.com/restaurants/freds
Chelsea | 101 7th Ave., 3rd Fl. (bet. 16th & 17th Sts.)
646-264-6402
"Not your usual department store restaurant," this Barneys staple is known for being the "quintessential spot for ladies who lunch," but its signature American dishes stand the test of time: "you can't go wrong with the Belgian fries or Freds Chopped Chicken Salad"; the "service is quick so you can get back to shopping"; and although it can feel "manic" at lunchtime, it's much more "sedate for dinner."

Freemans American   21 | 25 | 20 | $$

Lower East Side | Freeman Alley
(off Rivington St., bet. Bowery & Christie St.)
212-420-0012 | freemansrestaurant.com
You feel like you're "walking into another world" as you enter this "eerie secret hideaway" "tucked away on the LES" – "dimly lit," "woodsy" and decorated with "taxidermy animals"; the "home-cooked" comfort food will "make you want to become a regular"; with a brunch that is a "must" and a "late-night bar" upstairs, many consider this a "go-to date spot."

French Louie French   23 | 20 | 22 | $$

Boerum Hill | 320 Atlantic Ave.
(bet. Hoyt & Smith Sts.) | Brooklyn
718-935-1200 | frenchlouienyc.com
At this Boerum Hill spot, you'll "feel like you stepped into a café in the French countryside," with "straightforward and consistent" Gallic fare; diners appreciate the "nice-but-not-too-formal spot" not only for the food but also the staff's "kindness"; it's best to aim for lunch in the "pleasant garden."

🅩 Frenchette French   24 | 22 | 23 | $$$

TriBeCa | 241 W Broadway (bet. Walker & White Sts.)
212-334-3883 | frenchettenyc.com
It's "as close as you can get to Paris" at this "funky," "attractive," "sceney" TriBeCa bistro with "adventurous takes" on French recipes, plus a "fun natural wine list" that some love and others find "a little difficult to navigate"; it does get "roaringly busy," so you may want to "bring a bullhorn" for conversation, and while "premium prices" can lead to blanching, the "courteous" staff will help chill you out – most say it's "cool just to be there."

Fresco by Scotto Italian 23 | 21 | 24 | $$$

East 50s | 34 E 52nd St. (bet. Madison & Park Aves.)
212-935-3434 | frescobyscotto.com

This "Midtown Italian stalwart" is "always crowded at lunch" by "a solid core of regulars" that "feels related to the Scottos," an "incredibly welcoming" bunch famed for its TV ties and local fame; it's "a place to see and be seen and boast who has the deeper pockets" as you dine on the "delightful," "pricey" fare within a lemon-hued "modern setting" graced by the "beautiful" titular artwork on the walls.

Friedman's American 21 | 16 | 20 | $$

West 30s | 450 10th Ave. (35th St.)
212-268-1100 | friedmansrestaurant.com
West 30s | 132 W 31st St. (bet. 6th & 7th Aves.)
212-971-9400
West 40s | 228 W 47th St. (bet. 7th Ave. & B'way)
646-876-1232
West 70s | 130 W 72nd St. (Columbus Ave.)
646-864-2289
Morningside Heights | 1187 Amsterdam Ave. (118th St.)
212-932-0600
Chelsea | 75 9th Ave. (bet. 15th & 16th Sts.)
212-929-7100

For that always "hard-to-find" "gluten-free" brunch, or simply for "classic American breakfast fare" "served all day," this minichain of casual diners serves "generous" portions with a smile; it's "frequently hard to get in" on weekends and during peak lunch hours, but "comfortable decor" and "polite" service make it worth a possible wait, and overall the "convenient locations" around the city make "reliable" refuges for a "quick bite."

NEW The Fulton Seafood – | – | – | $$$

South Street Seaport | 89 South St. (Fulton St.)
212-838-1200 | thefulton.nyc

Jean-Georges Vongerichten has docked at the South Street Seaport in a grand space with Brooklyn Bridge views; serving drama through opulent raw bar towers and whole fish en croute, the menu goes relatively light on French food, but reveals other influences from the chef's previous restaurant ventures, all unified under the flag of dockside seafood; tabs are what you might expect of a celebrity chef restaurant on a touristy pier.

Fushimi Japanese/Sushi 22 | 21 | 21 | $$

Williamsburg | 475 Driggs Ave. (bet. 10th & 11th Sts.)
Brooklyn | 718-963-2555 | fushimigroup.com
Bay Ridge | 9316 4th Ave.
(bet. 93rd & 94th Sts.) | Brooklyn
718-833-7788
Grant City | 2110 Richmond Rd (bet. Colfax & Lincoln Aves.)
Staten Island | 718-980-5300
M Tottenville | 17 Page Ave. (S. Bridge St.) | Staten Island
718-356-3333

The specialty sushi rolls stand out on the menu at these "fun" and clubby Japanese spots that also serve fusion (for instance, Parmesan-crusted chicken breast alongside teriyaki shrimp) and classic sashimi for lunch and dinner, plus a set menu for weekend brunch; the Las Vegas–lounge interior is "over the top," but the "young" crowd doesn't mind the vibe and keeps it "busy."

❷ Gabriel Kreuther ⑤ French   28 | 27 | 28 | $$$$

West 40s | 41 W 42nd St. (bet. 5th & 6th Aves.)
212-257-5826 | gknyc.com

"Genius cooking" and "wonderful textures and flavors" define
the eponymous chef's "cutting-edge" Alsatian food, which is
"one part haute cuisine and one part magic act," with "delectable concoctions" inside "smoke-filled glass cloches" and
topped with "truffles shaved tableside"; "uniformly gracious"
service ensures a serene Midtown experience among "elegant
surroundings," with hand-painted walls and an upscale modern-
farmhouse sensibility.

Gaia Italian Cafe ⑤ Italian   26 | 15 | 14 | $

Lower East Side | 251 E Houston St.
(bet. Norfolk & Suffolk Sts.)
212-350-3977 | gaiaitaliancafe.com

The prices for "earthy Italian food" at this LES café are such
a "steal" that diners are "not sure how it exists" – it must have
something to do with the "weird hours," "gruff service," "strict
rules," and the "cramped quarters"; in exchange, you get "exceptionally good" homemade pasta and bread with a no-charge
BYO policy; but "don't make special requests" – the chef-owner
"will treat you very well if you follow her rules."

Gallaghers Steakhouse Steakhouse   25 | 22 | 24 | $$$$

West 50s | 228 W 52nd St. (bet. B'way & 8th Ave.)
212-586-5000 | gallaghersnysteakhouse.com

"They don't make them like this anymore," sigh devotees of this
"legendary," circa-1927 Theater District steakhouse, an "old
New York" "red-meat experience" pairing "generous portions"
of "butter-tender," hickory-grilled beef ("ogle" it in the dry-aging
locker out front) with an "extensive wine list" in a "historic,"
"upscale" setting; "traditional and friendly" service mitigates the
"noise"-making crowds, and while it costs "plenty," the "central
location" pleases showgoers bent on "walking to their plays."

Galli Italian   17 | 17 | 17 | $$

SoHo | 45 Mercer St. (bet. Broome & Grand Sts.)
212-966-9288 | gallirestaurant.com

You "can't go wrong" for "tried-and-true" Italian basics at this
SoHo stop with a "neighborhoody" feel, "friendly" service, and a
"large selection" of pasta and salads; the exposed-brick "decor
isn't terribly creative," and the overall experience can feel "boring," but it's "date-friendly" as well as a safe lunch choice, and the
"consistent" food and fair prices may "force you to come back."

Gaonnuri Korean   22 | 26 | 23 | $$$

West 30s | 1250 Broadway, 39th Fl. (32nd St.)
212-971-9045 | gaonnurinyc.com

Visit this "swanky" Korean "penthouse" in an office tower for
"drop-dead gorgeous" views of nearly every skyscraper in Midtown; the "gourmet" tabletop BBQ is "probably double what it
would be" at the smoke-filled places down below in K-town, but
it still seems "affordable" for such a "high-end" experience, and
considering the "gracious," polished service, and "spacious"
tables, it is a memorable "place to take out-of-town guests" or
anyone you want to impress.

Gargiulo's Italian
22 | 20 | 23 | $$

Coney Island | 2911 W 15th St.
(bet. Mermaid & Surf Aves.) | Brooklyn
718-266-4891 | gargiulos.com

This "stalwart standby reflecting the glory days of Coney Island" offers what "may be the definition of red-sauce Italian" fare, "served in an unhurried manner" with an "old-fashioned touch" amid a chandeliered interior "that looks like a catering hall"; it's an experience "not of this decade," but "if you crave tradition, this is the place for you"; P.S. "valet parking across the street is an added plus."

Gato Mediterranean
24 | 23 | 22 | $$$

NoHo | 324 Lafayette St.
(bet. Bleecker & Houston Sts.)
212-334-6400 | gatonyc.com

Chef-owner Bobby Flay delivers "consistency all around" at his NoHo hot spot for "innovative" Spanish-inspired fare, including small plates and a decent selection of vegetarian options; they all come with "assertive but balanced" flavors and are paired with "yum" drinks; it's a "bustling," "upscale" place with a "gorgeous" bar area, and sure, it's "noisy," "but who cares with such good food?"

Gazala's Place Middle Eastern
21 | 12 | 20 | $$

West 40s | 709 9th Ave. (bet. 48th & 49th Sts.)
212-245-0709 | gazalasrestaurant.com
West 80s | 447 Amsterdam Ave. (81st St.)
212-787-1800

The "value-packed menu" "invites sharing" at this "tiny" duo near the Theater District and in the West 80s, with dishes of the Middle Eastern Druze people; the menu features myriad meze and "oh so addicting," "paper-thin" pita; space is "cramped," but "service is friendly"; N.B. BYOB.

Gemma ◖ Italian
21 | 24 | 21 | $$

East Village | 335 Bowery (bet. 2nd & 3rd Sts.)
212-505-7300 | theboweryhotel.com/dining

At this affable Italian joint in the Bowery Hotel, the pleasant staff aim to please a "hip, young crowd" with "reasonable prices" and prime "outdoor seating" to soak up the "lively" East Village scene; inside, things get more "romantic," with "candles galore," "large" comfy booths, and "reliable" pizza and pasta, plus "complimentary banana bread" at brunch.

Gennaro ⌑ Italian
25 | 16 | 22 | $$

West 90s | 665 Amsterdam Ave.
(bet. 92nd & 93rd Sts.)
212-665-5348 | gennaronyc.com

It's like "getting a home-cooked meal every time" at this UWS "red-sauce" wonder, "where the locals congregate" for a "long list of specials" at a "reasonable price," and which the "friendly servers" "know by heart"; as a result, it's "always crowded" and "noisy, but cozy" (some say "cramped"); note that they "only take cash," and serve just "beer and wine."

NEW Gertie American

—| —| —| $$|

Williamsburg | 58 Marcy Ave.
(Grand St.) | Brooklyn
718-636-0902 | gertie.nyc

A California-style all-day counter-service spot, this colorful café brings to Williamsburg freshly baked bread, house-cured meats, and plenty of salads and vegetarian options; for those who aren't quite ready to go full West Coast, there are New York touches like sandwiches stacked to Brooklyn standards, Seinfeld references on the menu, and a lively selection of wine, beer, cocktails, and happy-hour specials.

Gigino Trattoria Italian

23| 22| 22| $$|

TriBeCa | 323 Greenwich St. (Duane St.)
212-431-1112 | gigino-trattoria.com
Battery Park City | 20 Battery Pl. (Little West St.)
212-528-2228

The "reliable" Northern Italian dishes, which are "well prepared" and offer "something for everyone," rarely disappoint here, especially when the "large" spread comes at a "fraction of the price" of comparable places; while "unpretentious," "neighborly" hospitality charms the "touristy" crowds, it's the feeling of "being in Italy" – and in the case of the Battery Park trattoria, the "unbeatable" New York Harbor "backdrop" – that really clinches things here.

Gino's Ⓜ Italian/Pizza

25| 18| 23| $$|

Bay Ridge | 7414 5th Ave.
(bet. Bay Ridge Pkwy & 74th St.)
Brooklyn | 718-748-1698 | ginosbayridge.com

"There is no way to go wrong with what you order," promise fans of this 1964 Bay Ridge mainstay that serves wood-fired pizzas at the front counter (a holdover from its beginnings as a slice shop) alongside seafood plates, specialty sandwiches, and pastas with some of the "best vodka sauce money can buy"; the space is always "crowded," so prepare for a "long" wait, but the service is "like a fine-tuned machine."

Giorgio's of Gramercy American

23| 18| 24| $$|

Flatiron | 27 E 21st St. (bet. B'way & Park Ave. S)
212-477-0007 | giorgiosofgramercy.com

"When you get thumbs-up from the real Italians," one fan says, "you know you are doing something right," with a menu of American classics that also incorporates lots of pasta and seafood; despite its "romantic atmosphere," this "lovely" spot has remained "under the radar"; newcomers and regulars say the owner makes sure you don't feel rushed and the servers "make an effort to ensure good times."

Glady's Caribbean

26| 20| 22| $$|

Crown Heights | 788 Franklin Ave.
(Lincoln Pl.) | Brooklyn
212-622-0249 | gladysnyc.com

"When it comes to good Caribbean food" and "sweet tropical drinks," this "intimate" turquoise-hued site with lots of "low-hanging lamps" and plants in Crown Heights is "the real deal," cooking dishes with "the perfect combo of spices"; "you need to be OK with cramped communal seating," and the "staff get overworked" on occasion, but "relax" and have a rum drink "if you can make it to happy hour" – "it's tasty while packing a punch."

Glasserie Mediterranean   24| 22| 21| $$|
Greenpoint | 95 Commercial St.
(bet. Box St. & Manhattan Ave.)
718-389-0640 | glasserienyc.com
Housed in an "out-of-the-way" old glass factory, this industrial-chic dining room draws lots of long-term fans, turning it into a Greenpoint "staple" for "communal feasts" of "modern takes on Mediterranean food," like a "meze brunch" with grilled flatbreads and vegetables "kissed by fire"; this buzzy place gets very "noisy," but a "knowledgeable" staff and a "small but thoughtful" wine list help soothe things.

Gnocco Italian/Pizza   21| 17| 20| $$|
East Village | 337 E 10th St. (bet. Avenues A & B)
212-677-1913 | gnocco.com
For gnocchi fritto, thin-crust pizza, and other "homey" special-ties from Emilia-Romagna come to this East Village eatery boasting all-season "backyard seating" in the "hidden garden" out back (it beats the "casual" interior); even though "service isn't great when they're busy," it remains a "neighborhood standby" for "proper Italian" and light apps.

NEW Golden Diner Diner/Korean   –| –| –| $$|
Lower East Side| 123 Madison St. (Market St.)
goldendinerny.com
Momofuku and Major Food Group alum Sam Yoo brings modern creativity and flair to a menu that combines classic diner fare with Asian accents (katsu chicken club), vegan options (a Caesar salad variant), and Jewish nods (matzo ball soup); early signs point to an appealing breakfast and lunch counter with house-made baked goods and elevated greasy-spoon specials for reasonable prices.

Golden Unicorn Chinese   22| 14| 15| $$|
Chinatown | 18 E Broadway (Catherine St.)
212-941-0911 | goldenunicornnyc.com
"Popular" for just about "forever," this Chinatown "stalwart" plies both tourists and locals with "satisfying" dim sum (plus "an extensive menu providing classic Cantonese") delivered via roll-ing carts throughout a multifloor banquet hall that's "fun, noisy, and crowded"; servers "move fast" among the "shared tables," but it's a slam dunk for "big groups."

Good Enough to Eat American   19| 14| 17| $$|
West 80s | 520 Columbus Ave. (85th St.)
212-496-0163 | goodenoughtoeat.com
The "name says it all" at this "reliable" UWS "brunch staple" with a "compact" but "sweet country-style environment"; sure, the "simple," home-style comfort food, including "all-day breakfast,"

especially the "pancakes, French toast, and eggs," is "good enough to eat," "but is it good enough to wait?" ask those who find the long "lines that form on weekends" "a bummer" ("better to come during the week").

The Good Fork Ⓜ American/Korean   25 24 24 $$
Red Hook | 391 Van Brunt St.
(bet. Coffey & Van Dyke Sts.) | Brooklyn
718-643-6636 | goodfork.com

"This awesome American restaurant with Korean flair" is a true "hideaway" in Red Hook in part because of the difficulty in getting here; your reward is the "unique and flavorful" dishes that emerge from the chef's crafty fusion of ingredients (start with pork dumplings); you can expect an unusually "relaxing and calm" mood in the "eclectic" diner car–style interior and "industrial garden."

Gotham Bar and Grill American   – – – $$$$
Greenwich Village | 12 E 12th St.
(bet. 5th Ave. & University Pl.)
212-620-4020 | gothambarandgrill.com

Change is afoot at a longtime favorite: after 35 years at the helm, chef Alfred Portale has left this Greenwich Village standby, making way for a new chef, a reworked menu, and some stylistic updates to the space; Victoria Blamey, who previously worked at Chumley's, Upland, and Il Buco Alimentari, is serving entirely new dishes, many of them featuring global ingredients and influences, plus a burger and other options available on a bar menu; a lengthy wine list is still on offer.

Gradisca Ⓜ Italian   23 18 23 $$$
West Village | 126 W 13th St.
(bet. 6th & 7th Aves.)
212-691-4886 | gradiscanyc.com

If you're lucky enough to come on a night when the chef's Bologna-born mother is rolling out the pasta, "order anything she is making"; that said, any of the "homemade" dishes are sure to "satisfy your cravings" here; inside a brownstone on a "quiet street" in the West Village, this longtime favorite, named for a Fellini beauty, is "friendly" and "casual," with "attentive" servers and a "beautiful selection of wine (all Italian)."

🄩 Gramercy Tavern American   28 27 28 $$$$
Flatiron | 42 E 20th St. (bet. B'way & Park Ave. S)
212-477-0777 | gramercytavern.com

"Fine dining at its peak" continues to "delight" devotees of Danny Meyer's "standard-setting" Flatiron "classic," this year's second Most Popular eatery, where "spectacular" New American prix fixe supper menus and "first-rate" wines are showcased in an "elegant," rustic main room with "astonishing" flowers and a "magnificent" staff; while it might seem like "parting with a portion of your life savings" when paying the bill, the "casual," no-reservations tavern area in front has "moderately priced" à la carte options; N.B. tips are included.

Gran Electrica Mexican
21 | 21 | 20 | $$

Dumbo | 5 Front St. (Old Fulton St.) | Brooklyn
718-852-2700 | granelectrica.com

"Enclosed by impossibly tall wooden fences" and lit by "fairy lights," the "beautiful" vine-covered garden of this "upscale" taqueria is in a "historic building" "right under the Brooklyn Bridge" in Dumbo; the "welcoming vibe," "killer margaritas," and studious selection of tequila and mezcal help keep it a scene, but some say the "slow" service, long waits, and just "OK" food prevent it from being truly electrifying.

NEW Gran Tivoli (Italian
—| —| —| $$$

NoLita | 406 Broome St.
(bet. Centre & Lafayette Sts.)
917-714-8832 | grantivoli.com

One focal point at this Italian-Mediterranean hot spot from Australian restaurateurs is the beautiful long bar, but other draws are the steaks shipped from Tasmania, plenty of seafood, vegan options, and a buzzy brunch worthy of NoLita; it stays noisy and crowded most of the time, but after dinner you can sneak downstairs to Peppi's Cellar, a wine and craft cocktail den with regular live music and events.

Grand Army (Seafood
20 | 21 | 19 | $$

Boerum Hill | 336 State St. (Hoyt St.) | Brooklyn
718-643-1503 | grandarmybar.com

Boerum Hill regulars "come often for the drinks" at this "cramped" local hang, where the cocktails with under-the-radar spirits change seasonally; while the "atmosphere holds up better" than some of the dishes coming out of the kitchen, "fun towers of seafood" and smart accoutrements like "eye droppers of different mignonettes" are worth coming back for.

Grand Banks (Seafood
17 | 28 | 15 | $$$

TriBeCa | Hudson River Park, Pier 25 (N Moore St.)
212-660-6312 | grandbanks.nyc

"Bring your sea legs and enjoy the view" from the Sherman Zwicker, a 1940s schooner floating in the Hudson at TriBeCa's Pier 25 that's popular with the "well-dressed" and "sunglass-clad"; the seafood and thoughtful "wine and beer selection" are best enjoyed "during summer," although it's usually open from late April through October; it can be "tough to get in," the service isn't first class, and prices may "shipwreck your wallet," but "if you like oysters" "as fresh as you can get," climb aboard.

Z Grand Central Oyster Bar & Restaurant S Seafood
23 | 20 | 19 | $$$

East 40s | 89 E 42nd St. (Park Ave.)
212-490-6650 | oysterbarny.com

"A cultural and culinary institution," this "golden oldie" "in the bowels of Grand Central" continues to turn out "blissfully reliable" seafood "throwbacks" (pan roasts and a "wonderful oyster selection" among them); in the "cavernous," "brightly lit" space you'll find "intricately tiled" vaulted ceilings, "unique counter seats," and a "buzzing" saloon, and while "erratic" service, "loud, crowded" environs, and "expensive" tabs irk some, if you wanna "pretend to be Don Draper," it's still a real "pearl."

Grand Sichuan Chinese

22 | 12 | 17 | $$

Chelsea | 229 9th Ave.
(bet. 24th & 25th Sts.)
212-620-5200 | Grand-Sichuan.com
Forest Hills | 98-108 Queens Blvd.
(bet. 66th & 67th Aves.) | Queens
718-268-8833
Grand Sichuan Eastern
Chelsea | 172 8th Ave. (bet. 18th & 19th Sts.)
212-243-1688 | grandsichuaneasternnyc.com
East 50s | 1049 2nd Ave. (bet. 55th & 56th Sts.)
212-355-5855

"Pick your pleasure" at this "unusual" Sichuan spot, with
food lovers "going out of their way" for soup dumplings "better
than you'll get at most dim sum places" and "consistently
fresh and tasty" spicy dishes that'll "treat you nice"; servers
are not always that attentive at the Midtown East location,
but Forest Hills residents consider theirs a "local treasure"
that's "well-run," with "fast and efficient" waiters and delivery
people.

The Grange ◖ American

22 | 20 | 22 | $$

Harlem | 1635 Amsterdam Ave. (141st St.)
212-491-1635 | thegrangebarnyc.com
A "charming" "neighborhood hangout" for gastropub-style,
"farm-to-table" Americana, this Hamilton Heights spot serves
a "small but varied" "seasonal" menu of "creative" food with
some vegan options, brought to you by "chummy" servers and
"friendly" bartenders shaking "artisan cocktails"; it works well
for a boozy brunch or hanging with a "fun dinner crowd" above
140th Street.

Great NY Noodletown ◖ Chinese

23 | 6 | 13 | $

Chinatown | 28 Bowery (Bayard St.)
212-349-0923 | greatnynoodletown.net
When you're craving Cantonese classics, this "longtime legend"
"hits the spot, especially at 3 AM"; "try anything salt-baked"
or something from the "wide selection" of namesake noodle
dishes, and it'll be "served quickly" at "big bang-for-the-buck"
prices; the less impressed note the "not particularly inviting
decor," warn of the possibility of being "seated with strangers,"
and call the staff "gruff" (or perhaps just "efficient") – "you have
to know what you want!!"

Greenpoint Fish
& Lobster Co. Seafood

23 | 18 | 19 | $$

Greenpoint | 114 Nassau Ave. (Eckford St.) | Brooklyn
718-349-0400 | greenpointfish.com
Set sail for North Brooklyn to indulge in "all things seafood" at
this "low-key" fish market with "decent" prices; sit at the "small
diner counter," "ask the cooks what's good" that day, and then
watch as they prepare "fresh" catches, raw-bar favorites, and
lobster rolls; "be prepared to wait" for "tight" seating, as locals
consider it a top pick "perfect for a quick bite."

| | FOOD | DECOR | SERVICE | COST |

Gregory's 26 Corner
Taverna Greek/Seafood
▼ 25 | 15 | 23 | $|

Astoria | 26-02 23rd Ave. (26th St.) | Queens
718-777-5511 | gregoryscornertaverna.net

"My go-to Greek in Astoria," proclaim partisans of the "casual taverna" "that serves baby shark and wine by the ewer," plus more conventional fish, meats, and classic Hellenic spreads – all "consistently simple and delicious"; the setting is "no-frills" and the service can be too ("sometimes you have to remind them you need something"), but folks "always return."

☑ The Grill Ⓢ American
25 | 28 | 26 | $$$$|

East 50s | 99 E 52nd St.
(bet. Lexington & Park Aves.)
212-375-9001 | thegrillnewyork.com

Mario Carbone and friends "hit it out of the ballpark with this" "fabulous-looking" Seagram Building steakhouse in the former Four Seasons' second-floor space, where the "grand" interior complements the "old-school" American dishes sporting "updated flourishes," "craft" martinis, and "top-notch" service; "just bring a wheelbarrow full of money" – the "suits" and "people-watchers" in attendance certainly do – and this "Mad Men" "restaurant theater" is yours to "savor" too.

Grimaldi's ⌿ Pizza
23 | 13 | 16 | $$|

Dumbo | 1 Front St. (bet. Dock & Old Fulton Sts.)
Brooklyn | 718-858-4300
Flatiron | 656 6th Ave. (bet. 20th & 21st Sts.)
646-484-5665 | grimaldis-pizza.com
Coney Island | 1215 Surf Ave.
(bet. Stillwell Ave. & 12th St.) | Brooklyn
718-676-2630
Douglaston | 242-02 61st Ave. (Douglaston Plaza
Shopping Ctr.) | Queens | 718-819-2133

"Patience rewards the palate" of 'za zealots braving the "long lines" anxious to enter the original location this "storied" pizzeria near the Brooklyn Bridge, where "solid" coal-fired thin-crust pies loaded with "flavorful" tomato sauce and "plentiful" toppings "satisfy even the pickiest of eaters"; less fulfilling is the cash-only, no-reservations, no-slices policy, and the decor is merely basic, although fans acknowledge the "friendly" service and the potential for "quieter" meals at the chainlet's other locations in Flatiron and Coney Island.

Guan Fu Chinese
▼ 26 | 23 | 23 | $$$|

Flushing | 39-16 Prince St. (39th Ave.) | Queens
347-610-6999 | guanfuszechuan.com

"A festive" special-occasion vibe prevails at this "high-end spot for Sichuan food" in Flushing, where "spicy, unusual offerings, like fried yolk corn" or braised turtle and lots of seafood are served amid latticed panels, carved wood furnishings, and stone floors; "be prepared to wait" at peak times, perhaps browsing through the photo-filled menu, unless you book one of the "private event spaces" popular with families.

GupShup Indian

| 23 | 23 | 18 | $$ |

Gramercy | 115 E 18th St.
(bet. Irving Pl. & Park Ave. S)
212-518-7313 | gupshupnyc.com

Bombay meets Big Apple at this "innovative" Indian destination in Gramercy, which fusions up street food with "unique" chutneys, tacos made with chickpea flour, and "off-the-charts" midnight-black daal; the "in-crowd" is a huge fan of the "craziness" happening inside the "glitzy" space, filled with dramatic lighting fixtures and vivid life-size murals, although the loud, "not so appealing" soundtrack can be a turnoff.

NEW Haenyeo Korean

▼ | 27 | 22 | 22 | $$ |

Park Slope | 239 5th Ave.
(bet. Carroll & President Sts.) | Brooklyn
718-213-2290 | haenyeobk.com

The food shines at this Korean Park Slope "gem" from the mind behind the East Village's legendary (and now closed) Dok Suni; here, "tasty," traditional seafood dishes and other staples have diners feeling the "love"; "innovative" cocktails, "warm" service, and reasonable pricing offset the compact space, and if it's not the fanciest spot in the area, it is a very welcome addition.

Hakkasan New York Chinese

| 24 | 26 | 23 | $$$ |

West 40s | 311 W 43rd St. (bet. 8th & 9th Aves.)
212-776-1818 | hakkasan.com

You "feel like royalty" as soon as you enter the "architecturally terrific," "dungeon-chic" London export in the Theater District to feast on "artful presentations" of "high-end Chinese," like "fabulous duck"; even if it is "expensive for the portions" and feels a bit like "clubbing," the open space allows you to "see the chefs in action," and the servers "get you to the curtain on time."

Han Dynasty Chinese

| 23 | 15 | 18 | $$ |

East Village | 90 3rd Ave. (bet. 12th & 13th Sts.)
212-390-8685 | handynasty.net
West 80s | 215 W 85th St. (B'way) | 212-858-9060
Downtown Brooklyn | 1 Dekalb Ave. (Fleet St.) | Brooklyn
718-858-0588

"Spiciness rules" at the NYC "branches of a Philadelphia" favorite offering "genuine Sichuan flavors" with spice levels going from "hot to OMG"; if you "don't let the waiting crowds discourage you," and don't mind "food that arrives when it's ready," you can bask in a "festive atmosphere" that works for groups and others after a "lazy-Susan experience" with prices that "won't break the bank."

The Handpulled Noodle Chinese

▼ | 26 | 10 | 19 | $ |

Harlem | 3600 Broadway (148th St.)
917-262-0213 | thehandpullednoodle.com

Though the exposed-brick digs are "tiny and cramped, the food more than makes up for it" at this humble Harlem site, where the noodles, prepared in Northwest Chinese style, are chewy, irregularly shaped, and "delicious" (good dumplings as well); ordering up front, you pair your choice with different stir-fries and soups, then slurp 'em down seated at counters along walls covered with vintage newspapers.

| | FOOD | DECOR | SERVICE | COST |

Z Hangawi Korean   28 | 25 | 26 | $$$

Murray Hill | 12 E 32nd St. (bet. 5th & Madison Aves.)
212-213-0077 | hangawirestaurant.com

"Leave your shoes at the front and sink into the relaxing atmosphere" at this "transportive" K-town vegetarian, where the "tasty" Korean specialties are so "delectable" that "you don't miss the meat," although the "original cocktails" may assist in that regard; "helpful" servers and a "serene," pillow-softened setting counteract the "pricey" tabs, making it a "place to linger" and create "everlasting memories"; N.B. vegan and gluten-free options are available, too.

Hanjan Korean   23 | 20 | 20 | $$$

Flatiron | 36 W 26th St. (bet. 6th Ave. and B'way)
212-206-7226 | hanjan26.com

Kimchi fried rice is the dish everyone remembers at this Korean favorite, but it's hard to go wrong with any of the "beautifully conceived and prepared dishes" accompanied by "really fresh banchan" (traditional sides) and "friendly service," adding up to a meal that's "completely satisfying"; reviewers also note the "excellent" cocktails and a "surprisingly good wine list," so take a cue from locals and "try happy hour at the bar."

Hanoi House Vietnamese   25 | 19 | 22 | $$

East Village | 119 St. Marks Pl.
(bet. 1st Ave. & Avenue A)
212-995-5010 | hanoihousenyc.com

The "fragrant," "rich," yet minimally dressed pho "provokes gasps of pleasure" and the "proprietary beer" hoi (fresh beer) as well as the rest of the large menu are true to Vietnam, but the "trendy" scene is pure East Village; get a reservation for this noodle house or else you'll have long waits for a seat at "little tables" in the "cramped" space – although "speedy" service does keep things moving.

NEW Hanon Japanese   – | – | – | $$

Williamsburg | 436 Union Ave.
(bet. Devoe & Keap Sts.)
Brooklyn | 347-799-1433

Destination-worthy udon has arrived in Williamsburg at this second branch of a Japan-based restaurant specializing in handmade versions of the slippery thick wheat noodles, and an eye-catching green variation made with bamboo and barley leaves; available in both hot and chilled preparations, there's a slurp for all seasons, served alongside the typical accompaniments, like tempura, tea, rice balls, and karaage (fried chicken).

Hao Noodle Chinese   23 | 22 | 19 | $$

Chelsea | 343 W 14th St. (Hudson St.)
646-882-0059 | haonoodle.com
West Village | 401 6th Ave.
(bet. Greenwich Ave. & Waverly Pl.)
212-633-8900

Showcasing "modern takes" on various Chinese regional "classics," these "cool" West Village and Chelsea joints feature "big" menus of "wonderful," often-"spicy" ("my mouth was on fire") dishes, including hand-pulled noodles, as well as dinner-only BBQ options at the 14th Street location; the "airy," "inviting" rooms have individual and communal tables, and while the "service isn't perfect," the "quality and taste" are both high, and reflected in prices.

The Happiest Hour ◖ American   19| 23| 17| $$|

West Village | 121 W 10th St.
(bet. Greenwich Ave. & Patchin Pl.)
212-243-2827 | happiesthournyc.com

With a tropical space that "feels like a Miami vacation," this "vibrant" West Village hangout serves "configurable-by-spirit" cocktails, plus burgers and other Americana basics to a youthful crowd seeking "happiness" via "a lively evening of drinking"; given the crowd's focus on "meeting people," the "noisy" digs and blah service are borderline irrelevant"; P.S. the "cool" cocktail bar downstairs is called Slowly Shirley.

Harlem Shake American   20| 19| 17| $$|

Harlem | 100 W 124th St. (Lenox Ave.)
212-222-8300 | harlemshakenyc.com

"Travel back in time" for "cheap, quality" burgers and diner breakfasts at a "retro" "hipster" counter joint that's "popular" with locals and others who find the "smash burgers" "much more satisfying" than eating at a chain (even if the greasy-spoon service isn't much different); on a nice day, you can sit out front, since there's "plenty of outdoor seating" and, as if this had to be said, "be sure to have a shake" too.

Harry's NYC ◖ American/Steakhouse   23| 22| 23| $$$|

Financial District | 1 Hanover Square
(bet. Pearl & Stone Sts.)
212-785-9200 | harrysnyc.com

"Housed in the historic India House," the former Cotton Exchange, this "warm," "cozy," clubby "old-timer" coddles expense-accounters with "fast service" and highly "tasty" steak, pastas, and other "nostalgic" American and Continental dishes, including a "famous beef Wellington"; although prices skew on the high end, "you get what you pay for here," and who knows better than the wizards of Wall Street?

Hart's American   26| 21| 23| $$$|

Bedford-Stuyvesant | 506 Franklin Ave.
(bet. Fulton St. & Jefferson Ave.) | Brooklyn
718-636-6228 | hartsbrooklyn.com

"Feel like you're in on the secret" when you scope out this "super-tiny" Bed-Stuy space; from the American eats – "simply made" but "executed with flair and finesse"– to the "thoughtful staff" to the woody, whitewashed brick interior (dominated by bottles of "interesting wines"), "nothing is fussy" here, making it "the perfect date restaurant" or perhaps the "neighborhood spot that everyone wishes they lived around the corner from."

Haru Sushi Japanese/Sushi   20 | 16 | 18 | $$
Financial District | 1 Wall St. Ct.
(Beaver St. & Pearl St.)
212-785-6850 | hartsbrooklyn.com
(**West 40s** | 229 W 43rd St. (bet. 7th & 8th Aves.)
212-398-9810
West 50s | 559 9th Ave. (56th St.) | 212-301-4440
(**West 80s** | 433 Amsterdam Ave. (bet. 80th & 81st Sts.)
212-579-5655
"You know what you're getting" at this "reliable" and "enjoyable"
mini-chain with "ordinary but consistent" maki and sashimi as
well as some "interesting" specialty rolls, along with lots of options for "non–sushi lovers" and popular happy hour deals; it's
modern and simple inside, and the service is generally "friendly"
and "efficient," though "noisy and crowded" at peak times; P.S.
additional locations are at Wall Street, Times Square, and Hell's
Kitchen.

NEW HaSalon Ⓢ Ⓜ Middle Eastern   – | – | – | $$$$
West 50s | 735 10th Ave. (50th St.)
212-495-9024 | hasalonnyc.com
This Hell's Kitchen branch of a festive Tel Aviv original is a
real adventure, with seasonal menus and DJs who transform
the dining room into a dance club after the second seating;
the party scene, the showy, photogenic food, and the intense
overall experience may lead to some serious sticker shock,
but if you're looking for dinner and a night out dancing, this
reservation-only spot will deliver both in one of the splashiest
ways possible.

Hatsuhana Ⓢ Japanese/Sushi   26 | 18 | 23 | $$$
East 40s | 17 E 48th St. (bet. 5th & Madison Aves.)
212-355-3345 | hatsuhana.com
Rather than flashy rolls and "flamethrower" theatrics, you'll get
"pure" "fresh fish with little fanfare" in a simple setting at this
Midtown East "survivor"; "you'll be surrounded" by business-
people who've been coming here for years and appreciate the
"attentive" service, the "approachable" chefs at the sushi bar,
and getting in and out "without paying a lot," especially for the
extra-value "lunch special."

Hearth American   25 | 23 | 24 | $$$
East Village | 403 E 12th St. (1st Ave.)
646-602-1300 | restauranthearth.com
"Put your phone in a box on the table" and prepare to "share"
your meal at this "zen"-infused Tuscan-American East Village
spot, where the "vibrant," seasonal small plates – including
"healthy options" flavored with "herbs you may have never
heard of" – and "seriously interesting wine list" make for "special" dining; some say it's "a bit overpriced," yet with staff who
"remember your name," plus the "warm" atmosphere, it really
does feel to most "like home."

Heidelberg German   21 | 19 | 19 | $$
East 80s | 1648 2nd Ave. (bet. 85th & 86th Sts.)
212-628-2332 | heidelberg-nyc.com
Yorkville hasn't been Kleindeutschland for a long time, but
at one of the neighborhood's few remaining German spots,

they still cook "stick-to-your-ribs" spaetzle and schnitzel "like Grandma's," pour "massive" beers in glass boots, and slather pork shanks in deep gravies full of "Teutonic goodness"; servers donning "dirndls and lederhosen" are "gemütlichkeit personified," making many feel like they are "virtually experiencing the country."

Hell's Kitchen (Mexican

19 | 17 | 18 | $$

West 50s | 754 9th Ave. (51st St.)
212-977-1588 | hellskitchen-nyc.com

This "reliable" Mexican cantina in Midtown West comes with a full "guacamole bar" menu; the "roomy" booths, crowds, and high "decibel level," and tasty margaritas and other "varied" drinks make it a good place to let loose, so it's better for post-theater or later than pre-curtain – boosters are happy that it's still "under the radar" and provides "bang for your buck."

Henry's End American

25 | 16 | 23 | $$$

Brooklyn Heights | 72 Henry St.
(bet. Orange & Pineapple Sts.) | Brooklyn
718-834-1776 | henrysend.com

This Brooklyn Heights institution, which moved in 2019 "to larger quarters" down the street, is the place to try "unique" seasonal plates featuring kangaroo and elk (plus more "exotic" options during its annual game festival) alongside an American menu that includes a "killer" fried chicken, all paired with an "excellent" wine list; the "terrific" staff are "beyond welcoming," too.

Her Name is Han Korean

25 | 19 | 22 | $$

East 30s | 17 E 31st St.
(bet. 5th & Madison Aves.)
212-779-9990 | hernameishan.com

"Her name should be 'delicious,'" say admirers of this "creative" spot, which supplies "a robust menu" of "super-satiating Korean soul food" and can "still knock out the classics with finesse," along with house-infused sojus, in a "down-to-earth," and often "busy" space that "can feel a bit cramped"; thankfully, "affordable" prices – including lunch-set "deals" – and "personable" service carry the day: "bring friends to try everything."

Hibino Japanese/Sushi

24 | 17 | 22 | $$

Cobble Hill | 333 Henry St. (Pacific St.) | Brooklyn
718-260-8052 | hibino-lic.com
Long Island City | 10-70 Jackson Ave.
(bet. 49th & 50th Aves.) | Queens
718-392-5190

The "understated, laid-back" neighborhoods of Cobble Hill and Long Island City are also home to these "unassuming" and "small" spaces, offering "fairly hard-to-find" varieties of sushi and Kyoto-style small plates at "remarkably reasonable" prices, not to mention some "wonderful sake specials"; the open kitchen concept helps make the interior "cozy and comfortable" – one that's "pleasant" from your first step inside.

Hide-Chan Ramen Japanese/Ramen   24 | 15 | 18 | $$

East 50s | 248 E 52nd St. (bet. 2nd & 3rd Aves.)
212-813-1800 | hidechanramen.nyc
West 50s | 314 W 53rd St. (bet. 8th & 9th Aves.)
212-969-0066

With branches in Midtown East and Hell's Kitchen, this "favorite ramen haunt" is known for its "fabulous chewy" noodles and "richly flavored" broth; meals are "consistently delicious and quick, without skimping on quality"; with masks of cartoon characters hanging on the walls, the interior is best described as "interesting," but clearly the room full of Japanese expats and tourists are really here for the "satisfying" bowls.

High Street on Hudson American   22 | 19 | 21 | $$

Meatpacking District | 637 Hudson St. (Horatio St.)
917-388-3944 | highstreetonhudson.com

"Take a loaf" of the "fabulous" bread and a bag of "fresh-baked goods" on your way out of this "comfortable" Meatpacking offshoot of a Philadelphia resto-café with "eclectic" decor, an "open kitchen," and "friendly" service; it's a neighborhood "go-to" during brunch, but it's also an "all-day" place that provides a "good value" for current, "fresh," seasonal American with Mediterranean influences.

Hillstone American   23 | 21 | 23 | $$$

East 50s | 888 3rd Ave. (54th St.)
212-888-3828 | hillstonerestaurant.com
NoMad | 378 Park Ave. S (27th St.)
212-689-1090

"It may be a chain, but it's a good chain," proclaim advocates of this NoMad/East 50s pair, a draw for "upscale American food that always delivers," plus a "willing-to-please" staff and "vibrant bar scene"; the "cozy, dark, cool atmosphere" "can be crowded," and "the prices go up just about every time you blink," but it's "a sure bet for groups looking to please everyone," or for times when "you just need" some spinach artichoke dip (a "must have").

Ho Foods Taiwanese   23 | 16 | 21 | $$

East Village | 110 E 7th St. (bet. 1st Ave. & Avenue A)
347-788-0682 | hofoodsnyc.com

At this "welcome addition" to the East Village, a limited menu provides the means for slurping down "deep, rich, and nuanced" beef soup and noodles ("al dente perfection") that taste "as if you were eating in Taipei"; while the "tiny" space is packed "all the time," tables turn over "quickly," and "brisk yet friendly" hospitality makes the wait worthwhile.

Holy Ground ☾ Barbecue   ▼ 25 | 28 | 27 | $$

TriBeCa | 112 Reade St. (W B'way)
646-882-0666 | holygroundnyc.com

If you like the idea of upscale BBQ, this "trendy" TriBeCa "subterranean lair" should be a "staple in your rotation"; the decor reads vintage steakhouse, with red-leather banquettes and dark wood-paneled walls covered with antique prints and mirrors, but the "robust menu" specializes in slow-smoked meats, augmented by serious sides (in particular, the "roasted brussels sprouts and crispy potatoes are great options") and cocktails both innovative and "classic."

⊉ Hometown Bar-B-Que Ⓜ Barbecue   28 | 19 | 19 | $$

Red Hook | 454 Van Brunt St. (Reed St.) | Brooklyn
347-294-4644 | hometownbbq.com
"You can smell the smoker from blocks away," say diehards, some of whom "crave this place nonstop"; you might want to "bring a bib" to sample the "fantastic" "Texas-style" BBQ, the brisket "full of nicely rendered fat," "exceptional ribs," and "messy and satisfying Asian-style glazed wings," and get in line with the passionate folks who believe "lamb belly is everything"; dining is at shared tables in a huge Red Hook warehouse space, and meats do run out.

Hop Kee ◖ 🖪 Chinese   22 | 9 | 16 | $$

Chinatown | 21 Mott St.
(bet. Chatham Sq. & Mosco St.)
212-964-8365 | hop-kee-nyc.com
"They've been nailing it for over 30 years," say diners who've been going since childhood to this "casual and consistent" Chinatown institution" for "basic old-fashioned Cantonese food made well," and offered at "low prices because it's cash-only"; though "fast," the "waiters can be grumpy," and the below-ground surroundings feel old, but most folks "ignore the atmosphere and just eat."

The House American   21 | 23 | 22 | $$$

Gramercy | 121 E 17th St.
(bet. Irving Pl. & Park Ave. S)
212-353-2121 | hospitalityholdings.com
This "charming hideaway" takes up two floors of a restored carriage house from 1854, making a "romantic setting"; it's worth asking for a table by the enormous front window or on the front patio to bring the "street and skyline" into view; the American fare is "refined," and while it "doesn't do anything adventurous," it's hard to complain about elevated classics like truffle mac and cheese, especially when it's served by "attentive" staff.

Houseman American   23 | 20 | 22 | $$$

Hudson Square | 508 Greenwich St. (Spring St.)
212-641-0654 | housemanrestaurant.com
The menu changes daily at this "tucked-away" Hudson Square "neighborhood joint," where offerings range from the "vegetable-forward" to a "fabulous" burger at a fair "value for the dollar," all cooked with "modern" "hipster restraint" in a "lively place"; although the "tables are very close together," the "civilized" service and "reasonable" decibel level (it works for those who "still want to hear themselves think") help make this house "feel like your own home."

Hudson Clearwater ◖ American   19 | 19 | 20 | $$$

West Village | 447 Hudson St. (Morton St.)
212-989-3255 | hudsonclearwater.com
This "perfectly cute" West Village "go-to" is a "casual jewel" – "great" for date night – offering a concise menu of "solid" eats

(duck confit, ricotta gnocchi, grilled hanger steak) for brunch, lunch, and dinner; the "charming" backyard garden terrace is much "loved," as is the chef's counter, where they "take their prep and presentation quite seriously."

NEW **Hudson Yards Grill** American — | — | — | $$$
West 30s | 20 Hudson Yards
(10th Ave. & 33rd St.)
212-545-7600 | hudsonyardsgrill.com
Come as you are to this crowd-pleasing yet elevated tribute to American comfort food, with a kid's menu, a picture-perfect cheeseburger, and a signature cocktail list; don't expect much innovation, just classics developed from the repertoire of Chef Michael Lomonaco of Porter House fame; you won't find the views here that some of the other Hudson Yards restaurants enjoy, but lunch prix fixe menus take some of the pricey edge off.

Huertas Spanish 22 | 18 | 23 | $$$
East Village | 107 1st Ave. (bet. 6th & 7th Sts.)
212-228-4490 | huertasnyc.com
For the "Basque experience" of snacking on pintxos with "imaginative" cocktails, such as "homemade vermouth" and gin and tonics on tap, this "cozy," wood-paneled tapas bar offers dishes "not easily found outside of Spain," tempting "happy-hour specials" (the garlicky "hot dog is simply not to be passed up"), "warm service" with a "no-tipping" policy, and a "family-style menu for groups."

Hunan Slurp Chinese 22 | 23 | 20 | $$
East Village | 112 1st Ave. (7th St.)
646-585-9585 | hunanslurp.com
You can tell that the "owner is an artist" by the sleek setting and fabulous decor at this "bustling East Villager" – take it all in while enjoying Hunan cuisine featuring "complex spices," elevated, "well-prepared" rice noodle soups and other "flavorful" dishes; the gorgeous presentations and the "friendly" service are two more pluses.

NEW **Hunky Dory** ℂ American — | — | — | $$
Crown Heights | 747 Franklin Ave.
(Sterling Pl.) | Brooklyn
516-418-2063 | hunkydorybk.com
Crowd-pleasing and open late, this Crown Heights spot serves all-day meals and innovative cocktails on a menu that rides the line between creative and comfortable, offering coddled eggs or oatmeal in the morning, and house-fermented vegetables or roasted cod at night; the friendly prices and happy-hour specials are targeted toward neighborhood regulars as well as those looking for a quick break from exploring Prospect Park or the Brooklyn Museum.

Hunt & Fish Club Steakhouse 21 | 24 | 22 | $$$$
West 40s | 125 W 44th St. (bet. 6th & 7th Aves.)
212-575-4949 | hfcnyc.com
Steak (and, to a lesser degree, seafood) hunters who "don't mind braving Times Square" congregate at this "glittery"

Midtowner, a quasi–supper club where the "big," "opulent" interior – complete with "high ceilings" and dramatic lighting – "better-than-average cocktails," and a "see-and-be-seen" crowd overshadow the uneven cuts; given that it's "super expensive," it's a haven for "business lunches," but also for pre-theater.

Hwa Yuan Szechuan Chinese   24 | 23 | 23 | $$$

Chinatown | 42 E Broadway
(bet. Catherine & Market Sts.)
212-966-6002 | hwayuannyc.com

This "upscale" reboot of the 1980s original takes its "tried-and-true Sichuan plates" to a "higher level" with carefully tuned favorites like "to die for" Peking duck and the cold sesame noodles its first chef made famous; the refurbished space is "pretty elegant" and well suited for "hosting business meals" – with "discreet and friendly service" (and higher than average prices) to match.

Hwaban M Korean   ▼ 23 | 24 | 26 | $$$

Flatiron | 55 W 19th St. (bet. 5th & 6th Aves.)
917-261-2020 | hwaban.com

Though somewhat under the radar, this refined Flatiron Korean is lauded as "a lovely experience" by those who've found it; often adorned with flowers, the dishes – modern takes on classics like bibimbap and kimchi stew – are pops of color within the bright, streamlined, beige-on-white surroundings; whether you opt for the prix fixe dinner or go à la carte, the "flavors are delicious."

Z I Sodi Italian   28 | 21 | 25 | $$$

West Village | 105 Christopher St.
(bet. Bleecker & Hudson Sts.)
212-414-5774 | isodinyc.com

Dining at this "blink and you'll miss it" West Village eatery means you'll have to "come early or late" or "snag a seat at the bar"; even diehard fans admit it's "annoyingly hard to get into" and reservations are "hard to come by," but the "imaginative, tasty, and well-prepared" Tuscan food – "stripped to the essentials and prepared and served with care and love" – make it "one of the best restaurants in the city," as do the "wonderful wines" and the "lively" mood.

I Trulli S Italian   22 | 21 | 23 | $$$

Murray Hill | 124 E 27th St.
(bet. Lexington & Park Ave. S)
212-481-7372 | itrulli.com

"Solid regional Italian food from Puglia" and a well-chosen wine list draw diners as much as the mellow space itself: the room between tables and a "roaring fireplace" in winter accommodate diners "not on a timetable," as does the "peaceful oasis of the backyard" in summer; by any measure, it's "a wonderful spot for gatherings," but "if flashy and trendy are your thing," regulars warn, "look elsewhere."

	FOOD	DECOR	SERVICE	COST

Ichiran ☾ Japanese/Ramen   23 | 18 | 21 | $$

West 30s | 132 W 31st St. (bet. 6th & 7th Aves.)
212-465-0701 | ichiranusa.com
West 40s | 152 W 49th St. (bet. 6th & 7th Aves.)
646-964-4294
Bushwick | 374 Johnson Ave. (bet. Bogart St. &
Morgan Ave.) Brooklyn | 718-381-0491

Ramen aficionados "become one with their bowls" and "forget the world for a little" at these Bushwick and Midtown outposts of a Japan-based chain known for its "customizable" noodles and "varied" accoutrements as much as its "silent, eat-by-yourself booths" that allow customers to savor the flavors in peace; if the concept seems "gimmicky," "the card-ordering process is easy," and regular tables are still available; N.B. no tipping.

Ikinari Steak   Japanese/Steakhouse   19 | 10 | 13 | $$

Greenwich Village | 90 E 10th St.
(bet. 3rd & 4th Aves.)
917-388-3546 | ikinaristeakusa.com
West 40s | 37 W 46th St. (bet. 5th & 6th Aves.)
917-409-5783

Seekers of carnivorous "instant gratification" head to these "fast"-moving Village and Midtown steakhouses, branches of a Japanese chain serving "decent," "inexpensive" cuts that are sold by weight while diners "stand" at tables for the privilege; some find 'em "too gimmicky," and these "casual" joints aren't known for stunning decor or service, but if you're looking "to bury yourself in a pound of meat," they're handy enough.

Il Bambino   Italian   24 | 16 | 20 | $$

Astoria | 34-08 31st Ave.
(bet. 34th & 35th Sts.) | Queens
718-626-0087 | lbambinonyc.com

"Creative," "delicious," "decently priced" paninis are the draw at this casual destination in Astoria, which also offers salads, a long list of creative crostini (chorizo, apricot butter, and goat cheese; peanut butter, parmesan, and chili oil) and wine; it's "fairly basic" inside, but the spacious garden out back is "nice" in the warmer months.

Il Brigante   Italian   22 | 16 | 18 | $$

South Street Seaport | 214 Front St.
(bet. Beekman St. & Peck Slip)
212-285-0222 | ilbrigantenyc.com

Calabrian specialties are offered from this somewhat "cramped" spot with an unbeatable waterside location at South Street Seaport; on the menu are wood-fired pizza, seafood pasta, and antipasti centered around spicy salami; the service and exposed-brick interior aren't big draws, but "fair prices" and a kid-friendly environment make it a "sleeper" in the neighborhood; the bar is "wine and beer only."

il Buco   Italian   27 | 24 | 24 | $$$

NoHo | 47 Bond St. (bet. Bowery & Lafayette St.)
212-533-1932 | ilbuco.com

"Close your eyes, and you're back in Florence" by way of this "romantic" NoHo Italian, which augments its "Tuscany-on-the-Bowery" feel with "outstanding," "delicately balanced" fare (including Spanish influences and "perfectly al dente" pastas), plus a "lovely," "earthy" space resembling a "wood"-decorated "inn"; this "feast for the eyes" brings with it a "scene," and the resulting "noise" can be distracting, but the "kind" staff and "cool" wine cellar help shore things up.

il Buco Alimentari & Vineria Italian 25 | 22 | 22 | $$$

NoHo | 53 Great Jones St. (bet. Bowery & Lafayette St.)
212-837-2622 | ilbuco.com

"Country"-style Italian food with a "modern" twist helps energize this "engaging" NoHo spinoff, which offers those "terrific" il Buco touches (including "OMG"-eliciting short ribs), plus a "robust wine list," in quasi-"rustic" surroundings made "boisterous" and "electric" by the "communal tables" and an "attractive crowd"; it works for "date nights" and before or after visits to the nearby Public Theater; there's also a market area/coffee bar in the front.

Il Cantinori Italian 25 | 24 | 25 | $$$$

Greenwich Village | 32 E 10th St. (bet. B'way & University Pl.)
212-673-6044 | ilcantinori.com

It "feels like you've been transported to Rome" at this "gem" in the Village that "has stood the test of time"; an "elegant" brownstone is the setting for "delicious" Italian cuisine with "perfectly cooked" pastas, fresh seasonal specials, and classic Tuscan dishes; "friendly" and "attentive" service is part of its charm; "impressive flower arrangements" add to the "romantic" feel, and if you have room left, the "desserts are worth the calories."

Il Cortile Italian 24 | 23 | 24 | $$

Little Italy | 125 Mulberry St. (bet. Canal & Hester Sts.)
212-226-6060 | ilcortile.com

The "aroma of garlic" wafts into the courtyard, drawing crowds to this "transporting," "relaxing" Italian "icon" that continues to "sustain its high level" and go "well north of red-sauce" mediocrity; "accommodating," "entertaining" servers and "live music" make it work for "business," "romance" or "out-of-town friends"; fans say it's "not like the cliché tourist traps" found elsewhere in Little Italy.

Il Falco Restaurant 🖪 Italian 25 | 19 | 22 | $$$

Long Island City | 21-50 44th Dr. (23rd St.) | Queens
718-707-0009 | ilfalcolic.com

A sort of unofficial "offshoot of Il Mulino" (where the chefs earned their chops), this "intimate, quaint" eatery near Court Square offers "old-school" "pastas made tableside" and other "excellent" Italian dishes served by staffers who "know what they're doing"; it may be "pricey for Long Island City," but it's one of "the best" choices of its kind there too; P.S. in summer, check out the "lovely garden in back."

Il Gattopardo Italian 25 | 23 | 24 | $$$$

West 50s | 13-15 W 54th St. (bet. 5th & 6th Aves.)
212-246-0412 | ilgattopardonyc.com

"If I were to be executed tomorrow, I'd want their pasta as my last meal," say fans of the classic Southern Italian dishes that "won't let you down," but another big draw of this "romantic boîte" in a Beaux Arts townhouse is its location behind MoMA; you can unwind in a minimalist, low-ceilinged white-cube space after an afternoon on your feet; the prices do "hit your wallet," but waiters are pleasant, and the wine list is long.

Il Mulino New York Italian · 26 | 21 | 24 | $$$

East 60s | 37 E 60th St. (bet. Madison & Park Aves.)
212-750-3270 | ilmulino.com
Greenwich Village | 86 W 3rd St.
(bet. Sullivan & Thompson Sts.) | 212-673-3783
TriBeCa | 361 Greenwich St.
(bet. Franklin & Harrison Sts.) | 646-649-5164

"You feel as if you traveled back to a kinder, gentler time" when the "complimentary appetizers," "served as soon as you sit," start hitting the table at this "retro" source for red sauce; "over-the-top service" of "family-style" portions laced with "lots of garlic" is a "gluttonous experience," and despite the "chain restaurant" feel and "long wait even with a reservation," the food remains "old-school Italian at its best."

Il Riccio Italian · 20 | 16 | 21 | $$

East 70s | 152 E 79th St. #5 (Lexington Ave.)
212-639-9111 | ilriccionyc.info

A "longtime neighborhood favorite" on the UES, this "solid" "reliable" serves "superior seafood" and other "simple and good" dishes inspired by the Amalfi Coast, along with a "reasonably priced" wine list; expect decent service from a staff overseen by an owner who cares about customers; the long, narrow space is "tight," so those in the know opt for a seat on the "pleasant" enclosed terrace.

Ilili Mediterranean · 25 | 23 | 21 | $$$

NoMad | 236 5th Ave. (bet. 27th & 28th Sts.)
212-683-2929 | ililinyc.com

Some of the most "addictive" Lebanese bites "this side of Beirut" bring diners to this "grown-up" NoMad spot – a "see-and-be-seen scene" furnishing "high-end" Mediterranean available via "easy-to-share plates" in an "upscale, modern" space with wood accents; "hit-or-miss service," "pricey" tabs, and "deafening" noise levels are drawbacks, but the "boisterous," "well-heeled" crowd isn't deterred, and you can always head upstairs, where it's "quieter."

Inakaya NY Japanese · 20 | 19 | 20 | $$$

West 40s | 231 W 40th St. (bet. 7th & 8th Aves.)
212-354-2195 | inakayany.com

"When you can't go to Japan," try this New York outpost of the popular Tokyo restaurant group, which serves robata-style charcoal grilled meat, seafood, and vegetables as well as some standout sushi; the "theatrical atmosphere" of chefs "calling out loudly in unison," waiters banging on drums, food served on long-handled paddles, and sake served out of a large barrel make it feel like you're getting "dinner and a show."

⊇ Indian Accent   Indian   27 | 25 | 25 | $$$$

West 50s | Parker New York, 123 W 56th St. (6th Ave.)
212-842-8070 | indianaccent.com

Many dishes reach "stratospheric" levels at this "high-end"
Midtown Delhi import for "inspired" fusion fare that "explores
the edges of a great cuisine but still remains Indian at heart";
these "addictive flavors" come via prix fixe and tasting menus
(à la carte options at lunch, or in the bar or patio areas) in a
"lovely, serene setting" with modern touches; it all adds up to "a
splurge," though the "courteous" staff help justify it.

Indochine   French/Vietnamese   23 | 23 | 20 | $$$$

NoHo | 430 Lafayette St.
(bet. Astor Pl. & 4th St.)
212-505-5111 | indochinenyc.com

Fans of this "NYC institution" propose that it's "still as hot as
ever" and "never lets you down, even after 35 years"; the "wonderful flavors" of Vietnam "blended with French influences"
are "consistently good" even if some feel the "menu needs
updating"; "celebrity spotting" is common among the "iconic"
"demilune banquettes and palm leaf wallpaper," and as you'd
hope for a place "situated across the street from the Public
Theater," there's a well-regarded pre-theater menu; stop by
after the show for the "sceney" "nighttime atmosphere."

Industry Kitchen   American/Pizza   16 | 20 | 18 | $$

South Street Seaport | 70 South St. (Maiden Ln.)
212-487-9600 | industry-kitchen.com

"It's the location and view that make this place worthwhile,"
since this South Street Seaport restaurant is "right on the water," making it an impressive "place to take visitors" or cowork-
ers for "after-work" drinks, especially in summer; centering on
wood-fired pizza, the menu is "basic" and just "OK," and the
"friendly" service "can be slow," so don't come if you don't want
to go with the flow.

Insa   Korean   24 | 21 | 23 | $$

Gowanus | 328 Douglass St. (4th Ave.) | Brooklyn
718-855-2620 | insabrooklyn.com

"Great for groups," this Gowanus venue with a "super-cool vibe"
offers "another good variation on Korean BBQ," grilled at communal tables within an "open, modern dining area"; however,
some say "it's just as fun to sit in a plush booth at in the loungey
bar and order soju and dishes to share"; either way, the servers
make you feel "most important" – and, to round out the evening,
"they have private karaoke rooms in back."

Ippudo   Japanese/Ramen   25 | 19 | 21 | $$

Greenwich Village | 65 4th Ave.
(bet. 9th & 10th Sts.)
212-388-0088 | ippudony.com
West 40s | 24 W 46th St. (bet. 5th & 6th Aves.)
212-354-1111
West 50s | 321 W 51st St. (bet. 8th & 9th Aves.)
212-974-2500

The "bustling" New York branches of this Japanese chain "live
up to the hype" for an "upscale" "traditional ramen experience,"

featuring a signature "smooth tonkotsu broth" that will have you "slurping" "excellent" noodles alongside "pork buns straight from heaven"; while there are "no reservations" and it "fills up fast," the "fast, attentive service" and authentically boisterous greetings from the staff make it "worth the wait."

Ivan Ramen Japanese/Ramen

23 | 17 | 20 | $$

Lower East Side | 25 Clinton St.
(bet. Houston & Stanton Sts.)
646-678-3859 | ivanramen.com
West 40s | 600 11th Ave. (bet. 44th & 45th Sts.)
212-582-7942

You'll quickly understand why "Ivan became a celebrated chef in Japan" when you taste the "umami-rich" "fusion" ramen that respects "tradition" yet still finds room for "innovation" (like using rye flour in the noodles for a "pleasant chew"); whether in the food court of Gotham West Market or the "madhouse" "nightlife scene" of the LES shop, food outshines atmosphere, service is "friendly" but hurried, and "craft beers" offer a break from "slurping down the broth."

Jack the Horse Tavern American

23 | 19 | 21 | $$

Brooklyn Heights | 66 Hicks St.
(Cranberry St.) | Brooklyn
718-852-5084 | jackthehorse.com

Known for "reliable" American dishes, this Brooklyn Heights standby "keeps it fairly simple and does it well" with a menu of salads – the smoked trout is "always wonderful" – and grilled meats and seafood, plus "wonderful" options for the "homey" brunch on Sunday; inside there's "lots of wood" to create that "low-key," "cozy" "old-fashioned pub look."

Jack's Wife Freda Mediterranean

21 | 19 | 20 | $$

SoHo | 224 Lafayette St. (Spring St.) | 212-510-8550
Chelsea | 116 8th Ave. (bet. 15th & 16th Sts.)
646-454-9045 | jackswifefreda.com
West Village | 50 Carmine St. (Bedford St.)
646-669-9888

"A haven for millennials seeking Mediterranean cuisine at moderate prices," this "quirky little" café trio "brings in crowds at all times" with its "variety of healthy and not-so-healthy options"; still, skeptics are "not sure why it has the buzz it does," claiming it "doesn't deliver on ambiance or service with the throngs" – could be the price of becoming "too popular."

Jacob's Pickles ℂ Southern

23 | 18 | 19 | $$

West 80s | 509 Amsterdam Ave. (85th St.)
212-470-5566 | jacobs.picklehospitality.com

At this elevated Southern on the UWS, everything's amped up, and its "twangish" grits and fried green tomatoes, "tough-to-beat" fried chicken, and "beyond delicious" biscuit sandwiches will feed you for "two days straight" – don't make ambitious plans for after, since you'll definitely be going "to sleep" post-brunch; inside the rustic room, quiet chats are "impossible" and it's "always crowded" – regulars keep finding themselves back for the comfort food "again and again."

James American   23 | 21 | 21 | $$

Prospect Heights | 605 Carlton Ave.
(St. Marks Ave.) | Brooklyn
718-942-4255 | jamesrestaurantny.com
"Can't-miss" burgers and an "excellent brunch" has made this
"all-American" Prospect Heights bistro a reliable local haunt
for those who appreciate an easy and "unpretentious" but
"creative" market-driven meal (and Monday's "burger night is
a steal"); the mellow space feels larger thanks to the picture
windows in front, high, pressed-tin white ceilings, and welcoming long bar across from soft leather banquettes.

Jams American   19 | 20 | 19 | $$

West 50s | 1414 6th Ave. (58th St.)
212-703-2007 | jamsrestaurant.nyc
Inside the 1 Hotel Central Park, this modern rustic all-day café
with an emphasis on "farm-fresh" ingredients – Jonathan Waxman's revival of his 1980s haunt – is marred by some "mediocre" dishes, although Waxman's famed chicken with salsa verde
(the only spot to get it now that Barbuto is closed) remains
"legendary"; although it's mostly "filled" with tourists, it's "lively"
but always "pleasant."

Jane American   19 | 16 | 19 | $$

Greenwich Village | 100 W Houston St.
(bet. LaGuardia Pl. & Thompson St.)
212-254-7000 | janerestaurant.com
This "dependable" Greenwich Village "staple" with a "re-
strained," wood-filled interior is "particularly good for brunch";
its "homey, comforting" food" is "reasonably priced," and the
"friendly service" and "retro bar" also help make it a decent
option "if you're in the neighborhood," especially if you seek
somewhere that's "not as noisy as typical NY spots."

Japonica Japanese/Sushi   24 | 16 | 22 | $$

Greenwich Village | 90 University Pl. (12th St.)
212-243-7752 | japonicanyc.com
There's "always fresh fish for the palate and beautiful flower
arrangements for the eye" at this Japanese " standby," "as
close to a serene dining experience as New York offers"; open
since 1978, it's "cherished" by Village residents; the dishes are
"consistently delicious," but check out the daily specials for the
"freshest and most interesting" options; the "space is small"
and "there are no reservations," so arrive early or expect a wait.

Ⓩ Jean-Georges French   28 | 27 | 28 | $$$$

West 60s | 1 Central Park West (61st St.)
212-299-3900 | jean-georgesrestaurant.com
Delivering a "world-class experience" since 1997, celebrity chef
Jean-Georges Vongerichten "pulls out all the stops" at his flagship across from Central Park, with an "elegant" dining room
that some call "the most beautiful in the city"; the "inventive"
French fare, from the "amazing appetizers" to the "tantalizing" desserts, is "served with flair but without attitude" by an
"incomparable" staff who "always leave you in awe – and so do
the prices."

Jeepney Filipino 20 | 15 | 16 | $$

East Village | 201 1st Ave. (bet. 12th & 13th Sts.)
212-533-4121 | jeepneynyc.com
"Enjoy various native Filipino dishes," some traditional, some "innovative," at this East Village joint with a "friendly" vibe and a plant-festooned interior; the "solid spot's" Kamayan feast – "a huge pile of food you eat with your hands" and share with the rest of your table, is perfect for festive parties, and the drinks "are a blast to share," too.

The Jeffrey Craft 23 | 21 | 23 | $$
Beer & Bites Gastropub

East 60s | 311 E 60th St. (bet. 1st & 2nd Aves.)
212-355-2337 | thejeffreynyc.com
Emitting "downtown vibes" from a Midtown East location under the Queensboro, this "perfect neighborhood joint" has a "knowledgeable staff" to help decipher an ever-"rotating beer list" while also serving enjoyable "small bites" on a comfortable back patio with prime outdoor seating; although it does everything from serving craft "coffee by day," to becoming a "cocktail lab" at night, to serving "lazy weekend" brunches, there's no question that "outstanding" selection of brews remains the big draw.

Jeffrey's Grocery American 22 | 21 | 22 | $$$

West Village | 172 Waverly Pl. (Christopher St.)
646-398-7630 | jeffreysgrocery.com
"Bustling with a young, hip crowd"; this "quaint neighborhood corner" destination pretty much "epitomizes the charm of the West Village"; with its "personable" servers, "consistently inventive cocktails," and menu that "changes often enough that it doesn't get tired," it's "always busy," and "there's not a lot of seating," but the place still manages a "low-key" feel – it makes you "want to brunch every weekend."

Jeju Noodle Bar Korean/Ramen ▼ 27 | 22 | 21 | $$

West Village | 679 Greenwich St. (Christopher St.)
646-666-0947 | jejunoodlebar.com
This "trendy" West Village Korean spot puts a contemporary "spin" on ramyun/ramen, plus other dishes featuring "unique, tantalizing flavor and texture combinations"; the "unassuming" space can be "hard to get into," but if you do manage to nab seats at the counter, you can "watch the preparation of the food" – the chef and staff are "meticulous" in their efforts, and the dishes on the "limited" menu are a good "value."

Jewel Bako 🅢 Japanese/Sushi 25 | 21 | 24 | $$$

East Village | 239 E 5th St. (bet. 2nd & 3rd Aves.)
212-979-1012 | jewelbakosushi.com
From the easy-to-miss entrance to the "elegant and refined" "minimalist" interior, this "intimate" East Village sushi bar operates with style and simplicity; even with a "professional" service staff explaining the "top-quality" selection of fish and thoughtful wine and sake pairings, it's still best to sit at the "chef's counter" for the "high-end omakase"; in spite of its accolades, it's also surprisingly good for the everyday sushi dinner sets, which are a "deal."

Z JG Melon ◖ Burger Joint   23 | 17 | 19 | $$

East 70s | 1291 3rd Ave. (74th St.)
212-744-0585 | jgmelon-nyc.com
Greenwich Village | 89 MacDougal St. (Bleecker St.)
212-460-0900
West 80s | 480 Amsterdam Ave. (83rd St.)
646-895-9388 | jgmelonnyc.com
A "preppy classic" since 1972, this old "reliable" "satisfies any
burger craving" with "juicy" patties and "terrific" cottage fries,
plus booze, dispensed to both "locals and tourists" (along with
that "frat-house" crowd); "cheesy melon"-themed decor, often
"curt" servers, and an "annoying cash-only policy" at the UES
original aren't pluses, but the separately owned UWS and Village locations take plastic, and "you can easily go at an off time
and walk right in" to avoid the lines.

NEW Jiang Diner Chinese   – | – | – | $$

East Village | 309 E 5th St.
(bet. 1st & 2nd Aves.)
646-484-5999 | jiangdiner.com
This East Village arrival celebrates the vast northwestern
Chinese province of Xinjiang with the traditional flavors of lamb
and cumin and weighty banquet dishes like a noodle-lined and
potato-studded big plate chicken; it's popular for takeout, but
the enormous entrees may be best enjoyed fresh in the dining
room, with enough friends to conquer the portions.

Jin Ramen Japanese/Ramen   24 | 16 | 19 | $$

West 80s | 462 Amsterdam Ave. (82nd St.)
646-657-0755 | jinramen.com
Morningside Heights | 3183 Broadway
(bet. 125th St. & Tiemann Pl.) | 646-559-2862
"You can't help" but "slurp away" when it comes to these
"seductive" noodles, and the pork buns are so "little, but oh
my!"; these two "heaven-sent" ramen nooks on the UWS and
Morningside Heights treat their "addictive" offerings like "an art
form"; the "small and cramped" spaces means your ears will be
filled with uptowners and Columbia students enjoying their own
dishes, but consider the "hectic" atmosphere part of the whole
experience.

Jing Fong Chinese   21 | 14 | 15 | $$

Chinatown | 20 Elizabeth St.
(bet. Bayard & Canal Sts.)
212-964-5256 | jingfongny.com
West 70s | 380 Amsterdam Ave. (78th St.)
646-678-5511
Come prepared for the "high energy" at these Cantonese
spots offering "consistently tasty" Hong Kong–style dim sum
with "lots" of variety and "speedy" service; the "huge" "red
and gold all over" Chinatown original with "classic" roving carts
is a "zoo on weekends" but "worth" the wait, while the "more
modern" UWS "mini-version" lacks carts and weekday lunch
service.

Joe & Pat's Pizza   26 | 16 | 22 | $$

Castleton Corners | 1758 Victory Blvd.
(bet. Manor Rd. & Winthrop Pl.) | Staten Island
718-981-0887
East Village | 168 1st Ave. (bet. 10th & 11th Sts.)
212-677-4992 | joeandpatsnyc.com

This pair of "neighborhood staples" is a "pioneer" in "cracker-crust" pizza, and although the rest of the dishes on the menu are "tasty," locals find themselves going "back to the pies time and again"; be warned: the Staten Island original is "worth the ferry ride" but the deecor is "nothing special," the seating is "not comfortable," and "parking a serious problem" – "thank God there's a Manhattan outpost!"

Joe Allen ☾ American   20 | 20 | 22 | $$$

West 40s | 326 W 46th St. (bet. 8th & 9th Aves.)
212-581-6464 | joeallenrestaurant.com

This "pre- or post-theater hangout" attracts a crowd happy for "no-nonsense service" that gets you out in time for curtain; people come for "star sightings" and a "bustling Broadway atmosphere," down to the posters of famous flops that paper the walls; the American menu is "elevated diner fare" ("love the meatloaf and martinis"), with the burger and banana cream pie both stars.

Joe Junior Diner   18 | 12 | 17 | $

Gramercy | 167 3rd Ave. (16th St.)
212-473-5150

"No surprises, but lots of nostalgia" is in store at this Gramercy Park "greasy spoon like in the olden days," down to the "counter-seating with swivel stools" and wood- and mirror-paneled walls; they're "well-known for their burgers," all-day breakfasts, and other diner delights, offered at "unbelievable prices" – all in all, it's "terrific" to find such a place for "real food."

Joe's Ginger ⊄ Chinese   20 | 10 | 16 | $

Chinatown | 25 Pell St. (Mott St.)
212-285-0333 | joeginger.com

"Not as crowded" as its sister joint, Joe's Shanghai, this Chinatown spot is also known for its "signature" xiao long bao (soup dumplings) that "are little bundles of goodness," as well as other "better-than-average" dishes served in "large portions"; "you don't go for the decor" and it's cash-only, but "good prices" keep that from being much of an issue.

Z Joe's Pizza ☾ Pizza   25 | 11 | 17 | $

Greenwich Village | 7 Carmine St.
(bet. Bleecker St. & 6th Ave.)
212-366-1182 | joespizzanyc.com
West 40s | 1435 Broadway (bet. 40th & 41st Sts.)
646-559-4878
Union Square | 150 E 14th St. (bet. Irving Pl. & 3rd Ave.)
212-388-9474
Williamsburg | 216 Bedford Ave. (5th St.) | Brooklyn
718-388-2216

"Pizza pros" have considered this "New York institution's" "straightforward" slices and pies "heaven on a paper plate" since 1975, with "perfect crackable crusts" and "fresh ingredients done right"; securing a stool here "provides entertaining people-watching," and while the lines are long, they "move quickly" regardless of whether you're craving some "2 PM or 2 AM slices."

Joe's Shanghai Chinese

| 23 | 10 | 16 | $$ |

Chinatown | 9 Pell St. (bet. Bowery & Doyers St.)
212-233-8888 | joeshanghairestaurants.com
Flushing | 136-21 37th Ave. (bet. Main & Union Sts.) | Queens
718-539-3838

The "outrageous" Shanghai soup dumplings are "always the star of the meal" at these "simple, unpretentious" Chinese spots; large communal tables make it the "perfect place for group dinners and family-style meals" or to start a conversation with strangers; it's "not a place to linger," but "portions are generous and prices are modest."

John Brown Smokehouse Barbecue

| 23 | 14 | 20 | $$ |

Long Island City | 10-43 44th Dr.
(bet. 10th & 11th Sts.) | Queens
"347-617-1120 | johnbrownseriousbbq.com

This LIC BBQ baron dishes up "awesome" smoked meats – "the delicious smell will hit you as you approach the building"; "a craft beer bar," "nice backyard area," and "funky, friendly atmosphere" all make "the whole thing go down easy," and don't miss the "burnt ends that are like candy."

John's of Bleecker St. Pizza

| 24 | 16 | 18 | $ |

West Village | 278 Bleecker St. (bet. 6th & 7th Aves.)
212-243-1680 | johnsbrickovenpizza.com
John's of Times Square
West 40s | 260 W 44th St. (bet. 7th & 8th Aves.)
212-391-7560 | johnspizzerianyc.com

"The hype is real" for the coal-oven thin-crust pizzas "charred to perfection," and the "no-slices" policy may tempt you to eat "the whole succulent pie"; expect "lines out the door" at both the original "old-school" West Village "institution" ("do not come here if you want to linger") and the multilevel Theater District location, a repurposed church perfect for "heavenly" 'za.

John's of 12th Street Italian

| 22 | 17 | 20 | $$ |

East Village | 302 E 12th St. (2nd Ave.)
212-475-9531 | johnsof12thstreet.com

Serving "archetypal" Italian-American fare in the East Village, this is a "neighborhood institution"; the "jovial" "old-world" atmosphere, "large" portions, and "accommodating," if "slow," service may remind you of "Brooklyn in the '50s," but the "vegan menu" will bring you back to the present; sure, the decor is "dated," (the centerpiece candles have been burning for decades) but "it's all about tasting that tomato sauce."

Johnny's Reef 🖘 Seafood

| 18 | 10 | 13 | $$ |

City Island | 2 City Island Ave. (Belden Pt.) | Bronx
718-885-2086 | johnnysreefrestaurant.com

Be "the envy of the gulls" "swooping overhead" at this "right-on-the-water" City Island stalwart, a cash-only, "cafeteria-style" "shack" dispensing "piles of fried and steamed seafood" that you bring to the picnic tables outside; no need to reflect on "the complete lack of ambiance" indoors or the "chaotic" setting and near-nonexistent service: when you're "enjoying the view of sailboats" on the Sound while nursing a "cold beer" on a "hot summer day," it's a genuine "value."

JoJo French — 25 | 23 | 23 | $$$

East 60s | 160 E 64th St. (bet. Lexington & 3rd Aves.)
212-223-5656 | jojorestaurantnyc.com

"Excellent" French plates "presented with care" remain the forte of Jean-Georges Vongerichten's longtime but recently renovated UES "standard," notable for its "creative" locavore menu and the "intimate" townhouse it's in; the "minimalist," "casually elegant" and brightly crisp interior can feel "cramped" and "crowded" at times, and while it's "expensive," it continues to be "a winning date destination," as well as suitable for a lunch with friends; P.S. the "upstairs seating is quieter."

Jones Wood Foundry British/Gastropub — 18 | 21 | 20 | $$

East 70s | 401 E 76th St. (bet. 1st & York Aves.)
212-249-2700 | joneswoodfoundry.com

You might expect the bangers and mash and other standards on the menu at this London-style "clubby-pubby" place on the UES, but there's also a more surprising "contemporary" seasonal menu that gets mixed reviews; the "friendly neighborhood bar" in the front is filled with "football watchers grabbing a pint" from the "solid" beer list, but past them is a "spacious" wood-paneled dining room and "amazing" garden in back.

Jongro BBQ ℂ Korean — 22 | 18 | 17 | $$

West 30s | 22 W 32nd St. (bet. B'way & 5th Ave.)
212-473-2233 | jongrobbqny.com

This "popular" Korean BBQ den in the West 30s serves "melt-in-your-mouth" meats charred on tabletop grills by servers who "do a great job cooking" before your eyes; the "spacious" multilevel layout allows for "more breathing room" and less smoke inhalation than other options, making it "good for beginners" who still want a true experience; it's "crowded," but you can avoid waits by going at lunch.

Joseph Leonard ℂ American — 23 | 23 | 22 | $$

West Village | 170 Waverly Pl. (Grove St.)
646-429-8383 | josephleonard.com

Regulars extol the virtues of this "cute and cozy place in the West Village," a "great neighborhood spot" where the atmosphere is "energetic without being overwhelming"; the dining room is a "tight squeeze" and the wait "can be long," "but luckily there are plenty of places nearby for a cocktail while you wait"; the chef is "always adding something special" to the "American with a twist" dishes.

Joya Thai — 23 | 19 | 20 | $

Cobble Hill | 215 Court St.
(bet. Warren & Wyckoff Sts.) | Brooklyn
718-222-3484 | joyabrooklyn.com

What keeps Cobble Hill regulars coming back to this "no-brainer go-to" is the "fresh and delicious" "everyday Thai" food;

in the "pleasant" contemporary interior there's a "cool vibe," but the backyard offers refuge from the "earsplitting din"; portions are large and a good value, an invitation for crowds eager for an "affordable date night or a great group outing."

Jue Lan Club Chinese
18 | 19 | 16 | $$$

Flatiron | 49 W 20th St. (6th Ave.)
646-524-7409 | juelanclub.com
Locals remember when this former church housed one of the city's hottest nightclubs, and say the "hip" space is still "always crowded," serving "exceptional" cocktails and blasting "fun but too loud" music – for something quieter, the umbrella-shaded patio is lovely in warm weather; the menu of dim sum and other Chinese classics gets mixed reviews, with some impressed but many arguing it's "overpriced and mediocre"; the less said about the often "unwelcoming" service, the better.

Juliana's Pizza
27 | 17 | 21 | $$

Dumbo | 19 Old Fulton St.
(bet. Front & Water Sts.) | Brooklyn
718-596-6700 | julianaspizza.com
Tucked under the Brooklyn Bridge is this "bucket-list" Dumbo pizzeria from pie maestro Patsy Grimaldi, whose "spectacular" coal-fired-oven version elicits praise for its "char," "crisp crust," and "simple toppings of excellent quality"; just "bring War and Peace to read during the waits" (there are no reservations), and remember: "you're not going for the ambiance."

Jungsik Korean
29 | 28 | 28 | $$$$

TriBeCa | 2 Harrison St. (Hudson St.)
212-219-0900 | jungsik.com
Tucked away on a quaint TriBeCa street, this hushed Korean spot is a way to get "Seoul in Manhattan," with "revolutionary" modern served via a "mind-blowing" tasting menu that balances "nuance" and "art" while "never losing sight of its origins"; enhancing the transcendental dining experience is "subtle, elegant" service with "sleek," "unobtrusive" servers who flow by "without missing a beat."

Junoon Indian
25 | 25 | 24 | $$$$

Flatiron | 27 W 24th St. (bet. 5th & 6th Aves.)
212-490-2100 | junoonnyc.com
The "inventive" Indian food is "elevated but true to its roots" at this "elegant" Flatiron standout, a "cavernous space" with "oversized fixtures" where the service is obliging and the atmosphere is described as "soothing" and "serene"; at dinner, a "high-quality tasting menu" plus two- or three-course set options are served in the main dining room, while the front room is à la carte; there's also a prix fixe lunch that's a "very good deal."

Kajitsu Ⓜ Japanese
27 | 22 | 24 | $$$$

Murray Hill | 125 E 39th St.
(bet. Lexington & Park Aves.)
212-228-4873 | kajitsunyc.com
"Hidden in a small building on a quiet East Side street," this "tranquil" eatery serves a vegetarian menu, based on Japanese temple cuisine, that "changes according to the seasons," with

"each dish carefully crafted" "to let the ingredients shine"; all this artistry comes at a price, but it does make for a "special treat," with a "nice selection of sake and beer" and "seamless" service.

Kang Ho Dong Baekjeong ⦅ Korean   26 | 15 | 18 | $$$

East 30s | 1 E 32nd St. (5th Ave.)
212-966-9839 | baekjeongnyc.com

Those "craving galbi" and banchan (the small traditional sides), or after "well-marinated" meats with "strong flavors," bring their friends to this stateside branch of the Korean barbecue chain; when stacked up against the dozens of K-town joints nearby, many say it's "hands-down" the best in town – so what if it gets "noisy and hectic" at times?

Kanoyama Japanese/Sushi   24 | 14 | 17 | $$

East Village | 175 2nd Ave. (bet. 11th & 12th Sts.)
212-777-5266 | kanoyama.com

The secret's out, so reservations are tough for this once "underrated" chef-driven Japanese East Village destination, where the draw is high-quality sushi "at an affordable price"; the "cramped" interior and "sometimes slow" service aren't noticeable if you sit at the bar for the "intimate omakase" with "unusual offerings," as well as fresh oysters on ice.

Kappo Masa ⑤ Japanese/Sushi   29 | 26 | 27 | $$$$

East 70s | 976 Madison Ave. (76th St.)
212-906-7141 | kappomasanyc.com

Born from a decades-long friendship between chef Masayoshi Takayama and art dealer Larry Gagosian, this "stylized Japanese eatery" in the basement below the Gagosian's Madison Avenue gallery is "sublime"; everything on the "innovative menu" is "artfully presented," and the "elegant" minimalist dining room is softened with "stunning floral displays"; in keeping with the quality and its creators, the prices are predictably "astronomical," but this is definitely a place for "special-occasion sushi."

Kashkaval Garden ⦅ Mediterranean   22 | 15 | 19 | $$

West 50s | 852 9th Ave. (bet. 55th & 56th Sts.)
212-245-1758 | kashkavalgarden.com

This "dimly" candlelit Hell's Kitchen nook is a standby for sharing Eastern Mediterranean mezes and skewers "with a date"; although it's "small" and "cramped," and the service isn't always quite as "warm" as the signature fondue here, there's a tiny "garden in back" that makes it a "well-priced" retreat for a glass of wine, and a thrill for any eaters yet to taste the Balkan cheese this place is named for.

ⓏKatz's Delicatessen ⦅ Deli   26 | 13 | 15 | $$

Lower East Side | 205 E Houston St. (Ludlow St.)
212-254-2246 | katzsdelicatessen.com

So "the echoey room hasn't changed in a bazillion years" and the staff get "grumpy" it's the heaping portions of corned beef and pastrami" that make this "landmark" LES deli, an "only-in-New-York experience" that "serves as much nostalgia as food"; "go during off hours" "to avoid the crush of tourists," "go for table service" "if you don't want to wait on line," but you "must go here at least once in your lifetime."

NEW **Kāwi** Korean — | — | — | $$$

West 30s | 20 Hudson Yards
(10th Ave. & 33rd St.)
646-517-2699 | kawi.momofuku.com

David Chang's Momofuku empire stakes its claim in Hudson Yards with this modern Korean kitchen, serving creative takes on homestyle dishes gilded with luxurious enrichments like truffle and foie gras; the windowless environment is dark, but the slick presentations ensure the dining room lights up with mobile phone flashes; expect a trendy atmosphere and beverage program, and prices that cash in on the magnetic setting, well suited for a special group meal.

Z KazuNori: The Original 28 | 23 | 26 | $$
Hand Roll Bar Japanese/Sushi

NoMad | 15 W 28th St. (bet. 5th Ave. & B'way)
212-594-5940 | handrollbar.com

"Hand-roll heaven" comes to earth at this "quality" NoMad Japanese from LA's Sugarfish team, an "efficient" business model in which customers "wait in line for seats" at the "small" sushi bar, then check off menu items that include the "exceptional" nori rolls of "extremely fresh fish," "warm" rice, and condiments, all delivered "quickly"; no reservations and no tipping, and it's pretty "affordable" – it "won't be a long meal, but it will be memorable."

Z Keens Steakhouse Steakhouse 27 | 25 | 25 | $$$

West 30s | 72 W 36th St. (bet. 5th & 6th Aves.)
212-947-3636 | keens.com

Take "a step back into the 1880s" at this "true New York steakhouse" in Midtown, where "succulent steak" and an "enormous mutton chop" are as "rich" as the history; beneath "thousands of clay pipes hanging from the ceiling," "welcoming staff" serve the cuts sliced and dripping "with buttery juices," alongside "phenomenal apps and sides" and a superb "selection of single malts"; it's a "go-to pre-Garden spot," a meal, and "tourist attraction" all in one.

Kefi Greek 21 | 17 | 19 | $$$

West 70s | 222 W 79th St.
(bet. Amsterdam Ave. & B'way)
212-873-0200 | michaelpsilakis.com

A flood and a subsequent move had many worrying about this restaurant for "traditional" and "hearty Greek," but with a menu doubling as a "meat-lover's delight," seafood prepared "just as one requests," and vegetables that aren't afterthoughts, it all still "satisfies fully"; the "tightly packed," "country-like" setting "looks like Greece" to many, and – judging by the "exhilarating" noise and upbeat aura – feels like it, as well.

Kellari Taverna Greek 23 | 21 | 22 | $$$

West 40s | 19 W 44th St. (bet. 5th & 6th Aves.)
212-221-0144 | kellariny.com

You'll feel like you're "eating in Greece" inside this "always reliable" tavern, where the fresh seafood is "prepared simply and presented at its peak"; "very personal service" and a "festive "atmosphere" make this establishment ideal for "Midtown workers and tourists" seeking pre-theater bites and post-work drinks; the "elegant, airy space" has "an intimate feel," but a lavish fish display is what really "transports you" to a seaside Mediterranean village.

Kesté Italian/Pizza 24 | 15 | 19 | $$

Financial District | 66 Gold St. (bet. Ann & Fulton Sts.)
212-693-9030 | kestepizzeria.com
West Village | 271 Bleecker St. (Morton St.)
212-243-1500

If you're craving "Napoli-style pizza" with "mouthwatering" toppings and "wonderful" crusts, then put your trust in these "pizza artists"; choose among dozens of "phenomenal" pies, or combine your favorite ingredients to make your own (sardines aren't available, although you might feel "packed in like one" in the "small and cramped" dining room with "unbearable" decibel levels); the prices are "incredibly affordable," and the gluten-free pizza might be "the best on the planet."

Khao Kang Ⓜ Thai ▼ 28 | 16 | 18 | $

Elmhurst | 76-20 Woodside Ave. (77th St.) | Queens
718-806-1807 | khaokangnyc.com

This "counter-service place" resembles the typical takeout joints of Bangkok and serves "some of the best Thai food in NYC"; you point to whatever looks good – the "affordable" dishes range from "mild to crazy hot," and the curries, stews, and other dishes all come with a heaping spoonful of jasmine rice – and then head to one of the simple wooden tables.

Khe-Yo Laotian 24 | 19 | 21 | $$$

TriBeCa | 157 Duane St. (bet. Hudson St. & W B'way)
212-587-1089 | kheyo.com

"Traditional Laotian sauces" that "make one's heart go bang-bang" elevate this "hip" spot in TriBeCa, where the "excellent," sometimes-"spicy" food (laab salads, satays, currys) pairs with cocktails in "casual," "cozy" surroundings; service may "lack the finer touches" expected of such an upscale place, and the tabs could use some cooling down, but most feel the "burn" is "completely worth it"; N.B. there's also a daytime café, Khe-Yosk, dispensing banh mi.

Ki Sushi Japanese/Sushi 26 | 19 | 23 | $$

Boerum Hill | 122 Smith St. (bet. Dean &
Pacific Sts.) | Brooklyn
718-935-0575 | kisushigroup.com
Park Slope | 282 Flatbush Ave. (Prospect Pl.) | Brooklyn
718-230-1381

"There's a reason there's always a crowd" at this slick neighborhood spot with locations in Brooklyn's Boerum Hill and Park Slope: it's the "consistently fresh," "better than average," "well-prepared sushi" served by a "welcoming" staff who can "accommodate young palates"; it "gets crowded," especially for weekday lunches and weekend dinners, but you can always sidle up to the sushi bar.

NEW **Kichin** ◖ Korean _–|_ _–|_ _–|_ $$|

Bushwick | 1264 Myrtle Ave. (Cedar St.) | Brooklyn
347-405-8948 | kichin.nyc

After a slew of popups and short-term locations, this Korean fried chicken specialist has found a home in Bushwick, with a multilevel space, promoting after-hours drinking and dancing with a house DJ; for those who don't bother with bird, the menu also includes other modern classics, such as kimchi fried rice, japchae, and other savory comforts that'll tempt you to order another round.

Z **Kiki's** ◖ Greek 25| 22| 19| $$|

Lower East Side | 130 Division St. (Orchard St.)
646-882-7052

This "cool" LES haunt "hits all the right notes for tastiness, value, and energy," producing Greek and Med classics that include "top-notch" seafood and "delicious" small plates to be paired with carafes of wine; sure, the waits are "long" and the space can get "jam-packed" (at times with a "faux-influencer crowd") but the atmosphere is "fun" and prices "don't break the bank."

King French/Italian 26| 24| 26| $$$|

Hudson Square | 18 King St. (6th Ave.)
917-825-1618 | kingrestaurant.nyc

You could eat at this "charming" Italian-inspired "neighborhood oasis" in Hudson Square "every day," since the "small," carefully "curated" menu "constantly changes," but is always "homey" and quick to jump on whatever's "fresh" and "seasonal"; considering that, and the "romantic," "attractive" surroundings, "savvy" staff and well-selected wine list, it's not surprising that so many call their visits here "memorable."

Kings County Imperial Chinese 25| 20| 20| $$|

Lower East Side | 168½ Delancey St. (Clinton St.)
212-475-0244 | kingscoimperial.com
Williamsburg | 20 Skillman Ave. (Meeker Ave.) | Brooklyn
718-610-2000

Fans of this "cool" Chinese eatery with branches in Williamsburg and the LES speak highly of the "hearty portions" of "incredible noodles" or "even better dumplings," served with a house-made soy sauce that's "good enough to drink on its own"; a few find it "overrated and overpriced," but most enjoy the "clever," "bold" dishes paired with "excellent cocktails" and an upbeat "atmosphere" enough to "bring friends."

Koi Japanese/Sushi 24| 23| 21| $$$|

West 40s | Bryant Park Hotel, 40 W 40th St.
(bet. 5th & 6th Aves.)
212-921-3330 | koirestaurant.com/new-york

Reeling in its share of the "pretty folk," this "hip restaurant serves much more than" "high-quality" sushi, with "upscale," "consistently good" Japanese fare" that "appeals to most everyone," although the "drinks may be more interesting" than the rolls; all in all, this favored place near Bryant Park is "good for business meals or meeting out-of-towners" as long as they don't mind the "ear-shattering" sound levels.

Kopitiam Malaysian

20 | 12 | 16 | $

Lower East Side | 151 E Broadway
(bet. Pike & Rutgers Sts.)
646-609-3785 | kopitiamnyc.com

Malaysian-dish mavens tout the "well-made street-food" specialties at this "unique" LES spot, which offers both "sweet
and savory options" (including "solid" breakfast choices, along
with coffees, teas, and house-made sambals) in a "small,"
"super-casual" space with counter service; it's "generally not
too crowded," despite the "handful of tables" available, and it's
"fast" and "cheap" enough "for a quick lunch with a friend or
small group."

NEW Krok Thai

– | – | – | $$$

Carroll Gardens | 117 Columbia St.
(Kane St.) | Brooklyn
718-858-8898 | k-r-o-k.com

Southeast Asian returns to the former Pok Pok space on the
Columbia Street Waterfront, but this time the food leans Isan,
the region in northeast Thailand, with several versions of papaya
salad and a menu of regional street specialties served alongside
craft beer and cocktails; the interior is basic, but there's an outdoor courtyard and the option for takeout or delivery.

Kubeh Middle Eastern

22 | 21 | 22 | $$

Greenwich Village | 464 6th Ave.
(bet. 11th & 12th Sts.)
646-448-6688 | eatkubeh.com

Serving "good and tasty Middle Eastern," dishes that are "closer
to home cooking," this Village storefront has a menu "built
around dumplings of various kinds" that are paired with broths;
the offerings may be "good enough for a special occasion, but
better for a low-key meal" in the "delightful" dining room, and
the prices are "reasonable"; the service is also "friendly," but
the "tin ceiling keeps the noise level high."

KumGangSan Korean

21 | 16 | 17 | $$

Flushing | 138-28 Northern Blvd.
(bet. Bowne & Union Sts.) | Queens
718-461-0909 | kumgangsanflushing.com

At this "solid" Korean BBQ haunt with tasty banchan as well
as sushi and noodle dishes, the grilling goes on "twenty-four
hours a day," and the lengthy list of lunch specials is a consider-
able draw, costing "a lot less than you would think"; although
"abrupt" waiters have a tendency to "rush" diners through
cooking their meats, they do attempt to "do their best" while
catering to the Flushing crowds.

Kung Fu Little Steamed Buns
Ramen Chinese/Ramen

22 | 8 | 14 | $

East 50s | 146 E 55th St. (bet. Lexington & 3rd Aves.)
212-804-8556 | kfdelicacy.com
West 30s | 610 8th Ave. (bet. 39th & 40th Sts.)
212-951-1934
West 40s | 811 8th Ave. (49th St.)
917-388-2555

Locals say this trio of noodle joints is their "secret spot for dining on a budget in Midtown"; although the space is "crowded"

and feels "utilitarian"; all is forgiven when it comes to the soup dumplings and the hand-pulled noodles that are (nearly) "as long as the Empire State Building is tall"; another plus: it's "open earlier and later than other places," making it good for a "quick and tasty pre-theater dinner."

The Kunjip ⊂ Korean   19│ 9│ 12│ $$│
West 30s | 32 W 32nd St. (5th Ave.)
212-564-8238 | thekunjipnyc.com
For a menu with a "wide range" of "hearty" Korean casseroles, "spicy" stews, and BBQ meats served alongside the standard array of banchan (side dishes) that "sufficiently satisfies" a multitude of cravings at "reasonable prices," try this West 30s spot; the "hit-or-miss" service and basic interior make this best for "quick," "affordable" meals before "MSG events," or as a 24-hour refuge on the weekends.

Kurumazushi ⑤ Japanese/Sushi   26│ 13│ 23│ $$$$│
East 40s | 7 E 47th St., 2nd Fl.
(bet. 5th & Madison Aves.)
212-317-2802 | kurumazushi.com
Climb the "rickety" steps to the second floor of a "nondescript" townhouse in Midtown East to enter a "comfortable" art-filled room for a "touch of high-end Tokyo," including some of "the best sushi in town" à la carte or via omakase and other set menus; true, it's expensive – you better be "able to afford Ginza prices" – but, "OMG" it's "well worth it."

Kyma Greek   25│ 24│ 24│ $$$$│
Flatiron | 15 W 18th St. (bet. 5th & 6th Aves.)
212-268-5555 | kymarestaurants.com
"Fabulous" "nouvelle" Greek food is what's on the menu at this "lively," "buzzy but not hectic" Flatiron location, a branch of the Long Island original; its "simple" preparations "let ingredients speak for themselves and shine," with "freshly prepared" fish flown in daily from the Mediterranean; the "light, bright, and airy" dining room attracts a "well-dressed crowd," who find its staff "gracious" and "attentive."

Kyo Ya Ⓜ Japanese   28│ 24│ 27│ $$$$│
East Village | 94 E 7th St. (1st Ave.)
212-982-4140 | kyoyany.com
You'll want to "eat more than you planned" so you can catch the "subtleties" lurking in "perfectly prepared" clay pot rice, miso-glazed proteins, and other Japanese delights that continue to "shine" in this basement restaurant; waiters leave you to "relax" in the "serene" surroundings, although eating at the counter will let you watch the chefs show off their "full set of skills."

L'Amico Italian   21│ 21│ 19│ $$$│
West 30s | 849 6th Ave. (bet. 29th & 30th Sts.)
212-201-4065 | lamico.nyc
A standout among the chain restaurants crowded around Madison Square Garden, this Italian eatery is a "breath of fresh air"; the atmosphere is upbeat and "hip" (or perhaps "crowded and noisy"), and the "delicious coal-oven pizzas" and other dishes

have a "modern and creative flair"; if you're there before a show you can take a break in the "lively bar" or cool your heels on the "awesome patio" before heading home at Penn Station.

2 L'Artusi Italian   28 | 25 | 26 | $$$

West Village | 228 W 10th St.
(bet. Bleecker & Hudson Sts.)
212-255-5757 | lartusi.com

"Get all the pastas," the "star of the show" at this West Village standout, where the "lovely" staff pair "consistently" "outstanding" Italian fare with an "extensive" wine list that offers "endless opportunity to explore"; the "sophisticated" bilevel space that's "great for dates" is "super busy all the time" and it's "tough to score a table," but "the counter seats overlooking the kitchen are the best seats in the house to watch the magic happen" and they are available for walk-ins.

L'Atelier de Joël Robuchon Ⓢ Ⓜ French   28 | 26 | 27 | $$$$

Chelsea | 85 10th Ave. (bet. 15th & 16th Sts.)
212-488-8885 | joelrobuchonusa.com

"Master" chef Joël Robuchon's "spirit and talent live on" at this small French chain's "superlative" Chelsea outpost, where "out-of-this-world" small plates (including tasting menus and vegetarian choices) dazzle diners in a "magnificent" red-hued space highlighted by counter seating that lets them watch the "innovation" happening in the kitchen; mix in the "extraordinary service," "sceney" vibe, and appropriately high cost, and you've got a place that "lives up to its name."

L'Express ◖ French   18 | 17 | 18 | $$

Gramercy | 249 Park Ave. S (20th St.)
212-254-5858 | lexpressnyc.com

Open around the clock and "what every neighborhood needs" but rarely has, this Gramercy Park brasserie is "great for late-night" cravings, including the "best steak frites you can find at 1 AM"; French classics like onion soup and croque madame are "not haute cuisine," but still "tasty," and the burgers and fries are popular for a reason; the noise level can be "overwhelming," so this is "not for conversation or a leisurely dinner."

L&B Spumoni Gardens Italian/Pizza   25 | 13 | 19 | $$

Gravesend | 2725 86th St. (bet. 10th & 11th Sts.)
718-449-1230 | spumonigardens.com

It's "worth the schlep" to this "institution" for a "true pizza pilgrimage," where the "out-of-this-world" square Sicilian pies are "huge" and the homemade spumoni is "delicious"; "friendly" staffers serve the crowded outdoor picnic-table seating area in the summer, while the "casual" interior – is it "Nonna's dining room"? – welcomes patrons year-round.

La Bonbonniere ⬚ Diner   19 | 12 | 19 | $

West Village | 28 8th Ave. (bet. 12th & Jane Sts.)
212-741-9266

The "neighborhood secret" is out: "there's nothing finer" than the "awesome hangover-curing" eggs and pancakes served at "non–West Village prices" inside this "old-timey" diner that "seems out of place in New York"; "you sure don't go here for the decor," and service is "nothing fluffy or high end," but patrons "thank god" that this "no frills" staple is still here and remains "packed" in a time when many "little places have disappeared."

🄰 La Contenta ⟨ Mexican   27 | 20 | 22 | $$

Lower East Side | 102 Norfolk St.
(bet. Delancey & Rivington Sts.)
212-432-4180 | lacontentanyc.com

Enthusiasts claim this LES "neighborhood" Mexican "has it all," including tacos, nachos, enchiladas, and other "crave-worthy" and traditional offerings, plus numerous drinks (including agave-enhanced cocktails and micheladas) – all in a "small" "cute setting"; still, the "quick service," "location," convenience, and moderate prices, along with late hours, keep this joint on the ball.

La Contenta Oeste ⟨ Mexican   22 | 20 | 21 | $$

Greenwich Village | 78 W 11th St. (6th Ave.)
212-533-2233 | lacontentanyc.com

A "much-appreciated addition" to the Village, this corner spot, larger than the LES original, serves "unique Mexican food" (including some "excellent vegetarian options") and "well-crafted cocktails"; come for the "outstanding" brunch, when a guitarist may be playing softly in the background, or on weekend evenings, when it's a "pretty lively place"; the staff are "charming and accommodating" no matter when you stop by.

La Esquina ⟨ Mexican   21 | 23 | 18 | $$

East 70s | 1402 2nd Ave. (73rd St.)
646-861-3356 | esquinanyc.com
NoLita | 114 Kenmare St. (bet. Cleveland Pl. & Lafayette St.)
646-613-7100
West 50s | 200 W 55th St. (bet. 7th Ave. & B'way)
646-707-3950

The Downtown flagship hosts "three restaurants in one"; walk past the bustling street-level taqueria to reach the "speakeasy" and dining club downstairs serving mezcal cocktails and "innovative," "quirky nuevo Mexican"; it's more of a party scene than a culinary one, but it makes a "fun experience" for a "celebration," to "impress someone" new in town, or just to take the sort of "friend who wants to do shots at dinner"; smaller taquerias are in the UES and Midtown West.

La Fonda Del Sol ⧆ Spanish   20 | 20 | 20 | $$$

East 40s | 200 Park Ave.
(enter on 44th St. & Vanderbilt Ave.)
212-867-6767 | patinagroup.com/la-fonda-del-sol

"A mix of atmospheres" characterizes this eatery adjacent to Grand Central Terminal: "a casual lounge for after-work drinks and tapas" and, "six steps above the hectic crowd," a "quiet," "formal dining room where you can get huge paellas and suckling pig" (the "better option," some say); pity that the space seems "more corporate conference room than Spanish restaurant" and that both food and service can be "spotty."

La Goulue French

22 | 22 | 21 | $$$

East 60s | 29 E 61st St. (bet. Madison & Park Aves.)
212-988-8169 | lagouluerestaurant.com
Everything's "très French" at this "old friend" that reopened in 2018; the address is new, but "fashionable" bistro "standards" still satisfy a "classy crowd" in a "pleasant," mirror-filled space that "gets loud" and busy – it "would be nice if you didn't have to dine with the table next to you"; that said, there's "mega-people-watching" to be had and the "social" atmosphere remains strong.

2 La Grenouille 🖫 Ⓜ French

28 | 28 | 28 | $$$$

East 50s | 3 E 52nd St. (bet. 5th & Madison Aves.)
212-752-1495 | la-grenouille.com
Serving "French cuisine at its finest," "this "longtime classic" in Midtown transports you to a "bygone time of luxury and sophistication," with an "elegant" and "aristocratic" dining room where you're "mesmerized by the lavish display of flowers" that "soar to the ceiling"; fans say "no one does old-style dining better" via "genteel and impeccable service," and while the prices definitely make it a "splurge," dinner here is "worth your last dollar."

La Masseria ⟨ Italian

24 | 21 | 23 | $$$

West 40s | 235 W 48th St. (bet. B'way & 8th Ave.)
212-582-2111 | lamasserianyc.com
Masseria dei Vini ⟨ Tues–Sat
West 50s | 887 9th Ave. (bet. 57th & 58th Sts.)
212-315-2888 | masseriadeivini.com
These upscale "farm-to-table" trattorias offer the kind of "transporting experience" that is rare in Midtown; although pricey, the Puglian food is "consistently superb" ("lasagna that made me cry"), complemented by an "extensive wine selection" and "friendly waitstaff who don't hover."

La Mela ⟨ Italian

21 | 15 | 21 | $$

Little Italy | 167 Mulberry St.
(bet. Broome & Grand Sts.)
212-431-9493 | lamelarestaurant.com
"Big plates" of Southern Italian fare is what you'll find at this "long-standing," "old-style" eatery "in the heart of Little Italy," where tourists and others scarf down à la carte and "family-style" multicourse "red-sauce" staples "till they're full"; sure, it can all be a little "cheesy" (in every sense), but the "energetic vibe," "chatty" servers, and "reasonable" tabs even things out; P.S. "go late enough" on the weekend for the "singing waiters."

La Mercerie French

23 | 27 | 24 | $$$

SoHo | 53 Howard St. (Mercer St.)
212-852-9097 | lamerceriecafe.com
It's not often you get to eat in a "gorgeous space with artistic floral decorations," but this café, "modeled on French tearooms of the '50s and '60s," is inside the "swanky" Roman and Williams Guild design store and is a "one-of-a-kind" experience; it gets "buzzy and busy," especially during the "boisterous" brunch, but inspired dishes, from "unrivaled buckwheat crêpes" to "sophisticated" breakfast "delicacies," are "delicious," though typically in "smallish portions."

La Mirabelle French
24 | 19 | 26 | $$$

West 80s | 102 W 86th St.
(bet. Amsterdam & Columbus Aves.)
212-496-0458 | lamirabellenyc.com

Bringing "old-fashioned French bistro food with old-fashioned dignity and service," this "charming," "intimate" UWS "standby" is "unpretentious," family-run, and skilled in effortlessly delivering "well-prepared," "traditional" dishes, overseen by servers that "go the extra mile"; sure, the room's a bit "dated," and the bill gets "expensive," but the "older crowd" here doesn't seem to mind, and "if you're lucky," the servers "will belt out a song for you."

La Morada 🖹 Mexican
▼ 27 | 7 | 23 | $

Mott Haven | 308 Willis Ave.
(bet. 140th & 141st Sts.) | Bronx
718-292-0235 | lamoradanyc.com

Connoisseurs "go for the moles" (there are six in all) at this family-owned Mott Haven spot, which serves traditional Oaxacan dishes as well as burritos, quesadillas, and the like in a compact, utilitarian space with a counter and, unusually, a community-geared lending library; prices are reasonable, and the staff is on point, so you might want to "bring friends" to "sample" the specialties.

La Pecora Bianca Italian
21 | 20 | 19 | $$$

East 50s | 950 2nd Ave. (bet. 50th & 51st Sts.)
212-899-9996 | lapecorabianca.com
Flatiron | 1133 Broadway (26th St.)
212-498-9696

At this pair of "hip," "informal" "farm-to-table" eateries with "reliable" and "fresh" "homemade pasta," "reservations are a must"; some diners report being "overwhelmed" by the "noisy" energy, while others are underwhelmed by the "spotty" service and a "limited menu" of "basic" dishes that are a bit "expensive for what they are," but locals definitely find comfort in the "lovely neighborhood" vibes and "rocking" weekend brunches.

La Sirène French
22 | 17 | 22 | $$$

Hudson Square | 558 Broome St. (Varick St.)
212-925-3061 | lasirenenyc.com
West 80s | 416 Amsterdam Ave. (80th St.)
917-261-5279

This worthy pair of "neighborhood brasseries" in Hudson Square and the UWS serve "basic French and Continental food" that's "a cut above," with memorable cassoulet and other classics; at its best it's stylish, "like dining in St. Barth," and with that come the crowds and the cozy (sometimes "too-tight") quarters; note that the Downtown location takes only American Express credit cards.

La Vara Spanish
27 | 19 | 23 | $$$

Cobble Hill | 268 Clinton St.
(bet. Verandah Pl. & Warren St.) | Brooklyn
718-422-0065 | lavarany.com

"Bold flavors" infused with "creative" Sephardic and Moorish touches "dazzle" at this "irresistible" Spanish outpost in Cobble

Hill, which turns out "elevated" yet "approachable" tapas and other dishes from a "helpful" staff; yes, "the tab can soar quickly," and "popularity" translates to a "cramped space" that's often noisy, but if you "book ahead," you'll almost certainly find a "shining example of a kind of cuisine most New Yorkers don't know enough about."

La Vigna Italian 22| 18| 23| $$|
Forest Hills | 100-11 Metropolitan Ave.
(70th Ave.) | Queens
718-268-4264 | lavignany.com
"Surprisingly good" and "well-prepared" Italian food at "affordable outer-borough prices" shines at this "pleasant" "neighborhood" spot in Forest Hills, a "small, quiet" "homey" brick-walled space; the setting may be due "for an uplift," but "warm" and "helpful" service prevails, and regulars like the handy location near the movie theater; they have decent lunch specials, too.

La Villa Italian/Pizza 23| 17| 21| $$|
Dyker Heights | 1529 86th St.
(bet. Bay 10th St. & 15th Ave.) | Brooklyn
718-256-3100 | lavillapizza.com
Mill Basin | 6610 Avenue U (66th St.) | Brooklyn
718-251-8030
Park Slope | 261 5th Ave. (bet. 1st St. & Garfield Pl.) | Brooklyn
718-499-9888
Howard Beach | 8207 153rd Ave. (82nd St.) | Queens
718-641-8259
This "old-school bustling pizza joint" satisfies with its wood-fired pies, and the large portions of "uncomplicated Italian cuisine" – everything from focaccia to rice balls to pasta – "will have you loosening a notch or two on your belt"; each of the Brooklyn and Queens locations offer surprises ("soup like Grandma used to make"), crowds, and a no-reservations policy; they're "always crowded, and understandably so."

Lafayette French 22| 23| 21| $$$|
NoHo | 380 Lafayette St. (Great Jones St.)
212-533-3000 | lafayetteny.com
At this "grown-up" all-day NoHo eatery-and-bakery, the "sprawling," "cinematic" setting with "huge banquettes" evokes "brasseries in Paris" – as do the "standard" French "bistro fare" and "see-and-be-seen" vibe; the "upbeat" feel, "warm-weather" outdoor seating, and a location handy for "trips to the Public Theater" are all a relief.

Lakruwana Ⓜ Sri Lankan ▼ 26| 27| 26| $$|
Stapleton | 668 Bay St.
(bet. Broad & Thompson Sts.) | Staten Island
347-857-6619 | lakruwana.com
Stepping inside the "beautiful" space in Staten Island is like entering a "museum," decorated with one-of-a-kind art, statues, furnishings, and household items from Sri Lanka; if you're ready to "fall in love" with its cuisine, a visit here is "worth it," especially during the "excellent" cash-only weekend buffet, which showcases dozens of dishes, many warmed over a flame in clay pots.

NEW LaLou M Wine Bar — —| —| —| $$$|

Prospect Heights | 581 Vanderbilt Ave.
(bet. Dean & Pacific Sts.) | Brooklyn
718-857-9463 | laloubrooklyn.com

Prospect Heights adds a natural wine bar to the bustling scene on Vanderbilt Avenue, helmed by a veteran sommelier from L'Artusi and the chef de cuisine at The Grill; they pair organic, biodynamic wines from around the globe with a small menu of mostly small bites inspired by the market, like fried olives and potato dumplings.

NEW Lamalo Middle Eastern — —| —| —| $$$|

East 30s | 11 E 31st St.
(bet. 5th & Madison Aves.)
212-660-2112 | lamalonyc.com

Gadi Peleg of Nur and Breads Bakery takes a fresh approach to modern Israeli cuisine in the Arlo NoMad Hotel with all-day meals centered around pillowy laffa bread, baked directly on lava rocks and perfect for scooping up colorful spreads and bright salads; reasonable prices for Midtown and arak cocktails served in wine bottles are also draws for groups who understand the pleasures of schmoozing over meze.

The Lambs Club American 23| 25| 23| $$$|

West 40s | Chatwal Hotel, 132 W 44th St.
(bet. 6th & 7th Aves.)
212-997-5262 | thelambsclub.com

Though the locale is perfect for pre-theater, "once inside you forget Times Square is just out the door," given the "cozy elegance" of this Art Deco–inspired space, "all decked out in red leather" with whimsical "NYC-based" touches, like skyscraper-shaped chrome light fixtures; this is chef "Geoffrey Zakarian's showcase," so expect "rich" riffs on American classics, served by "professional" staff; and if it all seems "too expensive," bear in mind the "upstairs bar is more casual," both cuisine- and price-wise.

Land Thai Kitchen Thai 22| 13| 18| $$|

West 80s | 450 Amsterdam Ave.
(bet. 81st & 82nd Sts.)
212-501-8121 | landthaikitchen.com

"High-quality," "plentiful" Thai specialties that are "better than expected" and "reliably good" await here – in fact, sometimes they reach "another level of tastiness," and the "bargain" lunch specials put the emphasis on "special"; the "tiny" wood- and brick-lined interior is best for takeout, but those "comfortable" enough to get "in the spirit" of dining communally will have a "good time."

LaRina Pastificio & Vino Italian 25| 19| 22| $$|

Fort Greene | 387 Myrtle Ave.
(bet. Clermont & Vanderbilt Aves.) | Brooklyn
212-852-0001 | larinabk.com

Supplying a "pasta-focused" menu highlighted by house-made options as well as a strong list of antipasti, this Italian "on the edge of Fort Greene" pairs "rustic but sophisticated" dishes with a store that sells its noodles, sauce, and other items; the rest of the space is "cozy" more than luxurious, but the "lovely" outdoor patio in back feels like an "escape from the city," and the fair prices and "welcoming" service are big pluses.

Lattanzi Italian   22 | 20 | 22 | $$$

West 40s | 361 W 46th St. (bet. 8th & 9th Aves.)
212-315-0980 | lattanzinyc.com

Known for its Roman cuisine with a Jewish tilt, this Restaurant Row mainstay – a standout within the craziness serves "reliable" Italian favorites (including a "terrific" veal chop and "loved" fried artichokes) in a "beautiful" converted townhouse with "old-world" furnishings; most agree the service is "welcoming" and "polished," and while it's "not cheap," it remains a "solid' option for pre- or post-theater dining.

Laut Malaysian/Thai   23 | 15 | 18 | $$

Union Square | 15 E 17th St.
(bet. B'way & 6th Ave.)
212-206-8989 | lautnyc.com

The "party in your mouth" can last a long time at this Union Square spot, turning out "flavorful" Malaysian, Singaporean, and Thai curries, stir fries, and noodles in a "casual," "funky" space that's "always packed with appreciative diners"; given its "popularity," the joint can get "noisy," and "tight quarters" may frustrate (it's "not a place for a long, relaxed meal"), but "affordable" prices and "before-the-movies" convenience make eating here "easy."

Lavagna Italian   24 | 20 | 21 | $$

East Village | 545 E 5th St. (bet. Avenues A & B)
212-979-1005 | lavagnanyc.com

An "early leader and continuing champ" among the packed scene of East Village Italian restaurants, this "small," charming trattoria features "knockout," "well-priced" pastas and an encyclopedic wine list in a romantic, if "cramped," setting; service can be "brusque," but once they get to know you, you're "family"; don't forget to "make a reservation" at peak times – they're "always crowded on the weekend."

Lavo ☾ Italian   17 | 18 | 17 | $$$

East 50s | 39 E 58th St. (bet. Madison & Park Aves.)
212-750-5588 | lavony.com

At least as much a "place to be seen" as a place to get mounds of pasta, giant meatballs, raw and grilled seafood, and "standard Italian favorites" as well as "decadent" fried Oreos, this white-tablecloth spot sits "atop a nightclub" "near Bloomie's" in Midtown East; it serves a "smooth crowd" of "promoters," "twentysomethings," "expense-account" business lunchers, and others who can swallow the "slow service" and big tabs for the sake of being in a "loud, crowded" "hot spot."

⯐ Le Bernardin ⑤ French   29 | 29 | 29 | $$$$

West 50s | 155 W 51st St. (bet. 6th & 7th Aves.)
212-554-1515 | le-bernardin.com

A longtime "temple to finned gastronomy," this "transcendent" Midtown French "icon" – which ranks #1 on this year's Most Popular and Top Food lists – continues to "astound," with "magician" chef Eric Ripert's "sublime" seafood tasting menus that "elevate fish onto a pedestal," in addition to an "unbelievable wine list," "stunning" decor, and an "extraordinary" staff; sure, such "perfection" may require "the market going up 1,000 points," but for cuisine "that satisfies all your senses," "nothing else compares to it" in town.

Le Bilboquet French

22| 22| 21| $$$|

East 60s | 20 E 60th St.
(bet. Madison & Park Aves.)
212-751-3036 | lebilboquetny.com

"Ground zero for the UES Euro set," this French bistro adorned with "festive" artwork is best known as a "kissy kissy place"; but if it's "a teeny bit snobby," it's also a "goody," with "tasty" eats (the signature "Cajun chicken always delivers") and a Gallic wait staff – "it's all about the vibe, man."

Le Colonial French/Vietnamese

23| 23| 22| $$$|

East 50s | 149 E 57th St.
(bet. Lexington & 3rd Aves.)
212-752-0808 | lecolonialnyc.com

"A couple of hours among the palm frond–filled room utterly transports one to another time and place" – specifically, 1920s French Indochina – at this venerable and "quiet Midtown retreat"; "the decor is spot-on for" the "fine if predictable" French-Vietnamese specialties; although there are a few dissenters, most call the service "expert" and the "movie set"–like interior "spot on" and "delightful" – "if it ever changes, I won't go back."

Le Coq Rico French

24| 20| 23| $$$|

Flatiron | 30 E 20th St. (bet. B'way & Park Ave. S)
212-267-7426 | lecoqriconyc.com

"Fantastic fowl dishes in a whimsical environment (feathers and eggshells everywhere)" sums up the experience at this "sleek" "French outpost in the Flatiron arrondissement" that "pays homage to poultry" and "eggy" fare, backed by servers who make "spot-on recommendations"; however, "you have to really love chicken" to love this place – the rest of the "menu is limited" – and not mind that it "costs a wing and a leg."

🅩 Le Coucou French

27| 28| 27| $$$$|

SoHo | 138 Lafayette St.
(bet. Canal & Howard Sts.)
212-271-4252 | lecoucou.com

"As good as anything in Paris," this "ethereal" SoHo "dream" gets its power from chef Daniel Rose's "spectacular" French fare plus an "off-the-charts" wine list in a "stylish," "romantic" setting where "you're treated like royalty" amid exposed brick walls, "perfectly high ceilings," and an open kitchen surveying the "vibrant scene"; "trying to nab a reservation" drives some patrons "cuckoo," and customers should "expect to spend their paychecks" here, but given the "gastronomic extravaganza" (including a "relative bargain" prix fixe lunch), it's "a knockout" overall.

Le French Diner ◖ French

28 | 22 | 27 | $$

Lower East Side | 188 Orchard St.
(bet. Houston & Stanton Sts.)
212-777-1577
"It's shocking how much quality food can come out of such
a small kitchen," marvel fans of this "hidden" and "cozy"
LES "boîte," where the "original" but traditional French food,
"cooked with love," includes a hanger steak to "haunt your
dreams"; combine this with a "short but killer" list of wines and
"fantastic" service, and you have the "coziest little date spot
there ever was."

Le Gigot French

25 | 19 | 24 | $$$

West Village | 18 Cornelia St.
(bet. Bleecker & 4th Sts.)
212-627-3737 | legigotrestaurant.com
Serving Provençal cuisine that feels like "home cooking," this
French "dream" is "romantic" and "perfect for a quiet date
night"; after more than two decades, it's become a "quintessential neighborhood place" with "a gracious and attentive" staff
that's been there for years; the "postage stamp–size" dining
room can feel "slightly cramped," but for many, it's at "the top of
the list of places to return to again and again."

Le Marais ◖ Kosher/Steakhouse

22 | 16 | 19 | $$$

West 40s | 150 W 46th St. (bet. 6th & 7th Aves.)
212-869-0900 | lemarais.net
Ask three different people to describe this spot, and you'll
probably get three different answers: a "welcoming French restaurant," a "convenient" Theater District option, and a "steakhouse that happens to be kosher" – and they'd all be correct;
the "lively and vibrant" two-story Midtown space is "packed
before a show" for the "best kosher steaks around" and bistro
classics (minus dairy, shellfish, or pork, of course); N.B. closed
Friday night.

Le Parisien Bistrot French

25 | 16 | 22 | $$

Murray Hill | 163 E 33rd St.
(bet. Lexington & Park Aves.)
212-889-5489 | leparisiennyc.com
"A real Left Bank experience without having to worry about the
exchange rate," this "neighborhood" Murray Hill bistro "brings
back delicious memories" with its "excellent" Gallic fare, "served
quickly and efficiently" to "budget" specifications; "tiny" quarters means it's "not a place for a romantic dinner" ("unless you
don't mind the next table hearing all your mots d'amour"), yet the
joint's "French feel" is so "old-fashioned" that most can't avoid
being "charmed."

Le Relais de Venise

22 | 17 | 20 | $$

L'Entrecôte French
East 50s | 590 Lexington Ave. (52nd St.)
212-758-3989 | relaisdevenise.com
"You'd better want steak frites" because that's the only thing on
the menu at this Midtown East bistro spinoff from a Paris original, pairing its signature dish ("completely reliable") with salad,

wine, "generously" poured cocktails and dessert; service can
be lackadaisical at times, but most reviewers like its "old-world
feeling" and say you "can't beat the formula."

Le Veau d'Or French   21| 18| 20| $$$

East 60s | 129 E 60th St.
(bet. Lexington & Park Aves.)
212-838-8133
Flying "under the radar," this UES "time capsule" from "old New
York" supplies "well-prepared" French "classics" at "fair prices"
in a "quiet," "intimate" environment (dig those "red banquettes")
beloved by "locals," who say it has some "dishes not available
anywhere else"; no, it's "not fancy," and some say it might be "a
bit past its prime," but if you're "dining or lunching in or around
Bloomie's," this "warm" trip down "memory lane" is relatively
"satisfying."

Lee's Tavern ◖ ⌺ Gastropub/Pizza   24| 12| 21| $

Dongan Hills | 60 Hancock St.
(Garretson Ave.) | Staten Island
718-667-9749
Pizza lovers travel far and wide for Lee's "excellent" bar pies with
"crispy," cracker-thin crusts, and it doesn't hurt that its free-
flowing beer and buffalo calamari are also "excellent"; billed by
some as the "'Cheers' of Staten Island," this Dongan Hills "dive"
is "always worth a trip," and a "neighborhood staple" that attracts
a "family-friendly" crowd of "all ages," N.B. cash only.

Left Bank American   20| 17| 20| $$

West Village | 117 Perry St. (Greenwich St.)
212-727-1170 | leftbanknewyork.com
This neighborhood place in the West Village is "unassuming,"
with a French-influenced menu that includes moules frites and
dinner salads as well as pastas; the chefs make their own sausage and seek out local produce at farmers' markets; if you're
just in the mood for takeout, the next-door sister restaurant,
Poulet Sans Tête ("headless chicken"), serves dry-rubbed rotisserie birds that get raves.

Legacy Records American   23| 26| 22| $$$

West 30s | 517 W 38th St. (bet. 10th & 11th Aves.)
text only 929-418-0115 | legacyrecordsrestaurant.com
An airy, emerald-hued space accented with grass cloth, gold
fixtures, and leather-topped tables, "the setting is the true
strength" of this "addition to the West 30s area" run by "familiar
faces from the Pasquale Jones and Charlie Bird team"; empha-
sizing pastas and roasts, the Italian-accented American food
(crudos, pastas, roasts) is "surprisingly delicious for such a
cool, trendy place," if not quite worth the "high prices."

NEW Leña Spanish   –| –| –| $$$

West 30s | 10 Hudson Yards
(10th Ave. & 30th St.)
646-495-1242 | littlespain.com
Occupying a corner of Hudson Yards' not-so-little Mercado
Little Spain, this venture from José Andres and the Adrià

brothers (of El Bulli fame) is dedicated to fire, with almost everything on the northern- and coastal-inspired menu cooked over wood embers, including heritage Ibérico pork and whole turbot; the wines hail from every corner of Spain, and there are several tasting menu options; prices are fair, considering the ingredients and prestige of the chefs.

Leonti ⑧ Italian   25| 25| 27| $$$$|
West 70s | 103 W 77th St.
(bet. Amsterdam & Columbus Aves.)
212-362-3800 | leontinyc.com
"For a pampered experience," head to this "formal," "fine-dining" UWS Italian establishment serving a "limited menu" of "creative," "elegant" plates that reveal "dedication" to every detail – "from the amuse-bouche to the dessert, everything is an event" – paired with a "superb" wine list and finished with "unique, delicious" sweets; the rustic-chic space feels "enchanting," and while the prices seem "slightly insane" to some, they also admit "no place tries harder to please."

The Leopard at des Artistes Italian   23| 27| 25| $$$$|
West 60s | 1 W 67th St. (bet. Columbus Ave. & CPW)
212-787-8767 | theleopardnyc.com
Still "wonderful to behold" long after "its heyday as the Café des Artistes" ended, this "historic" Lincoln Center–area "tradition" oozes "romance" with its "fantastic" murals of "nude maidens frolicking," which remain a major "source of conversation" despite the "excellent" Italian menu; the "sophistication" (coupled with the "high" prices) attracts an "older clientele," and most everyone is on board when it comes to the "coddling" staff, "civilized" jazz brunch, and "pre-theater dining" options, while no-corkage-fee BYOB Sundays feel like a "bargain."

Leuca Italian   25| 26| 26| $$$|
Williamsburg | 111 N 12th St.
(bet. Berry St. & Wythe Ave.) | Brooklyn
718-581-5900 | leuca.com
If any diehard Manhattanites are "still apprehensive about Williamsburg," the "creative," "high-end" Southern Italian fare and smart wine selection served by a staff that "keep their cool" in an "elegant" dining room at the William Vale Hotel should reassure them; the "large scale" means "lots of room to keep conversations going," and even though it's open all day, it's best for a pasta or wood-fired pizza dinner and "a fancy cocktail or two."

NEW Leyla Mediterranean   -| -| -| $$$|
West 70s | 108 W 74th St. (Columbus Ave.)
347-334-7939 | leylanyc.com
Move over pizza, the UWS can now feast on brick-oven pide and lahmacun at this modern, upscale Turkish newcomer with plenty of vegetarian choices; the moody, date-worthy interior and a shareable menu of meze, make this a wise place to keep in your back pocket for impromptu Uptown dinners or brunches with a Mediterranean twist.

Lhasa Fast Food Tibetan
▼ 28 | 10 | 20 | $

Jackson Heights | 37-50 74th St.
(bet. B'way & 37th Ave.)
Queens | 718-256-3805

The momos, especially the beef and chive varieties, at this "hidden" Tibetan counter-service spot are worth discovering: you'll find them by going down a narrow hallway inside a Jackson Heights storefront: the dumplings are "flavorful" and true to form, with traditional Himalayan flavor, as are the thenthuk (hand-pulled noodle soups), cold beef noodles, and other offerings on the limited menu.

LIC Market American
21 | 16 | 20 | $$

Long Island City | 21-52 44th Dr.
(23rd St.) | Queens
718-361-0013 | licmarket.com

With a "quaint" "café vibe" and a lovely backyard, this tiny farm-to-table choice near MoMA PS1 in Queens serves "clean, fresh" "well-prepared" American standards "with a few twists" alongside craft beer and natural wine; the service is casual, and the rustic decor doesn't exactly feel upscale, but it does feel "charming," and you'll be "lucky to get a table" for the "fantastic brunch" or the regular chef's dinners.

Lido Italian
24 | 19 | 23 | $$

Harlem | 2168 Frederick Douglass Blvd. (117th St.)
646-490-8575 | lidoharlem.com

This is the Uptown "neighborhood spot" you should go to "impress your parents" and show off some of Harlem's charms; come for the sunny "bottomless mimosa" brunches "for a very reasonable price" on the "outdoor patio," and eat "comfort" Italian dishes like the "must"-order meatballs at dinner in a "lively" exposed-brick dining room; "friendly" servers "know the menu and the community" well.

Lil' Frankie's (⌧ Italian/Pizza
25 | 20 | 20 | $$

East Village | 19 1st Ave. (bet. 1st & 2nd Sts.)
212-420-4900 | lilfrankies.com

"The lemon pasta and rigatoni are the moves" at this East Village eatery, which also serves a fine pizza, but it's never not a scene, so "come here if you're turning 25 and you have 25 friends" or you want an outstanding "boozy brunch" or a "wine-fueled family-style group dinner," and be ready for "crazy wait times and crowds"; N.B. cash only.

⊡ Lilia Italian
27 | 25 | 25 | $$$

Williamsburg | 567 Union Ave. (Frost St.) | Brooklyn
718-576-3095 | lilianewyork.com

Missy Robbins and Co. "never fail to deliver" at this "sophisticated" Williamsburg establishment with a "first-class menu of Italian-cuisine heaven," including wood-fired mains and "incredible" handmade pastas, in an "inviting" interior bolstered by a "large open kitchen," a roomy bar, and "energetic" scene; some call the options "overpriced," although most think it "exceeds" their "lofty expectations" – "a rare find" that justifies at least considering "selling your soul" to get that res.

Limani Mediterranean   25| 24| 22| $$$|

West 50s | 45 Rockefeller Plaza (5th Ave.)
212-858-9200 | limani.com

For "stylish" Greek dining at Rockefeller Center, the lunch prix fixe is "a real bargain" and an opportunity to enjoy "perfectly simple" "fresh seafood" like grilled octopus so tender it "melts in the mouth"; the "open, light room" with a "stark, white interior" and serene marine highlights is framed by a stunning, contemplative "central pool"; detractors point out that the crowds are "noisy and the service can be "spotty."

Z Lincoln Ristorante Italian   25| 26| 26| $$$$|

West 60s | 142 W 65th St.
(bet. Amsterdam Ave. & B'way)
212-359-6500 | lincolnristorante.com

"Location! Location! Location!" say those in tune with this "ridiculously convenient" restaurant, "where you can virtually "fall off your chair into a Lincoln Center performance"; happily, it's also "spectacular" and "serene," with a sophisticated menu of "innovative Italian cuisine" and "superior wine selections"; when merged with "top-drawer" service and "expansive windows" providing "lovely views onto the plaza," it amounts to a "hidden gem" for locals; the prix fixe dinner menu is "pricey, but worth it."

Lincoln Square Steak Steakhouse   19| 20| 20| $$$|

West 70s | 208 W 70th St. (Amsterdam Ave.)
212-875-8600 | lincolnsquaresteak.com

"Convenient" for Lincoln Center, this "solid" and "friendly" UWS steakhouse is in a "large" space decorated with a mural of party-goers; "fair" dishes, "earnest" but "spotty" service, and "pricey" bills rub some the wrong way, but "an affordable fixed-price menu," happy-hour deals, and half-price wine Sundays are all part of what makes it "pleasant."

Little Alley Chinese   23| 15| 18| $$|

Murray Hill | 550 3rd Ave.
(bet. 36th & 37th Sts.)
646-998-3976 | littlealley.nyc

Come to this Murray Hill Shanghainese specialist for soup dumplings, including one that's so big and juicy that it requires a straw to slurp down the broth, as well as other "creative and interesting" options; the room is "modern" but still fairly spare, with service that's "helpful" but sometimes distant – overall, a "cut above" most Midtown competitors.

Little Owl Mediterranean   24| 19| 23| $$$|

West Village | 90 Bedford St. (Grove St.)
212-741-4695 | thelittleowlnyc.com

"Squeeze on in for a delicious meal" at this "jewel box" on a "charming West Village corner" (in the iconic Friends building) for a "small and seasonal menu" of "Mediterranean cuisine at its best"; "waitstaff treat you like an old friend," and the "warm, cozy ambiance" "makes for a perfect romantic" night out; sure, the "food is worth the cramped space," but come at lunch to get more elbow room.

Little Park American
23 | 21 | 22 | $$$

TriBeCa | 85 W Broadway (Chambers St.)
212-220-4110 | littlepark.com
"Who knew vegetables could be" as "beautiful" and "intriguing" as they are on the "seasonal" menu at this "healthy" "organically inclined" "straightforward fancy" New American spot in TriBeCa; this locavore haven for "artistic" plates serves morning to night in a "beautiful" setting that's "comfortable," and the "attentive," "accommodating" service typically delivers, so the "high-end bills" are generally "worth the price."

Little Pepper Chinese
▼ 24 | 11 | 23 | $$

College Point | 18-24 College Point Blvd.
(bet. 18th & 20th Aves.)
Queens | 718-939-7788
"Fiery is hardly the word" to describe the "tingly" cumin lamb and "legit spicy" mapo tofu at this Sichuan spot in a College Point business strip; the hospitality at the "family-run" place "aims to please" with lightning quick service and an upbeat atmosphere.

Littleneck 🍽 Seafood
20 | 17 | 20 | $$

Gowanus | 288 3rd Ave. (bet. Carroll & President Sts.)
Brooklyn | 718-522-1921 | littleneckop.com
Greenpoint | 128 Franklin St. (Milton St.) | Brooklyn
718-383-3080
Williamsburg | 855 Grand St. (bet. Bushwick Ave. & Olive St.)
Brooklyn | 929-480-8349
"You won't regret sitting at the bar and eating oysters" "all night long" in this cash-only "Montauk sea shack" a few blocks from the Gowanus Canal, even if the feelings for many dishes here seesaw between "to die for" and "never stellar"; best to stick with the basics at this "low-key seafood joint"; you can join "plenty of hipsters" for all-day breakfast or sandwiches for lunch at the Outpost in Greenpoint.

🆕 Llama Inn Peruvian
26 | 25 | 23 | $$$

Williamsburg | 50 Withers St. (Meeker Ave.) | Brooklyn
718-387-3434 | llamainnnyc.com
"From the tiniest bites to the entrees, there are no misses" on the "yummy" Peruvian menu at this "lively" spot near the BQE – it's "one of Williamsburg's best," in fact, and one also blessed with a colorful, "fancy," "plant-filled interior" and a "friendly wait staff"; throw in "terrific" cocktails and "reservation availability" and you've got a "magical combination."

The Lobster Club 🍽 Japanese/Sushi
22 | 26 | 22 | $$$$

East 50s | 98 E 53rd St.
(bet. Park & Lexington Aves.)
212-375-9001 | thelobsterclub.com
Located in the Seagram Building in the space once inhabited by Brasserie, this "expensive" Japanese-inspired spot from Major Food Group turns out sushi as well as teppanyaki and lots of lobster and other sharing-friendly options, plus a lesser-known breakfast menu; the "lavishly decorated" interior is meant to impress, with acid-green banquettes, orangey-pink chairs, and a Jackson Pollock–esque floor that makes even the hard-to-impress say "visit once to say you've been."

Locanda Verde Italian
25 | 23 | 21 | $$$

TriBeCa | 377 Greenwich St. (N Moore St.)
212-925-3797 | locandaverdenyc.com

The "rocking scene" is the thing at this "buzzy" all-day restaurant in TriBeCa's Greenwich Hotel; "celeb sightings" lend sparkle to "wow"-inducing Italian fare and "imaginative" cocktails; true, it's a "tough table" to get and the noise can make it "hard to talk," but the "sexy" vibes and "courteous" staff guarantee "you won't want to leave when the meal is done."

Locanda Vini & Olii Italian
26 | 24 | 23 | $$

Clinton Hill | 129 Gates Ave. (bet. Cambridge Pl. & Grand Ave.)
Brooklyn | 718-622-9202 | locandany.com

Most diners "seem like regulars" at this "time capsule" in Clinton Hill inside a reclaimed apothecary; the building is the only old-fashioned thing about it, though, with a hip, "accommodating staff" serving "fantastic" pastas and Northern Italian specialties with modern flair; there's an entire Negroni menu that's tempting, but this food is built for vino, as showcased at their semiannual wine dinners.

The Loeb Boathouse American
19 | 27 | 20 | $$$

Central Park | E 72nd St. (Park Dr. N)
212-517-2233 | thecentralparkboathouse.com

The "magnificent" lakeside setting in Central Park is "wonderful for proposing" and "great for a celebratory meal," especially if you're eating al fresco on the patio; diners agree that it's "touristy but fun" and sometimes "an absolute madhouse" – but the "service and ambiance are worth it any time of year," and the menu of "Americana" is decent; to avoid crowds, try late-afternoon cocktails and watch the rowboats (or rent one).

NEW Lokanta Ⓜ Turkish
— | — | — | $$

Astoria | 3116 Broadway (32nd St.) | Queens
718-728-4477 | thelokanta.com

This emerging neighborhood favorite serves a vegetarian-friendly mix of traditional Turkish breakfast dishes (eggs, flatbreads, cheese) in the morning, and in the evening elevated versions of the homey Anatolian stews (a nod to those you'd find in Istanbul lunch cafeterias); the palm-leaf wallpaper and reasonably priced menu create a comfortable, casual experience.

Lolo's Seafood Shack Seafood
22 | 14 | 18 | $$

Harlem | 303 W 116th St. (Frederick Douglass Blvd.)
646-649-3356 | lolosseafoodshack.com

"If you can't make it out to the shore," get a taste of the tropics, "even in the dead of winter," at this "quaint" "Caribbean beach shack" in Harlem with seafood boils, smoked meat, sandwiches, and fried baskets served to "covered, all-weather" "picnic tables."

Lombardi's 🍴 Pizza
23 | 15 | 18 | $$

Chelsea | 290 8th Ave. (25th St.) | 212-256-1973
NoLita | 32 Spring St. (bet. Mott & Mulberry Sts.)
212-941-7994 | firstpizza.com

Grab your "NY history in a pizza" (thin-crust edition) at this "legendary" NoLita parlor, a "consistent" purveyor of "old-fashioned" coal-oven pies since 1905 (it claims to be America's first pizzeria); of course, "lines of tourists" mean "long waits for tables," but the "crazy-busy" atmosphere "is part of the charm," though the basic setting and service aren't – thankfully, it's not that expensive, and "they deliver"; N.B. no individual slices and cash only.

ⓩ Loring Place American   25| 23| 24| $$$

Greenwich Village | 21 W 8th St.
(bet. 5th & 6th Aves.)
212-388-1831 | loringplacenyc.com

"Carnivores and vegetarians alike" find something to enjoy at this "buzzy" Greenwich Village café, where "complex yet coherent" flavors inform an "inventive" seasonal menu grounded in local products – such as "crispy pizzas" made from house-milled flour; "cordial" service and "homey," "farmhouse" decor in a 19th-century building counteract the "high decibel counts," as well as "not-inexpensive" tabs, although the "beautiful people" in attendance don't seem to mind.

Los Mariscos Mexican   25| 20| 18| $

Chelsea | 409 W 15th St. (bet. 9th & 10th Aves.)
212-920-4986 | losmariscos1.com

A takeout joint for homemade tortillas, potent margaritas, and the "best fish tacos in New York," this cantina calls to mind a "hot summer day in Baja California," and no matter what you order, the "seafood is always perfectly fresh and prepared to perfection"; it's well "worth a visit," even if the location inside Chelsea Market means "you're lucky if you can sit down."

ⓩ Los Tacos No.1 Mexican   27| 12| 17| $

Chelsea | Chelsea Market, 75 9th Ave.
(bet. 15th & 16th Sts.)
212-256-0343 | lostacos1.com
West 40s | 229 W 43rd St. (bet. 7th & 8th Aves.)
212-574-4696

Lunch crowds line up and pack in for "killer" tacos served "street-style" with "simple, fresh ingredients" ("run, don't walk, for the carne asada") at these Chelsea Market and Times Square storefronts; fans gripe about the "crazy lines," "food court atmosphere," and lack of seating, but insist that even with "barely room to stand up and eat, it's worth it all" – "order everything," and "get extra napkins."

Loukoumi Taverna Greek   25| 18| 22| $$

Astoria | 45-07 Ditmars Blvd.
(bet. 45th & 46th Sts.) | Queens
718-626-3200 | toloukoumi.com

Diehards say this Queens staple has "the best Greek food in Astoria and therefore on earth," but at the very least it's "a cut above," dishing up classic mezes, the "freshest fish and seafood," "amazing" lamb chops, and decent salads, dips, and baklava; whether sitting in the "charming" dining room or in the back garden, the taverna's "welcoming" staff make you feel like you're eating on some Mediterranean isle.

The Loyal American   21 | 21 | 21 | $$$

West Village | 289 Bleecker St. (7th Ave. S)
212-488-5800 | loyalrestaurant.com

The music, blaring so loudly that you can "barely have a conversation," is all part of the "awesome scene" at this West Village hot spot; it's a "fun" (if a bit "too dark") space that resembles a midcentury supper club, drawing a "trendy" crowd; the bar section, overlooking 7th Avenue, is "perfect for sunset happy-hour drinks," but the thing most people remember are the DIY choices, like a make-your-own-sundae option.

☑ Lucali Pizza   28 | 22 | 23 | $$

Carroll Gardens | 575 Henry St.
(bet. Carroll St. & 1st Pl.) | Brooklyn
718-858-4086 | lucalibrooklyn.com

"Does better pizza exist?" – the thin-crust pie "strikes dead center between Neapolitan and NYC utility slice" – both it and the calzone (the only options) are "A++"; with passion like that, the "bonkers wait time" doesn't seem to keep many people away, and instead folks "get in line at 4 PM for a 6 PM opening" just to get on "the list" for this cash-only BYOB, a tiny room in Carroll Gardens; P.S. it's closed on Tuesday.

Lucien ℭ French   24 | 18 | 20 | $$

East Village | 14 1st Ave. (1st St.)
212-260-6481 | luciennyc.com

Like a "neighborhood bistro in a French village" but with East Village "cool-kid street cred," this "charming in a boho kind of way" "sliver of a restaurant" will have you "cheek to jowl" with an "eclectic" crowd hunkering down for old "standbys" at the "long bar" decorated with "lots of old photos"; service is "knowledgeable and friendly" and the mood is "informal and fun" – "on a rainy night, you won't want to leave!"

Lucky Strike ℭ French   18 | 17 | 18 | $$

SoHo | 59 Grand St. (bet. W B'way & Wooster St.)
212-941-0772 | luckystrikeny.com

This Keith McNally "SoHo institution" has been "bustling since the late '80s," and "quite frankly, not much has changed (decor included), but that's not necessarily a bad thing"; the menu combines French bistro fare with American standards including "a sturdy martini and a decent burger" served until late night; you'll also find "one of SoHo's best-kept happy hour secrets" daily at the long copper bar.

Luigi's Italian   23 | 18 | 23 | $$

Glen Oaks | 265-21 Union Tpke. (266th St.) | Queens
718-347-7136 | luigisnewhydepark.com

"Consistent" and "genuine" homemade pasta, wood-fired pizzas, fritto misto, and other classics, along with Negronis ("on tap") keep regulars coming back to this "old red-sauce" ristorante at the Queens–Long Island border for the "warm, homey, welcoming" atmosphere and an ever-present management that's "always there for whatever you need"; P.S. reservations are "a must."

Lupa Osteria Romana Italian 26 | 20 | 25 | $$$

Greenwich Village | 170 Thompson St.
(bet. Bleecker & Houston Sts.)
212-982-5089 | luparestaurant.com

"If you can't get to Rome," try this "charming" Greenwich Village trattoria "standby," which continues to showcase "earthy" yet "dynamic" fare from the Eternal City, plus a "deep" wine list featuring Italian vintages; a "welcoming" staff enhances the "local" feel, and while you may be "packed in like sardines" within the "cramped" (and often "noisy") and "simple" space, chances are you'll "leave stuffed like shells."

Lure Fishbar Seafood 24 | 23 | 22 | $$$

SoHo | 142 Mercer St. (Prince St.)
212-431-7676 | lurefishbar.com

"Fresh fish" and "sushi with a creative spin" (and a "killer lobster roll") in underground digs "styled to resemble the interior of a yacht" are what keep the "beautiful people" and groups filling up the tables and "large booths" and the bar; with all these passengers on board, it's one "crazy-loud" "cruise ship," but if you can handle the noise, it's a much-better-than-decent port of call when in SoHo.

Z Lusardi's Italian 24 | 19 | 23 | $$$

East 70s | 1494 2nd Ave. (bet. 77th & 78th Sts.)
212-249-2020 | lusardis.com

"Old-school Italian done right" is what you get at this "reliable" and "slightly stiff" UES "institution," "still going strong after all these years" and serving "consistently" "well-prepared meals" that include some "unusual" dishes; it's "particularly popular with an older, well-heeled crowd" of "steady regular patrons" who appreciate its "knowledgeable" waiters; the "elegant" space can get "crowded," but it's always a "warm place," and the "food never disappoints."

Luzzo's La Pizza Napoletana Pizza 24 | 14 | 19 | $$

East Village | 213 1st Ave. (bet. 12th & 13th Sts.)
212-473-7447 | luzzosgroup.com
Luzzo's BK
Brooklyn Heights | 145 Atlantic Ave.
(bet. Clinton & Henry Sts.) | Brooklyn
718-855-6400

"Without any pretentious nonsense," the chef-owner, a third-generation baker, turns out coal-fired Neapolitan-style pizzas with upscale ingredients to marvel at ("prosciutto and truffle sauce go well together") as well as "classic pies" with a "crust that's some of the best anywhere" at these "lively" East Village and Brooklyn Heights trattorias; the menus at both locations also encompass pastas and other traditional red-sauce favorites.

M. Wells Steakhouse French 26 | 23 | 26 | $$$

Long Island City | 43-15 Crescent St.
(bet. 43rd Ave. & 44th Rd.) | Queens
718-786-9060 | magasinwells.com

"O Canada," proclaim devotees of this "off-the-wall" yet completely "on-target" Long Island City steakhouse, which pairs an "excellent" Québécois-infused French menu with a "cool," "upscale" backdrop in what was once an auto-body shop and that now includes an open kitchen featuring a live trout tank; add it all up, and you've got a "lovely" (albeit "expensive") way to "feed your inner glutton."

Mable's Smokehouse Barbecue

23 | 17 | 18 | $$

Williamsburg | 44 Berry St. (11th St.) | Brooklyn
718-218-6655 | mablessmokehouse.com

For that hard-to-find roadhouse atmosphere in the big city, with lively "crowds" and smoked meats, like "tender brisket" "done to perfection," visit Williamsburg and go hog wild; the "nothing-fancy" interior is like a "mess hall," and the service, while "timely," is more bar than restaurant, but the honest prices, Southern charm, and come-as-you-are approach make it all worth it.

Madame Vo Vietnamese

23 | 17 | 20 | $$

East Village | 212 E 10th St. (bet. 1st & 2nd Aves.)
917-261-2115 | madamevonyc.com

"Sublime" "smells take over all your senses" as you enter this "always-packed" East Village restaurant, which entices with "homestyle Vietnamese" fare (most feel the "fabulous, filling" pho's the way to go); "tiny" and "noisy," it "does not stand out decor-wise," but the staff "gets the job done," "and the bill won't make you regret ordering the whole menu."

NEW Madame Vo BBQ Vietnamese

– | – | – | $$$

East Village | 104 2nd Ave. (6th St.)
917-675-7570 | madamevonyc.com

At this spin-off a few blocks south of the original, the focus is on a set menu celebrating beef seven ways, grilled for you at the table and served with the rice paper and vegetables you need to form them into tasty rolls; there's also a large à la carte menu that includes other meaty selections as well as a popular whole catfish dish; the vivid interior is decorated with tropical plant prints, aqua walls, and pop art.

NEW Madre M American/European

– | – | – | $$$

Greenpoint | 214 Franklin St. | (bet. Green & Huron Sts.)
718-389-8700 | madrenyc.com

This pan-European nook in the Greenpoint's Franklin Guest-house feels as boutiquey and cozy as the little hotel it's in; the wood paneling, a modern, globe-trotting, seasonal menu, and a creative mezcal cocktail list also do a fine job representing the diversity and trendiness of North Brooklyn; sit by the large front windows to take in the scene, or dine in the palm-shaded booths.

Z Maialino Italian

26 | 25 | 25 | $$$$

Gramercy | Gramercy Park Hotel
2 Lexington Ave. (21st St.)
212-777-2410 | maialinonyc.com

"Danny Meyer knows his stuff," declare devotees of his "classy" Italian spot overlooking "the trees of Gramercy Park" – a "special place" dispensing "scrumptious" Rome-inspired farm-to-table fare and "amazing" wines in a "charming farmhouse setting" with a fireplace; the "vibrant" feel is bolstered by "expert service," plus walk-in seating at the bar, and although tabs are "costly," the "no-tipping policy" is "a plus."

Maiella Italian   24 24 22 $$$

Long Island City | 4610 Center Blvd.
(46th Ave.) | Queens
718-606-1770 | maiellalic.com

"Right on the water in LIC" ("amazing Midtown and East River
views"), this "elevated Italian" enchants with its "mix of old and
new" dishes, including pizzas and the "must-have" house pasta,
swirled in a flaming cheese wheel tableside; it's "a little campy,
but still a place for a nice night out" with a date on the "delight-
ful patio" – and the "big circular bar is always inviting for single
diners to saddle up to" too.

Maison Harlem French   22 21 23 $$

Harlem | 341 St. Nicholas Ave. (127th St.)
212-222-9224 | maisonharlem.com

Diners come to this "easygoing" and "solid" bistro a few blocks
from the Apollo for its "nice," "almost-French-countryside" feel;
"quintessential" Parisian eats like "divine" mussels, "darn good"
steak, and quiche Lorraine might be expected, but some "less
common" fare stands out on the already "creative" menu;
inside, "lovely" servers float around the "warm," brick-covered
dining room.

Maison Pickle American   22 22 22 $$$

West 80s | 2315 Broadway (84th St.)
212-496-9100 | maisonpickle.com

"Enormous" French dips, fourteen-layer cakes that'll take you
to "carb heaven," "gigantic" dishes from an "eccentric menu,"
and "New Orleans speakeasy" cocktails help Upper West
Siders "eat, drink, and be merry" from breakfast through late
at this spinoff of Jacob's Pickles; a trendy crowd that includes
"leisurely" eaters rarely mind the "overwhelming" social com-
motion surrounding them, especially when it's all so "festive"
and framed by "gorgeous" lighting fixtures.

Maison Premiere Seafood   26 28 25 $$$

Williamsburg | 298 Bedford Ave. (1st St.) | Brooklyn
347-335-0446 | maisonpremiere.com

"Are we in New Orleans?" some ponder as they step into this
"lovely locale" – and "attractive" back garden – modeled after
the vintage cocktail haunts sprinkled up and down Magazine
and Bourbon Streets; you'll have to "fight the crowds" for
"always-fresh" oysters and "astounding" absinthe cocktails, but
linger for the sharply dressed bartenders who "put on a show"
and chat about "food, wine, cocktails, and life."

NEW Maison Yaki Ⓜ French/Japanese   _ _ _ $$$

Prospect Heights | 626 Vanderbilt Ave.
(Prospect Pl.) | Brooklyn
718-552-2609 | maisonyaki.com

The team behind Prospect Heights' Olmsted has opened this
French-influenced Japanese yakitori spot across the street,
with a menu of playful small plates, such as duck à l'orange
transformed into an addictive skewered meatball, and a drink
list with wine, sake, and cocktails inspired by Europe as well
as Asia – the retro bar overlooks a backyard with appealing
pétanque (lawn bowling) courts, and the prices are reasonable,
although the small plates can add up.

⚡Majorelle ⑤ French   27 | 29 | 28 | $$$
East 60s | 28 E 63rd St. (bet. Madison & Park Aves.)
212-935-2888 | lowellhotel.com/restaurants-and-bar
"Pricey but what an experience!"; escape from the "busy New York streets" into this "serene" UES getaway with the Top Decor rating—the "prettiest in town," blooming like an "architectural garden" with "to-die-for" flower arrangements; what takes the Lowell Hotel's signature dining room to the "highest caliber" is the "see-and-be-seen" crowd – "wear your jewels" here – and "hard-to-beat" French fare, "served beautifully" and with slightly Moroccan-influenced flavors.

MáLà Project Chinese   24 | 20 | 20 | $$
East Village | 122 1st Ave. (bet. 7th & 8th Sts.)
212-353-8880 | malaproject.nyc
West 40s | 41 W 46th St. (bet. 5th & 6th Aves.)
917-261-7520
"You pick the ingredients and they mix it up" for the "chilihead"-friendly dry pots here; those, along with "mix-and-match" accompaniments and dessert rice balls, provide a delightful "textural trip" that will "challenge what you think you know" about Sichuan cuisine; these spots in the East Village and near Bryant Park are "game changers" for those ready to "eat everything," with "huge" portions that'll thrill "each of the five senses."

Malaparte Italian/Pizza   22 | 18 | 20 | $$
West Village | 753 Washington St. (Bethune St.)
212-255-2122
The "out-of-the-way" location of this "cozy" and "genuine" neighborhood trattoria in the West Village adds to its "low-key," "any-day" allure; the kitchen specializes in the cuisine of Italy's Emilia-Romagna region, and its homemade pastas, grilled calamari, pizzas, and other dishes are "consistently well prepared" and "served by a friendly and efficient staff"; on top of all this, its prices "won't break the bank."

Malatesta Trattoria ⊘ Italian   25 | 19 | 22 | $$
West Village | 649 Washington St. (Christopher St.)
212-741-1207
For "casual, cheap, tasty Italian" and pastas to "dream about," including "pillowy" gnocchi, this is the "perfect cozy, candlelit spot"; "a sidewalk table here on a warm summer night is a thing of beauty," and the outdoor seating adds even more value to the "incredibly reasonable prices" on the wine and food; note that reservations are only for four or more, and only cash is accepted.

Malecon ℂ Caribbean   23 | 10 | 17 | $$
Washington Heights | 4141 Broadway (175th St.)
212-927-3812 | maleconrestaurants.com
West 90s | 764 Amsterdam Ave. (bet. 97th & 98th Sts.)
212-864-5648
Kingsbridge | 5592 Broadway (231st St.) | Bronx
718-432-5155
It's all about the "heavenly" rotisserie chicken with "oh that garlic slather" at these casual and "lively" Dominican joints; their portions are "huge" ("plan to nap afterward"), their value is "great," the so-so interiors make it most popular for takeout,

and service can be inconsistent, but overall it's a "lively" spot that's made for a "hungry group gathering" – major lunch specials, too.

Maloney & Porcelli Steakhouse   25 | 22 | 24 | $$$
East 50s | 37 E 50th St. (bet. Madison & Park Aves.)
212-750-2233 | maloneyandporcelli.com
"A power dining experience" is yours at this "old-school" Midtown steakhouse, a "high-quality" establishment for "excellent" dry-aged meats (plus the "famous" crackling pork shank) and "fabulous" martinis in a "clubby" space featuring balcony seating (along with a "lively" bar scene); you may need "an expense-account budget" to pay, but its business-lunch "convenience" and "strong" service remain strong, and there's always the nightly prix fixe dinner that includes wine – a relative deal.

Mama's Too Pizza   25 | 10 | 17 | $
West 100s | 2750 Broadway
212-510-7256 | mamastoo.com
"Pepperoni fans are ecstatic" about the "splendid" rectangular slices baked to "crackly-crisp perfection" at this UWS "takeout joint"; the counter service is distracted and the interior feels "cramped" because of "crazy lines," but most find this slice heaven "exceeds the hype"; this is pizza so good that "you might want to eat it alone" – and not just because of the danger of grease appearing on your chin.

Manducatis 🖾 Italian   25 | 18 | 25 | $$
Long Island City | 13-27 Jackson Ave. (47th Ave.)
Queens | 718-729-4602 | manducatis.com
Manducatis Rustica
Long Island City | 46-33 Vernon Blvd.
(bet. 46th & 47th Sts.) | Queens
718-937-1312 | manducatisrustica.com
From the "scent of roasted garlic" to the "flavor of ripe, red tomatoes," the "dependable and delicious homemade Italian food" at this LIC mainstay will make you "feel like you're in your grandparents' home"; it's "old school" in all the right ways, including "hearty portions" and a "good wine list"; the second location's a "more youthful version" of the original.

Manetta's Ristorante 🖾 Italian/Pizza   26 | 21 | 25 | $$
Long Island City | 10-76 Jackson Ave. (11th St.) | Queens
718-786-6171 | manettaslic.com
More than 25 years old, this family-owned site "continues to impress" with its "consistent" "real homemade" "Manhattan-quality Italian fare for LIC prices," including wood-fired brick oven pizza, served by "excellent" staff amid a "rustic," "comforting atmosphere"; "in the winter sit next to the roaring fireplace" and in summer go for a sidewalk seat; either way, you'll feel "at home."

🛿 Manhatta French   24 | 28 | 25 | $$$$
Financial District | 28 Liberty St., 60th Fl.
(bet. Nassau & William Sts.)
212-230-5788 | manhattarestaurant.com
Danny Meyer's latest offers a "breathtaking" "bird's-eye view of FiDi" and beyond, "looking north to the Empire/Chrysler

buildings and south to the harbor" from an "elegant yet relaxed" space 60 floors up; if the "glorified French bistro" prix fixe (the only option) "doesn't quite live up to the surroundings," it's "far better than one might expect," and presented with "warm, welcoming," and "high-energy" service; P.S. tips are included.

Manzo Italian   26 | 18 | 22 | $$$
Flatiron | Eataly, 200 5th Ave. (bet. 23rd & 24th Sts.)
212-229-2180 | eataly.com

"Superb and unique" is how fans describe the offerings at this Italian steakhouse, whose name translates as "beef"; its "tasty" plates of "quality" food include bone-in NY strip steak, tagliatelle Bolognese, and "exceptional" steak tartares, and come with "excellent" service; walled off from the rest of the Eataly market, the rustic space has a full dining room that overlooks its glass-enclosed butcher room.

Mapo Korean B.B.Q. Korean   ▼ 26 | 12 | 21 | $$
Flushing | 149-24 41st Ave. (149th Pl.) | Queens
718-886-8292

"Flavorful" kalbi (ribs) and "premium" meat cuts are cooked on a charcoal grill at your table at this Korean BBQ; you "get what you pay for" here, given the "limited" options but "scrumptious" quality that's served; the Flushing dining room is worn around the edges, but the many families that head here don't seem to mind.

NEW Mar Seafood/Spanish   — | — | — | $$$
West 30s | 10 Hudson Yards
(10th Ave. & 30th St.)
646-495-1242 | littlespain.com

At this full-service offering at José Andres and the Adrià brothers' expansive Mercado Little Spain food court and market, the haul includes seasonal fish dishes, including large-format paella, and prawn recipes resurrected from El Bulli, with a wide selection of Spanish wine meant to match the marine flavors; the on-site fishmonger sells fresh catches with the recipes and other ingredients necessary to re-create favorites at home.

Marc Forgione American   26 | 24 | 24 | $$$
TriBeCa | 134 Reade St.
(bet. Greenwich & Hudson Sts.)
212-941-9401 | marcforgione.com

The food is "endlessly inventive" at this TriBeCa mainstay, where the "ethereal" roast chicken (cooked under a brick, and portioned to share) reigns supreme, along with other "exciting" seasonal New American fare and a "thoughtful" wine list, all accompanied by "top-notch" service ("Forgione can often be spotted on the premises"); flickering candles keep things "cozy" and "romantic" in the crisp, brick-walled space with wood tables and "troves of culinary treasures."

Z Marea Italian   28 | 26 | 26 | $$$$
West 50s | 240 Central Park S (bet. B'way & 7th Ave.)
212-582-5100 | marearestaurant.com

"An oasis of civility" on Central Park South, Michael White's "sophisticated" West 50s Italian "masterpiece" showcases "pristine" seafood, "unbelievable" house-made pastas, and other "sublime" eats – along with "outstanding" wines, a "cool" bar and "solicitous" servers – in a "sexy," "buzzy" space frequented by "A-listers"; while the tab may "make your eyes water," lunch is a relative "bargain," and with brunch choices rounding things out, it's a "special occasion" spot that's sure to elicit "swoons."

Mari Vanna Russian   24 | 24 | 20 | $$$ |
Flatiron | 41 E 20th St. (bet. B'way & Park Ave. S)
212-777-1955 | marivanna.ru
Decorated like a "kitschy" "country house," this "comfy," "soulful" Flatiron charmer is "like eating in your Russian grandmother's" place; although it "can be noisy" during the weekend brunch buffet, and the service is "not so good when you're unknown," it's "still one of the best parties in town," with "well-prepared" Slavic classics to be chased with "many varieties" of vodka.

Maria Pia Italian   21 | 18 | 21 | $$ |
West 50s | 319 W 51st St. (8th Ave.)
212-765-6463
For "friendly, neighborhood" "homestyle" Italian cooking, consider this casual, "cozy" "good bet" in Midtown West with "efficient" service; because it is so "small," you "may have to wait for a table," but the "budget" pre-theater prix fixe is "a deal" in just the area "where you need" to find one, making it "worth walking a few extra blocks" north away from the madness of Times Square.

Mario's Ⓜ Italian   23 | 17 | 23 | $$ |
Arthur Avenue/Belmont | 2342 Arthur Ave.
(bet. Crescent Ave. & 184th St.) | Bronx
718-584-1188 | mariosarthurave.com
"If you want Neapolitan food in this legendary Italian neighborhood," come to this Arthur Avenue icon, where "top-notch" servers "know their regulars"; sure, the somewhat tired white-tablecloth "decor could use an upgrade," and it gets pretty "crowded," but when you're digging into the "hearty food with heart" – pizza and pasta and lots more – you remember that they've "been around about 100 years" for a reason.

The Mark Restaurant ℂ French   23 | 24 | 23 | $$$ |
East 70s | 25 E 77th St. (bet. 5th & Madison Aves.)
212-606-3030 | themarkrestaurantnyc.com
A hotel restaurant that comes with the imprimatur of Jean-Georges Vongerichten, this "sophisticated" spot near the Metropolitan Museum of Art is "on par" with his other crowd-pleasers, drawing a "cool clientele" ("don't be surprised if you see celebrities, particularly on weeknights") for the "impressive" American menu and an equally fine wine list; ask for a table under the skylight in the "fabulous" atrium.

Market Table American   22 | 19 | 22 | $$$ |
West Village | 54 Carmine St. (Bedford St.)
212-255-2100 | markettablenyc.com
"Tucked away" on the two and a half blocks that make up Carmine, this is a handy spot for dinner before or after jazz at the

nearby Village Vanguard; the farm-to-table menu packs in "lots of variety" and is "gluten-free friendly" – it "tends toward the healthy but does not go overboard"; through the "large picture windows" facing the street you can "watch the West Village crowd walk by," and the service is always "attentive."

Marlow & Sons American ▼ 24 | 23 | 23 | $$$
Williamsburg | 81 Broadway (Berry St.) | Brooklyn
718-384-1441 | marlowandsons.com
"Farm-to-table" provisions mark this long-standing, all-day Williamsburg New American, acknowledged for its seasonally changing dinner menu of consistent "tasty treats," along with its "no-nonsense style," with a small, wood-filled interior that's equal parts farmhouse and old-timey tavern; still going strong, it attracts locals and tourists who dig the bar options and good service, as well as the casual outdoor seating.

The Marshal American 22 | 17 | 21 | $$$
West 40s | 628 10th Ave. (bet. 44th & 45th Sts.)
212-582-6300 | the-marshal.com
Fans of this "quirky" Hell's Kitchen neighborhood hang come for the "imaginative" American farm-to-table fare (there's a "famous" meatloaf) prepared with "always fresh" seasonal ingredients and paired with wine from New York state; it's a "tiny corridor of a restaurant," so some find themselves "packed in like sardines," while others appreciate the "cozy," "homey" feel and "friendly" service.

Marta Italian/Pizza 23 | 21 | 21 | $$$
NoMad | The Redbury Hotel, 29 E 29th St.
(bet. Madison & Park Aves.)
212-651-3800 | martamanhattan.com
"Interesting" "thin-crust" Roman pizzas and wood-fired Italian fare coexist with "lots of buzz" at Danny Meyer's "stylish" joint in NoMad's "oh-so-hip" Redbury New York hotel, where the "great" pies feed an "eclectic crowd" within a "large, bustling space" anchored by the open kitchen; you may "have to yell to be heard by your dinner companion" and some find tabs (which include tips) "expensive," but the overall "convenience" is a plus.

Mary's Fish Camp Seafood 24 | 14 | 21 | $$$
West Village | 64 Charles St. (4th St.)
646-486-2185 | marysfishcamp.com
"The fish is the star" at this "rustic," transporting" spot that brings a "taste of rural Florida" to the West Village; the "no-frills" menu focuses on "the very best seafood": "you can't go wrong with the lobster roll"; the "staff are kind" and for some it even feels like you're "eating right on the water," but be forewarned that "it is small and it is crowded."

Masa Japanese/Sushi 27 | 24 | 27 | $$$$
West 50s | Time Warner Center, 10 Columbus Cir.
(bet. 58th & 59th Sts.)
212-823-9800 | masanyc.com
Sushi exists in "another dimension" at Masayoshi Takayama's Time Warner Center omakase destination, one where you'll pay a "pretty price tag" (around $600 a person) for an "incredible"

meal complete with "amazing" food and "excellent" service; clean lines and Japanese-style greenery keep things "zen," topping off an experience that's "totally worth it," at least for some.

Mastro's Steakhouse Steakhouse 25 21 23 $$$$

West 50s | 1285 6th Ave. (52nd St.)
212-459-1222 | mastrosrestaurants.com

The steaks "cut like a hot knife through butter," but save room for the butter cake that's also sold at the Theater District location of this national chain of "upscale" steakhouses, where tasty seafood options are also available; take a seat in the upstairs lounge for "fabulous live music" while staff "politely" and "professionally" serve; the prices do give reviewers pause, but don't worry, at least the "great bread basket" is free.

Maya Mexican 22 20 20 $$

East 60s | 1191 1st Ave. (bet. 64th & 65th Sts.)
212-585-1818 | eatmaya.com

"Good" Mexican dishes with "modern" stylings stand out at this "festive" UES kitchen and tequileria, known as much for its cuisine as its "flowing" drinks (check out the bottomless brunch), happy hour deals, and bar scene populated by "young people gathering after work"; it is predictably "noisy beyond belief," and some think the decor's "due for an update," but the "hospitable" staff raise spirits, and you can easily eat, drink, and be merry without "breaking the bank."

◪ Meadowsweet Mediterranean 27 24 26 $$$

Williamsburg | 149 Broadway
(bet. Bedford & Driggs Aves.) | Brooklyn
718-384-0673 | meadowsweetnyc.com

Come here for an "artful," seasonal Mediterrranean menu that changes daily, "amazing cocktails" with herbs come from an indoor garden, and a popular, "well-priced" brunch; the "casual, cool, and comfortable" laid-back space functions so well thanks to the "informative," personable team behind the scenes, who run this "hip, young" destination with lots of energy like it's "their living room."

The Meatball Shop Italian 20 15 18 $$

Chelsea | 200 9th Ave. (bet. 22nd & 23rd Sts.)
212-257-4363 | themeatballshop.com
East 70s | 1462 2nd Ave. (bet. 76th & 77th Sts.)
212-257-6121
☾ Lower East Side | 84 Stanton St. (bet. Allen & Orchard Sts.)
212-982-8895
☾ West 50s | 798 9th Ave. (53rd St.) | 212-230-5860
West Village | 64 Greenwich Ave. (11th St.) | 212-982-7815
Williamsburg | 170 Bedford Ave. (bet. 7th & 8th Sts.)
Brooklyn | 718-551-0520

"If it's round, they serve it" at this "fairly priced" mini-chain with a "mix and match" menu of "quick comfort food" that's "basic but delicious," in a "hopping place" with "upbeat service"; grab some for takeout or dine in for "weeknight dinners" that "the kids will thank you" for – they'll have the choice of "every kind of meatball imaginable," including impressive "alternatives for vegetarians and gluten-free diners."

Meijin Ramen Japanese/Ramen ▼ | 28 | 19 | 25 | $$ |

East 80s | 1574 2nd Ave. (82nd St.)
212-327-2800 | meijinramen.net

Not many UES competitors can match this neighborly ramen joint's "Osaka-quality" beef broths and "yummy" noodles "cooked to perfection," but don't count out the "solid" steamed buns and shishito peppers appetizer, either; consistent and strong hospitality is delivered by "attentive" servers aiming to please, giving an extra shine to the "low-key" dining room.

Melba's Southern | 26 | 20 | 23 | $$ |

Harlem | 300 W 114th St. (8th Ave.)
212-864-7777 | melbasrestaurant.com

This Harlem "institution" for Southern comfort food is chicken and waffles heaven, where the "fresh," "well-seasoned" menu is executed with "finesse" and presented with warm service – especially "if you are lucky enough to meet Melba" herself, "the most gracious host in town"; the "high-energy" space is so "small" and "packed" that it can barely fit the "huge" portions, but the "drinks are nice and strong," making it all go down easy.

MeMe's Diner Ⓜ Diner | 23 | 24 | 24 | $$ |

Prospect Heights | 657 Washington Ave.
(bet. Bergen St. & St. Marks Ave.) | Brooklyn
718-636-2900 | memesdiner.com

"They start you off with a little bowl of mixed cereals for the table to munch on" at this welcoming, "unpretentious" space; what you get is "creative," market-driven, "elevated" comfort food – the weekend brunch standouts include an "amazing Dutch pancake" and biscuits – in a "seamlessly modern-retro" Prospect Heights space lined with leather banquettes and brightened by expressive portraits on the walls; P.S. no lunch weekdays, and no reservations.

Mercato ◖ Italian | 24 | 19 | 22 | $$ |

West 30s | 352 W 39th St. (bet. 8th & 9th Aves.)
212-643-2000 | mercatonyc.com

This is "a real NY find" in the "shadow of the Port Authority," where you'll dine on a "fairly priced" menu of Italian specialties like "fab" seared octopus and "homemade" gnocchi with "fragrant ragù" as you sit "elbow to elbow with the table next to you"; this brick-walled trattoria's service is "efficient," and the "old posters" adorning the walls feel quite rustic for Midtown.

The Mercer Kitchen ◖ French | 22 | 22 | 20 | $$$ |

SoHo | Mercer Hotel, 99 Prince St. (Mercer St.)
212-966-5454 | themercerkitchen.com

Jean-Georges Vongerichten's iconic spot may "be underground, but the food is uplifting," with a well-regarded burger and other "accessible," "consistently" tasty dishes available from morning through late night, when the bar becomes the place to be seen; if the "dark" basement location, a "hip and trendy" destination since its inception two decades ago, makes you "claustrophobic," the upstairs café is a brighter option.

| | FOOD | DECOR | SERVICE | COST |

☑ The Mermaid Inn Seafood   23 | 19 | 21 | $$$

East Village | 96 2nd Ave. (bet. 5th & 6th Sts.)
212-674-5870 | themermaidnyc.com
West 80s | 570 Amsterdam Ave. (bet. 87th & 88th Sts.)
212-799-7400
Mermaid Oyster Bar
Greenwich Village | 79 MacDougal St.
(bet. Bleecker & Houston Sts.) | 212-260-0100
Serving "creative, delicious iterations of seafood favorites,"
including "reasonably priced" oysters, clams, and fish tacos,
these "comfy" "charming" neighborhood locations are also
known for "fantastic cocktails"; "drop anchor" for the oyster
happy hour (all night on Mondays) and in summer head to the
"lovely patio" in the East Village to feel like "you're outside
NYC"; complimentary chocolate pudding is a "sweet sendoff."

Mexico Lindo Ⓜ Mexican   23 | 17 | 22 | $$

Murray Hill | 459 2nd Ave. (26th St.)
212-679-3665 | mexicolindonyc.com
Now in its second generation of family ownership, this Murray
Hill classic for "old-fashioned" Mexican standbys, like "A+
guacamole," has been sizzling fajitas "since the '70s," and "forty
years later, the margarita pitchers are still flowing" in "warm,"
"friendly" surroundings; the decor could use a bit of sprucing
up, but the portion sizes and cheery service still work just fine.

Mezzaluna Italian   21 | 15 | 20 | $$

East 70s | 1295 3rd Ave. (74th St.)
212-535-9600 | mezzalunanyc.com
Open since 1984, this UES classic is "always packed and always
serving consistently" appealing Italian food, including wood-
fired pizzas and "pasta like Grandma made in her kitchen in Italy"; too many tables mean you "need a shoehorn to be seated,"
and the atmosphere is "frantic" and the staff often "harried," but
the "reliable" offerings are "worth a bit of discomfort."

Michael's Ⓢ American   23 | 23 | 24 | $$$

West 50s | 24 W 55th St. (bet. 5th & 6th Aves.)
212-767-0555 | michaelsnewyork.com
At this "classic New York–LA" "who's-who kind of place" in
Midtown, the attractions are "fresh, inventive, and breezy" Italian
dishes, modern art (yep, that's a Hockney), and a vibe that moves
from "power lunch" ("club atmosphere and a tab to match") to
"tranquil and civilized evenings"; "movers and shakers" prefer the
front room, but out back you get a view of the garden.

Mile End Delicatessen Deli   23 | 15 | 19 | $$

Boerum Hill | 97 Hoyt St.
(bet. Atlantic Ave. & Pacific St.)
Brooklyn | 718-852-7510 | mileenddeli.com
Showing locals "a thing or two about the deli experience,"
this "Montreal–New York hybrid with plate-licking poutine and
house-made smoked meats" will "satisfy your inner bubbe," if
you can handle "lines out the door" for the Jewish comfort food
(latkes, matzo ball soup) and "creative sandwiches" at this Boerum Hill café ("don't sleep on the brisket hash," either); "shared
tables are friendly and social" in the "cramped space."

Milkflower Italian/Pizza   25| 20| 22| $$|

Astoria | 34-12 31st Ave. (bet. 34th & 35th Sts.) | Queens
718-204-1300 | milkflowernyc.com

"Funky" "Neapolitan-style" pies with a "slight chew," "fun"
starters, and a "small" and carefully curated beer selection
keep "energetic" crowds coming to this Astoria pizzeria; the
"main focus" of the "simple" "neighborhood" setting is the large
"wood-fired" pizza oven – and you'll hear plenty of "loud" conversations about it, given the "not huge" space.

Mill Basin Deli Deli   24| 15| 19| $$|

Mill Basin | 5823 Avenue T
(bet. 58th & 59th Sts.) | Brooklyn
718-241-4910 | millbasindeli.com

An "unsung hero" of the "fading," "no-nonsense" Jewish deli
scene, this Mill Basin spot serves chopped liver, salads, and so
much else for a "loyal, aging" fan base; "from the pickles" to
the "mouthwatering" pastrami on "big, thick" rye, "everything
is finely crafted" – and "the soups (and we're not just talking
matzo ball) are quite flavorful and comforting"; the "old era" interior, with Erté-style art deco paintings mounted on the walls,
hasn't changed much through the decades.

The Milling Room American   23| 24| 22| $$$|

West 80s | 446 Columbus Ave.
(bet. 81st & 82nd Sts.)
212-595-0380 | themillingroom.com

Regulars don't want to "share the secret" of their "handsome"
"haunt" in the "restaurant-dense" part of the UWS, partially to
keep the dramatic glass atrium views to themselves, but mainly
to avoid "amplifying the sound" in the "terribly noisy" space,
though the tavern-like area is quieter; the "interesting" American dishes blend "locally sourced" ingredients with "simple
but creative" platings, but the happy hour and once-weekly
corkage-free "perk" get many diners most excited.

Mimi French   24| 19| 23| $$$|

Greenwich Village | 185 Sullivan St.
(bet. Bleecker & Houston Sts.)
212-418-1260 | miminyc.com

"Expect decadence in every small bite" at this "quaint" Greenwich Village "gem" dishing up a rotating menu of "surprising"
"riffs" on French classics available for an "affordable" prix fixe
or à la carte; "personable," "engaging" waiters add to the "intimate" atmosphere that some feel can be "cramped and noisy,"
while others say is "perfect for a romantic dinner à deux."

Mimi Cheng's Chinese   21| 15| 18| $|

East Village | 179 2nd Ave. (12th St.)
212-533-2007 | mimichengs.com
NoLita | 380 Broome St. (bet. Mott & Mulberry Sts.)
212-343-1387

"Modern," "lighter" jiaozi-style Taiwanese dumplings may be
highly "Instagrammable" at this "boutique" fast-casual concept,
but "cool" monthly collaborations and watching the team assemble each mouthful "by hand" in the open kitchen prevents these

"better-than-expected" bites from seeming too basic; you're better off eating them on the go, though, since the "uncomfortable" seating is "not built" for leisurely "hanging and chatting."

Mimi's Hummus   Middle Eastern   23 | 12 | 22 | $$
Ditmas Park | 1209 Cortelyou Rd.
(bet. Argyle & Westminster Rds.) | Brooklyn
718-284-4444 | mimishummus.com

"Sublime" hummus meets meze, "tons" of "warm" pita bread, kebabs, and salads "galore," all in "generous portions," at this "pleasant" vegetarian-friendly Middle Eastern café in Ditmas Park that's open all day for breakfast, lunch, and dinner; "friendly" servers work the "unassuming" space, which can get "crowded," but the consensus is that it's worth it.

⚡ Minetta Tavern ◖ French   25 | 23 | 23 | $$$
Greenwich Village | 113 MacDougal St. (Minetta Ln.)
212-475-3850 | minettatavernny.com

The "historic" tavern's Black Label Burger makes "grown men cry," but "excellent French bistro" dishes ("big slabs" of côte de boeuf, homemade chocolate soufflé) are also "worth the splurge"; the Greenwich Village destination's interior is a throwback to "the speakeasy days," with "swanky" red vinyl upholstery and dark wood embellishments; it's nearly always "crowded and happening," but you'll "never feel cramped" inside this "festive and special" spot.

Miriam   Middle Eastern   24 | 18 | 20 | $$
Park Slope | 79 5th Ave. (Prospect Pl.) | Brooklyn
718-622-2250 | miriamrestaurant.com

"Brunch lines may reach Tel Aviv" at this "solid" Park Slope café near the Barclays Center "that goes beyond flapjacks and eggs Benedict" ("they have perfected the chicken schnitzel") and includes "delicious Israeli-inspired dishes" ("top-notch shakshuka"), "reliable healthy food," and "tasty vegetarian options"; the style is "warm and welcoming," and suited to everyone from "date types" to groups of 10 and beyond.

Misi   Italian   26 | 24 | 24 | $$$
Williamsburg | 329 Kent Ave.
(bet. 3rd & 4th Sts.) | Brooklyn
347-566-3262 | misinewyork.com

Try to "save room for gelato" at this "sleek, modern space," but holding back might be impossible, because the "astonishing vegetables" almost eclipse the "mouthwatering pastas"; the "artistry and creativity" of chef Missy Robbins (also behind the nearby Lilia) is "impressive," and the enamored say it's "everything that the hype told me it would be"; the servers are "attentive and knowledgeable about the menu," but "even with a reservation the wait can be extreme."

⚡ Miss Ada   Middle Eastern   27 | 22 | 24 | $$
Fort Greene | 184 Dekalb Ave. (Carlton St.) | Brooklyn
917-909-1023 | missadanyc.com

"Fill your table with little bowls of dips" and get ready to "share" your chow at this Fort Greene Middle Eastern hangout, where the "flavorful," "high-quality" Mediterranean preparations are

augmented by herbs from the on-site garden, which doubles
as a charming patio; suffice it to say the "small" space "can
get crowded," but it's "romantic" enough for "a cool date" –
especially with such "friendly" service and "decent prices."

Miss Korea BBQ (Korean   20 | 16 | 15 | $$
West 30s | 10 W 32nd St. (bet. B'way & 5th Ave.)
212-594-4963 | misskoreabbq.com
"Come to chow down" on "huge" portions of Korean BBQ served
24 hours a day at this bustling three-story behemoth in the West
30s, where "each floor has a different vibe"; the first, "loud" and
touristy, is "fun" for after-hours fill-ups, the second ("fancy")
offers "a prix fixe feast of Imperial cuisine," and the third is a
modern bar; detractors find the "spacious" interiors a bit hokey
and call the service "friendly" but "too busy to care" about fixing
issues.

Miss Lily's 7A Cafe (Caribbean   20 | 22 | 19 | $$
East Village | 109 Avenue A (7th St.)
212-812-1482 | misslilys.com
Miss Lily's
Greenwich Village | 132 W Houston St (Sullivan St.)
212-812-1482
"If you're in the mood for a party," follow the "amazing dancehall
music" to this "playful" Jamaican staple that's always "super
fun" for people-watching and overflowing with "good vibes"; the
"homestyle" Caribbean menu stands out for being "better than
it needs to be," particularly the "off-the-charts" side dishes and
a frozen Dark 'n' Stormy that's "not to be missed."

Miss Mamie's Spoonbread   22 | 14 | 18 | $$
Too Southern
Morningside Heights | 366 W 110th St. (Columbus Ave.)
212-865-6744 | spoonbreadinc.com
"Down-home" soul food is the specialty at this "relaxed" Morningside Heights destination, where the fried chicken is a "favorite" accompanied by "traditional" sides (including collard greens
and some of the "best" mac and cheese), with coconut cake or
peach cobbler for dessert; "friendly" servers work around the
formica tables in the "little" space, where waiting times can be
"long, long, long," but "worth" it.

Mission Chinese Food Chinese   21 | 18 | 17 | $$$
Lower East Side | 171 E Broadway
(bet. Jefferson & Rutgers Sts.)
917-376-5660 | missionchinesefood.com
Bushwick | 599 Johnson Ave.
(bet. Gardner & Scott Aves.)
Brooklyn | 718-628-3731
"Unique spins on Chinese food" bring adventurous eaters to
these "innovative" LES and Bushwick spots, where spicy dishes
("wings are the must-order") balance out cool drinks, and the
"sceney" space feels "quirky" to some and "bonkers" to others;
the level of service and noise that comes with the territory
won't work for everyone, but if you go with a "big group," it is an
"impressive" (but "pricey") way to experience "original" and "delectable combinations"; P.S. the Brooklyn location is dinner-only.

Miznon Middle Eastern   25 | 12 | 16 | $

Chelsea | Chelsea Market, 435 W 15th St.
(bet. 9th & 10th Aves.)
646-490-5871 | miznonnyc.com

NEW West **70s** | 161 W 72nd St.
(bet. Amsterdam & Columbus Aves.)

"There is always a line" at this "casual" Tel Aviv–based chain, so grab a seat at the counter if you can for creative sandwiches on "cloud-like" pita bread and a "whole roasted cauliflower" that makes kebab lovers wonder how "vegetables could taste so good"; service is street-food "fast," and the "chaotic" atmosphere and minimal decor are standard for Chelsea Market, further nailing down its position as a "welcome addition to the cheap eats scene." N.B. a new UWS location opened this year.

Modern Love   ▼ 23 | 18 | 23 | $$

Brooklyn Ⓜ Vegan/Vegetarian
Williamsburg | 317 Union Ave. (1st St.) | Brooklyn
929-298-0626 | modernlovebrooklyn.com

The vegan "re-creations" of American dishes here, like steak made out of cauliflower and cashew-based mozzarella sticks, are "creative," all while staying "pretty affordable"; this bold dining room (Parisian-style seating, industrial-style lighting fixtures, plants and cut mirrors adorning the walls) and charmingly illustrated bathrooms are suitably modern, too.

❷ The Modern American   28 | 27 | 27 | $$$$

West 50s | 9 W 53rd St. (bet. 5th & 6th Aves.)
212-333-1220 | themodernnyc.com

The "wonderful, inventive" contemporary French cuisine at this "Danny Meyer triumph" is "as beautiful and precise as the art" in the Museum of Modern Art upstairs; the "most romantic tables overlook the museum's sculpture garden," but no matter where you're seated in the "elegant" room, the "polished" "service exceeds all expectations"; try the "buzzy" casual bar for an "equally delicious" but less expensive option; the restaurant has a no-tipping policy.

Molly's ℂ Gastropub   20 | 18 | 21 | $$

Gramercy | 287 3rd Ave.
(bet. 22nd & 23rd Sts.)
212-889-3361 | mollysshebeennyc.com

When in the mood for a "sawdust-on-the-floor" "casual" meal served by staff who "engage patrons with a true brogue," come to this "comfortable" Gramercy Park pub that is as ideal for "hearty dining" as it is for "a beer, burger, and watching the game" alongside "Irish memorabilia" and a fireplace that's "cozy in the winter"; here the formula "never changes": "music, food, and Guinness – the holy trinity."

Molyvos Greek   23 | 20 | 22 | $$$

West 50s | 871 7th Ave. (bet. 55th & 56th Sts.)
212-582-7500 | molyvos.com

"Classic Greek food with modern twists and an award-winning all-Greek wine list" make this roomy West 50s taverna, decorated in a rustic but minimalist style, an easy choice if you're heading to Carnegie Hall or City Center; despite being in "tourist territory," dishes are "prepared with finesse," the "service is solid, and the prices are doable."

☑ Momofuku Ko Ⓜ American   28 | 24 | 26 | $$$$

East Village | 8 Extra Pl. (1st St.)
212-203-8095 | ko.momofuku.com

"You feel part of the kitchen" at the East Village "crown jewel" of David Chang's empire, with "one of the best tasting menus in the city" and an "innovative" "challenge to the echelon of haute cuisine"; the "sleek, minimalist setting" and service that leaves "nary a napkin left unfolded" makes for "special occasions sans stuffiness"; the prices are "steep" and it's "very hard to get in," but they do serve walk-ins at the "underrated" bar, which offers à la carte ordering.

Momofuku Nishi Italian   22 | 18 | 21 | $$

Chelsea | 232 8th Ave. (22nd St.)
646-565-4109 | nishi.momofuku.com

Everyone has a favorite dish on David Chang's "take on Italian" menu, but it's the ceci e pepe (chickpea-derived miso and pepper), a riff on cacio e pepe, that comes up again and again; the whole menu is "unbelievably creative" in its integration of ingredients, and the cocktails and wine selections are also fine, but the storefront location is "extremely noisy" and you might find yourself "sitting way too close to strangers."

☑ Momofuku Noodle Bar Ramen   24 | 20 | 22 | $$

East Village | 171 1st Ave. (bet. 10th & 11th Sts.)
212-777-7773 | momofukunoodlebar.com
West 50s | Time Warner Center (3rd Fl.)

There is still "always a wait" for the "O.G. NYC ramen experience" at this pair of destinations in the East Village and Time Warner Center; "hop up on a stool, cozy in at a communal table," and "try the specials," but don't miss the "fluffy buns," "bouncy, fresh noodles," and "rich broth" that made them famous; more than the "knowledgeable" staff and "standard" decor, you come here for reliable "late-night eats" and an "affordable way to eat David Chang's food."

☑ Momofuku Ssäm Bar Pan-Asian   26 | 19 | 22 | $$$

East Village | 207 2nd Ave. (13th St.)
212-254-3500 | ssambar.momofuku.com

The "pork buns are still as good as ever" at this East Village icon and outpost of the David Chang empire, but the "eclectic" and "creative" menu also continues to evolve over time and "doesn't miss a beat"; the place has a "jovial atmosphere" and remains "cool," making it "great for dinner dates or drinks at the bar"; "reservations can be tough" at peak times still, leading some regulars to suggest it's "a good place to stop for lunch."

Momosan Ramen   25 | 18 | 22 | $$
& Sake Japanese/Ramen

Murray Hill | 342 Lexington Ave.
(bet. 39th & 40th Sts.)
646-201-5529 | momosanramen.com

You'd expect such "fine ramen" from the original Iron Chef, Masaharu Morimoto, but reasonable prices are a welcome surprise, especially in a Murray Hill joint so close to Grand Central, and there's "often a wait" to squeeze into the "narrow," casual, "izakaya-like setting"; on offer are the standard Japanese noodle shop dishes, like pork buns, but there are also "imaginative" and cheffy twists, like a combination of dan dan noodles and curry ramen, as well as a broad selection of sake.

Momoya Japanese/Sushi   24 | 19 | 21 | $$$
Chelsea | 185 7th Ave. (21st St.)
212-989-4466 | momoyanyc.com
West 80s | 427 Amsterdam Ave.
(bet. 80th & 81st Sts.)
212-580-0007
This "Japanese standout" with UWS and Chelsea locations is "more than a neighborhood standby," managing to be "chic and upscale without being too posh," with "comfortable banquettes"; fans praise the "attentive service," the "lengthy sake menu," and especially the "consistent" fish and "wide variety" of other items on the "beyond-sushi menu" of "high-quality" dishes, served in "large portions"; there are "no reservations, so get here early" or "be prepared to wait."

The Monkey Bar ⑤ American   21 | 24 | 22 | $$$
East 50s | 60 E 54th St. (bet. Madison & Park Aves.)
212-288-1010 | monkeybarnewyork.com
At what amounts to a "throwback to Mad Men–era NYC" in Midtown's Hotel Elysée, there's a classic "cocktail scene," "comfortable booths" where you can "actually have a conversation," and "friendly, efficient service"; the main attraction is the "delightful" interior itself, with "walls of caricatures" and wood-carved primates; most come to experience a "relic" of "classic New York" firsthand, but the updated menu, mainly inspired by midcentury classics, are "better than they have to be."

Montebello ⑤ Italian   24 | 20 | 25 | $$$
East 50s | 120 E 56th St. (bet. Lexington & Park Aves.)
212-753-1447 | montebellonyc.com
"They make you feel at home" with their "welcoming" "old world" service at this Northern Italian mainstay in the East 50s that serves "fantastic" iterations of classic plates (antipasti, pasta, grilled meat), with a strength in seafood; while it may be "getting a little aged around the edges," most still agree that it's a "lovely" "neighborhood spot."

NEW Montesacro Pinseria Italian   – | – | – | $$
Williamsburg | 432 Union Ave.
(Devoe St.) | Brooklyn
347-916-1062 | montesacrobk.com
This San Francisco original planting a flag in Williamsburg specializes in Roman pinsa (hand-stretched flatbread with toppings similar to pizza), using dough made from an easy-to-digest blend of soy, rice, and wheat flour; they also offer a hearty selection of Italian meats, cheeses, and wine, and a small menu of pasta; the modern yet romantic plant-filled space includes a serene all-weather patio made for date night.

Morandi Italian

| 21 | 20 | 21 | $$ |

West Village | 211 Waverly Pl.
(bet. Charles St. & 7th Ave. S)
212-627-7575 | morandiny.com

Keith McNally certainly "knows how to design a mood and a flavor," say fans of his "extremely popular" Village "neighborhood
staple," which makes "all the right moves"; a visit here means
"simple," "reliable" dishes served in "rustic," "lively" surroundings "that spill outside" in fair weather; "reasonable prices"
and "consistent" service boost its appeal, though if you took
away the "celeb"-studded "people-watching," it might be a fairly
"average" culinary experience.

Morgan's Barbecue C Barbecue

| 23 | 19 | 20 | $$ |

Prospect Heights | 267 Flatbush Ave.
(St. Marks Ave.) | Brooklyn
718-622-2224 | morgansbrooklynbarbecue.com

This "authentic taste of Texas" arrived "in the heart of Brooklyn"
via an alum of Austin's famous Franklin Barbecue; the "outdoor
space" is "picnic tables" plain, and the service is perfunctory,
but they smoke "divine" brisket; whether for friendly gatherings or to watch sports on TV , it's "always a good time," and
perfectly positioned in Prospect Heights for pre-gaming before
"events at the Barclays Center."

Morimoto Japanese/Sushi

| 26 | 27 | 25 | $$$$ |

Chelsea | Chelsea Market, 88 10th Ave.
(bet. 15th & 16th Sts.)
212-989-8883 | morimotonyc.com

Iron Chef–style "culinary wizardry" is on tap at Masaharu
Morimoto's "sophisticated" Chelsea outpost, which features
"creative," "delicately made" takes on Japanese cuisine,
coupled with "refreshing cocktails" and numerous sakes in a
"sleek, futuristic" setting; even if the tab is hard to absorb; the
"extremely friendly" service is just the shiso on top.

Morso Italian

| 25 | 22 | 24 | $$ |

East 50s | 420 E 59th St. (bet. 1st Ave. & Sutton Pl.)
212-759-2706 | morso-nyc.com

A visit to this "perfect neighborhood restaurant" – recognized
for its "sophisticated" food, "elegant" crowd, and a staff who
"treat customers like old friends" – is "like going to Rome"; locals
mention half a dozen favorite dishes, but swear it serves "the
best cacio e pepe (cheese and pepper) pasta in town"; it's also a
"summertime favorite," with a "beautiful" patio that relieves pres-
sure on the "stylish" dining room, where some find the "tables
too close together."

Morton's The Steakhouse Steakhouse

| 24 | 21 | 23 | $$$$ |

East 40s | 551 5th Ave. (45th St.)
212-972-3315 | mortons.com
Financial District | 136 Washington St. (Albany St.)
212-608-0171

A place for "expense-account carnivores," some call this one of
the best steakhouse chains in New York, although that means
every location comes "from the same cookie cutter"; expect
"generous portions" of "tender, juicy steaks prepared the way

you like," with a "wine list to create the perfect pairing" and "courteous" service; while many argue it's "overpriced," just as many say it's "always consistent" and "certainly a go-to."

Motel Morris American   19| 22| 20| $$|

Chelsea | 132 7th Ave. (18th St.)
212-880-4810 | motelmorris.com
With the marine-hued "look of an Atomic Era hotel," this "casually chic" "Chelsea meets South Beach" fauxtel has undeniable "charm," but some say it's best "for bespoke cocktails" at the "buzzy" bar, as the Asian-inflected American "menu is somewhat all over the place" and "the staff could use a little more training"; still, it's also well situated "for Joyce Theater-goers"; P.S. "don't miss" the "retro" bathrooms.

Moti Mahal Delux Indian   23| 15| 18| $$|

East 60s | 1149 1st Ave. (63rd St.)
212-371-3535 | motimahaldelux.us
"My go-to Indian," declare habitués of this corporate-looking branch of a New Delhi–based chain; it has spiced up the "East 60s restaurant scene" with "addictive" "versions of classic items," including "the ultimate butter chicken" (the chain's famous for it); "come with a big appetite" for the lunch special, "not a buffet, but AYCE," "with waiters bringing the dishes to your table" "so the food is fresh" – and a "remarkable value."

Motorino ℂ Pizza   23| 15| 19| $$|

East Village | 349 E 12th St. (bet. 1st & 2nd Aves.)
212-777-2644 | motorinopizza.com
West 80s | 510 Columbus Ave. (85th St.) | 917-675-7581
Williamsburg | 139 Broadway
(bet. Bedford & Driggs Aves.) | Brooklyn
718-599-8899
Thin-crust, wood-fired pies you'll surely devour "in just minutes" and "addictive" meatballs all help make this pizzeria (with three locations) perfect "for what it is"; "you're not there" for aesthetics, but it's obvious this joint is a "labor of love," with "courteous" service that strives to deliver "consistent" food "fairly fast" – although some diners prefer sticking around to fully embrace the "warm, intimate" setting.

Mountain Bird Ⓜ French   28| 19| 26| $$$|

East Harlem | 2162 2nd Ave. (111th St.)
212-744-4422 | tastingsnyc.com/mountain-bird
"Quite exceptional in every way," this "classy without pretension" East Harlem site serves "exquisitely prepared French food" "with a focus on game," although there's an "array of chicken and fish choices" too; the staffers "are really caring" as they welcome you into the rustic interior; the wine list "consists of bottles at the bar for you to select."

Moustache ℂ ⌦ Middle Eastern   26| 14| 22| $$$|

West Village | 90 Bedford St. (bet. Barrow & Grove Sts.)
212-229-2220 | moustachepitza.com
"Hidden" on a West Village side street, this "affordable" "tiny," sparsely decorated storefront serves "some of the best Middle

Eastern food in the city" – we're talking hummus, falafel, and the "fluffiest fresh-baked pitas you'll ever see"; the pitzas are also "interesting and tasty"; the service is "attentive," and the prices are "very reasonable," making it a "place to return to often."

Mr Chow Chinese   23 | 22 | 22 | $$$$
East 50s | 324 E 57th St. (bet. 1st & 2nd Aves.)
212-751-9030 | mrchow.com
TriBeCa | 121 Hudson St. (Moore St.)
212-965-9500
Remember "when this was the hippest place to be?"; the "elegant" East Midtown space, while "pretentious" to some, is still popular for "gourmet Chinese food at its best and most expensive"; a "group is always fun," so you can "order family style"; the TriBeCa location's "covered, elevated patio area actually makes eating outside in NYC enjoyable"; just be sure to "follow the advice of the waiters," and be ready for the bill to arrive with a thud.

Mu Ramen 🚫 Japanese/Ramen   25 | 18 | 22 | $$
Long Island City | 1209 Jackson Ave.
(bet. 47th Rd. & 48th Ave.)
Queens | 718-707-0098 | muramennyc.com
"Take your taste buds for a joyride" around Japan, as "an inspired chef" delivers "amazing appetizers" and "unbeatable ramen" that'll have you "slurping down like a madman" at this LIC locale; the small space contains little more than a few wood tables and a counter is "often packed, so expect waits"; luckily the "patient staff" "offer assistance in navigating the menu."

The Musket Room New Zealand   25 | 21 | 22 | $$$
NoLita | 265 Elizabeth St.
(bet. Houston & Prince Sts.)
212-219-0764 | musketroom.com
"Original" tasting menus inspired by New Zealand's cuisine and complemented by the country's wines are served with "top-notch" presentation and "wonderful" service at this "lovely" spot in NoLita; the "fine lamb dishes" and the rest of the food is "delicious," although portions are as "minimalist" as the "charming but not twee" interior of brick walls, dark wood, white ceilings, blue accents, and greenery and other "woodsy" touches.

Narcissa American   21 | 22 | 19 | $$$
East Village | 25 Cooper Square (bet. 5th & 6th Sts.)
212-228-3344 | narcissarestaurant.com
The "loveliest garden" in the East Village just might be this "hidden and romantic" spot within The Standard on the Bowery; featuring "fresh and seasonal offerings creatively presented," the menus are "pleasantly light," and include one that's entirely vegan; while the trendy scene yields noise that can be "tough to tolerate," and service becomes "harried when they're busy," it still "makes a great place to sit" "if you don't mind dropping some cash."

Nargis Cafe Uzbek
23 | 14 | 19 | $$

Sheepshead Bay | 2818 Coney Island Ave. (Avenue Z)
Brooklyn | 718-872-7888 | nargiscafe.com
"Delicious" Uzbek food "isn't easy to find" in NYC, but these
"interesting" Sheepshead Bay and Park Slope restaurants offer
"generous portions" of "solid" Central Asian "classics" that
"stick to your ribs (and the rest of you)"; they're "not fancy"
here, and service may be a bit weak, but "friendly" surroundings, "well-balanced cocktails," and "fair prices" help make
them "shining stars among the crowd."

The National American
17 | 19 | 17 | $$$

East 50s | 557 Lexington Ave. (50th St.)
212-715-2400 | thenationalnyc.com
In the Benjamin Hotel in Midtown East, this "utility knife"
works for "all occasions," from morning "power breakfasts,"
to a business lunch, to a nighttime nosh on its signature lamb
burgers; chef Geoffrey Zakarian's American brasserie churns
it out "fast" in tasteful (albeit sometimes "earsplitting") digs
that appeal to a business and vacationing crowd, and best
serves as an "inviting" "meeting spot" rather than a culinary
destination.

Natsumi Japanese/Sushi
20 | 17 | 20 | $$

West 50s | 226 W 50th St. (bet. B'way & 8th Ave.)
212-258-2988 | natsuminyc.com
You're likely not getting "top-drawer" sushi at this Theater District find, but you also "won't be sorry" when presented with its
"reliable-quality" rolls and "good-value"; "quick" servers tend to
turn "brusque when busy," so you won't "have a problem making
your curtain time," but they do manage to keep things "nice"
and "relaxed" despite the constant pre-theater rush.

Naya Middle Eastern
25 | 18 | 22 | $$

East 50s | 1057 2nd Ave. (bet. 55th & 56th Sts.)
212-319-7777 | nayarestaurants.com
"Fabulously delicious and fresh" Lebanese fare is the draw at
this Midtown East spot known for "delightful" mezes and other
"flavorful" Middle East favorites (kafta kebab, chicken shish
taouk), all brought by "accommodating" servers; the "tiny"
"futuristic" space is like "being in outer space" and it's "amazing" what they do in "such a small" setting; well-priced lunch
specials help make it a "go-to" for those seeking to avoid the
crowds in this part of town.

Neil's Coffee Shop Diner
16 | 10 | 18 | $

East 70s | 961 Lexington Ave. (70th St.)
212-628-7474 | neilscoffeeshop.com
At this "rare, traditional coffee shop" still surviving on the UES,
Hunter College students and other regulars cozy up in the
"old comfortable booths," sip out of courteously refilled mugs,
and order from a "typical, large diner selection" of "just-right"
Americana; the food is only "better than passable" ("okay is the
operative word"), but nobody can deny that it's the kind of "classic" that's disappearing.

Neptune Diner ✦ Diner
18 | 14 | 21 | $$

Astoria | 21-02 30th Ave.
(bet. 31st & 32nd Sts.) | Queens
718-278-4853

This 24-hour Greek diner, a "neighborhood institution," is known for "friendly" service and "classic" fare; the "extensive" menu has "a bit of everything," including burgers, gyros and other sandwiches, and breakfast anytime, all cooked to order and with "fair prices"; with a bar and counter and booth seating that's "always busy," it's an Astoria landmark – "What else is there to say?" – "it's the real thing."

Nerai ⑤ Greek
25 | 25 | 24 | $$$

East 50s | 55 E 54th St. (bet. Madison & Park Aves.)
212-759-5554 | nerainyc.com

With a "light and pretty" interior that evokes a breezy terrace overlooking the Mediterranean, this "top-notch" Greek restaurant serves "spectacular" seafood; the "gorgeous" and "classy" dining room, more "intimate" than you'll find at many nearby spots, draws a crowd that typically comes to relax either pre- or post-theater, though its prix fixe lunch menus are an attraction in their own right; a separate wine library is available for private parties.

New Park Pizza ✦ Pizza
25 | 12 | 20 | $

Howard Beach | 156-71 Cross Bay Blvd. (157th Ave.)
Queens | 718-641-3082 | newparkpizza.com

The dough stretching has been perfected "over sixty years" at this pizza parlor in Howard Beach, close to JFK; it's still run "by the same family," which has created what might be the "thinnest slice in NYC"; the service, while cordial, is straight from the counter, and seating in the no-nonsense interior is "limited" – it does lots of takeaway business.

New Wonjo ✦ Korean
20 | 12 | 16 | $$

West 30s | 23 W 32nd St. (bet. B'way & 5th Ave.)
212-695-5815 | newwonjo.com

They take a "traditional approach" at this open-late Korean BBQ, with marinated meats cooked over charcoal grills built into the table, helping justify the frequently "long waits" for a seat in this "smoky," casual room in the West 30s; the "lackluster" interior and "mediocre" service aren't as important at 3 AM, and the "quality and quantity" of meat is worth it anyway; plus, the large front windows allow amusing late-night people-watching.

Nha Trang One Vietnamese
23 | 10 | 18 | $

Chinatown | 87 Baxter St. (bet. Bayard & Canal Sts.)
212-233-5948 | nhatrangnyc.com

At this long-standing and "consistent" Chinatown favorite, the "classic Vietnamese dishes" like salt-and-pepper shrimp and sautéed frog's legs are "excellent" ("ask for fresh chilis on the side if you like your food hot"), and the pho is also a standout; even aficionados admit the "sparse" interior is "nothing to write home about," and the service varies, but they can't argue with the "reasonable prices."

Nice Matin French — 19 | 18 | 19 | $$$
West 70s | 201 W 79th St. (Amsterdam Ave.)
212-873-6423 | nicematinnyc.com
"Outside tables and windows that open to the street in warm weather," plus an "inviting as well as undulating bar," elevate this UWS "staple" with "food and service that are fine but nothing special" (although the "mind-blowing wine list" merits many mentions); still, being open from "breakfast through late night" ensures there's always "a lot of hustle and bustle" here.

NEW Niche 𝒮 Japanese/Ramen — — | — | — | $$
Lower East Side | 172 Delancey St. (Clinton St.)
929-274-1629 | nakamuranyc.com
After opening a self-titled restaurant that made him a shoyu ramen king of the LES, Shigetoshi Nakamura has dedicated his second location (next door) to mazemen – brothless noodles that can be topped with fish, veggies, Hudson Valley duck, or even a carbonara-inspired sauce; the space is tight and the seating is communal, but it works for quick, starchy fill-ups without the steam or weight of soup to slow you down.

NEW Niche Niche 𝒮 Wine Bar — — | — | — | $$$
SoHo | 43 MacDougal St. (King St.)
nichenichenyc.com
This SoHo concept from the owners of Tokyo Record Bar highlights wine instead of vinyl; its rotating list of regional vintages selected by guest sommeliers are paired with creative, complementary courses; the meal provides wine education as well as a forum for winemakers, importers, and other beverage experts, who act as nightly hosts; the breezy interior and manageable prices keep the experience approachable for curious newbies looking for a non-stuffy and social dinner.

Nick & Stef's Steakhouse 𝒮 Steakhouse — 23 | 20 | 23 | $$$
West 30s | 9 Pennsylvania Plaza
(bet. 7th & 8th Aves.)
212-563-4444 | patinagroup.com
"Reservations are a must" for "pregame" dinners, with a "private entrance" to Madison Square Garden that allows ticket holders to skip lines, but even on the off-season, the sizzling filets are worth a visit to this steakhouse chain, especially since "sports fans" won't be there to make it quite so "loud"; the decor is "simple," and the service is "welcoming," but be warned: it's priced for big wallets and "business lunch" "expense accounts."

Nick's Pizza Italian — 24 | 15 | 19 | $$
Forest Hills | 108-26 Ascan Ave.
(bet. Austin & Burns Sts.)
Queens | 718-263-1126
There are no individual slices on offer at this Forest Hills "neighborhood fixture," a "reliable," "family-oriented" joint for "thin-crust," "brick-oven" pies and a few other dishes (calzones, salads, "beyond compare" cannoli) at "reasonable prices"; while the "small," unexciting interior is "crowded most of the time," and the "service is hit-or-miss," the "tables turn over fairly quickly" – especially if you "get there when the kids and baby carriages have left."

Nicola's Restaurant (Italian   24 | 19 | 23 | $$$

East 80s | 146 E 84th St. (Lexington Ave.)
212-249-9850 | nicolasrestaurantnyc.com

"Frequent" patrons keep coming back to this "clubby" and casual throwback for what they call "real Italian in NYC," including the "best chicken parm" in the neighborhood, along with other northern dishes, and "lots of specials"; what makes this a true UES "destination for family and friends" is the "welcoming spirit" of the seasoned waiters, who are always happy to give "honest" recs when requested.

99 Favor Taste Chinese   21 | 15 | 17 | $$

East Village | 37 St. Marks Pl. (bet. 2nd & 3rd Aves.)
212-256-0480 | 99favortaste.com
Lower East Side | 285 Grand St.
(bet. Eldridge & Forsyth Sts.) | 646-682-9162
(Sunset Park | 732 61st St. (bet. 7th & 8th Aves.)
Brooklyn | 718-439-0578
Flushing | 135-41 37th Ave. (bet. Main & Prince Sts.)
Queens | 718-460-9699

"Massive amounts of food" for "super-affordable" prices power these "festive" "all-you-can-eat" mini-chain Chinese-Korean joints, where a "staggering variety of meats and veggies" lie in wait for "interactive" tabletop hot pot or BBQ dining; the "hectic" surroundings aren't fancy, and the service can be "lacking," but if you "bring a big crowd," "what's not to like?"; P.S. diners get a "free meal on their birthdays."

Nix Vegan/Vegetarian   24 | 21 | 22 | $$$

Greenwich Village | 72 University Pl.
(bet. 10th & 11th Sts.)
212-498-9393 | nixny.com

Chances are you've never had vegetarian/vegan food that "feels this special and this indulgent"; drawing on "various culinary traditions" (Indian, Japanese, Middle Eastern), the dishes have "flavors and colors" that approach the "mind-blowing," including ribbons of jicama and a deep-fried but light cauliflower – "it's not easy to make" them "taste so good"; the cocktails are "delicious and pair nicely," and the "chic" dining room is overseen by "quick and observant" servers.

ⓩ Nobu Downtown Japanese/Sushi   27 | 25 | 24 | $$$$

Financial District | 195 Broadway
(bet. Ann & Fulton Sts.)
212-219-0500 | noburestaurants.com
Nobu Fifty Seven
West 50s | 40 W 57th St. (bet. 5th & 6th Aves.)
212-757-3000

Several years after the original branch closed, the remaining locations from chef Nobu Matsuhisa, the "master of omakase," retain reputations as "justly deserved" as ever; even the "cooked dishes are excellent," so you "can pick blindfolded from the menu" and expect "beautifully prepared," "tastefully executed" "Japanese fusion dining," as well as a comprehensive sake list; while "reservations are a must" and "you shouldn't be surprised if you spend twice what you've planned," the "food and service remain top-notch."

| | FOOD | DECOR | SERVICE | COST |

Nom Wah Tea Parlor Chinese/Dim Sum   23| 14| 17| $|

Chinatown | 13 Doyers St.
(bet. Chatham Sq. & Pell St.)
212-962-6047 | nomwah.com
Nom Wah Nolita
NoLita | 10 Kenmare St. (bet. Bowery & Elizabeth St.)
646-478-8242

"Lines should not deter" "nostalgia buffs" hungry to experience
the "Chinatown of yesteryear" and to enjoy "piping hot," "freshly
cooked dim sum" and "specialty teas" at this "historic" parlor with
"1920s coffee shop vibes" (at the original Chinatown location);
although service is "not the strong point," eating at the "oldest"
such place in town is an "experience that everyone in New York
should have once" – a Cantonese-American "culinary landmark."

The NoMad Bar ⊂ S American   25| 27| 24| $$$|

NoMad | 10 W 28th St. (B'way)
212-796-1500 | thenomadhotel.com/new-york

For a taste of "utter refinement," tipplers take in this "sceney"
bar-restaurant in the NoMad Hotel, whose "dark, soaring" space
offers the chance to "linger" over "inventive cocktails" and
"luxurious" "comfort food" from Daniel Humm while engaging
in "intelligent conversation"; never mind the "pricey" tabs – the
"young, hip crowd" sure doesn't, and with such "attentive"
service, it's easy to put any "stressed-out" moments aside with
a few choice "nibbles and drinks."

2 The NoMad Restaurant American   26| 26| 25| $$$$|

NoMad | 1170 Broadway (28th St.)
212-796-1500 | thenomadhotel.com/new-york

"Fascinating people" complement the "trendy surroundings" at
this "classy" NoMad Hotel restaurant, where the "stylish crowd"
sits down for "spectacular" fare (including an "exemplary"
roasted chicken), "lovely" cocktails, and "excellent" wines; it's
an "elegant," multiroom space of "cozy corners and soft lighting," but you may feel like "wearing earplugs" to drown out the
"noise"; "doting service" and a "pitch-perfect" brunch help make
this "a memorable splurge."

Nonono Japanese   25| 20| 23| $$|

NoMad | 118 Madison Ave. (30th St.)
646-707-3227 | nonononyc.com

"Yesyesyes" – with a menu of small plates, you'll need to "order
many things" at this "modern" Japanese spot in NoMad; on
offer are "innovative" twists on yakitori (get the chicken oysters,
"a mouth carnival") as well as the usual grilled "powerhouses,"
along with tasty noodle dishes and other classic plates, the spacious, bilevel space feels "cool" and can handle big groups.

Noodle Pudding M ⊅ Italian   26| 18| 23| $$|

Brooklyn Heights | 38 Henry St.
(bet. Cranberry & Middagh Sts.) | Brooklyn
718-625-3737

"No reservations," "no sign," "no plastic" accepted –
nevertheless, this "neighborhood gem" is "still rocking it after
25 years," thanks to "ample portions" of "fresh" Italian dishes
"that excel" and "a warm, gracious host" (being situated "in a

section of Brooklyn Heights wanting for restaurants" doesn't hurt, either); yes, it can get "noisy and hectic," but "the food and prices are worth it."

Noreetuh Hawaiian   23| 18| 23| $$|
East Village | 128 1st Ave.
(bet. 7th St. & St. Marks Pl.)
646-892-3050 | noreetuh.com
This modern Hawaiian venture in the East Village pairs relaxed island vibes with an elevated, "inventive" menu (poke, crab tempura, kimchi fried rice with Spam) and low-key, "friendly" servers, along with a "deep, interesting wine list"; the low-key and "minimal" interior has casual decor, like Polaroids on the walls, that doesn't draw one's attention, but the "reasonable" prices and "free corkage Sundays" are much more "inspiring."

Norma's American   24| 19| 21| $$$|
West 50s | 119 W 56th St. (bet. 6th & 7th Aves.)
212-245-5000 | parkernewyork.com/eat
"Decadent breakfasts and brunches" set apart this American "treat" in Midtown's Parker New York hotel, where "spot-on" morning and afternoon specialties attract locals and "out-of-towners"; the basic contemporary decor, "inconsistent service," "frenzied" atmosphere, and "huge prices" are clearly not deal breakers when you get meals in such "ample portions" and "so tasty, you won't mind that you'll need to walk a few extra blocks afterward"; N.B. no dinner.

NEW North Fork American   —| —| —| $$$|
West Village | 122 Christopher St. (Bedford St.)
917-261-6598 | northforknyc.com
This spot for West Village bottomless brunch highlights ingredients sourced from area farms, in dishes like Long Island duck Benedict, and in dinners featuring local fish, game, and wild mushrooms foraged in Empire State woodlands, all served alongside New York state wine and beer; the prices and the plant-filled dining room are both relaxed, catering to neighborhood regulars and others whose healthy intentions may be tested by the temptation of unlimited prosecco.

North Square American   23| 18| 22| $$|
Greenwich Village | 103 Waverly Pl. (MacDougal St.)
212-254-1200 | northsquareny.com
"Get away from the hustle and bustle" in the Washington Square Hotel's "quiet haven," the "best-kept secret in Greenwich Village" for "nicely done" American meals offered by "anticipatory staff" (they "let us linger as long as we wanted") "in a subdued, adult environment"; it's particularly "pleasant" if you're "walking around Washington Square on a Sunday," when they do a "terrific" jazz brunch.

Z Nougatine at Jean-Georges French   27| 24| 26| $$$$|
West 60s | 1 Central Park W (60th St.)
212-299-3900 | jean-georgesrestaurant.com
The "secret is out" about this "gem" serving "lush" French-inspired dishes next to the Jean-Georges "mothership"; the "creative menu" of "delicious" dishes is a "bargain compared to

its sister restaurant" "but is no less wonderful"; the "sophisticated" space has "wonderful" views overlooking Central Park, and there's a "lovely outdoor terrace" in summer; the prix fixe lunch is "one of the best values in town."

Novitá Italian · 25 | 20 | 24 | $$$

Gramercy | 102 E 22nd St.
(bet. Lexington Ave. & Park Ave. S)
212-677-2222 | novitanyc.com

This "romantic hideaway" in Gramercy Park might be a little hard to find, but enough people have sought it out that it "fills up fast in the evening" and a reservation is a good idea; the "cozy" (sometimes "cramped") contemporary dining room manages to be "quiet enough to have a conversation"; the Italian dishes are "beautifully prepared and presented," the wine list pairs well, and the owner and staff are "gracious."

Nucci's Italian/Pizza · ▼ 23 | 17 | 25 | $$

Tottenville | 4842 Arthur Kill Rd.
(S. Bridge St.) | Staten Island
718-967-3600 | nuccissiny.com

From A (angel-hair primavera) to Z (zuppa de pesce), the "homestyle Italian food" classics are "never a disappointment" at this Staten Island standout ("you can't go wrong" with the varied pizzas, either); although the highly "friendly" staff are on point, the somewhat plain, institutional-looking digs lead some to say it's "best for takeout."

Nur Middle Eastern · 24 | 20 | 22 | $$$

Flatiron | 34 E 20th St. (bet. B'way & Park Ave. S)
212-505-3420 | nurnyc.com

The best strategy for ordering at this Israeli restaurant in Flatiron is to "bring all your friends and get one of everything"; "the breads and dips are the stars," says one fan, "but everything here shines"; if you don't mind the energetic and upbeat scene that leads to "high-decibel situations," then you're in for a "feast," "as even familiar-sounding foods are prepared in new ways that delight the palate."

Nyonya (Malaysian · 24 | 16 | 18 | $$

Little Italy | 199 Grand St. (bet. Mott & Mulberry Sts.)
212-334-3669 | ilovenyonya.com
Bath Beach | 2322 86th St. (Bay 34th St.) | Brooklyn
718-265-0888

This "old standby" dishes up "some of the best Malaysian food in the city," with "solid renditions of the classics," like the "light and crispy" roti canai; the interior is "no frills" and the staff "can be rushed," but the prices are "reasonable"; the place does get crowded, so "be prepared to wait" unless you opt for the less crowded Brooklyn branch.

O Ya S Japanese/Sushi · 27 | 25 | 26 | $$$$

Murray Hill | 120 E 28th St.
(bet. Lexington Ave. & Park Ave. S)
212-204-0200 | o-ya.restaurant

"Innovative" omakase is the draw at this "fantastic" Murray Hill sushi specialist in the Park South Hotel, where the "hyper-creative, hyper-delicious" Japanese dishes are available à la carte, too; factor in various cocktails and sakes, and all those tidbits "add up," although the "tranquil setting" and smooth service help assuage financial concerns; N.B. "sit at the counter to watch the masters at work."

Obao Thai/Vietnamese   20| 18| 17| $$|
East 50s | 222 E 53rd St. (bet. 2nd & 3rd Aves.)
212-308-5588 | obaony.com
Financial District | 38 Water St. (Broad St.)
212-361-6313
West 40s | 647 9th Ave. (45th St.) | 212-245-8880
The "very reasonable" fusion dishes here marry "comforting" Thai and Vietnamese flavors, especially in a "well-priced" lunch spread that'll keep you satiated for the rest of the day; the "casual" ambiance is most appreciated before the "hip" and "young" get out of work and fill it up, but the Hell's Kitchen location has space in back "roomy enough" for big groups.

Ocean Prime Seafood   25| 25| 25| $$$$|
West 50s | 123 W 52nd St. (bet. 6th & 7th Aves.)
212-956-1404 | ocean-prime.com
Coastal city-dwellers might suspect a "chain from the Midwest" (the original's in Columbus) "wasn't going to offer" stunning seafood, but this "upscale" surf-and-turf "throwback" fits right in, with Midtown-ready "hustle and bustle" perfect for "business lunches" or quick "theater-menu" dinners; the "austere, high-end" interior, reserve wine list, "prime beef," and "premier" service will make you feel like an admiral, but the prices are likely to "drain your wallet."

Oceana ⑤ Seafood   25| 25| 25| $$$$|
West 40s | 120 W 49th St. (bet. 6th & 7th Aves.)
212-759-5941 | oceanarestaurant.com
"Bill Telepan continues to be on top of his game," proclaim fans of the chef's Rock Center–area "fish emporium," where the "exciting" seafood specialties, "robust wine selection," and "inventive cocktails" find a home in a "cavernous" yet "elegant" setting patrolled by "accommodating" servers; while the "lively bar scene" creates "off-putting noise," many enjoy the patio seating.

The Odeon French   22| 21| 21| $$$|
TriBeCa | 145 W Broadway (bet. Duane & Thomas Sts.)
212-233-0507 | theodeonrestaurant.com
"Classic," along with "legend" and "institution," are words people associate with this longtime TriBeCa favorite, which first opened in 1980; it's "lively without being cramped or annoying," the service is also solid, and the kitchen "consistently delivers" "unpretentious bistro food," "from the mussels to the burger to the steak," "with no frills or fuss," accompanied by a well-chosen wine list and a bar that brings back memories.

NEW Odo Japanese   −| −| −| $$$$|
Flatiron | 17 W 20th St. (bet. 5th & 6th Aves.)
odo.nyc
For those looking to dive deeper into Japanese tasting menus, this house of kaiseki dining in Flatiron offers both traditional

versions at chef Hiroki Odo's bar, which features a variety of cooking techniques, and a sushi-focused menu at a separate table that's a unique omakase hybrid; prices are through the roof and portions are precious, but the chance to experience nine artistic courses in such an intimate space is rare.

Oiji Korean

26 | 22 | 24 | $$$

East Village | 119 1st Ave. (7th St.)
646-767-9050 | oijinyc.com

"Get the honey butter chips" for dessert at this "elevated" East Village spot serving "inventive" and "transcendent" Korean plates paired with "expertly made," "creative" cocktails that "complement the food well"; the "intimate," stylish brick-walled setting offers seats at tables sometimes plus a few at the bar, but it's compact, making reservations tough to get.

Okonomi / Yuji

26 | 23 | 24 | $$$

Ramen Japanese/Ramen
Williamsburg | 150 Ainslie St.
(bet. Leonard & Lorimer Sts.) | Brooklyn
718-302-0598 | okonomibk.com

"Once, you sit down, you're transported" to a Tokyo ramen bar (by night) or to a "unique" Japanese breakfast spot in the morning (with fish and egg custard working in "harmony"); either way, you'll have to wait (there are no reservations) for a seat at the "incredibly intimate" bar; it's "not for picky eaters," but the "out-of-the-box" artistry makes it a "true" "hip and delish" Williamsburg experience; N.B. no tipping.

Old Homestead

24 | 19 | 23 | $$$

Steakhouse Steakhouse
Chelsea | 56 9th Ave. (bet. 14th & 15th Sts.)
212-242-9040 | theoldhomesteadsteakhouse.com

The "grandaddy of New York City steakhouses," this "landmark" opened its doors in 1868; from an appropriate location near the Meatpacking District, they kick it old school here, with a "clubby atmosphere" and "waiters wearing white jackets," and it's still one of the best places for steer in town, serving "massive portions (with prices to match)"; if you're here for lunch, the burgers are also "wonderful."

Old Tbilisi Garden Georgian

23 | 14 | 19 | $$

Greenwich Village | 174 Bleecker St. (Sullivan St.)
212-470-6064 | oldtbilisigarden.com

From this "spacious" dining room emerges "good quality," "pleasantly surprising classic Georgian" and other Eastern European cuisine "you won't find elsewhere in Manhattan," including khachapuri (cheese-filled bread); other pluses include a garden tucked away from the street, and "fast" (albeit "not polished") service.

⚡ Olmsted American

27 | 24 | 26 | $$$

Prospect Heights | 659 Vanderbilt Ave.
(bet. Park & Prospect Pls.) | Brooklyn
718-552-2610 | olmstednyc.com

Deserving "kudos for making dinner interesting again," this "exciting" Prospect Heights restaurant gets patrons' "taste buds almost jumping off their tongues" with seasonal, "vegetable-forward" American meals – which often feature ingredients from its backyard garden – and "first-rate cocktails," all served by a "superkind" staff; P.S. since the "cozy," "bright" interior (highlighted by a live green wall and "neighborhood" vibe) can get "packed," fans advise "reserving well in advance."

NEW O:n Korean — — — $$$
East 30s | 110 Madison Ave.
(bet. 29th & 30th Sts.)
917-261-4326 | onnewyork.net

The team behind Her Name is Han brings a new creative take on Korean, but this time it's centered around hot pots cooked to order at your table; because the stewing process takes time, rice and snacks are served as it bubbles, along with an à la carte menu of tempting shareables; save room, as noodles can be added to the pot at the end to extend your meal.

One If by Land, Two If by Sea American 25 27 26 $$$$
West Village | 17 Barrow St.
(bet. 7th Ave. S & W 4th St.)
212-255-8649 | oneifbyland.com

You may feel like "popping the question" at this "enchanting" West Village standout in Aaron Burr's former carriage house, a famously "romantic" spot known for its "gorgeous setting" (candlelight, fireplaces, and "lovely music" from a baby grand), "stellar" service, and "wonderful" prix fixe and tasting menu fare, including a "heavenly" beef Wellington and other Continental and American fare; the price for such "sophistication" is "costly," but it's definitely a "special restaurant for a special occasion."

1 OR 8 M Japanese/Sushi 21 20 21 $$$
Williamsburg | 66 S 2nd St. (Wythe Ave.) | Brooklyn
718-384-2152 | oneoreightbk.com

Sushi mavens "love how secretish" this "cool" Williamsburg Japanese is, and the "interesting spin" it gives to omakase options and "quality" sushi has earned it a decent reputation; drinks ranging from sake to cocktails make the "casual, quirky" space more palatable, and although "lofty prices" get some reviewers down, the "friendly" staff help ensure it's "an acceptable spot" for the area, as do the value-priced lunch specials.

Ops ℂ Pizza 28 21 23 $$
Bushwick | 346 Himrod St. (Wyckoff Ave.) | Brooklyn
718-386-4009 | opsbk.com

With "chewy, tangy" sourdough crusts that emerge from a "sizzling" wood-fired brick oven, the pies here earn abundant praise, as do the Bushwick proprietors; "hip and dedicated to their craft," they're "creative" with their toppings, though even the "plain marinara is delicious," and their selection of natural wines, deciphered by "knowledgeable" servers and all priced the same, are another star attraction – so who cares if the "seating is cramped" and waits "long"?; N.B. tips are included.

Oriental Garden   Chinese

23 | 13 | 17 | $$

Chinatown | 14 Elizabeth St.
(bet. Bayard & Canal Sts.)
212-619-0085 | orientalgardenny.com

The fish tanks in the front window might attract tourists' attention, but locals know the "outstanding" seafood here – including scallops, clams, and soft-shell crabs – makes this a very strong Chinatown contender; frequent diners advise you to "go early" for the dim sum (served daily) and avoid the "long lines" that form outside at prime times; dishes are family-style, the prices are "reasonable," and the service is "friendly."

The Original Crab Shanty ☾ Seafood

24 | 19 | 21 | $$

City Island | 361 City Island Ave. (Tier St.) | Bronx
718-885-1810 | originalcrabshanty.com

"No need to go bankrupt for a lobster dinner for the family" at this "brash" "old reliable" on City Island; "don't expect fancy" here, just a satisfying meal with "enormous" plates of "tasty" seafood, "tropical, homemade drinks," and "friendly," "gracious" service; just remember: "if a sedate dining experience is what you are seeking, The Crab Shanty is not your port of call."

Orsay   French

20 | 21 | 20 | $$$

East 70s | 1057 Lexington Ave. (75th St.)
212-517-6400 | orsayrestaurant.com

The "brasserie environment" at this "little bit of Paris" on the UES draws "ladies who lunch" and a "loyal" neighborhood crowd for its all-day menu of "reliable" French classics, which some find "pricey"; service can be "iffy" and the atmosphere "noisy," so sitting on the patio during warmer months is the "perfect" option.

Osteria al Doge ☾ Italian

21 | 18 | 20 | $$

West 40s | 142 W 44th St. (bet. B'way & 6th Ave.)
212-944-3643 | osteriaaldogenyc.com

At what's "a step above the usual Theater District Italian," the "food is truly good," especially the Venetian specialties and the pizza and "homemade pasta," which make use of "subtle sauces"; the "welcoming staff" will "get you out quickly for a show," and you are just steps away from Times Square, but the bilevel space's "close quarters" mean it's "noisy and hectic at dinner"; go after curtain "to get a good table and better service."

Osteria Laguna   Italian

22 | 19 | 12 | $$

East 40s | 209 E 42nd St. (bet. 2nd & 3rd Aves.)
212-557-0001 | osterialagunanyc.com

"Efficient" sums up this "central" Italian standby's approach to hospitality: "fast service" for the midday "business crowd," providing gluten-free alternatives and always keeping the bar "fully stocked"; the "great variety" of specialties and "lovingly prepared" pizzas and pastas are enough to make diners take the prices in stride, and many find them "fairly decent."

Osteria Morini   Italian

25 | 21 | 23 | $$$

SoHo | 218 Lafayette St. (bet. Broome & Spring Sts.)
212-965-8777 | osteriamorini.com

"Phenomenal pastas" and "Italian meats and cheeses" are "the stars of the show" at this "exquisite" and "convivial" SoHo-rustic destination, a Michael White (Marea, Ai Fiori) spot where "huge portions" are "served with gusto," and Monday night half-price pastas are "the bargain of the city" – just be ready for a "super-noisy and very vibey" experience.

Otto Enoteca e Pizzeria Italian/Pizza   22 18 19 $$
Greenwich Village | 1 5th Ave. (8th St.)
212-995-9559 | ny.ottopizzeria.com
Resembling a train station in Italy – and not just because of the departures board on the wall – this "strangely giant" space is always "noisy, crowded, and festive"; the kitchen serves notable and "reasonably priced" thin-crust pizza and pasta, as well as a "huge" list of wines; fans say it's "good for a date night, a get together with old pals, or even to take the in-laws."

Otway American   ▼ 24 25 24 $$$
Clinton Hill | 930 Fulton St. (St. James Pl.) | Brooklyn
917-909-1889 | otwaynyc.com
This small restaurant on a pleasant corner – look for the twin wooden benches in Clinton Hill – serves American "classics" with a "delicious jolt" of flavor; brunch is a favorite here, and the wine list is surprisingly well traveled; the interior pretty much "drips with charm," from the penny tile floors to the two-story windows flooding the space with sunlight; P.S. there's a good weekday happy hour, too.

NEW Oxalis M French   ▼ 26 23 27 $$$
Prospect Heights | 791 Washington Ave.
(bet. Lincoln & St. Johns Pl.) | Brooklyn
347-627-8298 | oxalisnyc.com
The food is "melt-into-your-seat" "amazing" at this Prospect Heights destination serving a daily changing menu of season-ally inspired New American plates that are indeed "small" but "awesome," as well as a bar menu of inventive bites (a cheese plate with seasonal puree, little gem salad, pork neck); illumi-nated by a skylight and backed by an open kitchen, the space is bright, modern, and industrial.

Z Oxomoco Mexican   27 26 25 $$$
Greenpoint | 128 Greenpoint Ave.
(bet. Franklin St. & Manhattan Ave.) | Brooklyn
646-688-4180 | oxomoconyc.com
Prepare to be "shocked and awed" by this "proper, grown-up" "dining experience" in Greenpoint, a haven for "inspired," seasonal Mexican (including house-made tortillas), "fantastic cocktails," and "lots of mezcal and tequila," all served in a "bright," "vibey" space "filled with greenery"; you might need "a big budget to try everything," but when you consider the "professional staff" and "happening" atmosphere, it's "a total hit."

Pacific Palace Chinese   25 16 18 $$
Sunset Park | 813 55th St. (8th Ave.) | Brooklyn
718-871-2880 | pacific-palace.com
"Newly renovated" and "delicious as always," this grand Cantonese banquet hall in Sunset Park is "crowded" on the weekends, when the "endless" dim sum selection whizzes by

and the traffic of dumpling carts become a flurry; the service is quick and to the point, and the prices are moderate; don't be surprised if you run into a wedding event or other gathering of "celebrating families."

The Palm Court ◖ American   24| 26| 23| $$$|
West 50s | 768 5th Ave. (59th St.)
212-546-5300 | theplazany.com/dining

Treat yourself to "high tea at the Plaza" "at least once in your life," and experience the "white-glove service" of "old New York," where it "still feels like Eloise lives upstairs"; it's in full swing "during the holidays for the buffet," but any time you go, the "relaxed" "elegance" of the "historic dining room," filled with greenery and an iconic skylight, makes a special, albeit "very expensive" morning or afternoon.

The Palm Too Steakhouse   22| 20| 23| $$$|
East 40s | 840 2nd Ave. (bet. 44th & 45th Sts.)
212-697-5198 | thepalm.com
The Palm Tribeca
TriBeCa | 206 West St. (bet. Chambers & Warren Sts.)
646-395-6393
The Palm West Side
West 50s | 250 W 50th St. (bet. B'way & 8th Ave.)
212-333-7256

"Still a top steakhouse" after all these years, this "no-nonsense" "carnivores' castle" – a "tried-and-true" chain in the mold of the now-shuttered 1926 original – remains "consistently enjoyable" for its "abundant portions" of "well-aged" beef, along with "giant" lobsters, "killer drinks," and numerous wines in environs bolstered by "super caricatures on the walls" and "personalized service"; the "pricey" tabs aside, they remain "reliable" for meat mavens of all kinds.

Palma Italian   23| 24| 22| $$$|
West Village | 28 Cornelia St.
(bet. Bleecker & W 4th Sts.)
212-691-2223 | palmanyc.com

If possible, "snag a table in the backyard garden" (open year-round) of this townhouse on a quiet side street in the West Village; even if you are in the dining room you'll find it "warm," "inviting," and romantic – it's a "most darling spot" to "celebrate special occasions"; the kitchen serves a tightly edited selection of "unwaveringly tasty" Italian, with high marks for presentation, and the staff are "very accommodating."

Pampano Ⓢ Mexican/Spanish   21| 20| 21| $$|
East 40s | 209 E 49th St. (bet. 2nd & 3rd Aves.)
212-751-4545 | richardsandoval.com/pampano

A "kind of Spanish-Mexican mash-up" – the kitchen makes both paella and guacamole – this "high-end" "upscale" spot in a Midtown townhouse serves "tasty, refined" food; service is "polite and efficient," and fans call the space "inviting." Ask for balcony seating in the "beautiful and elegant" dining room, or in the summer escape to the "delightful terrace."

Paola's Italian   26 | 22 | 23 | $$$

East 90s | 1295 Madison Ave. (92nd St.)
212-794-1890 | paolasrestaurant.com

At this "old-style" Madison Avenue trattoria, "top-flight" pasta
options "just like Mama prepared" and Roman specialties are
the priority, and they make a "mean" Negroni; the "high-end,"
"somewhat older" regulars – perhaps with "a celebrity or politi-
cian" here and there – treat the "unrushed" room as a social
club, so anticipate waiting a bit when it's "mobbed," as diners do
take their time.

Pappardella Italian   20 | 18 | 19 | $$

West 70s | 316 Columbus Ave. (75th St.)
212-595-7996 | pappardella.com

Worrying "lest too many people catch on" to this UWS "survivor," its many neighborhood boosters say it "consistently
satisfies" with "unpretentious" "red-sauce" pasta dishes and
gluten-free alternatives, "rare" for an Italian joint; the "safe and
predictable" interior is scattered with rustic trinkets "resonant
of Tuscany," and the "affable, prompt" servers manage the
"crowded" space filled with feasting dates and local families.

🖪 Park Avenue American   25 | 26 | 24 | $$$

Flatiron | 360 Park Ave. S (26th St.)
212-951-7111 | parkavenyc.com

"Breathtaking interior design that changes with the season" is
just one highlight here, where everything from the menu to the
waitstaff's uniforms gets a makeover four times a year; menu
choices "are not only innovative, but absolutely delicious and
beautifully presented," and the wines, especially on the pairing menu, are "outstanding"; the staff are "on point" and "can
handle a large group, which is a plus."

Park Side Italian   25 | 20 | 23 | $$

Corona | 107-01 Corona Ave.
(bet. 51st Ave. & 108th St.) | Queens
718-271-9871 | parksiderestaurantny.com

Fans swear that the "bread basket alone is reason enough to
dine here," but this "hugely popular Italian" in Corona ("it can
be difficult to get reservations") is the kind of place where the
"prices are reasonable" and the portions are as "enormous" as
the personalities of the diners, many of whom seem like they
are out of a movie (politicians and celebrities are part of the
mix, too); it's been "family owned and operated for decades."

Parker & Quinn American   20 | 18 | 19 | $$

West 30s | 64 W 39th St. (6th Ave.)
212-729-0277 | parkerandquinn.com

There's something for everyone at this "cute," "simple," "casual," and "reasonably" priced all-day bar; from a "menu for all
dietary needs" to being an OK place to take kids, this gastropub
in the Refinery Hotel is always busy, which sometimes means
"average" food, "slow" service, and the "unbearably" loud
sounds of business and "happy hour" crowds, a side effect of
its convenient location off Bryant Park.

Parm Italian ___19__ __14__ __16__ _$$_

Battery Park City | Brookfield Place,
250 Vesey St. (North End Ave.)
212-776-4927 | parmnyc.com
NoLita | 248 Mulberry St. (bet. Prince & Spring Sts.)
212-993-7189
West 70s | 235 Columbus Ave. (71st St.)
212-776-4921

Those on a quest for "a damn good" version of the eponymous sandwich head to the Torrisi/Carbone team's "bustling" chain, which dishes out "big portions" ("fast before coming here") of "solid," "down-home" Italian-American grub; the menu's "limited," and the "minimal" "too-bright" surroundings may not impress, but the typically "affordable" check does; those who need to feed a family can opt for kids' menus.

Parma ◖ Italian ___22__ __17__ __23__ _$$$_

East 70s | 1404 3rd Ave. (80th St.)
212-535-3520 | parmarestaurantnyc.com

"Reliable" comes up over and over in reviews of this "welcoming" "red-sauce favorite" with "responsive" servers; it developed a "loyal following" as soon as it opened in 1977 for classic and "generous" portions of dishes like minestrone and eggplant parmigiana; it's still popular with families, often with several generations crowded around the same table ("this is our local kitchen").

Pascalou French ___23__ __16__ __20__ _$$_

East 90s | 1308 Madison Ave.
(bet. 92nd & 93rd Sts.)
212-534-7522 | pascalou.info

This "always welcoming" "diversion" on Madison Avenue in the East 90s has "outlasted" fellow French neighbors by being a "longtime asset" to the community, "reliably" preparing bistro "standards" and soufflés "worth waiting for"; diners shrug off the "cramped" layout and instead call it a "pleasing" "little bit of Paris" and the sort of place that "every neighborhood should have."

🏆 Pasquale Jones Italian/Pizza ___25__ __22__ __23__ _$$$_

NoLita | 187 Mulberry St. (Kenmare St.)
917-453-0339 | pasqualejones.com

"You have to love a place with two wood-burning ovens," used for the "delicious" clam pizza (along with other correctly "charred and chewy" varieties) and so much else, all of it served up in a soft-toned "small" NoLita setting with a "great vibe" and "attentive" service; the homemade pastas and other Italian fare are also well-received, as is the "terrific wine program" and the high-end glassware used – "go for the wine glasses alone."

NEW Pastis French ___-__ __-__ __-__ _$$$_

Meatpacking | 52 Gansevoort St.
(bet. Greenwich & Washington Sts.)
212-929-4844 | pastisnyc.com

This glamorous brasserie is back in MePa, down the street from its old location; the decor and menu have been freshened up, but it's also re-created what visitors loved about the chic original, including its status as a celebrity-fueled hot spot; as always, that means long waits, so make reservations to enjoy the people-watching and the steak frites that made it famous.

Pastrami Queen Deli   24 | 7 | 14 | $$

East 70s | 1125 Lexington Ave. (78th St.)
212-734-1500 | pastramiqueen.com

"Pastrami rules" at this "solid" UES deli known for its "succulent" meats, "monster-sized sandwiches" that can "feed two," and other "Jewish soul food" staples; the "small," usually "crowded" space is filled with "ugly, too-close tables and chairs," so take-out's a good idea; either way, "be prepared to pay more than you think you will" (even with such "perfunctory" service).

Patricia's Italian/Pizza   25 | 23 | 24 | $$

Morris Park | 1082 Morris Park Ave.
(bet. Haight & Lurting Aves.) | Bronx
718-409-9069 | patriciasofmorrispark.com

It's no wonder diners "come from all over" for this "old-fashioned" Bronx trattoria's "amazing" wood-fired pizza, "well-pounded" chicken cutlets, and bread that's "worth the carbs"; it's got an Italian layout – exposed brick, open kitchen, "not overstuffed" with tables – and the "on-site" owners are at your beck and call for "insider" dishes not featured on the menu.

Patsy's Italian Restaurant Italian   23 | 17 | 21 | $$

West 50s | 236 W 56th St. (bet. B'way & 8th Ave.)
212-247-3491 | patsys.com

"Calories and carbs be damned," say diners about this West 50s red-sauce veteran, where dining "is like having Sunday dinner with the family," with tasty and "rib-sticking" "old-fashioned" Southern Italian dishes; photos of entertainers, Sinatra among them, line the walls of the "rambunctious" white-tableclothed dining room, which "hasn't changed in years – keep it that way!" say the nostalgic – just don't "expect a quiet time."

Patsy's Pizzeria Pizza   22 | 15 | 18 | $$

🚩 **East Harlem** | 2287 1st Ave. (118th St.)
212-534-9783 | thepatsypizza.com
East 40s | 801 2nd Ave. (43rd St.)
212-878-9600
West 70s | 61 W 74th St. (bet. Columbus Ave. & CPW)
212-579-3000

"One of the original pizza joints in NYC," originally from East Harlem, and now with spin-offs across the city, they serve traditional pies that are "thin," "tasty," and "way above average," along with "red-sauce Italian"; it's a "family-oriented place," which often means noisy; through it all the staff remain "friendly and competent, if a little frazzled at times," and the no-reservations policy "sometimes results in long waits."

Paulie Gee's Pizza   26 | 19 | 20 | $$

Greenpoint | 60 Greenpoint Ave.
(bet. Franklin & West Sts.) | Brooklyn
347-987-3747 | pauliegee.com

"Believe the hype": this Greenpoint "wood-fired" "pizza mecca" features "eye-popping" toppings that are "novel" and

FOOD DECOR SERVICE COST

"mouth-watering," and fans of the hot honey says it's worth asking for a side of it "to dip your crust in"; despite all the innovation, it's still a place that "respects the sacred institution" – don't be discouraged by the "cavern-like" interior or their strict no-reservations policy; the welcoming servers "who care" and tableside chats with "Paulie himself" make it "worth even" "two-hour waits."

Peacefood Vegan/Vegetarian   21 15 17 $$
Greenwich Village | 41 E 11th St. (University Pl.)
212-979-2288 | peacefoodcafe.com
Peacefood Cafe
West 80s | 460 Amsterdam Ave. (82nd St.)
212-362-2266
Even carnivores "love" these storied vegan "retreats" in the Village and the UWS for the "straightforward palate pleasers" and "salads dressed perfectly," although "the star of the show is their desserts"; you may have to wait for a seat or for your waiter, but if you're contemplating "going down that old hippie highway," this is the ("noisy when crowded") place to do it.

Peaches HotHouse Southern   25 18 20 $$
Bedford-Stuyvesant | 415 Tompkins Ave.
(Hancock St.) | Brooklyn
718-483-9111 | bcrestaurantgroup.com
Fort Greene | 87 S Elliott Pl. (Lafayette Ave.) | Brooklyn
718-797-1011
This pair of urban country cafés answers the call for hot chicken and cold beer in Brooklyn; the Nashville-style fried bird glows red with spices and can be requested from mild to "numbing hot," and items like shrimp and grits and the various sides also get some love; reviewers say to "be prepared for a wait" in the casual surroundings, but that it's "well worth it" for a taste of this Southern soul food.

Z Pearl Oyster Bar S Seafood   27 17 23 $$
West Village | 18 Cornelia St.
(bet. Bleecker & 4th St.)
212-691-8211 | pearloysterbar.com
There's "no need to drive to Maine" for "top-quality lobster rolls," the specialty of this "unpretentious" West Village "standout," whose "supremely fresh," "New England–style" seafood is "served with enthusiasm"; the "small" space "ain't much to look at," and the no-reservation policy means you may have to "stand in a sad line" for seating, but if you want to feel like "the ocean's right outside the door" for a "reasonable price," this spot's a "pleasure."

Peasant M Italian   23 21 22 $$$
NoLita | 194 Elizabeth St.
(bet. Prince & Spring Sts.)
212-965-9511 | peasantnyc.com
"Creative" Italian fare, much of it "cooked in a wood-burning oven," is the lure at this "solid," dinner-only NoLita spot – its often "wonderful," food, such as lamb chops with polenta or the baby octopus, encourage "romance" in the "warm and intimate" interior; there's also a no-reservations cellar wine bar in case you need extra refueling.

Peking Duck House Chinese ⎮24⎮ ⎮15⎮ ⎮20⎮ ⎮$$⎮

Chinatown | 28 Mott St.
(bet. Chatham Sq. & Pell St.)
212-227-1810 | pekingduckhousenyc.com
East 50s | 236 E 53rd St. (bet. 2nd & 3rd Aves.)
212-759-8260

Large families and out-of-towners say it's "worth the trip" to the "Chinatown institution" for the "sublime" signature crispy duck, better than what's found at its "spiffier" Midtown location, and at the main branch you can BYOB with no charge; ceremonious tableside prep by "a carver with a cleaver" is enough to "forget the surroundings" and the "so-so service."

The Penrose ℂ Gastropub ⎮20⎮ ⎮21⎮ ⎮19⎮ ⎮$$⎮

East 80s | 1590 2nd Ave. (bet. 82nd & 83rd Sts.)
212-203-2751 | penrosebar.com

A "downtown feel" possesses this UES destination, a "crowded" bar with a "big social scene" catering to "your entire office," "twentysomethings," and "so many first dates"; the "craft cocktails, beards, and all" have made this joint "maybe too popular," but "ultra-creative" cocktails, "huge" portions, and a brunch made for a "good Sunday afternoon nap" cater to a neighborhood "that is a bit lacking" in other places like this.

Pepolino Italian ⎮25⎮ ⎮17⎮ ⎮23⎮ ⎮$$⎮

TriBeCa | 281 W Broadway
(bet. Canal & Lispenard Sts.)
212-966-9983 | pepolino.com

"Outstanding" homemade pasta, intriguing specials, and superb cheesecake are the draws of this "charming" Tuscan trattoria in TriBeCa – "provided you can find it"; the humble location is likely the reason it's "still not discovered by the masses," so regulars celebrate their secret and cherish "summer eating outside," an "accommodating" staff, and "reasonable" prices.

Z Per Se French ⎮28⎮ ⎮28⎮ ⎮27⎮ ⎮$$$$⎮

West 50s | 10 Columbus Cir.
(bet. 58th & 60th Sts.)
212-823-9335 | thomaskeller.com/perseny

"Bravo!" shout fans of "master" chef Thomas Keller's "gastronomic event" in the Time Warner Center, a jackets-required "pinnacle" of French–New American "cooking indulgence," with "divine" main-room tasting menus – plus lounge-area à la carte options – along with "superb wines" in a "thrilling setting" highlighted by "exquisite" Manhattan views; "first-rate" service also shines, and although it's "not for the weak of wallet" ("take your platinum card"), most agree that as "memorable" times go, this one's "world-class."

Pera Mediterranean ⎮21⎮ ⎮19⎮ ⎮19⎮ ⎮$$$⎮
Brasserie Mediterranean

East 40s | 303 Madison Ave. (bet. 41st & 42nd Sts.)
212-878-6301 | peranyc.com
Pera Soho
SoHo | 54 Thompson St. (Broome St.)
212-878-6305 | pera-soho.com

A taste of Istanbul awaits at these "pleasant" Mediterranean spots dishing up "a wide array" of dips, mezes, and grilled meat and fish plates with a side of house-made breads; the Midtown original is known for "noisy and busy" lunch and happy hour scenes, while its SoHo offshoot is beloved for its "fantastic" outdoor patio.

Periyali Greek
25 | 21 | 24 | $$$

Flatiron | 35 W 20th St. (bet. 5th & 6th Aves.)
212-463-7890 | periyali.com

"If you're craving fresh grilled fish and Greek food," join the "classy crowd" "at this perennial favorite in the Flatiron district"; from the "expertly cooked" classics to the "civil" staff to the "pretty," "tranquil" white-on-white environs with "fresh flowers all year round," all is "romantic" and "predictably excellent"; and if it's offered "nothing new in decades," "no one seems to care."

Perry St American
25 | 25 | 24 | $$$$

West Village | 176 Perry St. (West St.)
212-352-1900 | perrystrestaurant.com

"The food is delicious and the wines excellent," as you would expect from Jean-Georges Vongerichten, with "flawless execution" of "creative dishes" displaying French, American, and Asian influences; and unlike his self-titled "mother ship uptown," this "out-of-the-way" spot in the far West Village is "quiet and calm," so "you can have a conversation without screaming"; the "lovely, warm staff" match the "beautiful room"; don't miss the well-priced "lunch prix fixe."

Persepolis Persian
22 | 17 | 21 | $$

East 70s | 1407 2nd Ave. (bet. 73rd & 74th Sts.)
212-535-1100 | persepolisnewyork.com

You know a place is doing something right when people rave about the rice, in this case the "amazing" sour cherry version served at this "lively" Persian spot with a long and narrow dining room; those in the know come in the warmer months because the seats outside are "particularly nice"; the staff are "very attentive," and they "never rush you," even though "it can be crowded and noisy on weekends."

Pete's Tavern ℂ Gastropub
16 | 20 | 18 | $$

Gramercy | 129 E 18th St. (Irving Pl.)
212-473-7676 | petestavern.com

"Always packed," this is one of New York City's longest-running establishments; it's "nothing fancy," just a welcoming "neighborhood pub" in Gramercy Park serving "oversized portions" of "typical tavern food" and "generous" drinks; the atmosphere is "rich with NY history," from "O. Henry" on, but the perceptive say the "food is mostly just an excuse to keep drinking and hanging out" – "I've been going here for 100 years," claims one.

🔟 Peter Luger Steak House 🍴 Steakhouse
28 | 18 | 23 | $$$$

Williamsburg | 178 Broadway (Driggs Ave.) | Brooklyn
718-387-7400 | peterluger.com

An eternal pilgrimage site for carnivores, this "legendary" 1887 Williamsburg institution achieves the "pinnacle of porterhouse," but is also famed for other "divine," "properly aged" steaks "you can cut with your fork"; the "convivial," quasi– "German beer garden" setting is staffed by "grumpy" veteran servers, and the "crowded" space can be a "madhouse," but if you "book ahead," you'll certainly obtain that "primal protein fix"; just remember that credit cards aren't accepted, so bring "big wads of cash" or a debit card.

Philippe Chinese   22 20 20 $$$
East 60s | 33 E 60th St. (bet. Madison & Park Aves.)
212-644-8885 | philippechow.com
Meatpacking District | 355 W 16th St.
(bet. 8th & 9th Aves.)
212-885-9400

"For high-end Chinese cooking" presented with style, these "clubstaurants" in Meatpacking and the UES bring their fans to wax rhapsodic about dishes like the "tender" and "crispy" Peking duck, carved tableside, and the "buttery" chicken satay; the place "can get loud, but that's half the fun," and the prices make a meal here "a splurge, for sure."

Piccola Venezia Italian   25 18 24 $$$
Astoria | 42-01 28th Ave. (42nd St.) | Queens
718-721-8470 | piccola-venezia.com
Take a trip "back in time" at this "old-school" family-run Italian spot for "marvelous" Northern-style classics (like antipasti, pastas, and grilled meats and fish) with "super-sized" portions and "not-to-be missed" house-made desserts; everyone "feels like family" among the "white tablecloths," the "exceptional," buttoned-up waiters," and a "vintage" crowd of regulars – "Sunday dinners are a delight."

Piccolo Angolo Ⓜ Italian   25 16 23 $$
West Village | 621 Hudson St. (Jane St.)
212-229-9177 | piccoloangolo.com
"Red sauce the way it should be," declare devotees of this "warm, family-run" West Village café that's been serving "easy-to-understand Italian food" in "huge portions" ("meatballs the size of softballs") since 1992; although the ambiance could be a lot better" – "ridiculously tight quarters" – "you keep coming back because the food's always good and the house wine goes down easy."

Pier A Harbor House ◖ Gastropub   15 22 17 $$
Financial District | 22 Battery Pl. (Little West St.)
212-785-0153 | piera.com
Serving "quick" "drinks and oysters" from a "landmarked" "waterfront property" at the tip of Manhattan in Battery Park, the "ample" "biergarten-style outdoor seating" fills up after work, and there "are not a lot of waitstaff to keep up"; still, there are few better places for a "sunset and a glass of wine" without risking "high tabs"; just "seat yourself," "order at the bar," and "enjoy the view" of the Statue of Liberty.

Pies 'n' Thighs Southern   23 17 20 $$
Williamsburg | 166 S 4th St. (Driggs Ave.) | Brooklyn
347-529-6090 | piesnthighs.com
"The best kind of carbo-load" – "truly delicious desserts (the pies)," fried chicken that "melts in your mouth," and buttermilk

biscuits and other classic sides are all present at this Southern stand "not too far from the Williamsburg Bridge"; there's "always a crazy wait" and "not much in the way of ambiance," but all's forgiven when the food arrives – it's "always so good."

Pietro's Italian   25 | 16 | 26 | $$$

East 40s | 232 E 43rd St. (bet. 2nd & 3rd Aves.)
212-682-9760 | pietros.com

"Not glamorous" (but "not stuffy"), and certainly "not new," this "midcentury" Manhattan relic in the East 40s may make "you instantly want to order a martini"; while the "dusty" interiors could "use a little update," "you'll leave full and satisfied" from the "big portions" of steaks, chicken parm, and Caesar salad without "having to spend a fortune," and you'll appreciate the respectful service that ensures that most of the old-timer "patrons are regulars."

Pig and Khao Filipino/Thai   23 | 16 | 19 | $$

Lower East Side | 68 Clinton St.
(bet. Rivington & Stanton Sts.)
212-920-4485 | pigandkhao.com

"If you want a flavor bomb," come to this "quirky" LES stop serving "unique" Filipino- and Thai-inspired fare with "a strong kick," including sisig that's "incredible in all its fatty glory" as well as lots of other pork options; "there's not a ton of elbow room" – "be prepared to sit real close to strangers" – but service is solid, the vibe is "fun," and "trendy" cocktails help get the party started, especially if you're part of a group.

Pig Beach M Barbecue   20 | 20 | 16 | $$

Gowanus | 480 Union St.
(Gowanus Canal) | Brooklyn
pigbeachnyc.com

With the Gowanus nearby, it's more "concrete jungle" than beach at this "above-average," "affordable" BBQ "hangout"; it delivers on smoked meats, in "a huge space that's always packed" with Brooklynites keen on "day-drinking outside" on the "massive" patio, and maybe playing a round of cornhole; "lines run long," it's "noisy," and service lags, but if you're with "a big group" and don't mind the "preschoolers playing tag" around you, it's fun.

Pig Heaven Chinese   20 | 14 | 19 | $$

East 80s | 1420 3rd Ave. (bet. 80th & 81st Sts.)
212-744-4333 | pigheavennyc.com

"Don't pass on the ribs" at this "porcine-themed" neighborhood place for "old-school Americanized" Chinese food that is "just right" if you can manage to "get past their name" and the "friendly" but "slow" service – it's "worth the aggravation"; those less blissed-out say the "faded" dining room (with "hog decor" "less prominent than in the old days") "has a different feeling" ever since the original owners retired and the place moved one avenue over, but overall it's still a decent value.

Ping's Seafood Chinese

22 | 14 | 16 | $$

Chinatown | 22 Mott St.
(bet. Chatham Sq. & Mosco St.)
212-602-9988 | eatatpings.com

For dim sum that's served in traditional bamboo steamers, this Hong Kong/Cantonese classic in Chinatown is well worth a visit, especially if you go for the seafood dumplings and fish preparations; it's all "consistently well prepared and satisfying," and the service is "efficient," which is especially crucial during the frequent periods when it's "busy, especially on the weekend," and "you're crammed in with little space between tables."

Pio Pio Peruvian

23 | 15 | 19 | $$

East 90s | 1746 1st Ave. (bet. 90th & 91st Sts.)
212-426-5800 | piopio.com
Murray Hill | 210 E 34th St. (bet. 2nd & 3rd Aves.)
212-481-0034
West 40s | 604 10th Ave. (bet. 43rd & 44th Sts.)
212-459-2929
West 90s | 210 Amsterdam Ave. (94th St.)
212-665-3000
Gravesend | 282 Kings H'way (7th St.)
Brooklyn | 718-627-3744
Mott Haven | 264 Cypress Ave. (bet. 138th & 139th Sts.)
Bronx | 718-401-3300
⧉ Middle Village | 62-30 Woodhaven Blvd. (bet. Dry Harbor Rd. & 62nd Dr.) | Queens | 718-458-0606
Jackson Heights | 84-02 Northern Blvd.
(bet. 84th & 85th Sts.)
Queens | 718-426-4900

"Take your taste buds for a joyride" at these "lively" multiborough Peruvians, known for their "plentiful" portions of "flavorful" rotisserie chicken with a "wonderful" trademark green sauce; "quick service" and "fantastic prices" ensure "you'll be too busy eating to care" about the "bare-bones" interior, though since they're frequently "busy," takeout or delivery is a good option; N.B. the Jackson Heights location has live music every Wednesday night, while the Middle Village site is cash-only.

Pisticci Italian

25 | 19 | 23 | $$

Morningside Heights | 125 La Salle St. (B'way)
212-932-3500 | pisticcinyc.com

"If this were my neighborhood, I'd be a regular," say those smitten with this Morningside Heights mainstay for "simple," "like-Grandma-used-to-make Italian" dishes ("nice pasta" in particular), served by "friendly staff" in colorfully "quaint," homey digs; it's "accessibly priced" too, even if the locale's a bit "out of the way" for those not "in the Columbia University area."

PizzArte Italian/Pizza

21 | 16 | 18 | $$

West 50s | 69 W 55th St. (bet. 5th & 6th Aves.)
212-247-3936 | pizzarteny.com

Both the traditional Neapolitan and "gluten-free pizza crust" at this sleek space are as "fantastic" as the art gallery decor that references its proximity to MoMA; while the modern paintings might not make up for the "communal tables" and distracting "noise level," it's still an inspiring place to get an "upscale" wood-fired "pre-theater" pie, which you can count as a cultural experience.

Pizzeria Sirenetta Italian/Pizza

23 | 17 | 21 | $$

West 80s | 568 Amsterdam Ave.
(bet. 87th & 88th Sts.)
212-799-7401 | pizzeriasirenetta.com
"Not your typical pizza place," this "interesting" UWS Italian from the folks behind the Mermaid Inn pairs a "solid menu" of "high-quality" Neapolitan pies with "sophisticated" pastas and small plates, plus booze and brunch, in a "breezy," often "packed" white-brick-walled interior; "accommodating" service and moderate costs (there are "excellent" happy-hour "deals") compensate for the "noise," and the outdoor seating's "a real plus"; P.S. "it's smart to reserve a table."

P.J. Clarke's American/Burger Joint

19 | 17 | 19 | $$

Battery Park City | Brookfield Place,
250 Vesey St. (North End Ave.)
212-285-1500 | pjclarkes.com
C East 50s | 915 3rd Ave. (55th St.) | 212-317-1616
C West 60s | 44 W 63rd St. (Columbus Ave.)
212-957-9700
"An NYC classic," these "historic," "old-school" saloons showcase "satisfying burgers," plus "excellent" drinks, in "pub"-style interiors complete with "tables your grandfather ate at" (that's especially true of the 1884 Midtown East original); these days, the tabs are "soaring," and it's usually "noisy" and "frenetic," given the "active bar scene"; the Lincoln Center location works as a pre- or post-performance stop, while the Battery Park City site's outdoor area has "lovely views" of the Hudson.

Playa Betty's Mexican

17 | 18 | 16 | $$

West 70s | 320 Amsterdam Ave.
(Bet. 75th & 76th Sts.)
212-712-0777 | playabettys.com
You'll find a bit of "California in the middle of Manhattan" at this "always packed," "beachy" taqueria on the UWS; the "colorful," "funky" "decor is a hoot," it's "great for groups," and there's a kid's menu; though the service is suitably casual, and the food tends to seem "better after a few margaritas," it's a "lively" and "fun" spot for "cheap eats in a high-priced area."

The Polo Bar American

23 | 28 | 25 | $$$$

East 50s | 1 E 55th St. (5th Ave.)
212-207-8562 | ralphlauren.com/global-polo-bar
"Well-appointed luxury" is "everywhere you look" at this Midtown "portal into Ralphworld" (designer Lauren owns it) – from the "old-school glamour" of the gleaming-wood, green-and-plaid "horsey hunt club" interior to the "beautiful" patrons (please "try not to gawk"); "the staff are accommodating without being intrusive" and the cuisine is "quintessential American" "comfort food raised to the next level"; sure, it "reeks of entitlement," but "if you can score a reservation, run, don't walk," for the experience.

Pondicheri Indian

19 | 16 | 18 | $$

NoMad | 15 W 27th St. (5th Ave.)
646-878-4375 | pondicheri.com

Serving some of the "more creative Indian" in town, this "huge space" in NoMad makes "a good entry into more modern renditions" of subcontinental classics; the "inventive dishes" include curry bowls, non-traditional thalis, and "interesting twists on pastries" that help make the breakfast here (served till 3 PM) a "tasty and viable proposition"; although it gets points for being an "upbeat and happy place," the occasional long waits can be "painful."

Porsena Italian

25 | 20 | 23 | $$$

East Village | 21 E 7th St. (bet. 2nd & 3rd Aves.)
212-228-4923 | porsena.squarespace.com

From an inconspicuous East Village location, this "charming" and "modest" "hole-in-the-wall" "never disappoints" for "fine" "rustic" Tuscan cooking, with a "well-curated" menu of dishes like you'd "find in Italy," with impressive sausages and "serious pasta dishes" tossed with creative local ingredients and time-tested techniques; it's all ushered along by "knowledgeable servers" and a "friendly" bar pouring thoughtfully chosen wines.

⛶ Porter House Bar and Grill Steakhouse

27 | 26 | 27 | $$$$

West 50s | 10 Columbus Cir. (bet. 58th & 60th Sts.)
212-823-9500 | porterhousenyc.com

This "suave" Time Warner Center steakhouse teams "perfectly cooked," "butter"-smooth dry-aged meats and a "well-rounded wine list" with a "plush" interior known for its "stunning views of Columbus Circle and Central Park"; you may need a "fat wally" to handle the bill, but that's hardly a concern for business meals and "big occasions," and the "wonderful" service just adds to the overall "harmony."

Posto Thin Crust Italian/Pizza

23 | 13 | 18 | $$

Gramercy | 310 2nd Ave. (18th St.)
212-716-1200 | nycthincrust.com

"Cracker-thin crust" aficionados say this Gramercy Park spot has "absolutely nailed this kind of pizza," and some even swear you can skip the toppings, because a pie this "solid" can "can stand on its own" – other Italian dishes are available, but the 'za will always be the "default"; since the place is so "relaxed" and "casual" though sometimes "crowded and noisy," it's a decent "place to bring kids" as well as have a date night.

⛶ Prince Street Pizza Pizza

27 | 12 | 14 | $

NoLita | 27 Prince St. (bet. Elizabeth & Mott Sts.)
212-966-4100 | princestreetpizzanyc.com

Those square "Sicilian slices, man" – the "pillow-like" texture, "glistening" cupped pepperoni ("little circles of joy"), a "spicy and flavorful" sauce "smothered" atop the "crispy" cheese crust all "live up to the hype"; while the NoLita pizzeria itself doesn't "look like much," lines are often "down the block" – so consider ordering "a few extra" pies to justify the trip; the wait "goes quickly" thanks to the "stern" dough slingers and the lack of seats.

Prune American   25| 18| 22| $$$|
East Village | 54 E 1st St. (bet. 1st & 2nd Aves.)
212-677-6221 | prunerestaurant.com
"Idiosyncratic and bohemian," this East Village "landmark"
keeps crowds waiting for Gabrielle Hamilton's "seasonal," "creative," "deceptively simple" food with complex flavors, served
by a "warm and casual" staff; tables are so "tightly squeezed
together" some may feel they're "eating in their friend's
cramped apartment," but most find it "quaint" and well worth
the "moderately priced" cost, especially for the wildly popular
brunch, which is first-come, first-served.

Pure Thai Cookhouse Thai   26| 14| 19| $$|
West 50s | 766 9th Ave. (bet. 51st & 52nd Sts.)
212-581-0999 | purethaicookhouse.com
This "true standout in a sea" of other Hell's Kitchen Thai restaurants serves "addictive" dishes that are "always fresh and
perfectly spiced," helping newbies move beyond "just pad Thai
and curry"; "it's cramped but friendly" and "service is good,"
but "it's virtually impossible to get a seat at lunch," even though
many think the "uncomfortable chairs" exist "to ensure you eat
and leave"; try to "eat off hours," and "don't expect to linger."

Pylos ☾ Greek   26| 23| 23| $$$|
East Village | 128 E 7th St.
(bet. Avenue A & 1st Ave.)
212-473-0220 | pylosrestaurant.com
If you want to dine somewhere a little "swanky for the East Village" with effective service, a "buzzing" atmosphere, and "cool"
decor, where you'll be seated beneath hanging "clay pots," call
on this Greek Adonis; you can bring your crew for whole grilled
fish so fresh it's "as if they pulled it right out of the Aegean,"
and sit at "large communal tables" where "everyone asks their
neighbor" for recommendations – "just don't show up without
a reservation."

Quality Eats Steakhouse   22| 20| 20| $$$|
East 70s | 1496 2nd Ave. (78th St.)
212-256-9922 | qualityeats.com
NoMad | 3 E 28th St. (bet. 5th & Madison Aves.)
212-257-8882
West Village | 19 Greenwich Ave. (10th St.)
212-337-9988
This "millennial steakhouse" resembles an "Art Deco burger
joint," where the "crowds are beautiful but not snooty" and
"you need a shoehorn to get into your seat"; the "hand-crafted
cocktails" and the food, which really is "consistent" and "great
quality," both help distract from the noise level and the variable
service, which is friendlier earlier in the evening.

Quality Italian Italian   24| 21| 22| $$$$|
West 50s | 57 W 57th St. (6th Ave.)
212-390-1111 | qualityitalian.com
Between the "trendy" space and the chicken parm transmogri-
fied into a pizza, this "modern" Theater District "power scene"
puts on "quite a show" to enjoy "before a show," and the "innovative twists" and "Italian steaks done right" satisfy even those
unimpressed by gimmicks; it's "noisy" and "crowded," but the

"indulgent" portions, "top-drawer cocktails," and "welcoming" service provide a dinner "you will remember" – "a bit corporate, but still legit."

Quality Meats Steakhouse

25 | 23 | 23 | $$$$

West 50s | 57 W 58th St. (bet. 5th & 6th Aves.)
212-371-7777 | qualitymeatsnyc.com

The name says it all at this "second-generation Smith & Wollensky" in the West 50s, which updates the steakhouse experience with a "sleek," "sexy," "dark," cavernous setting full of artsy flourishes like meat cleavers on the walls and "special alcoves" for privacy; at its core, it's still a place for a "big steak dinner" of prime dry-aged tomahawks with all "the fixin's," and big-name red wines – "expensive but worth it."

Queen Italian

25 | 17 | 24 | $$$

Brooklyn Heights | 84 Court St.
(bet. Livingston & Schermerhorn Sts.) | Brooklyn
718-596-5955 | queenrestaurant.com

A little piece of the 1950s that's "alive and well," this Brooklyn Heights institution is known for its "delicious" "no-nonsense" Italian food (house-made mozzarella and a "must-order" chicken parm among them), all served by "courteous," "attentive" waitstaff; the white-tablecloth interior is "retro" without even trying, and often packed at lunch with "judges, juries, and attorneys" from the courts nearby.

Queens Comfort ⌿ Southern

24 | 21 | 20 | $$

Astoria | 3618 30th Ave.
(bet. Steinway & 41st Sts.) | Queens
718-721-3800

"Rocking the comfort-food scene," this Astoria spot is "wild," with a "super-funky" menu of down-home Southern staples (chicken and waffles), donuts, and "crazy dishes" in an informal, often "packed" house loaded full of "pop-culture memorabilia"; the lines and cash-only policy make some eyes roll, but it's definitely a place for those looking for "tacky fun" during brunch, lunch, or dinner, especially "if you're in the area" already.

NEW Queensyard British

– | – | – | $$$$

West 30s | 500 W 33rd St. (10th Ave.)
212-377-0780 | queensyardnyc.com

From the group behind the Time Warner Center's Bluebird London comes this Hudson Yards lounge, which attempts to breathe some calm into a frenetic mall; views of the Vessel are on display, as are audaciously dressed cocktails; the pricey menu traverses the Atlantic, featuring both buttermilk-dredged fried chicken and fish-and-chips at brunch, while preparing fowl and fin in more delicate ways during dinner service.

Racines NY Ⓢ French

21 | 16 | 21 | $$$

TriBeCa | 94 Chambers St.
(bet. B'way & Church St.)
212-227-3400 | racinesny.com

An "amazing list" of old vintages and small-production bottles found "nowhere else," effortless decor, "casual service," and a "low-key vibe" all help keep fans of this wine bar spinoff from

Paris in high spirits; the "eccentric" "French-inspired" small plates, "done in surprising ways," complement the offbeat pours – to match their natural ethos, the kitchen "works with the seasons" and "changes the menu often."

Radiance Chinese

19 | 19 | 19 | $$

East 50s | 208 E 50th St. (3rd Ave.)
212-888-8060 | radiancetea.com
Radiance Tea House & Books
West 50s | 158 W 55th St. (bet. 6th & 7th Aves.)
212-217-0442

For a "zen" respite from city life, head to these "serene" tea parlors for a "limited" menu of traditional bites and a wide selection of herbal infusions; most reviewers deem them "serene and cultured hideaways" for a "quiet" meetup with friends and say perusing the bookshelves at the Midtown West location is not to be missed – the Buddhist-themed collection is "one of the best in the city."

Rafele Italian

24 | 20 | 22 | $$

West Village | 29 7th Ave. S (Bedford St.)
212-242-1999 | rafele.com

Fans of this "relaxed Italian bistro" offer a lot of superlatives for the "classic" dishes, including "innovative," "creative," and "festive" – not surprising, as the chef grew up making pasta with his mother in Naples; the West Village eatery is "always busy and bustling," sometimes crossing the line to "crowded" and "noisy"; the service is "attentive," the prices "reasonable."

Rahi Indian

26 | 23 | 23 | $$$

West Village | 60 Greenwich Ave. (Perry St.)
212-373-8900 | rahinyc.com

This "not quite traditional" West Village favorite serves "innovative" and "inspiring" Indian dishes ("beautiful" presentation) that are a "creative mix" of influences: "with the incorporation of fiery spices and other heat-packed profiles, your taste buds are in for a treat," and the cocktails are equally "playful and bold"; it's good for groups, with small plates that are made for sharing, and the "professional" staff also get a nod.

Randazzo's Clam Bar Seafood

24 | 11 | 19 | $$

Sheepshead Bay | 2017 Emmons Ave.
(21st St.) | Brooklyn
718-615-0010

The reason so many decide to "pull off the Belt Parkway and go back in time" by a visit to this "legendary" Italian American in Sheepshead Bay is its "fresh" seafood plates, including "must-try" clams and "excellent" calamari, all with a side of its famed oregano-steeped hot sauce ("when in doubt, get the medium spicy"); sure, "it doesn't look like much" and service is minimal, but almost all say "it's old school, but never out of style."

Rao's Ⓢ Italian

23 | 19 | 22 | $$$$

East Harlem | 455 E 114th St. (Pleasant Ave.)
212-722-6709 | raosrestaurants.com

"Getting into Harvard Business School is easier than getting a table" at this "one-of-a-kind," East Harlem Italian, where "lucky" diners who "have a guy who knows" someone consume "lusty red-sauce" classics amid "festive, brassy" digs resembling "a tavern" – albeit one with frequent celebrities; the excitement of just being there is probably why "everybody's smiling," because the "exorbitant" tabs don't elicit such reactions, though "if you win the lottery and can score a seat," it's "a must-go."

Raoul's (French
26 | 22 | 24 | $$$

SoHo | 180 Prince St.
(bet. Sullivan & Thompson Sts.)
212-966-3518 | raouls.com

"Bohemian" since 1975, this "sexy" "old-school" SoHo "hangout" still has no trouble inducing patrons to "sit cheek-by-jowl with other diners amid a joyous din" for a "classic French-bistro menu," all while vibing on the "tiny," "funky" space and "eclectic art collection"; of course it's a "loud" night out, and waits can be significant, but the celeb-spotting potential, drink options, and "welcoming staff" keep things "intoxicating."

❷ Ravagh Persian Grill Persian
26 | 17 | 21 | $$

NoMad | 11 E 30th St. (bet. 5th & Madison Aves.)
212-696-0300 | ravaghrestaurants.com
East 60s | 1135 1st Ave. (bet. 62nd & 63rd Sts.)
212-861-7900
East Village | 125 1st Ave. (St. Marks Pl.)
212-335-0207

This elegant trio of Eastside Middle Eastern grills is the "best of its kind," serving "lots of kebab choices," "homemade bread," succulent stews, "strong tea," and "mounds of saffron rice" so "generous" they "seem to grow larger as you are eating"; it's "not too fancy," but the servers try hard and it's "fairly priced"; "go with friends so you can share more."

NEW Red Hook Tavern
– | – | – | $$$

Red Hook | 329 Van Brunt St.
(bet. Sullivan & Pioneer Sts.) | Brooklyn
917-966-6094 | redhooktavern.com

From the team behind Red Hook's beloved Hometown BBQ comes this long-awaited addition to the same neighborhood; here chef-owner Billy Durney's meat-cooking skills are used on burgers, steaks, a bacon-topped wedge salad, and more, all served in a neighborhood-y space designed to feel like it's been around longer than it has.

Red Rooster Southern
22 | 21 | 20 | $$

Harlem | 310 Lenox Ave. (126th St.)
212-792-9001 | redroosterharlem.com

Marcus Samuelsson's unique blend of soul by way of Scandinavia has become a Harlem "institution" – it's a "fun place to celebrate" among the "lively crowd," the "jumping" scene, and the curio-filled interior, or simply get a fix of Southern comforts like the Yardbird (fried chicken); the service is "proper," but "slow," and the place gets "crowded and loud," especially during musical performances downstairs at the speakeasy-themed Ginny's Supper Club or during gospel brunch on Sundays.

Redeye Grill American — | — | — | $$$
West 50s | 890 7th Ave. (bet. 56th & 57th Sts.)
212-541-9000 | redeyegrill.com
Reopened in 2019, this dependable diner is known for its menu of American classics, especially its burgers, as well as a handy Midtown location that's close to Carnegie Hall and convenient to the Theater District.

🔢 RedFarm Chinese   25| 17| 21| $$$
West 70s | 2170 Broadway (77th St.)
212-724-9700 | redfarmnyc.com
West Village | 529 Hudson St. (Charles St.)
212-792-9700
"Not your typical Chinese fare" – the "inventive" and "fresh" menu is an "elevated take on dim sum" "with a New York twist," including the "memorable" Katz's pastrami egg roll; the "buzzing" "farmhouse casual" atmosphere can translate to "long waits" at peak times "despite reservations," but it's "worth the trip."

The Regency Bar & Grill American   19| 22| 21| $$$
East 60s | 540 Park Ave. (61st St.)
212-339-4050 | loewshotels.com/regency-hotel
"The gossipy business breakfast crowd opens the day" at this "elegant" and spacious Art Deco-inspired refuge in the Loews Regency Hotel, known for "good people-watching," whether "sitting in the banquettes, looking outside, or at the bar"; true, the "pricey" American "food is surprisingly ordinary" and the service no better than "nice," "but it's all about the crowd" here, isn't it? P.S. reservations are required, even for breakfast.

Remi Italian   24| 24| 23| $$$
West 50s | 145 W 53rd St. (bet. 6th & 7th Aves.)
212-581-4242 | remi-nyc.com
The "traditional" Northern Italian dishes "do not disappoint here," and that includes "first-rate" Venetian classics; with a "pretty and sunlit" interior, it's a "respite from the hustle and bustle" of Midtown, and benefits from being right by MoMA and blocks from the Theater District; the airy main room, decorated with large murals of Venice, can be "noisy" on occasion, but the service tends to be "accommodating."

Restaurant Nippon 🆂 Japanese/Sushi   25| 20| 23| $$$
East 50s | 155 E 52nd St.
(bet. Lexington & Third Aves.)
212-688-5941 | restaurantnippon.com
First opened in 1963, this Midtown East standby attracts Japanophiles and expats and others convinced that it still "excels" in "classic" Japanese cuisine – "it ain't just sushi" – like sukiyaki, teriyaki plates, and soba and udon noodle dishes (plus sashimi), all at more "moderate" prices "than newer" competitors; "gracious" service and pleasant surroundings enhance the experience.

🆕 Reverence 🆂 Ⓜ American   — | — | — | $$$
Harlem | 2592 Frederick Douglas Blvd. (138th St.)
reverence.nyc
A chef known for his series of underground supper clubs in San Francisco has landed in Harlem, bringing a bit of the sunshine

state to this California-inspired restaurant serving a five-course tasting menu (with a vegetarian option) that diners prepay for online.

NEW Rezdôra Italian   —| —| —| $$$|
Flatiron | 27 E 20th St.
(bet. B'way & Park Ave. S)
646-692-9090 | rezdora.nyc
Emilia-Romagna cooking – like ravioli and prosciutto draped over gnocco fritto – is featured at this sensational Flatiron ristorante from an alum of Massimo Bottura's globally celebrated Osteria Francescana; other delights include dry-aged rib eye, house-made gelato, and a thoughtful list of Italian wines; make sure to make a reservation, and bring carb-loving friends so that you can try the pasta tasting as a table.

RH Rooftop Restaurant American   20| 28| 20| $$$|
Meatpacking District | 9 9th Ave.
(Little W 12th St.) | 212-217-2210
"Belle epoque charm" lives on, stories above the Meatpacking District, at this "beautiful, beautiful" terrace that "takes one's breath away" with "over-the-top" crystal chandeliers illuminating "high-quality" seating (no surprise there, since you're in a Restoration Hardware); you're "paying for the scene," so expect "good but not exceptional" food – as well as out-of-towners "taking pictures of their food for Instagram" – particularly the "sublime" and photogenic burger on the menu of American classics.

Ribalta Italian/Pizza   22| 18| 20| $$|
Greenwich Village | 48 E 12th St. (B'way)
212-777-7781 | ribaltapizzarestaurant.com
At this happening "neighborhood Italian," in the East Village, "deserving of its popularity," traditional dishes and "soccer games with Napoli spirit" on the TVs are what it's about – the pizza is a "winner" and the pastas and salads are worth a taste too; the vibe is "lively" (some call noise levels "deafening") and the space can get "crowded" at dinner, so if you want to speak to your dining companion, "order takeout."

The Ribbon American   20| 16| 19| $$$|
West 40s | 220 W 44th St. (bet. 7th & 8th Aves.)
212-944-2474 | theribbonnyc.com
West 70s | 20 W 72nd St. (bet. Columbus Ave. & CPW)
212-787-5656
The fried chicken, served Sunday and Monday nights, is "where it's at" in these "clubby" American hangouts also known for salads, burgers, prime rib, and "tasty" raw bar options paired with a long list of cocktails; the UWS location is known for its happy hour and "awesome" bar scene, all assisted by the "friendly" servers and bartenders – but "if you like quiet, go early."

Z The River Café American   26| 28| 26| $$$|
Dumbo | 1 Water St. (bet. Furman &
Old Fulton Sts.) | Brooklyn
718-522-5200 | rivercafe.com
You can't beat the "dreamy" setting at "one of NYC's most romantic restaurants," with "unmatched" views of the Brooklyn

FOOD DECOR SERVICE COST

Bridge from its Dumbo location and "stunning floral arrangements" that are "never less than lush"; "exquisite" "old school"
hospitality makes you feel like "the only guest in the restaurant," and dinner is "worth dressing up for" (which is good,
since jackets are mandatory for men); fans find the "new and
exciting" American dishes and "sublime" desserts are "off
the charts."

☲ Riverpark American   25| 27| 26| $$$
Murray Hill | 450 E 29th St. (1st Ave.)
212-729-9790 | riverparknyc.com
From a near-"secret location off the East River," Tom Colicchio's
"peaceful" New American, "hidden away" in an office park near
Bellevue, comes with "fabulous" waterside views in a "genteel,"
"modern" setting; the "delectable," "inventive" seasonal fare
is augmented by produce from its own farm; "superb" service,
"convenient" parking, and "reasonably quiet" surroundings help
make this a strong candidate for "celebrating special occasions," and the al fresco seating's "a plus."

Robert American   23| 26| 24| $$$
West 50s | Museum of Arts and Design,
2 Columbus Cir. (bet. B'way & 8th Ave.)
212-299-7730 | robertnyc.com
Serving "a smart menu offering American fare with twists and
turns," this restaurant, named after an eminent party planner,
sits atop the Museum of Arts and Design; its biggest attraction
is its floor-to-ceiling windows, the better to see the "stunning
views of Columbus Circle" and Central Park – "it's a sight to
behold"; the mood-cheering interior is part "1980s Art Deco"
and part "chic modernist"; "solid service" keeps it all running
smoothly.

☲ Roberta's ℂ American/Pizza   27| 20| 19| $$
Bushwick | 261 Moore St. (Bogart St.) | Brooklyn
718-417-1118 | robertaspizza.com
"There's a reason the crowds keep coming" to this "Bushwick
staple" with Manhattan food hall outposts: "some of the best
pizza in NYC – not your normal slice, but a fancier, more decadent" variety, with a "thin, delicious crust" and "really original
toppings"; the action unfolds in a "large rustic" space with
"quaint lighting," communal tables, and a Tiki bar/"massive beer
garden in back"; "waits are ridiculous" and the staff acts "hipper
than God," but it's still "a must-go."

Roberto's ⑤ Italian   25| 20| 24| $$$
Arthur Avenue/Belmont | 603 Crescent Ave.
(Hughes Ave.) | Bronx
718-733-9503 | robertosbronx.com
This Arthur Avenue/Belmont–area "class act" continues to turn
out "terrific homemade pastas" and other "creative" fare from
a "big menu" with "lots of specials" (plus wines) that lead fans
to question whether they're "in Italy or the Bronx"; "professional" service nixes any qualms about uninspiring decor and
"expensive-for-the-neighborhood" prices, and it's well located
for "post-Yankees game" meetups or after-zoo meals.

Rolf's German

15 | 24 | 16 | $$$

Gramercy | 281 3rd Ave. (22nd St.)
212-477-4750 | rolfsnyc.com
Roughly half of the year if feels like "walking into Christmas" here, with decorations that "cover every inch" of this German institution in Gramercy; its "dated menu" groans with schnitzels, wursts, and other hearty, "decent" dishes; expect to pay "top dollar" for "slow" service and "blast-from-the-past dining," and walk away with a colorful "Instagram photo" of you with your stein of beer.

Roll-N-Roaster Deli

22 | 11 | 17 | $

Sheepshead Bay | 2901 Emmons Ave.
(bet. Nostrand Ave. & 29th St.) | Brooklyn
718-769-6000 | rollnroaster.com
"You haven't truly had good fast food" until you've had the "melt-in-your-mouth" roast beef sandwich (it's "king") or the not-to-be missed cheese fries – "everything here is better with cheese" – at this Sheepshead Bay legend; "a complete throwback in a good way," this "classic spot for a quick bite" has powerful "1970s" energy and is quite "nostalgic for all born-and-bred Brooklynites" – "please, never change," plead its many fans.

Room Service Thai

19 | 18 | 16 | $$

West 40s | 690 9th Ave. (bet. 47th & 48th Sts.)
212-582-0999 | roomservicerestaurant.com
It's hard to rise above the high concentration of "endless, less-than-exciting" Thai joints in Hell's Kitchen, but this one does just that with "creative" dishes "not seen" on competitors' menus; "value value value" attracts pre-theater diners and the lunch crowd, as do dramatic mirrors and chandeliers that add to the "dark" atmosphere; the less impressed note occasional misfires that show it's not "living up to its promise," but for most it's still "a cut above."

Root & Bone Southern

24 | 18 | 21 | $$

East Village | 200 E 3rd St. (bet. Avenues A & B)
646-682-7076 | rootnbone.com
Head to Alphabet City for Mason jar bourbon cocktails and gut-busting "comfort" food in an "open and airy, homey" atmosphere that makes you "feel like you're in the South," eating takes on down-home classics like "deviled eggs that elevate the form" and "sweet tea–brined fried chicken"; there's usually "a line," and the "slow service" struggles to keep up at times, but if you're craving some soul food, this "biscuit heaven" is "hard to beat."

Rosa Mexicano Mexican

21 | 20 | 21 | $$

East 50s | 1063 1st Ave. (58th St.)
212-753-7407 | rosamexicano.com
Flatiron | 9 E 18th St. (bet. B'way & 5th Ave.)
212-533-3350
TriBeCa | 41 Murray St. (Church St.) | 212-849-2885
West 60s | 61 Columbus Ave. (62nd St.)
212-977-7700
"One of the first great Mexican restaurants in NYC" and still a "reliable" and "festive" "standby," this small chain has locations

all over the city, including one across from Lincoln Center that's "a good time"; the guac, prepared tableside, is "legendary," and the margaritas are "dynamite," especially the fresh pomegranate one.

Rose Water American
25 | 18 | 23 | $$

Park Slope | 787 Union St.
(bet. 5th & 6th Aves.) | Brooklyn
718-783-3800 | rosewaterrestaurant.com

The "market-driven" "locavore" menu that "changes with the seasons" is "limited but oh so delicious" at this "Park Slope stalwart," an "extraordinary neighborhood eatery" for sustainably raised and "interesting" American food; expect a "consistent quality experience" in the "minuscule" and minimalist room, or at breezy tables out front amid flowering plants in good weather; the prix fixe (Sunday through Thursday) is a "terrific deal."

Rosemary's Italian
21 | 23 | 20 | $$

West Village | 18 Greenwich Ave. (10th St.)
212-647-1818 | rosemarysnyc.com

"Situated on a lovely corner" in the West Village, this "great neighborhood place" is "full of trendy, beautiful people" who come for the "unassuming but not boring" handmade pasta dishes; the interior manages to feel "bright and lively" while remaining "not too loud for conversation," especially in the serene rooftop garden, where organic produce is harvested; service isn't always swift, but you'll find the staff "always cheery."

Rosie's Mexican
19 | 19 | 18 | $$

East Village | 29 E 2nd St. (2nd Ave.)
212-335-0114 | rosiesnyc.com

This is a "sceney" East Village casual Mexican cantina that's built for "pitchers of margs" and bowls of guac, "heightened by an upbeat, lively crowd" ready to take group photos on the front patio; the "noisy" "happy hour is a great deal," and even if it can be "difficult to get a table" and portions are "small," the "freshly made tortillas" "satisfy," and the tacos themselves are solid.

Rossini's Italian
23 | 20 | 24 | $$$

Murray Hill | 108 E 38th St.
(bet. Lexington & Park Aves.)
212-683-0135 | rossinisrestaurant.com

It's "not very trendy or innovative, but you know what you'll get" at this "dependable" Murray Hill veteran: "above-average, old-school" Northern Italian dishes, "fresh" and "served with formal flair"; true, the "traditional" interior is a "little dated," but the nightly live music adds "cheerful ambiance"; P.S. "particularly recommended: Saturday nights, when they have opera singers."

Rotisserie Georgette French
23 | 21 | 23 | $$$

East 60s | 14 E 60th St.
(bet. 5th & Madison Aves.)
212-390-8060 | rotisserieg.com

"Everyone feels welcome" at this "engaging" UES eatery, where "Parisian-style" rotisserie chicken and other "well-prepared" French specialties, plus a "strong wine list," attract an "older" crowd in a "frenzied and noisy NY setting" that "feels a little like an old-school brasserie"; the overall offering, once you've factored in the all-important "scene" and proximity to Central Park, makes for an "elegant" spot; N.B. Sunday brunch is available from late September through late June.

🄩 Rubirosa Italian/Pizza 26 | 18 | 21 | $$

NoLita | 235 Mulberry St.
(bet. Prince & Spring Sts.)
212-965-0500 | rubirosanyc.com

"Life-changing pizzas" with "crispy thin crusts" inspire admirers of this NoLita destination, "loved" for its "damn-special" pies, "addictive" house-made pastas, meatballs, and other Italian specialties that "far surpass your average mom-and-pop joint" fare; since the "casual" "rustic" space is "always packed," and reservations are "hard to come by," "expect waits" (along with "cramped" and "loud" surroundings), although "reasonable" costs, "friendly" service, and "super-delicious" gluten-free menu items are pluses.

Ruby's Cafe Australian 22 | 18 | 18 | $$

NoLita | 219 Mulberry St. (Spring St.)
212-925-5755 | rubyscafe.com
Murray Hill | 442 3rd Ave. (bet. 30th & 31st Sts.)
212-300-4245

These "cute" Australian cafés, which have reached the status of neighborhood "go-to's" in NoLita and Murray Hill, present good brunches, lunches, and "casual" dinners, with something to "please everyone" (there are "flavorful" burgers, "fresh" salads, and "crunchy" fries); the waits can be as long as the quarters are "tight," but the servers are "always friendly and efficient," making for a "lovely" experience.

Rucola ℂ Italian 25 | 22 | 22 | $$$

Boerum Hill | 190 Dean St. (Bond St.) | Brooklyn
718-576-3209 | rucolabrooklyn.com

"The best carrots I have ever eaten" is saying something, but fans mostly flock to this "rustic" farm-to-table Italian café in Boerum Hill to "be blown away by their fresh pastas and brilliantly juicy meats" ("cocktails are phenomenal" too); "if you can get in, it's a Herculean feat" – they don't take reservations for parties under five, and it's "very popular and very noisy," especially for dinner; breakfast here is another plus, as is the backyard.

Ruffian Wine Bar 25 | 23 | 25 | $$

East Village | 125 E 7th St. (bet. 1st Ave. & Avenue A)
212-777-0855 | ruffiannyc.com

"Crowded" and teeny-tiny, this East Village cave is perfect for a "wine night," with "natural" and unusual pours swirling to the beat of audacious music; "incredible" flavor descriptors on the list and a staff with "lots of enthusiasm" help you find the right bottle, and the constantly "changing menu" of small dishes is, like a fine wine, "well-balanced" and crafted with "refined" technique; N.B. they accept only small parties and don't take reservations.

Runner & Stone American

22 | 19 | 21 | $$

Gowanus | 285 3rd Ave.
(bet. Carroll & President Sts.) | Brooklyn
718-576-3360 | runnerandstone.com

Come for the "out-of-this-world" breads – fans say they have the "best baguettes in Brooklyn" – but be sure to "get there early, as they sell out quickly"; brunch and dinner options include house-made pastas and seasonal vegetables, and the full bar is a favorite destination for cocktails; a "hidden gem" in Gowanus, it feels "intimate and romantic," thanks to exposed brick and floor-to-ceiling windows that let in lots of light.

❷ Russ & Daughters Cafe Deli/Diner

26 | 19 | 21 | $$

Lower East Side | 127 Orchard St.
(bet. Delancey & Rivington Sts.)
212-475-4880 ext. 2
East 90s | The Jewish Museum,
1109 5th Ave. (92nd St.)
212-475-4880 ext. 3 | russanddaughters.com

For "a postmodern Jewish eats/deli experience," nothing's more "enjoyable" than this pair serving "inventive takes on old favorites" in "smartly done" cafés with "a touch of retro kitsch"; nearly fed-up diners say that both branches – one "in the heart of the LES" "not far from the original 1914 appetizing store," the other in the Jewish Museum – are "just too hard to get into" and "pricey for what they are, but that's soon forgotten when the nova is melting in your mouth."

The Russian Tea Room Russian

19 | 25 | 22 | $$$$

West 50s | 150 W 57th St. (bet. 6th & 7th Aves.)
212-581-7100 | russiantearoomnyc.com

Experience-seekers get revved up about the "blinis and borscht" classics (caviar tastings, beef Stroganoff, chicken Kiev) and 44 vodkas at this "extravagant" Midtown institution that "retains its old luster"; "everyone looks like they're descended from royalty," and you're sitting on cherry banquettes and among giant gold samovars under an "ornate" and "sumptuous" interior; it's all way too much, but worth a splurge, at least "once in a lifetime."

❷ Sadelle's Diner

23 | 22 | 19 | $$$

SoHo | 463 W Broadway
(bet. Houston & Prince Sts.)
212-776-4926 | sadelles.com

"If you can get manage to get a table," you'll enjoy a "decadent breakfast" at this "quintessential New York" spot for bagels, smoked fish, eggs, and other brunch fare; what amounts to an elevated diner is "pretty" and "chic but also inviting," with "everything designed down to the salt and pepper shakers"; it can be "very, very noisy" and is always "expensive," but the SoHo spot is "worth it for special occasions."

Safari African

▼ 26 | 13 | 21 | $$

Harlem | 219 W 116th St. (bet. Frederick
Douglass Blvd. & St. Nicholas Ave.)
212-964-4252 | safariharlem.com

"Let your taste buds wander" to East Africa by way of Harlem at this tiny, "crowded" café serving traditional stews and spiced tea;

it's an extremely casual operation with a basic space adorned with Osmanya (Somali) script on the walls – its servers go out of their way to help illuminate the cuisine for those who don't know it; plus, it's BYOB and "possibly the only place to get Somali food in NYC."

St. Anselm Steakhouse

27 | 19 | 22 | $$$

Williamsburg | 355 Metropolitan Ave. (4th St.) | Brooklyn
718-384-5054 | stanselm.net

"The best bang-for-your-buck steakhouse in NYC" (or at least "all of Williamsburg"), rave fans about this "unassuming, small" spot dominated by a massive-wood-planked bar; "they take a lot of care grilling and serving" the "amazing" meats – not just beef, but unusual veal and pork cuts – and that "makes up for no reservations and long wait time"; "get there early or just be prepared to grab a drink at the bar next door," regulars recommend.

St Tropez Wine Bar Wine Bar

20 | 20 | 21 | $$

SoHo | 194 Spring St. (Sullivan St.)
917-261-4441 | sttropezwinebar.com
West Village | 304 W 4th St. (bet. Bank & 12th Sts.)
917-388-3893

"See and be seen" at this "simple but chic" West Village wine bar with a "limited menu" (oysters, cheeses, stews, salads, etc.) and a "diverse" selection of "delicious" bottles that make it easy for malbec mavens and Bordeaux bros to pretend they are actually "in Paris"; the farmhouse-inspired dining room is "cozy" but "tight," and it's "a little tough to pop in" without a reservation, but "friendly" sommeliers always make sure your glass is full; the SoHo branch opened in 2019.

Sakagura Japanese

26 | 23 | 23 | $$

East 40s | 211 E 43rd St. (bet. 2nd & 3rd Aves.)
212-953-7253 | sakagura.com
East Village | 231 E 9th St. (bet. Stuyvesant St. & 2nd Ave.)
212-979-9678

"A touch of Tokyo in Midtown," the main branch's "windowless" dining room is in a "nondescript office building's" basement and "difficult to find," but the "melt-in-your-mouth" sashimi and sushi and "more varieties of sake than you knew existed" keep it "bustling" at lunch; open for decades, it's "one of the most outstanding and unusual Japanese restaurants in the city"; the much newer (and smaller) outpost in the East Village flies beneath the radar, but earns equally high ratings for its "wonderful" menu.

Sal and Carmine Pizza Pizza

25 | 8 | 18 | $

West 100s | 2671 Broadway (bet. 101st & 102nd Sts.)
212-663-7651

"Close your eyes" and "concentrate" on the "perfect" ratio between the "tangy" tomato sauce and the "just rich enough" cheese, and thin crust good enough to "eat on its own" at this "platonic ideal" of a counter-service pizzeria near the top of the UWS; it's "exactly what you would expect" from a "family-run" slice dive if you pictured it before going: not much talking, and "tiny" tables in an interior tailor made for takeout.

| | FOOD | DECOR | SERVICE | COST |

Salinas Spanish
27 | 26 | 24 | $$$

Chelsea | 136 9th Ave. (bet. 18th & 19th Sts.)
212-776-1990 | salinasnyc.com

It's not often a restaurant can truly be "sexy," but aficionados of this "hidden gem" in Chelsea say just that, in addition to terms like "romantic" and "intimate"; and it's not just because the dining room is "resplendent with roses" that provide a "fragrant backdrop to dinner" – it comes with "typical gracious Spanish hospitality," the wine list is "extensive," and the "fireplaces and plush finishes make the experience divine"; the "unique Basque-influenced" food includes "wonderfully inventive" tapas and "sumptuous" seafood.

Salumeria Rosi Italian
24 | 17 | 21 | $$$

West 70s | 283 Amsterdam Ave. (73rd St.)
212-877-4800 | salumeriarosinyc.com

"Small portions encourage a tasting approach to the abundant menu" of "high-quality" cured meats and cheeses and "well-prepared" pasta at this "casual" UWS Italian salumeria-cum-restaurant selling "items for either takeout or eat-in"; although creatively decorated with plaster-cast produce, "it's a smallish place, and they can be a bit annoying about how long you stay"; still, it's "molto bene" "for a midday snack" or ahead of a show at the Beacon.

San Matteo Pizza Italian/Pizza
26 | 14 | 18 | $$

East 80s | 1739 2nd Ave. (81st St.)
212-426-6943 | sanmatteopanuozzo.com

The "kitchen performs miracles nightly" at this "wood-fired" Neapolitan pizza on the UES baking divine personal pies and panuozzo (stuffed-dough sandwiches); "smaller than a postage stamp," it's "always jammed" and has a "nondescript" interior and "so-so service," but the food delivers exceptional "bang for your buck," especially for the neighborhood, and the frenetic energy is that of a "bustling eatery somewhere in Italy."

San Pietro ⑤ Italian
24 | 20 | 26 | $$$$

East 50s | 18 E 54th St.
(bet. 5th & Madison Aves.)
212-753-9015 | sanpietroristorantenyc.com

Instead of splurging for a flight to Rome, "you can drop the same amount for dinner" at this Midtown destination for haute Italian; this is "investment banker heaven," so "prepare to pay for the privilege" of rubbing elbows with those engaged in "corporate entertaining at its highest level"; in return, expect "impeccable service," "wonderful" food, and a suitably regal wine list; some prefer the open-air seating to the dining room.

Sandro's Ⓜ Italian
24 | 16 | 21 | $$$

East 80s | 306 E 81st St. (2nd Ave.)
212-288-7374 | sandrosrestaurant.com

The "charm is in the food" at this UES Italian "sleeper hit," where the list of daily specials is longer than the menu itself, making it "challenging" to choose among the "exquisite" pastas and other Roman classics; the "cozy" space can get "crowded" and "noisy," but service is always "warm." Don't be surprised if

FOOD | DECOR | SERVICE | COST

Chef Sando "wanders" through the dining room "making sure you're happy."

Sanfords ◖ American 22 | 21 | 22 | $$
Astoria | 30-13 Broadway
(bet. 30th & 31st Sts.) | Queens
718-932-9569 | sanfordsnyc.com
This "Manhattan-like addition" to Astoria is a "solid choice" for New American offerings that "occasionally break out of the mold" and "rare" whiskeys poured from a "bourbon bar of excellence" – it runs along the side of the "hip" and "pleasant" modern space, a former cafeteria; "expect to wait in lines on the weekends" for dinner and brunch, but once you get that coveted seat the service is "helpful" and "attentive."

Sant Ambroeus Italian 23 | 21 | 21 | $$$
East 70s | 1000 Madison Ave.
(bet. 77th & 78th Sts.)
212-570-2211 | santambroeus.com
NoLita | 265 Lafayette St. (Prince St.) | 212-966-2770
West Village | 259 W 4th St. (Perry St.) | 212-604-9254
"Ah to be seen" at these "upscale" cafés, where the food is "delicious and expensive – just like the crowd" (including "princesses of the UES"), which goes "to graze" on traditional Milanese plates, "divine" pastries and cookies, and for "perfect" espresso and other coffee; service can be "spotty," but sitting outside in warmer months "can't be beat."

Santina Italian 20 | 24 | 19 | $$$
Meatpacking District | 820 Washington St.
(Gansevoort St.)
212-254-3000 | santinanyc.com
This "airy, breezy" "glass box" on the Hudson in the Meatpacking District evokes the "seaside" vibes of Southern Italy and makes diners feel "fancy-free"; start with the "don't-miss" chickpea pancakes before moving on to "inventive" fresh grilled fish paired with a selection from the "highly curated" wine list, all suggested by capable but casual servers; most of the menu can be made gluten-free, too.

Sarabeth's American 20 | 18 | 19 | $$$
East 90s | 1295 Madison Ave. (92nd St.)
212-410-7335 | www.sarabethsrestaurants.com
Murray Hill | 381 Park Ave. S (27th St.) | 212-335-0093
TriBeCa | 339 Greenwich St. (bet. Harrison & Jay Sts.)
212-966-0421
West 50s | 40 Central Park S (6th Ave.) | 212-826-5959
West 80s | 423 Amsterdam Ave. (bet. 80th & 81st Sts.)
212-496-6280
Brunch is "king" at this NYC chain, known for its "divine" muffins, pancakes and omelets, "velvety" tomato soup, jams, and sweets "worth the caloric splurge"; the many branches share "lovely" "family-friendly" surroundings ("they are very quick with the food"), and "ladies who lunch abound"; sure, "weekends are a zoo," but most agree they're "always a safe bet," especially at the East 90s branch, handy to the Museum Mile.

Saravanaa Bhavan Indian
23 | 9 | 14 | $$

Murray Hill | 81 Lexington Ave. (26th St.)
212-684-7755 | saravanaabhavannyc.com
West 70s | 413 Amsterdam Ave. (80th St.)
212-721-7755

"When you need a thali or dosa fix," these spare and simple restaurants in Curry Hill and the West 70s provide options that are "very close to what you'll get in South India," including its frothy and perky filter coffee; "all vegetarian" and kosher too, "the food is much better than the environment," which tends towards the "scruffy," and the somewhat "weary" service.

Sardi's Ⓜ Italian
17 | 23 | 21 | $$$

West 40s | 234 W 44th St. #3 (bet. 7th & 8th Aves.)
212-221-8440 | sardis.com

"Part of Broadway's history," this Theater District "staple" from 1921 feels like "like eating in a museum," with "celebrity carica-tures" on the walls and "people-watching" opportunities (you may see "cast members of the plays" in the area, along with tourists, of course); the Continental-Italian dishes are "second-ary," and the service merely "decent," but it's "convenient," and the "lively" bar's "fine" for pre- and post-performance drinks while also "sopping up" the "traditional-showbiz" vibe.

Sarge's Delicatessen & Diner ℂ Deli
23 | 12 | 18 | $$

Murray Hill | 548 3rd Ave. (bet. 36th & 37th Sts.)
212-679-0442 | sargesdeli.com

"Jewish deli food at its most delish" ("mile-high hot pastrami sandwiches," "superior" chicken soup) is alive and well at this Murray Hill "go-to," a "true throwback" to diner days, from the "big menu" to the "traditional, brusque-but-with-love service"; the "prices are reasonable," and its 24/7 hours make it "a late-night lifesaver," although the "dingy, worn" interior "could use a refresh."

Sasabune Ⓢ Japanese/Sushi
27 | 14 | 23 | $$

East 70s | 401 E 73rd St. (1st Ave.)
212-249-8583 | sushisasabune.tumblr.com

"Fish nerds" swim uptown to this UES "respite" for a well-received omakase menu and "melt in your mouth" sushi ("for the purist") that'll make you say "wow"; the no-nonsense appearance is a slight turnoff, but "purists" find it a "real special treat"; the "polite, professional" staff are "gratifyingly willing" to discuss their process.

NEW Savida Mediterranean
– | – | – | $$$

TriBeCa | 139 Duane St.
(bet. Church St. & W B'way)
212-202-3175 | savidanyc.com

With this taverna with a Tel Aviv twist, TriBeCa has a new home for the Mediterranean tradition of sharing meze, along with freshly baked bread and tackling whole grilled fish and washing it down with bottles of wine; a comfortable, casual environment and impressively low prices for the neighborhood make this a candidate for treating a large group of friends or a date; the happy hour and shakshuka brunches are also gaining momentum.

Saxon + Parole American

NoHo | 316 Bowery (Bleecker St.)
212-254-0350 | saxonandparole.com

19 | 21 | 20 | $$$

"Whether you are looking for a full-blown dinner, just drinks at the bar, or something in-between," this woodsy, horse-themed "space works for almost any occasion" when you're trotting around NoHo; the staff "actually wants to befriend you" as they sling the meat-oriented American mains and "amazing" cocktails (don't miss the "intriguing" DIY Bloody Mary bar at brunch); P.S. head downstairs for The Poni Room, a quasi-speakeasy with Asian-influenced snacks and a rosé-heavy wine list.

Sayra's Wine Bar (Wine Bar

Far Rockaway | 91-11 Rockaway Beach Blvd.
(bet. Beach 91st & Beach 92nd Sts.) | Queens
347-619-8009

▼ 25 | 25 | 25 | $$

Furnished with myriad woods and other decorations that make it "feel like Spain or Italy," this breezy, narrow Far Rockaway bar teams its wines (and a few brews) with easy-on-the-wallet appetizers; responsive service and liberal open hours and and happy hours, plus outdoor beer garden–style seating when the weather's nice, are more points in this one's favor.

Scalinatella Italian

East 60s | 201 E 61st St. (3rd Ave.)
212-207-8280

21 | 17 | 20 | $$$$

Locals and celebs walk "down a flight of stairs" to this "small," "cave"-like UES Italian, a "neighborhood" spot that feels "old world" while still being "close to Bloomingdale's"; although the fare is "average" or a bit better (and that includes the specials), as is the service, the price can still induce "sticker shock"; still, it "can get pretty packed with customers," so it's clearly doing something right.

Z Scalini Fedeli Italian

TriBeCa | 165 Duane St.
(bet. Hudson & Staple Sts.)
212-528-0400 | scalinifedeli.com

27 | 26 | 28 | $$$$

"Old-world charm with service to match" informs this "exemplary" TriBeCa Italian, where "exquisite" dishes make up the prix fixe-only menus served in a "romantic" space that "oozes with elegant sophistication"; "fancy prices" don't seem to stem its "popularity with Wall Streeters on an expense account" or its appeal for "taking special guests," and the "quiet" atmosphere only reinforces its status as an NYC "treasure."

Scampi Italian

Flatiron | 30 W 18th St. (bet. 5th & 6th Aves.)
212-888-2171 | scampinyc.com

21 | 18 | 19 | $$$

"Inventive riffs on classics" are what draw the crowds to this seafood-focused Southern Italian favorite in the Flatiron district; "wonderful" crudos (Italy's answer to ceviche) are a "light way to start the meal," which often moves on to "surprisingly delicious" grilled fish and "some of the best pasta around"; as for the service, it runs a bit hot and cold, ranging from "excellent" to "not the best."

Scarpetta Italian   23| 22| 23| $$$|

NoMad | 88 Madison Ave. (bet. 28th & 29th Sts.)
212-691-0555 | scarpettarestaurants.com

At this "must-try" for "pasta lovers," enchanted eaters "wonder if they put a bit of black magic" in the spaghetti, because it's so tasty – as is the seafood; the "stylish interiors," "sexy room," and "deep wine list" lead to a "lively" night out, though some say it's not the same since chef Scott Conant departed, and the noise level makes it feel like you have to "scream over the table during dinner."

Scarr's Pizza Pizza   26| 20| 19| $|

Lower East Side | 22 Orchard St.
(bet. Canal & Hester Sts.)
212-334-3481 | scarrspizza.com

"It looks like a slice shop" judging by the facade, but it's more of a lounge with a "throwback" "1970s basement vibe" that celebrates the "old LES"; and while it may seem like a "cool kid" place, with hip service to match, the pizza is "superb" classic greasy NYC (with some "vegan options") – and it's fun to sit in the "comfy booths" and let the time warp wash over you.

Sea Thai   16| 19| 14| $$|

Williamsburg | 114 N 6th St. (Berry St.) | Brooklyn
718-384-8850 | seathainyc.com

Expect "young people" taking "tons of photos" in a "dark," moody interior that showcases a reflecting pool and Buddha statue; you should also expect "long waits" at peak times if you don't "reserve ahead," and drop-the-plates-and-go service even if you do; despite the "big" semi-Thai menu being full of average food, some find it's "worth the trip" to Williamsburg to experience the "elaborate decor" and "relaxing atmosphere" in a place "more presentable than most in its price range."

The Sea Fire Grill Seafood   26| 24| 26| $$$|

East 40s | 158 E 48th St. (bet. Lexington & 3rd Aves.)
212-935-3785 | theseafiregrill.com

With "tremendous" seafood "standards" and "succulent" steak, this "special-occasion" spot with prices to match in the East 40s treats diners "like royalty," and fans say to "look no further" to "turn back the clock" with a team that "understands" hospitality: "attentive" but "not overbearing" servers in "white jackets," "adult" but "no attitude," and "prompt" but "no one rushes you"; "try to sit in the back room by the fireplace."

The Sea Grill 🗷 Seafood   24| 25| 24| $$$|

West 40s | Rockefeller Plaza, 19 W 49th St.
(bet. 5th & 6th Aves.)
212-332-7610 | patinagroup.com/the-sea-grill

With a "dramatic" location "in the heart of" Rockefeller Plaza, this "classic" source for seafood features an "elegant" interior with "wonderful views" of the nearby ice rink's skaters in winter (as well as garden scenery come balmier weather); on offer from the "caring" staff is "high-quality" fish – including sushi – and "excellent cocktails," and although the "hefty" costs are a drawback, it's still a decent choice for fêting out-of-towners; get a window table "so you can watch NYC go by."

Seamore's Seafood   19 18 19 $$

NoLita | 390 Broome St. (Mulberry St.)
212-730-6005
Chelsea | 161 8th Ave. (18th St.)
212-597-9222 | seamores.com
Dumbo | 66 Water St. (bet. Main & Dock Sts.) | Brooklyn
718-663-6550
Financial District | 250 Vesey St. (North End Ave.)
646-585-7380

"It's always sunny" at this sustainable seafood chainlet, where you have the freedom to "design your own meal" with "lots of healthy sides" that don't weigh you down for the rest of the day; the "breezy Long Island shack" interior feels a little "Hamptons," but noise levels at the "bustling" Chelsea and NoLita locations can "throw off your meal" – "be ready to speak loudly" or hold your peace.

🅩 2nd Ave Deli Deli   24 13 18 $$

East 70s | 1442 1st Ave. (75th St.) | 212-737-1700
Murray Hill | 162 E 33rd St. (bet. Lexington & 3rd Aves.)
212-689-9000 | 2ndavedeli.com

"Traditional" "Jewish soul food" gets people kvelling at these "nostalgic" UES and Murray Hill delis, which offer "mile-high sandwiches," "winning" knishes, matzo ball soup "to cure any ailments," all in "huge portions"; of course, the check feels "closer to Park Avenue" than Bialystok, the interior basically "doesn't matter," and you "don't expect white-glove service" – but just "bring your appetite and a box of Alka-Seltzer": this "trip down memory lane" is "just what the doctor ordered."

2nd Floor Bar & Essen ◖ Gastropub   22 23 20 $$$

East 70s | 1442 1st Ave. (75th St.)
212-737-1700 | 2ndavedeli.com

"One of the city's best-kept secrets," 2nd Ave Deli's kosher upstairs bar feels a little bit "speakeasy"; the menu updates Jewish classics that come in "large portions" and are "not to be missed"; sure, it's a fine destination "to impress Bubbe with New World" fare, but most agree the "amazing cocktails" are the top draw, along with a "dark and cozy" room that "never seems to be too busy."

Sen Sakana 🅢 Japanese/Peruvian   21 20 24 $$$

West 40s | 28 W 44th St. (bet. 5th & 6th Aves.)
212-221-9560 | sensakana.com

The service is "exceptional" and "attentive" at this "high-end" Nikkei (Japanese–Peruvian fusion) Theater District location with a no-tipping policy; its influences "collide to create flavors" that impressed diners "would not have imagined," resulting in mind-opening takes "on the usual suspects" of sushi and sashimi – in contrast, most rice and meat dishes "are pretty standard"; Broadway-bound guests point out that "you can hear your companions' conversations," making it a good pre-show option.

Serafina Italian/Pizza

19 | 16 | 18 | $$

East 70s | 1022 Madison Ave. (79th St.)
212-734-2676 | serafinarestaurant.com
Meatpacking District | 7 9th Ave. (Little W 12th St.)
646-964-4494
West 70s | 2178 Broadway (77th St.)
212-595-0092
Expect "fairly typical Italian food" at these "casual" neighborhood hangouts known for thin-crust pizza and "standard,"
"nothing to write home about" pasta dishes; the staff is known
to be "accommodating," especially when the "nothing-fancy"
digs are packed with "lots of families and children"; the chain
has six more locations throughout Manhattan.

Serra by Birreria Italian

16 | 27 | 15 | $$$

Flatiron | Eataly, 200 5th Ave. (23rd St.)
212-937-8910 | eataly.com/us_en/stores/nyc-flatiron
Atop Eataly in Flatiron, this "magical" space has "stunning,"
"bright, airy" decorations that "change seasonally," but the
"pricey" menu is less inspiring; "overwhelmed bartenders" and
overrun waitstaff trying to serve a space "spanning an entire
city block" are usually "friendly," but sometimes "impossible
to find" – go "for the scene, not necessarily to have a mind-
blowing meal," advise rooftop mavens – maybe just an "Aperol
spritz" and some "Italian meats and cheese."

Sette Mezzo Italian

24 | 18 | 23 | $$$

East 70s | 969 Lexington Ave. (bet. 70th & 71st Sts.)
212-472-0400
A great place to spot celebs (and demi-celebs and industrial
titans), this clubby UES favorite is one place where a reservation is a must ("although if you aren't a regular, good luck");
habitués insist that the "expensive" and non-flashy Italian fare is
carefully prepared and served by a "considerate" staff, although
the "tables are a little too close together."

Sevilla ℂ Spanish

24 | 16 | 22 | $$

West Village | 62 Charles St. (W 4th St.)
212-929-3189 | sevillarestaurantandbar.com
The "heavenly" smell of garlic "hypnotizes you" as you walk into
this "oldie but goodie" Spanish eatery; open since 1941, it's a
"friendly neighborhood spot" where the servers "treat you like
family" and serve "huge portions" of "well-prepared" classics
like paella and shrimp in white wine sauce; the "decor is a little
tired" and the tables "a little crowded," but "you go for the food,
not the atmosphere."

Sfoglia Italian

24 | 18 | 21 | $$$

East 90s | 1402 Lexington Ave. (92nd St.)
212-831-1402 | sfogliarestaurant.com
"High-caliber" Italian fare inspired by "farmhouse" recipes –
"comforting" chicken under a brick that's "sheer nirvana,"
"fabulous" breads and pastas – warms up your soul, or at least
cozies you up for a "food coma pronto"; this Uptown "charmer"
is "snug," with the crowd of locals and those headed to the
92nd St. Y all sitting "close together" on the long tables under the
chandeliers, so "plan ahead" if you're looking to squeeze in too.

Shabushabu Macoron Japanese ▼ 28 | 16 | 29 | $$$$

Lower East Side | 61 Delancey St.
(bet. Allen & Eldridge Sts.)
212-925-5220 | shabushabumacoron.com

"Exquisite and intimate" is how fans describe this LES Japanese eight-seater, where diners sit along a counter and enjoy the "unique" experience of an omakase meal of hot pot "delicacies" cooked right in front of them – a rarity; the setting is simple, the service provides (and requires) lots of attention to detail, and even after eight courses "you will not want the meal to end."

NEW Shabushabu Mayumon Japanese – | – | – | $$$$

Lower East Side | 115 Division St. (Orchard St.)
646-476-7717 | www.shabushabumayumon.com

The team behind Shabushabu Macoron welcome an elegant new tasting-menu option in the LES, with a similar approach to high-end Japanese; the seasonally changing prix fixe menu emphasizes Wagyu beef hot pots and handmade soba noodles, but here, rather than focusing on traditional preparations, the menu is more internationally inspired, with dips like Piemontese bagna cauda; expect extravagant ingredients and intimate seating near the chef, as well as prices in line with such coddling.

Shake Shack Burger Joint 21 | 13 | 16 | $$

Flatiron | Madison Square Park
(Madison Ave. & 23rd St.)
212-889-6600 | shakeshack.com

"Hooray for Danny Meyer," exclaim aficionados of the restaurateur's "popular," "ubiquitous" now-global chain started in Madison Square Park, which delivers "moist, juicy" patties, "awesome" French fries, "fantastic" milkshakes, and other "elevated fast food," plus beer and wine, for a "reasonable price" to those who "can't live without their fix"; less lauded are the "crazy long lines," "no-frills" decor, and "frenetic" atmosphere, which often sparks "competitive seating"; branches now exist across NYC and around the world, but many agree "the original location is still the most appealing in good weather."

Shalom Japan M Japanese 25 | 19 | 24 | $$$

Williamsburg | 310 S 4th St. (Rodney St.) | Brooklyn
718-388-4012 | shalomjapannyc.com

"One of the most unique" and "super-creative" restaurants in a neighborhood constantly seeking after originality, its Jewish/Japanese fusion represents an "unexpected" but "beautiful melding of two cultures," with "well-executed" dishes like matzo ball ramen; the food and service are sincere, the decor is casual, the sake list is terrific, and with the option to order extra pork, it definitely doesn't keep kosher.

Shanghai You Garden Chinese ▼ 24 | 15 | 18 | $

Flushing | 135-33 40th Rd.
(bet. Main & Prince Sts.) | Queens
718-886-2286 | shanghaiyougarden.com

"One of the better Shanghainese restaurants in the city," say fans of this Flushing favorite, where the "xiao long bao (steamed soup dumplings) are excellent, but the other dishes are what separate it from the competition"; the "casual" digs are "typically crowded," and you should "be prepared to wait for a table" at peak hours, but "they let you place your order in advance, so once you sit down the food comes rather quickly."

Shuka Mediterranean   23| 24| 21| $$|

SoHo | 38 MacDougal St. (bet. Houston & Prince Sts.)
212-475-7500 | shukanewyork.com

The "vibe and price point," and "great-for-sharing" portions make this "high-energy" SoHo "brunch destination" the "perfect group gathering spot" for "meeting and greeting friends" and "ordering a ton"; the staff "helpfully walks you through" the "creative" menu of "fresh, inviting, and satisfying," Middle Eastern food with many "vegetarian-friendly" options.

Shuko Japanese/Sushi   28| 25| 27| $$$$|

Greenwich Village | 47 E 12th St. (B'way)
212-228-6088 | shukonyc.com

"Every bite is perfect and imaginative" at this Greenwich Village Japanese destination, serving an "unrivaled" and "heavenly" "parade of bites" via omakase and kaiseki menus; although the service is "attentive," it's overall casual and laid back, with music that's "off the hook" – "who knew sushi and hip-hop went so well together?"; it's also quite a "splurge," albeit a "memorable" one.

Shun Lee Palace Chinese   23| 22| 23| $$$|

East 50s | 155 E 55th St. (bet. Lexington & 3rd Aves.)
212-371-8844 | shunleerestaurants.com

This once-legendary destination for upscale Chinese food in the East 50s still commands a "loyal following" for dim sum and traditional dishes – the "lettuce cups and Peking duck are a must" – in "ritzy" and "cordial" surroundings, and although diners acknowledge dishes are "Americanized," they also find honest Hunan, Sichuan, and Cantonese coming out of the kitchen; this "solid choice" remains popular for family celebrations, with "professional" service.

Shun Lee West Chinese   21| 20| 20| $$$|

West 60s | 43 W 65th St.
(bet. Columbus Ave. & CPW)
212-595-8895 | shunleerestaurants.com

Though proximity to Lincoln Center and "excellent dim sum" are the main draws, you can have a "Chinese banquet on a grand scale" here, guided by "knowledgeable" servers who take "a cheerful approach" to the "vast menu choices" of "undeniably tasty Chinese-American classics"; the less enthused say the "lacquered black-and-white" decor is dated, some dishes have taken "a turn for the worse," and "tables can get overrun with children."

Silver Rice Japanese/Sushi   ▼ 26| 14| 19| $|

Crown Heights | 638 Park Pl.
(Franklin Ave.) | Brooklyn
718-398-8100 | silverrice.com
Prospect Lefferts Gardens | 575 Flatbush Ave.
(bet. Maple & Midwood Sts.) | Brooklyn
347-789-9874

This tiny pair of Brooklyn sushi bars serve "seasonal," made-to-order, creative Japanese, including vegetarian macrobiotic rolls and "fresh" fish combinations in handheld paper coffee cups (with the option of switching to flax seed–studded rice), with a cafe-like setting to match; the menu is designed for quick stops and "takeout" rather than dining, and the "high-quality" food and ample selection of beer and sake make it comfortable for small neighborhood meals.

Simon & The Whale American   20 | 23 | 21 | $$$
Murray Hill | 23 Lexington Ave. (23rd St.)
212-475-1924 | satw.nyc
"Funky and fresh" come to mind when you step into the "pleasing surroundings" of the Freehand Hotel's ground-floor space, even more so once you take in the "midcentury" design with "tons of wood elements" by the Roman and Williams studio; you'd expect nothing less from restaurateur Gabriel Stulman, whose signature elements include "thoughtful" hospitality from a "friendly, competent" staff and an expansive menu of Mediterranean-inflected seafood and American dishes.

⊞ The Simone ⑤ French   27 | 23 | 27 | $$$$
East 80s | 151 E 82nd St. (bet. Lexington & 3rd Aves.)
212-772-8861 | thesimonenyc.com
"If one wants quiet, fine dining on the UES," seek out this "secret" place, which is "like having dinner with a friend" who "happens to be an extraordinary cook," composing "classically prepared, mostly French" dishes "paired perfectly with wines" and served by staffers who "tend to your every whim" within "the coziness of an elegant townhouse"; with "only eleven tables," "reservations are hard to come by, but well worth the wait."

Sistina Italian   25 | 25 | 24 | $$$
East 80s | 24 E 81st St. (Madison Ave.)
212-861-7660 | sistinany.com
Set in "a lovely townhouse" – part palazzo, part "delightful glass-enclosed solarium" – this "elegant" UES destination "attracts a well-heeled and well-dressed older crowd" with an "enormous menu" of "superbly executed," lightened-up Italian classics, offered by "professional, charming" servers; it's "become a bit pricey," but still "worth the extra dollars" if you "save it for a special occasion" or big date night.

The Smile Mediterranean   18 | 19 | 16 | $$
NoHo | 26 Bond St. (bet. Bowery & Lafayette St.)
646-329-5836 | thesmilenyc.com
"Beloved by regulars," and with a "rustic and charming" "underground" setting that feels like it's in "someone's farmhouse," this all-day "neighborhood" Mediterranean in NoHo serves a "limited" menu of "decent" dishes; less of a joy are the "tight" seating and subpar service, but the reasonable prices are cheerful, as is the availability of breakfast served until mid-afternoon.

⊞ Smith & Wollensky Steakhouse   25 | 21 | 24 | $$$$
East 40s | 797 3rd Ave. (49th St.)
212-753-1530 | smithandwollenskynyc.com
"Old-school charm" is the hallmark of this Midtown East "staple," which many steakhouse lovers consider "a classic";

its "exceptional steaks," fresh seafood, and "superior sides" (including lauded hash browns) all help make it an "absolute favorite"; the "old-world style and service" includes "professional staff that know how to take care of their guests"; if you're not "on an expense account" try the Grill, where "locals" order burgers and lighter fare for "slightly more reasonable prices."

The Smith ☾ American   19 | 17 | 18 | $$

East 50s | 956 2nd Ave. (bet. 50th & 51st Sts.)
212-644-2700 | thesmithrestaurant.com
East Village | 55 3rd Ave. (bet. 10th & 11th Sts.) | 212-420-9800
NoMad | 1150 Broadway (27th St.) | 212-685-4500
West 60s | 1900 Broadway (63rd St.)
212-496-5700
The American food is "dependably" tasty at this "vibrant" and "energetic" mini-chain with a "something-for-everyone menu" that's "more bar style than fine dining" (oysters, burgers, mac n cheese, bibimbap) that really gets going at the "always-packed" brunch; as a "casual" "go-to" suited to groups, it can easily get "noisy" – bring your "earplugs" – but service is "fast" and "attentive"; it's also "one of the better options near Lincoln Center."

Snack Taverna Greek   20 | 15 | 18 | $$

West Village | 63 Bedford St. (Morton St.)
212-929-3499 | snacktaverna.com
On a "picture-perfect West Village corner," this "charming Greek taverna" is both "rustic and romantic"; the "classic" dishes, "done simply," often have an "innovative touch," and the servers are "warm and knowledgeable"; all in all, it's a "cozy neighborhood staple," though some locals admit they "wouldn't travel too far to come here."

Sobaya Japanese   25 | 20 | 24 | $$

East Village | 229 E 9th St. (bet. 2nd & 3rd Aves.)
212-533-6966 | sobaya-nyc.com
"Fresh, hand-cut, and "meticulously" made buckwheat noodles are the main attraction at this East Village soba shop that offers "filling" meals while maintaining "the highest of Japanese traditions," including dishes like tempura and eel that can be turned into combo "bento boxes"; while "there is almost always a wait," service is "efficient," the simple surroundings are "pleasant," and the "sake list is divine."

Socarrat Paella Bar Spanish   20 | 16 | 19 | $$

Chelsea | 259 W 19th St. (bet. 7th & 8th Aves.)
212-462-1000 | socarratnyc.com
East 50s | 953 2nd Ave. (bet. 50th & 51st Sts.)
212-759-0101
NoLita | 284 Mulberry St. (bet. Houston & Prince Sts.)
212-219-0101
You "might as well be in Seville" at this Spanish staple with "hot, tasty, fun, and fresh" tapas and paella "prepared in the traditional way" – it's the "real deal"; come ready for a popular happy hour that makes it "noisy at night" and also "be prepared to wait" for the namesake dish; the "friendly and welcoming" servers help ensure your enjoyment, though the memorable sangria doesn't hurt, either.

Sofreh Persian

▼ 26 | 22 | 24 | $$$

Prospect Heights | 75 St. Marks Ave.
(Flatbush Ave.) | Brooklyn
646-340-0322 | sofrehnyc.com

"Straight out of the souk" comes this "popular" Prospect Heights Persian "hot spot," which combines an "interesting menu" of "unusual" specialties with creative cocktails in a bright, simple, white-walled setting; often it's "hard to get" a reservation here, and the tabs do pile up, but "personal service" and outdoor seating help make this "a much-needed addition" to the local landscape.

Sojourn American

19 | 15 | 16 | $$

East 70s | 244 E 79th St. (bet. 2nd & 3rd Aves.)
212-537-7745 | sojournrestaurant.com

Brunch gets high marks at this UES hangout with Downtown DNA, where dishes like the lobster Benedict attract praise; the "always crowded, always fun" happy hour is popular with a crowd who come for the "tasty" and "diverse" small plates, well-chosen wine, and surprisingly robust live music scene; the noise can be "earsplitting" and the "service has never been great," so head elsewhere for a "serious dinner."

Somtum Der Thai

24 | 15 | 18 | $$

East Village | 85 Avenue A (bet. 4th & 6th Sts.)
212-260-8570 | somtumdertogo.com

At this East Village version of a Bangkok restaurant celebrated for Isaan food (from northeastern Thailand), it's "always packed," and "for good reason"; the "wonderful selection" of fried chicken, sticky rice, and the signature papaya salad make a balanced lunch that's a "go-to" combo; be advised that although the service and surroundings are casual, you should "make a reservation," and if you ask for "Thai spicy," you may leave "without being able to feel your tongue."

Sorbillo Pizzeria Italian/Pizza

22 | 15 | 17 | $$

NoHo | 334 Bowery (bet. Bond & Great Jones Sts.)
646-476-8049 | sorbillonyc.com

"Naples-style pizza" is the draw at this NoHo Italian, which "makes the cut" with not-too-pricey pies that use organic flour, natural yeast, and a long rise, accompanied on the menu by salads, apps, and pastas, although the crisp, wood-filled interior "could be better," as could the "average" service; the overall "cool vibe," a long bar and "outdoor seating" make it a decent choice for a "casual date" meal while in the area.

Sotto 13 Italian

17 | 17 | 17 | $$

West Village | 140 W 13th St. (bet. 6th & 7th Aves.)
212-647-1001 | sotto13.com

Thin-crust pizza, fresh pasta, "bottomless brunch" drinks, and tempting "happy hour deals" are some of the reasons diners beat a path to this "cozy" "neighborhood spot" in the West Village; those less into its charms say the "ordinary" Italian snacks are merely a "step above" "basic," deem the "small" space "strangely laid out" and often "noisy," and point out that service can be bumpy; still, it's "cute," and the specials are a "real bargain."

Sottocasa Italian/Pizza   26| 20| 22| $$|

Boerum Hill | 298 Atlantic Ave. (Smith St.) | Brooklyn
718-852-8758
Harlem | 227 Lenox Ave. (bet. 121st & 122nd Sts.)
646-928-4870 | sottocasanyc.com

"A little piece of Rome in Brooklyn," this literally "underground"
pizzeria serves "one of the best Neapolitan pies" in the city –
"don't sleep on the Amatriciana" – as well as some delicious
salads; the atmosphere is "cozy and friendly," with a "family
attitude," and it's "gently priced" for what you get; and while it's
"definitely a little trendy, but don't let that turn you off"; there's
also an "excellent" outpost in Harlem.

Souvlaki GR Greek   21| 18| 17| $$|

East 50s | 231 E 53rd St. (bet. 2nd & 3rd Aves.)
212-832-0395 | souvlakigr.com
Lower East Side | 116 Stanton St.
(bet. Ludlow St & Essex Sts.)
212-777-0116
West 50s | 162 W 56th St. (bet. 6th & 7th Aves.)
212-974-7482

"Incredibly flavorful" dips, "filling" pita wraps, and lamb chops
"sold by the kilo" available at "affordable" prices draw fans to
these Greek tavernas in Midtown and on the LES; the "cute
Mykonian" decor takes you on a "quick vacation," although the
"cheek-by-jowl" table "squeeze" can make for mild "claustrophobia" during peak hours; P.S. a roving food truck also belongs
to this growing group.

🄓 Sparks Steak House Ⓢ Steakhouse   26| 21| 24| $$$$|

East 40s | 210 E 46th St. (bet. 2nd & 3rd Aves.)
212-687-4855 | sparkssteakhouse.com

"Here's the beef," shout "carnivores" about this Midtown "living
legend," a circa-1966 steakhouse "throwback" featuring "giant,"
"incredible" cuts "with just the right sizzle," plus an "awesome
wine list" – delivered by servers "who know what they're doing";
"sky-high" tabs, "old-school" (or maybe just "out-of-date") surroundings, and the "need to shout to have a conversation" ruffle
feathers, yet "those with money and power" (along with mere
mortals) find it "enjoyable" for "schmoozing" while absorbing
the "history."

Speedy Romeo Italian/Pizza   23| 18| 19| $$|

Lower East Side | 63 Clinton St.
(bet. Rivington & Stanton Sts.)
212-529-6300 | speedyromeo.com
Clinton Hill | 376 Classon Ave. (Greene Ave.) | Brooklyn
718-230-0061

Pizzas covered with "innovative" toppings emerge from "wood-
fired madness" like champs – it's all "burnt" in "a good way";
"but don't miss the wings and burger either," say fans – this
Swiss Army knife of pizzerias in Clinton Hill also serves "amped-
up" antipasti, steaks, and "phenomenal" desserts; they're "upbeat" spots, but large groups here can leave waiters "stressed
and harried" on occasion.

Spicy Village ⑤ Chinese ▼ 28 | 8 | 12 | $ |

Lower East Side | 68 Forsyth St.
(bet. Grand & Hester Sts.)
212-625-8299 | spicyvillagenyc.com
"Wonderful" hand-torn noodles, "huge" portions of sheet-pan chicken, and cumin lamb make diners go "ahhh" at this "busy" microscopic LES/Chinatown staple; it doesn't matter if you're "crammed" into a "tiny" table with "strangers" when you're sinking your teeth into these "easy" and deeply flavorful eats.

The Spotted Pig (British/Gastropub 22 | 20 | 17 | $$ |

West Village | 314 W 11th St. (Greenwich St.)
212-620-0393 | thespottedpig.com
Many feel this West Village gastropub is "not what it once was"; still, stalwarts recommend it for the "yummy" Anglo-Italian eats (including "one of, if not the best, burgers in NYC") and the "cozy," plaid-centric, "genuine pub-style decor"; others note that the "staff is transactional" and they don't take reservations.

SriPraPhai Thai 27 | 14 | 20 | $$ |

Woodside | 64-13 39th Ave.
(bet. 64th & 65th Sts.) | Queens
718-899-9599 | sripraphai.com
It's an enviable trick to have both a "huge menu" ("including a separate vegetarian section") but also make it possible to "close your eyes and point to a random page and land on something delicious," but this Thai legend has kept its rep for "absolutely terrific" dishes with "ample spice"; service is "efficient" while the space is "functional," and "the back patio is nice in warmer months."

The Standard Biergarten (German 15 | 20 | 14 | $$ |

Meatpacking District | The Standard, High Line
848 Washington St. (bet. Little W 12th & 13th Sts.)
212-645-4100 | standardhotels.com/new-york
It's "Oktoberfest every day" at this open-air hall underneath the High Line that's made for grabbing German beers on draft and snacks (sausages, "monster" pretzels); occupying its long picnic benches is a crowd that ranges (not widely) from "recent college grads" to "bros" to young bankers – "networking opportunities abound"; even though the noise here can turn off even the biggest fans, they also admit they "spend way too much time at this place, but never regret it!"

The Standard Grill American 22 | 23 | 21 | $$$ |

Meatpacking District | The Standard, High Line
848 Washington St. (bet. Little W 12th & 13th Sts.)
212-645-4100 | thestandardgrill.com
Scene-seekers "go for the people-watching" at this "hip" spot in the Standard Hotel, where Rocco DiSpirito is now at the helm; it comes with an "attractive" setting, "happy" crowd, and "lovely" New American fare, which includes raw-bar, vegetarian, and gluten-free options, plus "fantastic" drinks; "pleasant" outdoor seating and a "convenient location" make it a good option for "unwinding" after "a stroll on the High Line."

Stella 34 Trattoria Italian/Pizza

24 | 23 | 23 | $$

West 30s | Macy's, 151 W 34th St.
(bet. B'way & 7th Ave.)
212-967-9251 | patinagroup.com/stella-34

"Who would have suspected that you could find fine food and a light, bright dining room" offering "awesome Empire State Building views" "in Macy's, of all places," say fans of this "hidden gem" that specializes in "grown-up meals" of "wood-fired fresh pizzas" and other "imaginative" Italian delights, served by "relaxing, charming" staff; the "iconic location" makes it "ideal after or during a day of shopping" or before an event at Madison Square Garden.

STK Downtown C Steakhouse

22 | 23 | 21 | $$$

Meatpacking District | 26 Little W 12th St.
(bet. 9th Ave. & Washington St.)
646-624-2444 | stksteakhouse.com
STK Midtown
West 40s | 1114 6th Ave. (bet. 42nd & 43rd Sts.)
646-624-2455

"Nightclubby vibes" and "cool bar scenes" differentiate these "seductive" Midtown and Meatpacking District steakhouses, where the "glitzy," "spacious" surroundings and "jumping" crowd predominate, with the "excellent" cuts and "strong drinks" also competing for attention; some feel the "upbeat," music-enhanced settings err on the "noisy" side, but despite just-OK service, they "deliver a consistent product" – happy-hour options are decent, too; P.S. the Downtown location is dinner-only.

Storico M Italian

18 | 19 | 16 | $$$

West 70s | 170 Central Park W (77th St.)
212-485-9211 | storicorestaurant.com

"Convenience" to Central Park as well as the New-York Historical Society is one of the major reasons to head to this almost-"hidden" Italian inside the museum, where "shelves full of fine china" (part of the collection) overlook an "upscale" room that feels like "Sag Harbor or Southampton"; although "high prices," just-"adequate" service, and noise irritate some diners, it remains a decent "alternative" to other spots nearby, and the setting is hard to beat.

Strip House Steakhouse

23 | 22 | 22 | $$$

Greenwich Village | 13 E 12th St.
(bet. 5th Ave. & University Pl.)
212-328-0000 | striphouse.com
West 40s | 15 W 44th St. (bet. 5th & 6th Aves.)
212-336-5454

A "swanky," "blast-from-the-past" feeling lures the "crowds" to these "stylish" Village and Midtown steakhouses, where the steamy, red-hued interiors jibe well with "tender" meats, "well-done cocktails," and "proper wine" options; although it gets "boisterous," and the tabs run high, the "cool vibes" also lend themselves to "chilling" with your "carnivore friends" or a "date"; N.B. a speakeasy bar is next to the 12th Street original, while the Midtown site also serves lunch as well as bar food.

Sugar Freak Cajun/Creole   23 | 20 | 20 | $$
Astoria | 37-11 30th Ave. (37th St.) | Queens
718-606-1900 | sugarfreak.com

With "sensational" and "shareable" specialties like po'boys and red beans and rice, "strong" cocktails, and "must-try" beignets, this Astoria staple for Cajun/Southern is the "closest thing to being in New Orleans," with "funkiness" embodied everywhere, from the mismatched plates and tables to the beads hanging from the chandeliers; with no reservations it's no wonder the buzzy brunch is "always crowded."

Sugarcane Raw Bar Grill American   22 | 22 | 17 | $$
Dumbo | 55 Water St. (Old Dock St.) | Brooklyn
718-473-9555 | sugarcanerawbargrill.com

The views from the "outdoor seating" just might "eclipse" all others in Dumbo at this branch of a Miami-based mini-chain with an "unusual" menu of sushi, raw bar favorites, and seafood tapas, creating a medley of bite-sized things from the ocean, with additional options for non–fish-lovers; it has "spotty" service and an atmosphere that's "hectic" as well as "fun," but if you "roll with it" all, you'll enjoy.

Sugarfish by Sushi   25 | 19 | 21 | $$$
Nozawa Japanese/Sushi
Flatiron | 33 E 20th St. (bet. B'way & Park Ave. S)
347-705-8100 | sugarfishsushi.com
SoHo | 202 Spring St. (Sullivan St.)
212-847-7464

"Get in line early" and prepare for an "absurd wait" for "hyped" sushi from these branches of an LA-based chain; delivering an "omakase feel without an omakase price," it uses "set menus" with combo names like "Trust Me"; most are happy to do just that, and love that there is a "no tip" policy and find the "price quality unmatched," but purists bemoan service they say "rushes you" and a streamlined franchise-y feel.

Sunday In Brooklyn American   23 | 25 | 21 | $$$
Williamsburg | 348 Wythe Ave.
(S 2nd St.) | Brooklyn
347-222-6722 | sundayinbrooklyn.com

"No Sunday scaries here" – "charming" and "inviting," like a "cabin in the woods," this Williamsburg joint features an open kitchen, a greenery-filled area on the second floor, a private event space, and rooms "packed" with "hipsters" seeking "inventive" New American fare – including the "must-order" social-media-famous malted pancakes, "super-creative cocktails," and an "amazing" brunch; the lines get predictably "hellish," but "professional" service, outdoor seating, and reasonable tabs keep things appealing.

Superiority Burger Vegan/Vegetarian   25 | 13 | 20 | $
East Village | 430 E 9th St. (Avenue A)
212-256-1192 | superiorityburger.com

"Come for the veggie burger, stay for the innovative sides" and "incredible rotating specials" at this East Village white-tiled "hole-in-the-wall," where the "chill folks behind the counter" "do radical things with fresh vegetables and flavors"; "if you can score a seat, great; if not, Tompkins Square Park nearby makes for a good backup dining room."

Supper ⊄ Italian
24 | 19 | 21 | $$

East Village | 156 E 2nd St. (bet. Avenues A & B)
212-477-7600 | supperrestaurant.com

"So damn good and worth the wait" ("don't miss the chicken parm") say neighborhood fans of this long-lived cash-only East Village haunt ("this place still rocks!"); sure, "there are sexier Italian places" but it's "cheap, good, and just right" (it looks "like it's in an old home," after all), with "character" and "warm" service to spare.

Sushi Azabu Japanese/Sushi
▼ 28 | 16 | 20 | $$

TriBeCa | 428 Greenwich St.
(bet. Laight & Vestry Sts.)
212-274-0428 | sushi-azabu.com

"No frills, but fantastic sushi" sums up this "subterranean, unassuming place in TriBeCa" that features "absolutely off-the-charts omakase" – "premium price points" but also "worth every penny"; "be sure to sit at the bar," where you can chat with the chefs as they prepare your "exquisite" meal.

Sushi By Bou Japanese/Sushi
26 | 23 | 25 | $$$

East 30s | 32 E 32nd St.
(bet. Madison Ave. & Park Ave. S)
917-268-7268 | sushibybou.com
Flatiron | 49 W 20th St. (bet. 5th & 6th Aves.)
917-268-7268
Union Square | 118 E 15th St. (bet. Irving Pl. & Union Sq. E)
917-268-7268
West 40s | 132 W 47th St. (bet. 6th & 7th Aves.)
917-268-7268
Sheepshead Bay | 1811 Emmons Ave. (Sheepshead Bay Rd.)
Brooklyn | 917-268-7268

"Wildly affordable omakase" options are the draw of these "unique" sushi spots, where timed set menus featuring "fresh," "innovative" seafood get diners in and out "quickly"; perhaps it's "not a relaxing experience," and the "tiny," "funky" rooms aren't "fancy," but if you count in the "cool vibes," it sure does "feel like Japan." N.B. reservations by text only.

NEW Sushi By M Japanese/Sushi
27 | 17 | 26 | $$$

East Village | 75 E 4th St. (bet. Bowery & 2nd Ave.)
347-688-8101 | sushibym.com

"Next-level sushi" is the deal at this "closet"-size, counter-only East Village nook, where a "rapid-fire whirlwind" of "excellent," regularly changing omakase menus and other "innovative" Japanese fare delight diners during hourly timed seatings; it's all a bit "unceremonious," yet the "casual decor belies the seriousness of the food," and with the "affordable" prices, "attentive" staff, and "social" vibe, it "leaves patrons smiling"; reservations are recommended (it's "not a walk-in place").

| | FOOD | DECOR | SERVICE | COST |

Sushi Dojo ◖ Japanese/Sushi　　▼ 26 18 22 $$$
East Village | 110 1st Ave. (bet. 6th & 7th Sts.)
646-692-9398 | sushidojonyc.restaurant
"Unique" offerings, along with omakase options that are a
"terrific bang for the buck" are the chief virtues of this East
Village joint; "it feels like just another dinky sushi spot," but the
"nontraditional" raw fish and rolls are often adorned with "luxe
ingredients like foie gras or truffle foam," making for "a nice
change of pace from others in the city."

Sushi Ginza Onodera ⑤ Japanese/Sushi　29 28 29 $$$$
East 40s | 461 5th Ave. (40th St.)
212-390-0925 | sushiginzaonoderanewyork.com
"You never know what you're going to get" at this elegant
Japanese place in the East 40s, but you can count on "an out-
of-this-world experience" with "exquisite fish" (imported from
Japan's Toyosu Fish Market) and red vinegar-tinted, "always-
fresh rice" "served by professional" chefs you'll have "a really
nice time talking to"; offering omakase only, it's "pricey, but
worth it" for a slice of "sushi heaven."

Sushi Ishikawa ⑤ Japanese/Sushi　　27 24 28 $$$
East 70s | 419 E 74th St. (bet. 1st & York Aves.)
212-651-7292 | ishikawanyc.com
"High-end" omakase menus at "half the price" and "without the
pretension" are made even better thanks to the "friendliest"
chef behind the counter at this sushi spot in the East 70s; he's
"welcoming" and "easy to talk to" throughout dinner – and he
even has a few "funny" jokes up his sleeve; the "upscale" sushi
pieces are a "glutton's delight," using "incredible" ingredients
like gold flakes and foie gras to jazz up an already "fantastic"
presentation.

Sushi Kaito Ⓜ Japanese/Sushi　　▼ 27 18 28 $$$
West 70s | 244 W 72nd St.
(bet. B'way & West End Ave.)
212-799-1278 | sushikaito.net
This sushi bar is bringing Tokyo to the UWS with "terrific"
omakase dinners that vary in size but that always feature the
chef's choice for fresh fish of the day – one of the best such
"affordable" menus in the city; this is an elevated neighborhood
experience, with about a dozen places at the bar, name tags to
mark your seat, and direct communication with those preparing
your food – and the "price is reasonable for the quality."

Sushi Katsuei ⑤ Japanese/Sushi　　26 16 20 $$$
West Village | 357 6th Ave. (Washington Pl.)
212-462-0039 | sushikatsuei.com
Park Slope | 210 7th Ave. (3rd St.) | Brooklyn
718-788-5338
"The chefs here really know what they are doing" at this "unassuming" but bright duo in Park Slope and the West Village,
which bring "melt-in-your-mouth" sushi in combinations "that'll
have you dreaming for days afterward"; while it is "expensive"
overall, it's a notable "deal for quality" Japanese fare, especially
the "well-priced omakase" menu, "totally on par with the other
more expensive" options in the city.

Z Sushi Nakazawa Japanese/Sushi   29| 24| 28| $$$$|
West Village | 23 Commerce St.
(bet. Bedford St. & 7th Ave. S)
212-924-2212 | sushinakazawa.com/nyc
"Forget 'Jiro Dreams of Sushi' – New Yorkers dream of" Daisuke
Nakazawa, the "young apprentice to the Tokyo master" in the
documentary, who crafts a "delicious and thoughtful" omakase
experience that takes you on "a journey through the Japanese
sea" and leaves you "ruined for all other sushi"; "you will spend
serious money" for the "freshest fish," but "artful" presentations
from the maestros behind the counter ensure that this is "as
good as it gets" in this town.

Sushi of Gari Japanese/Sushi   26| 16| 22| $$$|
East 70s | 402 E 78th St. (bet. 1st & York Aves.)
212-517-5340 | sushiofgari.com
Sushi of Gari TriBeCa S
TriBeCa | 130 W Broadway (Duane St.) | 212-285-0130
Sushi of Gari 46
West 40s | 347 W 46th St. (bet. 8th & 9th Aves)
212-957-0046
Gari Columbus M
West 70s | 370 Columbus Ave. (bet. 77th & 78th Sts.)
212-362-4816
"Sushi purists and enthusiasts" flock to this "high-end"
Japanese mini-chain for its "inventive," "super-fresh" raw
fish showcasing "amazing flavors," along with "crazy-unusual
omakase selections," all served by an "accommodating staff";
"it ain't cheap," and the "plain," usually "crowded" digs can be a
turnoff, but aficionados make it clear that "even if you have no
idea what you're eating, you will love it."

Sushi Seki ℂ S Japanese/Sushi   26| 17| 21| $$$|
East 60s | 1143 1st Ave. (bet. 62nd & 63rd Sts.)
212-371-0238 | sushiseki.com
Chelsea | 208 W 23rd St. (bet. 7th & 8th Aves.)
212-255-5988
West 40s | 365 W 46th St.
(bet. 8th & 9th Aves.) | 212-262-8880
Serving "some of the freshest, tastiest sushi in town," this
chain racks up "repeat visits" for its "classic presentations"
and "creative techniques" that "bring out the flavors"; fans of
the "always packed" neighborhood places call out the "melt-in-
your-mouth" fish, and say the omakase menu (where the chef
chooses the courses) is the way to go; just "be prepared for a
hefty bill."

Sushi Yasaka Japanese/Sushi   26| 15| 21| $$|
West 70s | 251 W 72nd St.
(bet. B'way & West End Ave.)
212-496-8460 | sushiyasaka.com
"Always packed with hungry Upper West Siders" now that "the
word is out," this "reasonably priced" Japanese eatery is where
the "courteous, prompt, friendly service" is outdone only by the
"high-quality sushi"; true, it's "small, crowded, and noisy," but
fans "go for the food, not the atmosphere" – and it's "hard to get
a table if you don't have a reservation far in advance."

	FOOD	DECOR	SERVICE	COST

☑ Sushi Yasuda ⑤ Japanese/Sushi — 28 | 22 | 25 | $$$$

East 40s | 204 E 43rd St. (bet. 2nd & 3rd Aves.)
212-972-1001 | sushiyasuda.com
Expect "genuinely melt-in-your-mouth delicious" sushi at this
Japanese mainstay near Grand Central, where "only the highest
quality" fish is served, whether à la carte or via the "super special" omakase menu; although its namesake master returned
to Japan long ago, it's still "as good as it gets," combining
"heavenly" food, "attentive" service, and "beyond expensive"
but "totally worth it" tabs.

Sushi Zo ⑤ Ⓜ Japanese/Sushi — ▼ 29 | 23 | 27 | $$$$

Greenwich Village | 88 W 3rd St. (Sullivan St.)
646-405-4826 | sushizo.us
With the effort the omakase chefs here put into serving the
"freshest" "denizens of the sea" and presenting them in a "creatively constructed" manner, it's no wonder that many proclaim
them some of the most "phenomenal" sushi meisters in the
city – fans say they have mastered the "provenance" of fish too,
"tracking migration"; it doesn't hurt that the chefs are game for
"super fun" conversations while "delicately" slicing their fish at
this Greenwich Village spot.

Suzume ⟨ ⊟ Japanese — 24 | 20 | 20 | $$

Williamsburg | 545 Lorimer St. (Devoe St.) | Brooklyn
718-486-0200 | suzumebk.com
This "cozy little" Williamsburg "standby" is a "pescatarian's
dream," with salmon ramen, "refreshing" poke sushi, and other
"imaginative yet accessible" Hawaiian-Japanese creations,
making it a spot for a "creative date night"; the "easygoing" service and "fair" prices are nice enough, but mostly you come for
"those noodles," served in a "low-key" place to "eat in peace"
"and watch the chef work."

Sweet Chick ⟨ Southern — 23 | 18 | 19 | $$

Lower East Side | 178 Ludlow St. (Houston St.)
646-657-0233 | sweetchick.com
Prospect Heights | 341 Flatbush Ave. (Park Pl.) | Brooklyn
718-484-7724
Williamsburg | 164 Bedford Ave. (N 8th St.) | Brooklyn
347-725-4793
Long Island City | 46-42 Vernon Blvd.
(bet. 46th Rd. & 47th Ave.) | Queens | 718-433-4064
"Get your chicken-and-waffles fix" at these "stomach-expand-
ing" and "energetic" Southern restaurants, which also have
"mouthwatering" variations on the main theme; the "modern"
yet rustic settings are "nothing memorable," service can be
"slow," and "waits" may be "long," but it's a "solid" choice for
"filling" fare, as well as a "brunch standby."

Sylvia's Restaurant Southern — 21 | 16 | 20 | $$

Harlem | 328 Malcolm X Blvd.
(bet. 126th & 127th Sts.)
212-996-0660 | sylviasrestaurant.com
Probably the "most famous soul food restaurant in NYC," this
"Harlem mainstay does not disappoint" with "rib-sticking" "fried
chicken and Southern delights," say its many devotees – in
contrast to critics who declare that "the glory days have long

passed," citing "long waits" and "just eh" eats; even so, "the Sunday morning gospel brunch is something everyone should do once" – just "get there before the tour buses come in."

Szechuan House Chinese   ▼ 26 | 12 | 12 | $$

Flushing | 133-47 Roosevelt Ave. (Prince St.) | Queens
718-762-2664 | szechuanhouses.com

Diners seeking a "good meal" head to Flushing's oldest Sichuan haunt, daring tastebuds to keep up with tongue-tingling Chongqing chicken, fiery dan dan noodles, and a fried tilapia swimming in chili oil; an average-looking dining room – spruced up only with red tablecloths and a painting here and there – are nothing to write home about, but servers ensure just enough hospitality for big groups.

Szechuan Mountain House Chinese   ▼ 26 | 20 | 20 | $$

East Village | 23 St. Marks Pl. (bet. 2nd & 3rd Aves.)
917-388-3866 | szechuanmountainhouse.com
Flushing | 3916 Prince St. (39th Ave.) | Queens
718-888-7893

"An interesting range of fine Sichuan dishes," "beyond deli-cious" and "properly spicy upon request" (those "peppercorns are not used sparingly"), dominate the menu at this Chinese pair; both the Flushing and the East Village locales are "always crowded," but "the food is worth waiting for," and the rustic decor – wood furnishings and artifacts, straw screens, and bamboo dividers – is "visually pleasing."

NEW TabeTomo Japanese/Ramen   – | – | – | $$

East Village | 131 Avenue A
(bet. 9th St. & St. Marks Pl.)
646-850-6414 | tabetomonyc.com

This dipping-style ramen shop is from a veteran of LA favor-ite Tsujita Artisan Noodle; with that sort of pedigree, expect thick noodles, decadently rich 60-hour broth, fair prices, and long waits that keep you hungry enough to fool yourself into believing you could finish the eight-pound Megamori Tsukemen Challenge; cold beer is available to cool the broth, as well as hot stones to warm it back up if it cools too much.

Table d'Hôte French   24 | 17 | 25 | $$$

East 90s | 44 E 92nd St.
(bet. Madison & Park Aves.)
212-348-8125 | tabledhote.info

"The kind of unpretentious gem you hope to find in Paris," this "adorable" French-American in Carnegie Hill furnishes a "limited menu" of "spot-on" eats in a "tiny" space; given the dimensions, it's "not all that comfortable," and you will likely "need to book" ahead for a table, yet the "warm" service, "quiet" atmosphere, and not-so-bad prices soften the blow, and it's "handy" for UES museums.

Taboon Mediterranean   25 | 20 | 23 | $$$

West 50s | 773 10th Ave. (52nd St.)
212-713-0271 | taboononline.com

Middle Eastern food overlaps with Mediterranean at this "consistently remarkable" Hell's Kitchen café, named after the wood-fired oven used to cook many of the menu items; dishes are "made with the freshest ingredients" and prepared "with a twist of creativity" – fans say to "go for the stuffed breads" and meze; the "friendly" staff add to the charm of the brick-walled space, which is "bustling," "noisy," and with large windows facing the sidewalk.

Taci's Beyti Middle Eastern   23 | 15 | 19 | $$

Sheepshead Bay | 1953 Coney Island Ave.
(bet. Avenue P & Quentin Rd.) | Brooklyn
718-627-5750 | tacisbeyti.com

Fans say the Turkish food is "a level above" at this long-standing BYOB in Sheepshead Bay, where the "chicken shish is succulent," the "octopus is moist and tender, the fish is grilled to perfection," and the traditional coffee is a real "treat"; the simple interior is "always packed" with a "neighborhood crowd," keeping things "noisy and energetic."

Tacombi Mexican   20 | 21 | 18 | $$

NoLita | 267 Elizabeth St. (bet. Houston & Prince Sts.)
917-727-0179 | tacombi.com
Flatiron | 30 W 24th St. (bet. 5th & 6th Aves.)
212-242-3491
West 30s | 23 W 33rd St. (bet. 5th & 6th Aves.)
212-967-5555
West Village | 255 Bleecker St. (bet. Leroy & Cornelia Sts.)
646-964-5984

"California vibes" run through this "airy and festive" Mexican chain whose MO involves designing "cool industrial" spaces that make you feel like you're eating "inside of a taco truck"; "tasty but tiny" tacos, "amazing" hot sauces and "strong, spicy" pitchers of margaritas will "do the job" and set the mood for an "elevated casual dinner" with a group "of any size," or just when you need "a good place fast."

Tacos El Bronco ◖ Mexican   ▼ 25 | 9 | 18 | $

Sunset Park | 4324 4th Ave. (44th St.) | Brooklyn
718-788-2229 | tacoselbronco.com
Sunset Park | 860 5th Ave. (37th St.) | Brooklyn
917-405-5759

What started as a food truck has branched out to a Sunset Park brick-and-mortar delivering "superior" tacos "for the buck" with the works ("homemade" corn tortillas, "delicious" green salsa, garnishes like charred spring onions and radishes) and "homey" fillings like chorizo, pork skin, and beef tongue; it's always a party here, with Mexican tunes blaring from the jukebox and soccer games playing what seems like 24/7.

Tacuba Mexican   22 | 19 | 18 | $$

West 50s | 802 Ninth Ave. (53rd St.)
212-245-4500 | tacubanyc.com
Astoria | 35-01 36th St. (35th Ave.) | Queens
718-786-2727

The kind of place that inspires excess punctuation – "great cocktails!" "great tacos!" "tasty guac!" – also attracts young people looking for "drinks, noise, and a hip atmosphere" (it's "chaos on a Friday night"); while the Astoria location gets mixed reviews for the food (it's more a happy hour hang), its Theater District counterpart wins higher marks for the "killer margaritas," "friendly service," and "fresh"-tasting, often "elevated" Mexican dishes.

NEW TAK Room American   —| —| —| $$$$|
West 30s | 20 Hudson Yards
(10th Ave. & 33rd St.)
929-450-4050 | takroomnyc.com
Thomas Keller's arch tribute to country club cuisine at Hudson Yards sidesteps the last several decades of culinary trends, instead updating midcentury American fare with current presentations and prices; it's best for those with the thirst – and finances – to take advantage of an impressive bubbly list, with bottles served from carts, and even guests not drawn in by fine wines or nostalgic touches like complimentary caramel corn will appreciate the top-shelf service and architectural views.

Takahachi Japanese/Sushi   24| 15| 21| $$|
East Village | 85 Avenue A (bet. 4th & 6th Sts.)
212-505-6524 | takahachi.net
TriBeCa | 145 Duane St. (bet. B'way & Church St.)
212-571-1830
It's "hard to find higher quality" sushi for the money in NYC than what's rolled at these "dependable" "neighborhood standbys" with an "extensive menu for a small place," with both "classics" and some creative rolls; a casual, affordable meal that is "comparable to the best," with "friendly and attentive" service makes the sometimes long wait to eat here "totally worth it."

Takashi Japanese   26| 20| 23| $$$|
West Village | 456 Hudson St.
(bet. Barrow & Morton Sts.)
212-414-2929 | takashinyc.com
Fans of this "tight Japanese BBQ" say "this is the place" for a meaty good time – guests love that they can grill their own beef, which might include just about any part of the steer – it's a "magnificent" experience enhanced by a minimalist dining room, a low-key atmosphere, and "lovely" service, so it's no surprise that "reservations are a must; P.S. beef-broth ramen is served late on Friday and Saturday nights.

NEW Takeshi ⑤ Japanese/Sushi   —| —| —| $$$|
SoHo | 28 Grand St. (bet. 6th Ave. & Thompson St.)
917-675-0771 | takeshisushiny.com
While not exactly cheap, this omakase-focused sushi bar in SoHo is a great deal for splurge dinners or lunches; the chefs take their time to talk to customers and create raw fish tastings that feel special, all served alongside curated sake pairings designed for the evening's freshest cuts.

NEW Taladwat Thai   —| —| —| $$$|
West 40s | 714 9th Ave. (49th St.)
646-823-9815 | taladwat.com
This Hell's Kitchen star sets itself apart from other nearby Thai restaurants through its discount set meals, which allow you to

taste two different curries or other dishes from a big list for a nice price; the stew-centric menu is a change from the noodle- and stir-fry–centric fare of the chef's two previous restaurants, Pure Thai Cookhouse and Land Thai Kitchen – the dishes travel well for takeout or delivery if you're not into the dining room's simple bench seating and minimal decor.

Ⓩ Tamarind Tribeca Indian   27 | 27 | 27 | $$$

TriBeCa | 99 Hudson St. (bet. Franklin & Harrison Sts.)
212-775-9000 | tamarindtribeca.com
"The spice is right at this TriBeCa standout," where "lovers of modern Indian cuisine" delight in "high-end delicacies" "pre- pared with flair and panache" and served by "obliging," "grace- ful" staffers in an "airy," "elegant," yet "cheerful" wood-planked space; prices are pretty "upscale," but it's "worth it" for a slice of "culinary nirvana"; P.S. the lunch prix fixe garners praise as "one of NYC's last real bargains."

Ⓩ Tanoreen Ⓜ Middle Eastern   27 | 20 | 25 | $$

Bay Ridge | 7523 3rd Ave. (76th St.) | Brooklyn
718-748-5600 | tanoreen.com
"Throw on your stretch pants and hop on the R train" for this "delightful" Bay Ridge Mediterranean–Middle Eastern favorite; its "sensual" Palestinian-inspired dishes are served in "huge" portions by an "excellent" staff – its chef, Rawia Bishara, is likely to "talk to you like you're family" as she "circulates," and while the place is often "busy" and anything but palatial, com- menters say this "journey" to "expand your culinary horizons" is worthwhile.

Tanoshi Sushi Ⓢ Ⓜ Japanese/Sushi   29 | 15 | 26 | $$$

East 70s | 1372 York Ave. (bet. 73rd & 74th Sts.)
917-265-8254 | tanoshisushinyc.com
"You must trust the chefs" to take you on "a sushi experience like no other," feeding you "delicious jewels" of "melt-in-your- mouth," "top-notch" fish at a fraction of the cost at the more famous omakase spots; even more "sublime" is the "intimate" UES setting, with a "1:4 chef to customer ratio" and a generous "bring your own sake" policy: they'll even "chill it for you in an ice bucket."

Tao ☾ Pan-Asian   23 | 26 | 22 | $$$

Tao Downtown
Chelsea | 92 9th Ave. (bet. 16th & 17th Sts.)
212-888-2724 | taogroup.com
Tao Uptown
East 50s | 42 E 58th St. (bet. Madison & Park Aves.)
212-888-2288
"It's like eating in your favorite Instagram pic" at this pair of "multi-level" "pan-Asian" mega-restaurants, which provide "more of a nightclub experience than dinner," complete with "high-decibel" noise and "over-the-top decor" that features a "giant Buddha statue" – the "big and bold" flavors of "fusion bites" make "delicious plates to share," and though the sushi and "exciting cocktails" aren't cheap, you're "paying for the scene," one "perfect for groups" and "celebrations."

	FOOD	DECOR	SERVICE	COST

Taqueria St. Marks Place ◖ Mexican
East Village | 79 St. Marks Pl. (bet. 1st & 2nd Aves.)
646-964-5614

21 | 19 | 20 | $

Perpetually adorned with Christmas lights, this "funky dive" is a "neighborhood option for cheap Mexican food" when down St. Marks way; "the service is nice," but the place is "not particularly quiet," so it's "best for a quick bite" or a few rounds of "killer margaritas" or a Mexican beer along with its "absolutely-worth-getting guac" – it all provides major "bang for your buck for a sitdown dinner in the East Village."

Taqueria Tlaxcalli ◖ Mexican
Parkchester | 2103 Starling Ave.
(Olmstead Ave.) | Bronx
347-851-3085 | taqueriatlaxcalliny.com

▼ 27 | 13 | 23 | $

Now, "this is the real thing," declare fans of the burritos, tacos, and other Mexican mainstays served for breakfast, lunch, and dinner (there's also a menu for los niños) offered by this Parkchester site; both the dishes and the interior are decorated in bright colors that, along with the "rustic" artifacts and artwork, lend an upbeat, "fun atmosphere" to the small, narrow space.

Tavern on the Green American
Central Park | Central Park W (67th St.)
212-877-8684 | tavernonthegreen.com

18 | 25 | 20 | $$$

"Sylvan surroundings" that "hearken to a bygone era" remain the biggest reason to go to this "iconic" Central Park "destination for all seasons"; its "tremendous" greenspace views, courtyard, and "opulently" reimagined interior "enchant" tourists and some locals; it's true that the "decent" American fare is still "not as special as the decor," the service "could be better," and you'll have to swallow hefty prices along with the food – but as "landmarks" go, it's still "magical" overall.

ⓩ Taverna Kyclades Greek
Astoria | 33-07 Ditmars Blvd. (33rd St.) | Queens
718-545-8666 | tavernakyclades.com
East Village | 228 1st Ave. (bet. 13th & 14th Sts.)
212-432-0011
Bayside | 39-28 Bell Blvd. (40th Ave.) | Queens
718-631-2000

26 | 16 | 21 | $$

"Fish so fresh it seems like it was caught an hour ago" is the attraction of this "affordable" "Astoria institution," with "modern-taverna-like" branches in Bayside and the East Village; the "all-around friendly staff" serve "generous portions" of Greek fare, and while the "upscale" outposts improve on the original's "bare-bones" decor, the "no-rez" policy at all three means "waits can be a pain" – "be strategic and go for early lunch or weekday dinner."

Tavola Italian/Pizza
West 30s | 488 9th Ave. (bet. 37th & 38th Sts.)
212-273-1181 | tavolahellskitchen.com

21 | 17 | 20 | $$

For familiar "pre- or post-theater" Italian "with some new twists," try this West 30s Neapolitan trattoria that offers "moderately" priced wood-oven pizza and whole roasted fish, is decorated with "old-world" delicatessen touches, and has "knowledgeable" servers; it's "noisy," with "tight quarters" but the location near the Port Authority is "convenient" for coming and going, and the "welcoming" atmosphere might make you want to stay a while.

TBar Steakhouse

22 | 19 | 22 | $$$

East 70s | 1278 3rd Ave. (bet. 73rd & 74th Sts.)
212-772-0404 | tbarnyc.com

"Perfectly prepared steaks" are a big reason to head to this UES grill, but not the only one – the thin-crust pizzas win praise, as do the salads; it's a prime spot for "people-watching," which is handy, because "the tables are too close to each other" and "the din at dinner makes conversation impossible"; there's also an "extensive wine list" and "friendly and helpful" staff; you "definitely need a reservation," or "don't bother going."

Telly's Taverna ◖ Greek

25 | 16 | 19 | $$

Astoria | 28-13 23rd Ave.
(bet. 28th & 29th Sts.) | Queens
718-728-9056 | tellystaverna.com

"Why eat grilled fish anywhere else?" ask fans, given that the seafood is "consistently fresh and well prepared" at this Astoria staple owned and staffed by a "caring" Greek family; the interior is "pleasant," the backyard garden seating is "lovely," and the bill won't "break the bank"; it's also "accommodating" for all sorts of groups.

Tempura Matsui Ⓢ Ⓜ Japanese ▼

29 | 24 | 26 | $$$$

Murray Hill | 222 E 39th St. (Tunnel Exit St.)
212-986-8885 | tempuramatsui.com

Japanophiles seeking "a wonderful night out" congregate at this intimate and "unique" venue in Murray Hill, which specializes in "seasonal tempura" and various fried ingredients over rice, featured in several multicourse menus; under a slanted bamboo-beamed roof, you sit at the wood counter, where à la carte options are also available, or at tables; either way offers a sight of the frying chefs in action.

10 Corso Como Italian

24 | 24 | 22 | $$

South Street Seaport | 200 Front St. (Beekman St.)
212-265-9500 | 10corsocomo.com

"A trendy restaurant in Milan" transported to the South Street Seaport, this "fashionable," "avant-garde" "place to be seen" serves "expertly executed" Italian specialties; the "eclectic, chic," "open environment" "befits its location attached to the designer store of the same name"; the usually "attentive" service can get a tad "slow" when it's crowded, but the waterfront location filled with "beautiful people" makes it "worth it."

NEW Teranga Ⓜ African

– | – | – | $$

Harlem | 1280 5th Ave. (109th St.)
itsteranga.com

At this standout at Harlem's Africa Center, Chef Pierre Thiam, of Lagos's famed Nok by Alagra, prepares intriguing, affordable, and filling quick-service plates and bowls inspired by his native Senegal and beyond, all gluten- and dairy-free and cooked with ingredients largely sourced from his home continent; the attached café boasts an impressive array of juices as well as coffee with origins from Ethiopia to Rwanda.

Terroir Tribeca ◖ Italian/Wine Bar   20 | 20 | 23 | $$
TriBeCa | 24 Harrison St.
(bet. Greenwich & Staple Sts.)
212-625-9463 | wineisterroir.com

The servers are "super knowledgeable, passionate, and genuinely want to help" at this TriBeCa wine bar with a "punk-like attitude"; they pour a "huge" variety of wines by the glass, "letting you travel far and wide" while matching them with light Italian dishes; it's "lively" and always "buzzing" after work.

Tessa Mediterranean   22 | 20 | 21 | $$$
West 70s | 349 Amsterdam Ave.
(bet. 76th & 77th Sts.)
212-390-1974 | tessarestaurant.com

"Italian-based, but with enough other choices to please various palates" (there's a "delicious pork chop"), this Mediterranean relies on its "serious food" to make it a "happening spot"; it gets "a little loud at peak periods due to the narrow shape" and the "pleasant" but stern industrial-chic decor; still, servers exude a "welcoming vibe, making it a regular go-to" for "many UWS locals," as do the appealing happy hours and other deals.

Thai Market Thai   23 | 18 | 19 | $$
West 100s | 960 Amsterdam Ave.
(bet. 107th & 108th Sts.)
212-280-4575 | thaimarketny.net

It's worth seeking out this "well-kept secret" a couple blocks south of St. John the Divine; its menu expands beyond the "usual" Thai dishes seen so often around town to "excellent" rich curries, peanutty tofu pra-ram, and "inventive" starters inspired by street food; "Columbia kids" jam themselves into the "engaging" joint, partially to admire the "real-life images" repurposed as wallpaper and the bright umbrellas doubling as lighting fixtures.

Thalassa ◖ Ⓩ Greek   24 | 25 | 25 | $$$
TriBeCa | 179 Franklin St.
(bet. Greenwich & Hudson Sts.)
212-941-7661 | thalassanyc.com

Brick walls, white linens, and wood accents set the "gorgeous" scene at this "classy" Greek in TriBeCa, where "incredibly fresh" fish and seafood are paired with wines from a "first-rate" list; true, tabs can get "pricey" quickly, although prix fixe options can help mitigate that, and the "impeccable" service and overall "lovely" experience leave patrons happy.

Thalia American   20 | 18 | 21 | $$
West 40s | 828 8th Ave. (50th St.)
212-399-4444 | restaurantthalianyc.com

"Friendly" servers who'll "ensure you make your curtain" populate this "convenient" New American, located close to Broadway and therefore often quite "lively"; detractors wish that the food were a bit more exciting, and that the "big," bar-enhanced space didn't resemble "a time-warp to the early-'90s," but the availability of breakfast options, outdoor tables, and happy-hour drinks all ensure that it's an "adequate" pit stop; P.S. reservations are "a must" pre-performance.

Thursday Kitchen Korean — 25 | 20 | 23 | $$

East Village | 424 E 9th St.
(bet. 1st Ave. & Avenue A)
646-755-8088 | thursdaykitchen.com

You truly feel the "energy" of a Thirsty Thursday at this "awesome," "eclectic" spot in the East Village that blends European and "Korean influences" to create "inventive" dishes like kimchi paella and edamame dumplings, and inspires nostalgia with soju-enhanced "Capri Sun cocktails" in glowing pouches; the whimsical dishes make it feel like a bit of an "Instagram trap," and no reservations create "always long" waits, but an upbeat staff make you want to stay to order the "entire menu."

Tía Pol Spanish — 23 | 14 | 19 | $$

Chelsea | 205 10th Ave. (bet. 22nd & 23rd Sts.)
212-675-8805 | tiapol.com

Locals joke that the name "must mean 'teeny weeny' in Spanish" – the dining room in front really is "exceptionally small" – but this "literal hole-in-the-wall" serves "killer sangria" and some of "the best tapas in town"; it's busy whenever you drop by, but "especially at happy hour," when everyone bellies up to the long bar.

Tiella Ⓜ Italian/Pizza — 25 | 17 | 24 | $$

East 60s | 1109 1st Ave. (bet. 60th & 61st Sts.)
212-588-0100 | tiellanyc.com

The "small pizzas," plus house-made pastas and other "well-prepared" Southern Italian dishes, are the draws at this minuscule ("a postage stamp" size) eatery near the Queensboro Bridge; the staff are "sympathetic," and the "volume level is low" in the "unassuming," brick-walled space, but it's probably "not a place to dine if you're a party" of more than four; the "moderate" prices and location help keep its "picky" East 60s clientele "happy."

Tim Ho Wan Chinese — 22 | 13 | 17 | $$

Greenwich Village | 85 4th Ave. (10th St.)
212-228-2800 | timhowanusa.com
West 40s | 610 9th Ave. (bet. 43rd & 44th Sts.)
212-228-2802

Dim sum veterans instruct newbies to begin their "journey" with this Village and West 40s "taste of Hong Kong," presenting "classics" like "life-changing" pork buns and pan-fried turnip cakes "up to par" with any you'd find in Chinatown; time has "tamed" the "huge" crowds (although a "no-reservation" policy means that waits remain "long" at peak times).

Tiny's & The Bar Upstairs American — 20 | 22 | 17 | $$$

TriBeCa | 135 W Broadway
(bet. Duane & Thomas Sts.)
212-374-1135 | tinysnyc.com

The name is "very apt" for this "cozy" and "kooky" TriBeCa hangout with a concise seasonal menu of "well-executed"

New American small plates and more substantial dishes, often paired with both classic and creative cocktails; most find it a pleasant spot for breakfast, lunch, dinner, or weekend brunch and suggest snagging a seat by the fireplace for a real treat; there's outside seating in season, too.

Z Tocqueville 🖼 French   28 | 27 | 27 | $$$$

Flatiron | 1 E 15th St. (bet. 5th Ave. & Union Sq. W)
212-647-1515 | tocquevillerestaurant.com
Serving a "refined" French–New American menu, this "restaurant for grown-ups" provides "civilized dining" via "memorable" meals and a "fabulous wine list" in a "high-end, plush" setting that's "blessedly quiet" and that "lends itself to conversation"; of course, such a "bastion of excellence" – which includes "impeccable service" – "comes with a price to match," though prix fixe pre-theater and lunch menus work "if you don't want to splurge."

Tokyo Record Bar 🖼 Japanese   21 | 26 | 27 | $$$

Greenwich Village | 127 MacDougal St. (W 3rd St.)
212-420-4777 | tokyorecordbar.com
At this subterranean West Village spot, decorated like "your best friend's basement," "the food is good, but the experience is outstanding": "the DJ curates a vinyl jukebox playlist of old-school record classics based on guests' recommendations, while they enjoy a Japanese set menu" and "unique sakes" – and you can always "stop by for insane izakaya bites after the seatings have ended"; with only 18 seats, it's "notoriously difficult" to book, but "such a good time" if you do.

Toloache Mexican   23 | 18 | 20 | $$

East 80s | 166 E 82nd St. (bet. Lexington & 3rd Aves.)
212-861-4505 | toloachenyc.com
Greenwich Village | 205 Thompson St. (bet. Bleecker & W 3rd Sts.) | 212-420-0600
West 50s | 251 W 50th St. (bet. B'way & 8th Ave.)
212-581-1818
"Full of fabulous surprises," the "unconventional" Mexican menu includes a variety of "excellent" guacamoles, "delicioso" ceviches, and margaritas that will "kick your booty"; while the noise at the Uptown locations can be "deafening" during peak service, the "enthusiastic" waitstaff go "well out of their way to please"; the "casual cool" cantinas may be "cramped," but they remain the kind of well-loved standbys "every neighborhood dreams about."

Tomoe Sushi Japanese/Sushi   25 | 10 | 18 | $$

Greenwich Village | 172 Thompson St.
(bet. Bleecker & Houston Sts.)
212-777-9346 | tomoesushi.com
Although it's been open for decades and the "decor is dated," there are still "crazy long lines" outside this Village favorite known for "giant slices of sushi"; it's "not cheap anymore," but it's still a "bargain for what you get"; they don't take reservations, "so get there early, because they run out of sushi every night," and while this is "not a place to linger," it's worth it for Japanese fare with "none of the frills."

Tony's Di Napoli Italian

21 | 17 | 21 | $$

East 60s | 1081 3rd Ave. (bet. 63rd & 64th Sts.)
212-888-6333 | tonysnyc.com
◖ **West 40s** | 147 W 43rd St. (bet. 6th & 7th Aves.)
212-221-0100

"You'll never leave hungry" when you dine on the "terrific" family-style Southern Italian cooking, with portions "big enough to take home for the next day"; it's "always busy, and deservedly so," which for some means a "rollicking good time" and, for others, a "noisy" and "sometimes chaotic" scene in an "uninspired" dining room; still, the "attentive waitstaff" "get you in and out quickly," and prices are "not too hard on the purse."

Torishin Japanese

27 | 22 | 25 | $$$

West 50s | 362 W 53rd St. (9th Ave.)
212-757-0108 | torishinny.com

"They know what to do with chicken" at this yakitori joint in Hell's Kitchen, where skewered-meat "fanatics" "sit at the counter to watch the action" – chefs charcoal-grilling "high-quality" Japanese snacks "right in front of you"; add in myriad sakes and "attentive service," and you have a winning recipe – "it's a little easy to consume too much, so watch out"; P.S. there are omakase and delivery options as well.

Tørst ◖ Gastropub

24 | 23 | 25 | $$

Greenpoint | 615 Manhattan Ave. (Nassau Ave.)
Brooklyn | 718-389-6034 | torstnyc.com

It's "all about the beer" at this "inviting" Greenpoint gastropub, where the "fabulous" list of craft brews are all geared to "big-flavor seekers"; there is "surprisingly" tasty "food to boot" on the limited menu of snacks and sandwiches, and the "passionate" bartenders keep things moving in the "modern," wood-paneled room; P.S. happy-hour items are conducive to "bringing a crew" to sample the offerings.

Totonno's Pizzeria Napolitana Ⓜ ⊟ Pizza

26 | 11 | 15 | $$

Coney Island | 1524 Neptune Ave. (bet. 15th & 16th Sts.)
Brooklyn | 718-372-8606 | totonnosconeyisland.com

"What I'd have en route to the electric chair" is how fans feel about the "perfectly charred" coal-oven pizzas at this circa-1924 Coney Island cash-only institution known just as much for its "gruff" service as it is for "flavorful" pies (and some dissenters say the servers are not "nearly as snarly as they seem"); the "unadorned" space draws crowds and has inconsistent opening hours – be sure to call ahead – but it's "worth" the trip.

Totto Ramen ⊟ Japanese/Ramen

23 | 12 | 16 | $$

East 50s | 248 E 52nd St. (2nd Ave.)
212-421-0052 | tottoramen.com
◖ **West 50s** | 366 W 52nd St.
(bet. 8th & 9th Aves.) | 212-582-0052
West 50s | 464 W 51st St.
(bet. 9th & 10th Aves.) | 646-596-9056
Flushing | 38-09 Union St. (38th Ave.) | Queens
917-285-2505

"Slurp"-savorers "satisfy" their ramen "cravings" at these "solid" Japanese joints in Midtown, havens for "inexpensive" noodles bathed in "rich, creamy" broths; no, the so-so service and "matchbox"-size interiors don't exactly live up to the "amazing flavors," and "long waits" because of "crowds" are a "downside," but "when you need some serious comfort food," they're a suitable stop; "fast stop"; N.B. cash-only, and no reservations.

Tournesol French | 24 | 17 | 21 | $$ |
Long Island City | 50-12 Vernon Blvd.
(bet. 50th & 51st Aves.)
Queens | 718-472-4355 | tournesolnyc.com
"Although the LIC neighborhood has changed," this "stalwart" has not – it's "still serving the same delicious basic bistro food" in an interior that "feels like you're visiting your French family," and the "prices are an absolute deal"; however, while "still great, it's still tiny," so be prepared to love thy neighbor seated at the adjacent "crammed tables"; N.B. American Express is the only credit card accepted.

Tra Di Noi Ⓜ Italian | 26 | 15 | 23 | $$ |
Arthur Avenue/Belmont | 622 E 187th St.
(bet. Belmont & Hughes Sts.) | Bronx
718-295-1784 | tradinoi.com
"Come early, they run out" at this "classic red-sauce" standby for "homestyle nonna cooking" near Arthur Avenue; the "affable waitstaff," with "homey and warm" hospitality make it feel like you're "eating in someone's home," and it's no wonder, "with a husband and wife team running the place"; "affordable prices" and "personal" attention continue to ensure that "this is where the locals eat."

Traif Ⓜ American | 27 | 18 | 23 | $$ |
Williamsburg | 229 S 4th St.
(bet. Havemeyer & Roebling Sts.) | Brooklyn
347-844-9578 | traifny.com
"Inventive" and "whimsical," "studiously non-kosher" the "ever-changing variety of small plates" makes you "want to ooh and aah over every dish," with unusual flavor combinations that work so well they "make you wonder why no one has done this before"; "warmth and approachability" are everywhere, from the "welcoming service" to the shareable menu perfect for ordering "a bunch of dishes."

Trattoria Dell'Arte ◖ Italian | 23 | 21 | 22 | $$$ |
West 50s | 900 7th Ave. (bet. 56th & 57th Sts.)
212-245-9800 | trattoriadellarte.com
"Just steps from Carnegie Hall," this sunny "longtime fixture holds up" with "traditional Italian food" "prepared with care and attention," particularly the "amazing antipasto bar"; it's "pricey" and "tightly packed," but the "high-spirited staff" "help you cope"; besides, it can be entertaining "to eat under an oversized wall sculpture of an ear or breast."

🅩 Trattoria L'incontro Ⓜ Italian | 28 | 21 | 26 | $$$ |
Astoria | 21-76 31st St. (Ditmars Blvd.) | Queens
718-721-3532 | trattorialincontro.com
It's always a "celebration" at this "classic" Astoria "destination," where "phenomenal" Italian plates from an "encyclopedic

menu" complement the "endless specials" that the "courteous" servers "recite from memory"; although the setting is merely "comfortable," the "fairly reasonable prices" and the chance to "people-watch for local politicians and sports figures" up the ante, and "if you're lucky," "delightful" chef Rocco Sacramone will "come out to talk to you."

Trattoria Romana Italian/Pizza   25 | 20 | 24 | $$
Dongan Hills | 1476 Hylan Blvd.
(Benton Ave.) | Staten Island
718-980-3113 | trattoriaromanasi.com
"No airfare" is required for this "trip to Italy" via Staten Island, at this Dongan Hills joint with a "huge menu" of "quality" "red-sauce" dishes – including wood-fired pizzas, plus vino and weekly specials – in "tight quarters" that are frequently "noisy" and "crowded"; the "old-fashioned" quality here is enhanced by the "prompt, friendly" service (especially from the chef, "on hand to oversee everything"), although it's less reflected in the prices.

Trattoria Trecolori Italian   22 | 18 | 22 | $$
West 40s | 254 W 47th St. (B'way)
212-997-4540 | trattoriatrecolori.com
This "reasonably priced" trattoria, a smart choice in the Theater District, serves "good-sized portions" of pasta with a "generous amount of shaved parmigiano on top"; the "accommodating and professional" service means you'll get to your show before the curtain goes up, but "make sure you have a reservation," "because it gets crowded"; the dining room is good for conversation, which in this area is a "rare find."

Tribeca Grill American   23 | 22 | 22 | $$$
TriBeCa | 375 Greenwich St. (Franklin St.)
212-941-3900 | myriadrestaurantgroup.com
Each decade that passes further cements this "creative American" spot as an "NYC institution," with its menu of bistro classics, and even if it might not have the same star power, it's "still fun," has a "fashionable scene," "attentive service," and roomy seating – and you still may "see a celebrity or two"; the "top-notch" wine program and "beautiful," "historic" bar help it stand apart from other places Downtown.

TsuruTonTan Japanese   23 | 23 | 22 | $$
Union Square | 21 E 16th St.
(bet. Union Sq. W & 5th Ave.)
212-989-1000 | tsurutontan.com
West 40s | 64 W 48th St. (bet. 5th & 6th Aves.)
212-575-2828
"Giant" bowls of "tasty" udon are the main draw at these "sophisticated" noodle "palaces" (offshoots of a Japanese chain) that also serve a "diverse" variety of appetizers and sushi by "attentive" staff; both spaces manage to be "modern" and "classy," and while the Downtown location had big shoes to fill after taking over the former Union Square Cafe space, most find it a "worthy successor"; P.S. make a reservation, though you may still have to wait.

Tuome ⑤ Ⓜ American

26 | 19 | 22 | $$$

East Village | 536 E 5th St. (Avenue B)
646-833-7811 | tuomenyc.com

A "low-key" setting – "dimly lit, wooden chairs and close-set tables" – belies the "simple but excellent dishes" at this "intimate"
East Villager "patronized by a sophisticated young crowd of
knowledgeable diners"; whether you go for one of the seasonal
offerings or the signature pig out (Berkshire pork and spicy
peanut noodles) for two, the Asian-inflected American fare will
be "thoughtful, unique," and delivered with "on-point service."

Turkish Kitchen Turkish

23 | 18 | 20 | $$

Murray Hill | 386 3rd Ave. (bet. 27th & 28th Sts.)
212-679-6633 | turkishkitchen.com

This "bright-red" bilevel room in Murray Hill is a "neighborhood no-frills favorite for lavish," "dependable Middle Eastern
meals" at "real bargain" prices – particularly the prix fixes and
renowned Sunday brunch buffet "filled with Turkish delights"
("impossible to leave with weight-loss hopes intact"); the "staff
are attentive in explaining the menu" but "a bit lackadaisical
once you get served."

NEW The Turk's Inn Turkish

– | – | – | $$$

Bushwick | 234 Starr St.
(bet. Irving & Wyckoff Aves.) | Brooklyn
718-215-0025 | theturksinn.com

For this painstaking re-creation of a beloved circa 1934 Wiscon-
sin supper club, actual pieces of the original, which closed in
2014, were trucked out to Brooklyn and reassembled for what
amounts to a kitschy, bright spectacle of a place; the reborn
inn is part of a complex with a music venue, a kebab takeout
window, a rooftop bar, and a dining room serving Turkish and
other Middle Eastern dishes.

Tuscany Grill Italian

23 | 17 | 22 | $$

Bay Ridge | 8620 3rd Ave.
(bet. 86th & 87th Sts.) | Brooklyn
718-921-5633 | tuscanygrillbrooklyn.com

Patronized by locals for years "for good reason," this Bay Ridge
mainstay specializes in grilling meats, fish, and veggies in
Tuscan style, rounding out the menu with pizzas, antipasti, and
salads; reservations are a "must," and the "rustic" space gets
"crowded," but the service is "professional," and it's "lovely" and
"quiet" – a "solid performer" that rarely disappoints.

Tutto il Giorno ⑤ Italian

21 | 25 | 21 | $$$

TriBeCa | 114 Franklin St.
(bet. Church St. & W B'way)
212-274-8100 | wtuttoilgiorno.com

Fans rave about the "stunning" decor at this TriBeCa Italian
"neighborhood gem" (a Hamptons transplant) notable for
skylights and high ceilings, "romantic" lighting, and a stylish, "almost zen" atmosphere rounded out by "warm," "friendly" staff;
the traditional Neapolitan plates like risotto, pasta, and grilled
fish may run "pricey," but they are also "consistently" tasty.

12 Chairs Cafe Middle Eastern 23 | 18 | 20 | $$

SoHo | 56 MacDougal St. (bet. Houston & Prince Sts.)
212-254-8640 | 12chairscafe.com
Williamsburg | 342 Wythe Ave. (S 2nd St.) | Brooklyn
347-227-7077

"Charming, homey vibes abound" at this pair of "low-key"
Middle Eastern spots that offer "a taste of Israel like no other"
with "simple yet memorable food" (special shout-out to the
shakshuka, "amazing" eggs in a spicy tomato sauce) and
"above-par service"; true, the "tables are packed together, but
that only adds to a sense of community" at the SoHo original
(the younger "Williamsburg one is more spacious").

🅩 21 Club American 23 | 25 | 25 | $$$$

West 50s | 21 W 52nd St. (bet. 5th & 6th Aves.)
212-582-7200 | 21club.com

"Channel your inner Gatsby" at this "mythical" 1930 Midtown
"classic," a former speakeasy with a "clubby" interior sporting
celebrity-"donated knickknacks" plus "dependable" American
fare, "fine" wines, and "attentive" service; tabs may sometimes
veer "out of control," but if you want to sample New York's "rich
history" among "captains of industry" while "fantasizing" about
"Bogie" and "Bacall," this spot's "timeless"; N.B. jackets are
required (no jeans) in the bar room and upstairs.

21 Greenpoint Ⓜ American 21 | 22 | 22 | $$$

Greenpoint | 21 Greenpoint Ave.
(bet. West St. & Transmitter Park)
Brooklyn | 718-383-8833 | 21greenpoint.com

"Anything can happen" at this "hip" "American bistro" in Greenpoint "with a cozy vibe," bright, woodsy interior, solid service,
and a "beautiful bar up front"; you can sit and sample everything
from wood-oven "Neapolitan pizza to schnitzel," but the "one
consistency" is the "creativity" of the "seasonal menu," which
changes daily and extends to the "casual," "relaxing" brunch.

Two Hands Cafe Australian 22 | 22 | 21 | $$

Little Italy | 164 Mott St. (Broome St.)
twohandsnyc.com
TriBeCa | 251 Church St. (bet. Franklin & Leonard Sts.)

"Part of the wave of Australian restaurants" sweeping NYC,
these "cute cafés in Little Italy" and TriBeCa boast "healthy,"
"yummy breakfast options" and "light lunch bites" delivered by
"super-nice servers"; "the wait is not fun," but for many "the
food makes up for it," as do the "chill" decor and "hip vibe."

212 Steakhouse Steakhouse 21 | 18 | 19 | $$$

East 50s | 316 E 53rd St. (bet. 1st & 2nd Aves.)
212-858-0646 | 212steakhouse.com

Kobe beef straight from Japan is the star at this American-style
steakhouse in Midtown East – one of the few on the East Coast
certified to serve the imported cuts, which predictably "come
at a premium"; the grill turns out "tasty" plates and sides that
go beyond the usual to include grilled octopus, beet salad, and
a decent selection of seafood; steering away from the typical
dark-wood and hunting-lodge prototype of this genre, the
"pleasant" interior has a more modern look.

Txikito Spanish
26 | 17 | 23 | $$$

Chelsea | 240 9th Ave. (bet. 24th & 25th Sts.)
212-242-4730 | txikitonyc.com

This pintxos bar in Chelsea is a "culinary experience," capturing both the "tradition" and "current" relevance of Basque cuisine with creative "small plates," "warm" service, "friendly" owners, and touches like the proper pouring techniques of txakoli wine; even with "basic" surroundings and a "hefty bill" at the end, lots of adventurous daily "specials" "make it interesting" enough "to keep coming back."

Ugly Baby Thai
26 | 16 | 22 | $$

Carroll Gardens | 407 Smith St. (4th St.) | Brooklyn
347-689-3075 | uglybabynyc.com

"The spice levels are no joke" at this "tiny, humble" Thai dining room in Carroll Gardens with a "small but "interesting" menu of dishes like "rich and comforting" khao soi, and many other "heat bombs" ready to "clear out your sinuses" while still "staying true to traditional flavors"; "gaudy" "wall art spans" a buzzing interior with "knowledgeable" servers, but "be prepared to wait," as they take "no reservations" and Brooklyn loves this place.

NEW Uluh Chinese
– | – | – | $$

East Village | 152A 2nd Ave.
(bet. 9th & 10th Sts.)
917-261-5963 | uluh.business.site

The club-like environment fits right into the East Village, but it's unusual for a dim sum shop – even one with upscale touches like truffled soup dumplings and heated toilet seats; the tea list is full of expensive and exotic leaves; prices are fair and portions run large, making it a perfect spot for an affordable celebration.

Umbertos Clam House ◖ Italian
21 | 15 | 19 | $$

Little Italy | 132 Mulberry St.
(bet. Grand & Hester Sts.)
212-431-7545 | umbertosclamhouse.com

"If you love clams on the half-shell," there's this "one-of-a-kind" Little Italy "staple," with "old-fashioned" seafood (linguine and clam sauce, shrimp scampi) and other dishes that "Grandma" would appreciate; it's "nothing particularly special" from a culinary standpoint, and the setting and spotty service could be improved, but the tourists don't mind, and "late-night" options, plus the appeal of "walking around in the neighborhood," mean there's a lot to "enjoy."

Una Pizza Napoletana Ⓢ Italian/Pizza
25 | 18 | 20 | $$$

Lower East Side | 175 Orchard St.
(bet. Houston & Stanton Sts.)
646-692-3475 | unapizza.com

"Outstanding" Neapolitan pizza is the draw at this LES "stand-out," reborn after a nine-year sojourn in San Francisco; fans say "nobody makes a crust" like its pizzaiolo, Anthony Mangieri, who provides a menu of just a few classic combinations (they're "pillowy perfection") along with adventurous small plates and "divine" desserts in an industrial-chic space; many note that it's "really expensive" but "absolutely delicious."

Z Uncle Boons Thai

27 | 22 | 22 | $$$

NoLita | 7 Spring St. (bet. Bowery & Elizabeth Sts.)
646-370-6650 | uncleboons.com

Slinging dishes "big on flavor and spice" as well as some "melt-your-face-off" fare, this "fun" and "sceney" NoLita Thai restaurant is also known for "beer slushies" and "creative cocktails," all served in a "funky," "madhouse" basement resembling "a Bangkok secondhand store"; "loooong waits" (there are no reservations) are a drawback, but nearly all agree it's "worth it" for the "unbelievable food, perfectly executed"; N.B. Uncle Boons Sister on Mott Street has a counter and a more limited menu for eat-in, takeout, and delivery.

Z Union Square Cafe American

26 | 25 | 26 | $$$$

Gramercy | 101 E 19th St. (Park Ave. S)
212-243-4020 | unionsquarecafe.com

Danny Meyer's Gramercy Park "crown jewel" "hasn't lost its charm," say admirers of this "quintessential" NYC "mainstay," a "refined" yet "unpretentious" New American featuring "memorable" fare, plus an "endless wine list," in a "civilized setting" staffed by "polished" servers; despite the recent move to its current location, it retains a "downtown" vibe, and while it's undeniable "prices are high," most believe "this is how restaurants should be run"; P.S. patrons find the no-tipping policy "a pleasure."

Up Thai Thai

24 | 20 | 20 | $$

East 70s | 1411 2nd Ave. (bet. 73rd & 74th Sts.)
212-256-1188 | upthainyc.com

There's "always a line out the door" at this "go-to destination for Thai food on the UES"; locals swear it's hard to order wrong, but classics like pad thai get consistently high marks; vegetarians and vegans are pleased with the kitchen, which is good about "accommodating your requests"; and prices are "reasonable," but the "service is underwhelming."

Z Upland American

25 | 24 | 24 | $$$

Murray Hill | 345 Park Ave. S (26th St.)
212-686-1006 | uplandnyc.com

This "definition of a crowd pleaser" serves a "highly curated yet user-friendly menu" of "unique farm-to-table" Cal-Italian with "seasonal" flourishes in a "farmhouse-look" space that's "got a 'cool without even trying' kind of feel"; the "convenient location," "attentive" service, and "upscale yet comfortable" atmosphere keep it "next to impossible to get a reservation," but if you do manage, you'll find it "crowded, but worth the effort."

Upstate Seafood

25 | 14 | 20 | $$

East Village | 95 1st Ave. (bet. 5th & 6th Sts.)
646-791-5400 | upstatenyc.com

"Stop by after work" for an "excellent" "happy hour" "oyster experience" at this tiny East Village "raw bar" with exposed brick walls; try to make a reservation to avoid the "annoying waitlist" to get in; inside it's likely to be on the "noisy" side, but the "small," "ever-changing menu" of seafood delights is "fresh" and "flavorful" and ready to be paired with a smart list of New York State beer and wine.

	FOOD	DECOR	SERVICE	COST

Utsav Indian   22 | 20 | 20 | $$

West 40s | 1185 6th Ave. (bet. 46th & 47th Sts.)
212-575-2525 | utsavny.com

"Leave the craziness of Times Square" for this calm and reliable
Indian standby, where the curries, grilled items, and breads
"range from very good to ordinary"; expect "well-spiced flavors"
in a roomy saffron-toned space brightened by courtyard-facing
picture windows; the "gracious, efficient service" ensures you're
out in time for curtain.

Uva ℂ Italian   22 | 20 | 21 | $$

East 70s | 1486 2nd Ave. (bet. 77th & 78th Sts.)
212-472-4552 | uvanyc.com

A candlelit dining room, a handful of tables on the street, and
an "enchanting" covered garden in the back that "feels like you
are eating in Italy" are part of what make this "romantic" wine
bar the "definition of a perfect neighborhood restaurant," one
that's often "a little crowded, but understandably so"; it serves
"decent," "classic dishes, with a twist," all "consistent," tasty,
and in "good-size portions."

Valbella Italian   26 | 24 | 25 | $$$

East 50s | 11 E 53rd St. (bet. 5th & Madison Aves.)
212-888-8955 | valbellarestaurants.com

"Hidden back behind a big building" "in the heart of Midtown"
awaits "a treat": "exceptional Italian food" and "professional service" as you sit amid wall racks of bottles from an "extensive wine
list" or on the cobblestone patio; all told, it's an "extraordinarily
comfortable and elegant experience" "particularly if somebody
else is picking up the tab" (those "large plates" get "pricey").

Vandal American   18 | 23 | 18 | $$$

Lower East Side | 199 Bowery (Rivington St.)
212-400-0199 | vandalnewyork.com

Like dining in a "massive," mural-filled "urban museum," this
quasi-nightclub from the Tao Group attracts a "scene-seeking,"
"youthful" crowd that doesn't seem to mind the noise; while
the "diverse" selection of street food–inspired small plates are
a decent "concept," they are "hit or miss (but mostly miss)"
in execution, and bills add up fast; the all-important cocktails
(including boozy push-pops), pin it down further as a spot for
serious partiers.

Vanessa's Dumpling House Chinese   20 | 6 | 11 | $

East Village | 220 E 14th St. (bet. 2nd & 3rd Aves.)
212-529-1329 | vanessas.com
Lower East Side | 118A Eldridge St.
(bet. Broome & Grand Sts.)
212-625-8008
Williamsburg | 310 Bedford Ave.
(bet. 1st & 2nd Sts.) | Brooklyn
718-218-8809

"Line up" at this "inexpensive dumpling lover's staple," where
"really cheap" prices mean you "gotta try everything," particularly the "delightfully crisp" scallion pancake sandwiches
and the dumplings that are "little buns of pleasure"; it's best
to "overlook" the nothing-fancy space, "disposable plates

and splintery chopsticks," and "inattentive" service, but taking it to eat "on a curb" is always an option, especially during peak hours.

Vatan Indian | 26 | 20 | 21 | $$ |
Murray Hill | 409 3rd Ave. (29th St.)
212-689-5666 | vatanny.com
For "vegetarian done right," pay a set price, and this Murray Hill classic will serve unlimited refills of aromatic Indian curry on your thali plate, with "crispy breads" and some "rare Gujarati specialties" thrown in; the "oddball" jungle decor may seem "hokey," but this multicourse extravaganza is an "excellent value" for a "relaxing" heart- and soul-healthy night out.

Z Vaucluse 🗷 French | 25 | 27 | 25 | $$$$ |
East 60s | 100 E 63rd St. (Park Ave.)
646-869-2300 | vauclusenyc.com
Chef Michael White's "civilized," "elegant" UES brasserie is easy on the eyes, with a "lovely space" and a "comfortable, bright" color palette that attracts a "well-heeled clientele"; "food is always of the highest order," with "consistently" tasty French fare "with a twist" and an "impressive" wine list that "touches all the bases" – sommelier recs "pair perfectly with each course."

Veselka Ukrainian | 22 | 14 | 18 | $$ |
East Village | 144 2nd Ave. (9th St.)
212-228-9682 | veselka.com
Pierogis, blintzes, stuffed cabbage, and Ukrainian "dishes done with aplomb" ensure "there's almost always a wait" at this "convivial" "bit of old East Village history"; the "diner-like" digs can get "noisy" and "crowded," and "if it's too busy, the service is poor," but given that it's "open 24 hours" and "breakfast is served all day," "no one cares."

Vesta Trattoria ▼ | 27 | 23 | 25 | $$ |
& Wine Bar Italian/Pizza
Astoria | 21-02 30th Ave. (21st St.) | Queens
718-545-5550 | vestavino.com
Astorians and others head to this "upscale" trattoria to dine on Italian comfort dishes, accompanied by a list of affordable wines by the glass; the weekend brunch, which includes a potato-and-egg hangover pizza, brings in many locals to the "casual" spot, which has work by local artists on the walls, a touch as friendly as the service and "reasonable" prices, especially during happy hour.

Vesuvio ◖ Italian/Pizza | 23 | 14 | 20 | $$ |
Bay Ridge | 7305 3rd Ave.
(bet. 73rd & 74th Sts.) | Brooklyn
718-745-0222 | vesuviobayridge.com
A Bay Ridge staple since 1953, this "dependable" neighborhood Italian still serves the pizzas it did from the beginning, along with other "superb" classics like pastas, heroes, and grilled meats and seafood; with a dining room with white tablecloths as well as pizzeria-style seating, the setting remains simple and still feels "homey," despite having "grown" over the years.

	FOOD	DECOR	SERVICE	COST

Vezzo Thin Crust Italian/Pizza   24 | 14 | 18 | $$
Murray Hill | 178 Lexington Ave. (31st St.)
212-839-8300 | nycthincrust.com
Just about everyone seems to "love the crunch" of the "paper-thin-crust" pizzas at this "reliable" and "casual" Murray Hill Italian, whose "dreamy" pies (check out the Shroomtown), "generous" toppings, and "easy-on-the-wallet" tabs win praise, as do the "generous" salads; less fun is the "meh" interior and no-reservation policy, and it "can be loud and crowded at peak times," although it's usually "fast" enough.

2 Via Carota ☾ Italian   28 | 24 | 24 | $$$
West Village | 51 Grove St.
(bet. Bleecker St. & 7th Ave. S)
212-255-1962 | viacarota.com
Reviewers give "an A" to this "lovely" West Village Italian from Jody Williams (Buvette) and Rita Sodi (I Sodi), who proffer "spectacular" dishes featuring "bright" flavors (including "lovingly dressed" vegetarian options), plus "superb" cocktails in a "rustic" "country" setting; given the "thoughtful" service and "high-energy" vibe, fans are more than ready to "get there early," as the "no-reservations" policy means "long waits."

Via Quadronno Italian   22 | 16 | 20 | $$$
East 70s | 25 E 73rd St.
(bet. 5th & Madison Aves.)
212-650-9880 | viaquadronno.com
A "popular" "stop for lunch while visiting museums and galleries" and an "escape from the mean streets of the UES," this neighborhood Italian "feels like a bit of Europe"; it has "excellent salads and sandwiches," and some praise its spaghetti Bolognese, as well as its espresso and cappuccino, which are "the real thing"; it's "tight quarters" in the storefront space, but that doesn't deter its fans.

Vic's Italian   22 | 20 | 21 | $$$
NoHo | 31 Great Jones St.
(bet. Bowery & Lafayette St.)
212-253-5700 | vicsnewyork.com
At this NoHo source for seasonal Italian fare, standouts include wood-fired pizzas, house-made pastas and limoncello, "vegetables prepared to perfection"; the crowd-pleasing, "gutsy" "comfort" dishes keep this place "super busy" with a "hip," "lively" bar crowd huddling up for cocktails, and "efficient" service turns tables over quickly.

ViceVersa Italian   23 | 22 | 23 | $$$
West 50s | 325 W 51st St. (bet. 8th & 9th Aves.)
212-399-9291 | viceversanyc.com
Performance-minded patrons find this Theater District "veteran" a "perfect" choice before (or after) a show, primarily because its "reliable" and "traditional" Italian fare, assorted drinks, and "professional staff" don't suffer because of the "timely" turnarounds required by curtain times; the "tastefully decorated" digs (which include a "calming" garden area) add to the "comfortable" feelings and diners' overall "satisfaction."

| | FOOD | DECOR | SERVICE | COST |

Vietnaam Vietnamese   23 | 12 | 19 | $$
East 80s | 1700 2nd Ave. (88th St.)
212-722-0558 | vietnaam88.com
It "tastes like Hanoi" out on the UES; the "expansive menu" of
fresh "Viet specialties" at "reasonable prices" keep this place
"very popular," but "it's worth taking a long lunch from work";
the "tables move quickly," and the satisfying noodle soups
come out "Usain Bolt–level fast."

Villa Mosconi ⑤ Italian   25 | 19 | 26 | $$
Greenwich Village | 69 MacDougal St.
(bet. Bleecker & Houston Sts.)
212-673-0390 | villamosconi.com
The servers' charming personalities may "occasionally provide
some unexpected entertainment," but they always "make you
feel like family" at this "old-style" Greenwich Village "landmark";
the "basic red-sauce" fare is made from timeless recipes, and
the space recalls what the "Village was like" back in 1976, when
the family opened it: think Little Italy without being "surrounded
by tourists"; "save some room" if you hear whispers that
"Grandma made cannoli."

Vinateria Spanish   ▼ 25 | 21 | 24 | $$
Harlem | 2211 Frederick Douglass Blvd. (119th St.)
212-662-8462 | vinaterianyc.com
Try a glass of something new at this dark and romantic neighborhood enoteca in Harlem with modern decor and a "warm"
staff to guide you through the "constantly rotating" menu of
elegant Italian-Mediterranean dishes and handmade pasta, with
a "well-curated" list of wines from all over Europe; its street-
front patio is great for "outdoor drinks and people-watching,"
especially during the well-priced happy hour.

Vinegar Hill House American   22 | 20 | 20 | $$$
Dumbo | 72 Hudson Ave.
(bet. Front & Water Sts.) | Brooklyn
718-522-1018 | vinegarhillhouse.com
"Hidden" on "a quiet cobblestone street at the east end of
Dumbo, this "idiosyncratic" New American serves "inventive"
"farm-to-table" dishes that make "cute date-night" meals; "tiny,"
"quaint," and resembling a "countryside" cottage, complete with
"folk art" and a "lovely garden," it all seems very "idiosyncratic"
and unusual, which is probably what attracts the "lively crowd";
in contrast, the "thoughtful" staff and fairly accessible prices
keep things pretty down to earth.

Vini e Fritti ◖ Italian   24 | 25 | 24 | $$$
NoMad | 30 E 30th St. (bet. Madison & Park Ave. S)
646-747-8626 | vinifritti.com
This "casual" Italian wine bar – a "charming," "no-fuss" Danny
Meyer spot "hidden" in NoMad's Redbury New York hotel –
showcases its "versatility" with "perfectly crispy fried" snacks,
plus other "small bites" that patrons "wash down with bubbles"
or cocktails; "tips are included," so you don't need to do any
"arithmetic after your meal," and despite a no-reservation
policy, "excellent service" and organization mean you can "almost always get the seat you want."

| | FOOD | DECOR | SERVICE | COST |

Vinum Italian   ▼ _24_ _21_ _22_ $$

Stapleton | 704 Bay St. (Broad St.) | Staten Island
718-448-8466 | vinumnyc.com

This "cozy," "chic" wine bar in Stapleton has an "extensive" list
of bottles and you can "drop money like it's Manhattan" on re-
fined dining options that are closer to Italian than the "excess
of similar places"; it's "out of the way," halfway between the ferry
and the bridge, and it's "not easy to get a prime-time reserva-
tion," but it still attracts fans who say it's "worth the trip" for the
in-house baking and osteria feel.

NEW Violet American/Pizza   _19_ _21_ _21_ $$$

East Village | 511 E 5th St.
(bet. Avenues A & B)
212-850-5900 | violeteastvillage.com

Another place from the team behind Emmy Squared and Emily,
this "trendy but easygoing" East Village café specializes in so-
called "Rhode Island pizza," which resembles a flatbread," grilled
and sometimes verging on "oily," with various toppings; also on
offer from the "friendly staff" are "fancyish" American pastas,
seafood, and small plates, which, though "good for sharing,"
may "need some work" to reach their true potential.

Virginia's S M American   _23_ _21_ _23_ $$$

East Village | 647 E 11th St. (Avenue C)
212-658-0182 | virginiasnyc.com

"The space itself is pretty unassuming," "low key," and "out of
the way," but this East Village place with well-done cocktails
and " friendly bartenders" is "a lot of fun," "not too expensive "
and makes for a "romantic date spot"; while the "burger is
stellar, don't sleep on the other" elevated-but-unpretentious
pub classics here; it's best to "make a reservation, as waits can
get long."

Vitae S American   _25_ _22_ _25_ $$$

East 40s | 4 E 46th St. (bet. 5th & Madison Aves.)
212-682-3562 | vitaenyc.com

"Just off of Fifth Avenue" in the East 40s ("an area that doesn't
have a lot of good places," some say) this bilevel venue offers
an "interesting menu" of "elegant, seasonal American food,"
"well executed" and served by "an efficient staff" amid a
"comfortable," contemporary interior, encased in lamp-adorned
grillwork; it's "pricey but worth it" "for a business lunch," and fun
for celebrations and get-togethers as well.

Wa Jeal Sichuan Chili House Chinese   _24_ _17_ _19_ $$

East 80s | 1588 2nd Ave. (bet. 82nd & 83rd Sts.)
212-396-3339 | wajealrestaurant.com

"Keep it hot" if you want this "interesting" Sichuan spot "at its
best," though you can always "set your own level" of heat in
"high-quality" spicy wontons, mapo tofu, and whole fish; "ac-
commodating" but occasionally "spotty" service makes meals
in the dimly lit space "pleasant," although Sunday nights can
be tough, as the "takeout business overwhelms staff," and they
can't keep up.

Walker's American   18 | 18 | 22 | $$
TriBeCa | 16 N Moore St. (Varick St.)
212-941-0142 | walkersnyc.com
Filled with locals, this "long-standing" TriBeCa "neighborhood
haunt" offers an "old-timey," "Cheers"-like experience with its
"friendly" crowd and brews aplenty; although the dishes are
"typical bar food," and the atmosphere's "lacking" to some,
it's "folksy" enough to provide an effective "retreat" from the
everyday hustle-and-bustle, particularly when you consider its
"excellent value."

Wallsé Ⓢ Austrian   27 | 24 | 26 | $$$
West Village | 344 W 11th St. (Washington St.)
212-352-2300 | kurtgutenbrunner.com
A "little piece of Vienna" resides in the West Village, where
the "wunderbar" schnitzel, spaetzle, and strudel are "old-fash-
ionedly large" by today's standards and there's a "top-flight"
prix fixe meant to be savored "slowly"; the "tranquil" dining
space, an "oasis of Proustian elegance" and discreet service, is
decorated with "masses of flowers" and striking wall art – it's all
"adult in the best possible sense."

Walter's ◖ American   22 | 20 | 21 | $$
Fort Greene | 166 Dekalb Ave.
(Cumberland St.) | Brooklyn
718-488-7800 | waltersbrooklyn.com
If you're after a Fort Greene hipster hangout, well, "bearded
people drinking whiskey can be found here"; the service is
"sometimes iffy," but "the stomach-filling" American classics
(deviled eggs, oysters, pork chops, catfish) "really make up for
it," and the "Bloody Marys are on point"; there's an "eclectic"
and "energetic" vibe and the prices are "reasonable," so it's no
surprise that this neighborhood standby is "always crowded."

Waverly Inn American   21 | 22 | 20 | $$$
West Village | 16 Bank St. (Waverly Pl.)
917-828-1154 | waverlynyc.com
Those after "special occasion" dining head to this aristocratic
"old friend" inside an 1844 West Village townhouse kitted out
with "dark and cozy" period touches – especially "romantic" if
you "cuddle up" by the fireplace; the "high-end American comfort food" is "not exciting," but the plates are "presented well,"
and although service can be "stuffy," it's also "steady"; all in all,
time spent here feels like being "transported" to the English
"countryside," and it earns its spot on "bucket lists."

NEW Wayan Indonesian   ▼ 27 | 27 | 26 | $$$
NoLita | 20 Spring St.
(bet. Elizabeth and Mott Sts.)
917-261-4388 | wayan-nyc.com
You might "feel like you're on vacation" while dining at this "upscale" Indonesian-French hybrid in NoLita from Jean-Georges'
son Cedric that was inspired by his experiences growing up and
working in Southeast Asia; the "beautiful" space is as much an
attraction as the original food with lots of shareable options, like
satay skewers and "imaginative cocktails"; make sure to "book
ahead," and note the small plates can add up quickly.

NEW **Wayla** Thai

— — — $$

Lower East Side | 100 Forsyth St.
(bet. Broome & Grand Sts.)
212-206-2500 | waylanyc.com

This LES hot spot attracts diners hungry for the bold interpretations of Thai classics from a Bangkok expat chef, as well as those drawn by its tranquil outdoor space; those looking for relaxed, spicy dinners or an atypical weekend brunch will be treated to street stall–style dishes and cocktails with Southeast Asian flavors – that is, if you can find the hidden entrance to the unmarked basement that leads to its paradisiacal patio.

West-Bourne American

21 22 19 $$$

SoHo | 137 Sullivan St. (bet. Houston & Prince Sts.)
212-534-3050 | westbourne.com

The "fast-casual" vegetarian food here (grain bowls, chia pudding, and a beloved mushroom reuben), paired with a matcha latte or free seltzer, works "for brunch following yoga, so you can pretend you're healthy"; the "cute" glass-fronted communal space evokes living rooms fans have "always dreamed of but will never have," and you may even think you've "temporarily left NYC for California or Australia," although crowds and limited seating will quickly snap you back to SoHo realities.

Westville American

21 14 18 $$

Chelsea | 246 W 18th St. (bet. 7th & 8th Aves.)
212-924-2223 | westvillenyc.com
Dumbo | 81 Washington St. (bet. Front & York Sts.) | Brooklyn
718-618-5699
East Village | 173 Avenue A (11th St.) | 212-677-2033
Financial District | 110 Wall St. (bet. Front & South Sts.)
212-741-4780
West 50s | 809 9th Ave. (bet. 53rd & 54th Sts.)
Hudson Square | 333 Hudson St. (bet. Charlton &
Vandam Sts.) | 212-776-1404
West Village | 210 W 10th St. (Bleecker St.)
212-741-7971

This Manhattan mini-chain has been "doing healthy-ish since before it was trendy," with a "plethora" of "inventive," "seasonal" veggies, plus burgers, sandwiches, and "yummy" desserts, ensuring there's "something for everyone"; the spaces tend to be "small" and "cramped" and they don't take reservations, but the "friendly" staff keep things moving.

Wheated Ⓜ Pizza

▼ 27 21 21 $$

Ditmas Park | 905 Church Ave.
(bet. Coney Island Ave. & 10th St.)
Brooklyn | 347-240-2813 | wheatedbrooklyn.com

The namesake grain is celebrated in a couple of ways at this "always-packed" Ditmas Park pizza place: first, in the "always-inventive" pies, most of them "super vegetarian- and vegan-friendly" options, and second, in the extensive list of hard-to-find bourbons and other whiskeys, bottles of which dominate the "comfortable, albeit tiny environment" and much of the "great drinks" list as well.

White Bear Chinese   25 | 6 | 16 | $

Flushing | 135-02 Roosevelt Ave.
(Prince St.) | Queens
718-961-2322

"The #6 is what they're famous for" – "tender," "delicate,"
"meaty" "wontons in hot chili oil" – but this "mom-and-pop"
Chinese dumpling specialist also offers a few other satisfying
snacks that are impossibly "cheap"; it's a required stop on any
"Flushing food crawl," and even offers souvenirs in the form of
"a frozen bag to go" – a way to commemorate this somewhat
barren "hole in the wall," with "only four tables" and blithe
counter service.

NEW **Wild Ink** Pan-Asian   – | – | – | $$$

West 30s | 20 Hudson Yards
(10th Ave. & 33rd St.)
646-974-7305 | wildinknyc.com

In a slick, shiny space in Hudson Yards, this NYC debut from a
London-based restaurant group serves a menu of dishes with
inspiration from all over Asia, ranging from General Tso's sweet-
breads to crispy mapo tofu dumplings to curried lamb momos,
plus other options like crudos and roasted chicken; all this goes
down in a room with big windows overlooking The Vessel.

Wildair American   26 | 20 | 23 | $$$

Lower East Side | 142 Orchard St. (Rivington St.)
646-964-5624 | wildair.nyc

Taking LES visitors on a "culinary journey," this visionary "tapas-
style" bar for natural wines from small producers pairs them
with "unusual" versions of sharable New American plates made
to "impress"; it's all "delightful," "low-key" "charming," "modern"
– and "intimate" to a fault, with tables that make you party to
the "personal conversations" of those seated "right up next"
to your high-top; still, it's a memorable trip, and the service is
"helpful."

Win Son Ⓜ Taiwanese   27 | 21 | 23 | $$

Williamsburg | 159 Graham Ave.
(Montrose Ave.) | Brooklyn
347-457-6010 | winsonbrooklyn.com

This Taiwanese-American spot in East Williamsburg serves
standards "kicked up a notch" and "maximum" flavors through
dishes featuring "unique and impressive food combinations;
regulars say you'd be doing a grave "disservice" if you don't
get some pork buns for your group, but "even the marinated
cucumbers are fantastic"; it's all served in a "casual and fun
dining room," but be prepared to wait, as reservations are only
for groups of five or more; P.S. a bakery spin-off opened down
the block in 2019.

Wo Hop ☾ 🏷 Chinese   24 | 8 | 16 | $

Chinatown | 17 Mott St. (bet. Mosco & Worth Sts.)
212-962-8617 | wohopchinese.com

"You have to go at least once" to this circa-1938 Chinatown
"mainstay," a "diamond in the rough" dispensing "humongous
portions" of "dependable" "classics" at "ultracheap" prices to
"late-night" revelers and other folks; if the usually "crowded,"

photo-studded downstairs interior is "not much to look at" ("get a load of the dollar-bill-covered walls"), and the "gruff" service startles, the location "by the courts" soothes – "it's why I never mind being called for jury duty"; N.B. cash only.

Wokuni Japanese | 23 | 23 | 22 | $$ |
Murray Hill | 327 Lexington Ave.
(bet. 38th & 39th Sts.)
212-447-1212 | wokuninyc.com
"They have their own farm in Japan" where they raise fish sustainably, which explains the "very, very fresh sashimi" at this Murray Hill spot; expect "fresh" ingredients prepared in "interesting ways" and a serene, minimalist high-ceilinged dining room to match, and be sure to ask the "top-notch and knowledgeable servers" about the $1 oysters if it's happy hour.

Z Wolfgang's Steakhouse Steakhouse | 26 | 22 | 24 | $$$$ |
East 40s | 16 E 46th St. (bet. 5th & Madison Aves.)
212-490-8300 | wolfgangssteakhouse.net
East 50s | 200 E 54th St. (3rd Ave.) | 212-588-9653
Murray Hill | 4 Park Ave. (33rd St.) | 212-889-3369
TriBeCa | 409 Greenwich St. (bet. Beach & Hubert Sts.)
212-925-0350
West 40s | 250 W 41st St. (bet. 7th & 8th Aves.)
212-921-3720
Prepare to "loosen the belt a few notches" at this "old-school" steakhouse chain, where "huge portions" of "aged," "perfectly charred" beef lead fans to admit "they truly serve a mighty fine piece of cow" – although the "clubby atmosphere" and "professional" staff also win kudos; yes, it's "busy, loud, and frenetic," and you may have to "bring half of Fort Knox" to pay, but "for an important client meal" or other celebration, it's a "home run."

Wollensky's Grill ℂ Steakhouse | 26 | 21 | 24 | $$$ |
East 40s | 201 E 49th St. (3rd Ave.)
212-753-0444 | smithandwollenskynyc.com
"Say hello to the bartender" at "the friendliest steakhouse in NYC"; "more casual than the big-time Smith and Wollensky's" next door, the Midtown East tavern offers a "livelier scene and a lower price point" for "old-school" fare; "drinks are generous" and the bar area is a "favorite" for people-watching, especially "late night," when nighthawks settle into plates of "fantastic roast beef hash" and burgers that are "second only to the bartenders' personalities."

Wondee Siam Thai | 21 | 9 | 20 | $$ |
West 50s | 792 9th Ave. (bet. 52nd & 53rd Sts.)
212-459-9057
A "small and cozy storefront," this long-standing and "friendly" favorite in Hell's Kitchen impresses for its "tasty and inexpensive" menu of Thai favorites of noodles, curries, and soups as well as its BYOB policies and "fast service" at dinner "for the pre-theater, pre–Lincoln Center crowd"; it's also "good for a quick takeout" if you'd rather not stay for the "cramped conditions."

| | | FOOD | DECOR | SERVICE | COST |

The Writing Room American   20| 20| 18| $$$|
East 80s | 1703 2nd Ave. (bet. 88th & 89th Sts.)
212-335-0075 | thewritingroomnyc.com
"Perched amid rowdy bars," this friendly neighborhood local is an
"ode to the history of Elaine's," the fabled and feisty literary destination here for nearly 50 years; these days, the "straightforward"
American dishes served, like "above-average" fried chicken,
make you "forget you're on the UES," and the "vibrant and energetic" scene includes those who spend their nights drinking
dirty martinis; intimate conversations are best had in the "quiet"
back study, a "reminder of the old writers who imbibed."

Wu Liang Ye Chinese   24| 12| 16| $$|
West 40s | 36 W 48th St. (bet. 5th & 6th Aves.)
212-398-2308 | wu-liang-ye.com
"For those who like it hot," this longtime favorite near Rock
Center and "close to Broadway" serves "generous portions" of
"superb Sichuan food," much of it fiery – true, the second-floor
dining room in a brownstone "needs some TLC," but "you are
paying for the food, not the decor"; there's also a lot of "noise"
and "bustle," but "we will keep climbing those stairs," promise
its fans.

Wu's Wonton King Chinese   24| 10| 15| $|
Lower East Side | 165 E Broadway (Rutgers St.)
212-477-1111 | wuswontonking.com
A "no-charge" BYO wine policy is just the cherry on top at
this Cantonese spot on the edge of the LES, where the staff
stay busy roasting "legitimately delicious" meat ready to be
"devoured"; there's also a "vast" selection of dim sum and the
"eponymous" soup that "shouldn't be missed"; "large" groups
are lured in by "extremely affordable" prices, so the punishing
turnover rates can make the waitstaff "manic" on occasion.

Xi'an Famous Foods Chinese   23| 9| 14| $|
Chinatown | 45 Bayard St.
(bet. Bowery & Elizabeth Sts.)
212-786-2068 | xianfoods.com
West 40s | 24 W 45th St. (bet. 5th & 6th Aves.)
212-786-2068
Flushing | 41-10 Main St. (41st Rd.) | Queens
718-786-2068
"The food is what you're here for" at this "casual" and "reliable"
chain of hand-pulled noodle houses; the "fantastic" "tongue-
tingling" "flavor explosion" of lamb and cumin with "mouth-
numbing chili sauce" is the "real deal," and "could be served
at a street stand in Xi'an"; although you can get takeout, the
food should be "consumed on the spot, as the staff will insist,"
but you'll have to "fight for a table," additional branches are
throughout NYC.

Xixa Ⓜ Mexican   28| 21| 23| $$$|
Williamsburg | 241 S 4th St.
(Havemeyer St.) | Brooklyn
718-388-8860 | Xixany.com
Unassuming from the outside, "charming and intimate on the
inside," this dark, gold-accented Williamsburg venue has the

"classy, creative" vibe of nearby sister restaurant Traif, "but with a Mexican twist"; "you won't leave behind a crumb" of the "inventive" and unusual offerings, like snapper tempura tacos or Peking duck carnitas; "drinks are also a must-have" – "try building your own cocktail" from the many tequilas and mezcals on offer.

Yakitori Totto (Japanese · 24 | 15 | 18 | $$$

West 50s | 251 W 55th St. (bet. B'way & 8th Ave.)
212-245-4555 | tottonyc.com

"Get in line as soon as the restaurant opens" to "grab a counter seat and watch the master grill "succulent" chicken "over a charcoal fire" at this "skewer heaven" in Midtown; although the "small, cramped, and noisy interior" won't allow you to spread your own wings, and the service is basic, the experience "feels like you've been transported to Tokyo," and that includes an authentically "pricey tab."

Yama 49 ⑤ Japanese/Sushi · 24 | 12 | 19 | $$

East 40s | 308 E 49th St. (bet. 1st & 2nd Aves.)
212-355-3370 | yama-nyc.com
Yama 17
Gramercy Park | 122 E 17th St. (Irving Pl.)
212-475-0969

Bites "the size of your head" please sushiholics at these "reliable" Gramercy Park and East 40s joints, where diners "get their fill on huge pieces of fish," plus other "quality" Japanese fare, at "acceptable prices"; the "minimalist" surroundings can sometimes "feel like you're in a basement," it's always "out-the-door" "packed," and the service is meh, but when it comes to "neighborhood" spots, these "little holes-in-the-wall" provide quite a "mouthful."

Yefsi Estiatorio Greek · 22 | 17 | 20 | $$

East 70s | 1481 York Ave. (bet. 78th & 79th Sts.)
212-535-0293 | yefsiestiatorio.com

Regulars gush about the enjoyable fish and other dishes at this taste of Greece, especially if you snag a table in the "charming garden in the back"; start with one of the mezes (or "make a whole meal out of them"), then move on to one of the "classic, yet inventive" main courses; it's "always crowded," but the "tables are well spaced so you don't mind the noise" as much, and the "service is friendly and attentive."

Yemen Café Middle Eastern · 24 | 12 | 19 | $$

Bay Ridge | 7130 5th Ave. (72nd St.) | Brooklyn
718-745-3000 | yemencafe.com
Cobble Hill | 176 Atlantic Ave. (bet. Clinton & Court Sts.)
Brooklyn | 718-834-9533

Now's your chance to set a "personal best in stomach expansion"; it's hard not to "eat big" at these "tried and true" Middle Eastern cafés in Cobble Hill and Bay Ridge, compliments of "complex" whole roasted lamb, "incomparable" fava beans and other appetizers, and tea that "warms your soul"; though decor and service are fine, feasting is the point at these "casual" "drop-in" spots.

Yun Nan Flavour Garden 🍽 Chinese   ▼ 26 | 9 | 20 | $ |

Sunset Park | 5121 8th Ave.
(bet. 52nd & 53rd Sts.) | Brooklyn
718-633-3090

"Cross-the-bridge noodles," a traditional Yunnanese decon-structed chicken noodle soup, are served alongside other regional dishes at this soup, noodle, and dumpling specialist in Sunset Park, Brooklyn's Chinatown; it all comes with basic digs and cash-only payment, but the portions are "hearty," the prices are low, and the menu is composed of still relatively hard-to-find specialties you'll see at few other restaurants in NYC.

Yves American   20 | 18 | 17 | $$$ |

TriBeCa | 385 Greenwich St. (N Moore St.)
646-937-9055 | yves-nyc.com

Offering an "eclectic menu with something for all," this "trendy" TriBeCa hangout serves a "limited" selection of French-influenced American-Continental fare in a "casual," "pleasant" space; it does stay "busy," although "slow service," coupled with "pricey" tabs, "leave a lot to be desired"; that said, it's "invit-ing" enough for "date night," and you can "sit outside" in fine weather.

Zero Otto Nove Italian/Pizza   24 | 22 | 23 | $$ |

Flatiron | 15 W 21st St. (bet. 5th & 6th Aves.)
212-242-0899 | zerootonove.com
Ⓜ Arthur Avenue/Belmont | 2357 Arthur Ave.
(186th St.) | Bronx
718-220-1027

The pizza is "amazingly" turned out and the specials "note-worthy" at these "charming" Southern Italian spots, named for the area code (089) of Salerno, the owner's hometown; the Flatiron location is "cavernous" and "relaxed," while the Arthur Ave. original has an "old-world Italian feel" – and while that one doesn't take reservations, it's "worth the hassle"; at both branches, "affordable" prices and "friendly" servers keep regulars returning.

🆕 The Zodiac Room American   – | – | – | $$$ |

West 30s | Neiman Marcus, 20 Hudson Yards
(10th Ave. & 33rd St.)
646-562-3599 | neimanmarcus.com/restaurants

The Neiman Marcus at Hudson Yards includes its own branch of the department store's chain of cafés with a menu of standards aimed at highbrow shoppers, such as caviar with fingerling chips, elegantly composed salads, and lobster club sandwiches, all served with complimentary chicken consommé, puffy popovers, and strawberry butter; the views facing Midtown and the genteel airs at its afternoon tea service both increase its qualities as a welcome refuge.

Zum Schneider NYC German   20 | 17 | 20 | $$ |

East Village | 107 Avenue C (7th St.)
212-598-1098 | nyc.zumschneider.com

"If you like bratwurst, it's worth making the trip" to Alphabet City's "small but great" "real beer house with real food that goes along with it," primarily Bavarian classics (schnitzel, pretzels, potato pancakes) paired with "towering" steins of German beer, including many hard-to-find brands on tap; you can join the crowd watching soccer at the long wooden tables inside or the smaller ones spilling out onto Avenue A; it's "fun," it's "inexpensive," and it "makes a great party."

Zum Stammtisch Ⓜ German

27 | 21 | 25 | $$

Glendale | 69-46 Myrtle Ave.
(bet. 69th Pl. & 70th St.) | Queens
718-386-3014 | zumstammtisch.com

"The huge portions of traditionally prepared German delights" – real "stick-to-the-ribs comfort food" – are why you head to this "wunderbar" Glendale destination; the Bavarian classics like goulash soup and jaeger schnitzel, the "steins of beer served by waitresses in their dirndls," and the hunting-lodge interior all work together to make it "feel like you're sitting at a table for Oktoberfest"; P.S. their next-door store sells "excellent wursts" and other specialty items.

Zuma Japanese

24 | 26 | 21 | $$$$

Murray Hill | 261 Madison Ave.
(bet. 38th & 39th Sts.)
212-544-9862 | zumarestaurant.com

You can feel the "buzz" at this "posh" Murray Hill Japanese destination, a "glitzy," "sceney," "over-the-top" space (it's part of a global chain) with bilevel seating areas – including an upstairs lounge – and an "excellent, wide-ranging selection" of izakaya-inspired and robata-grilled dishes as well as "creative" cocktails; while the service can border on "amateurish," it all works out for folks "trying to impress" and OK with the price tag.

ZZ's Clam Bar Ⓢ Ⓜ Seafood

25 | 22 | 23 | $$$$

Greenwich Village | 169 Thompson St.
(bet. Bleecker & Houston Sts.)
212-254-3000 | zzsclambar.com

"Exquisite" "small plates of fresh seafood and – of course – clams," plus cocktails that are near "perfection" keep folks clamoring for this "tiny" Village joint with a "supper-club feel" from the Carbone team; it charges pretty "eye-popping prices," but it's a "fantastic experience if you can swing it financially" and if you can get a reservation, counter seats are much easier to nab than tables.

RESTAURANT INDEXES

Cuisines

Includes restaurant names, locations, and Food ratings.

AFRICAN

Safari | Harlem	26
NEW Teranga | Harlem	–

AMERICAN

A Summer Day | TriBeCa	17
Z ABC Kitchen | Flatiron	25
Abigale's | West 30s	19
Acme | NoHo	19
Allswell | W'burg	21
Aretsky's Patroon | East 40s	25
Asiate | West 50s	25
Atera | TriBeCa	28
Atrium Dumbo | Dumbo	20
NEW Au Cheval | TriBeCa	26
Z Aureole | West 40s	26
Aviary NYC | West 60s	20
NEW Babs | G'wich Vill.	26
Bar Centrale | West 40s	17
Bar Pleiades | East 70s	22
Bar Sardine | W. Vill.	23
Beauty & Essex | LES	22
NEW Belcampo | West 30s	–
Bernie's | Greenpoint	25
Black Barn | NoMad	21
Z Blanca | Bushwick	29
Blenheim | W. Vill.	21
Z Blue Hill | G'wich Vill.	28
Blue Ribbon Brasserie | multi.	25
Blue Ribbon Federal Grill | FiDi	21
Boat Basin Cafe | West 70s	15
Brooklyn Farmacy | Carroll Gard.	22
Bryant Park Grill | West 40s	20
Bubby's | multi.	21
Burger & Barrel | SoHo	21
Burger & Lobster | multi.	19
Burke & Wills | West 70s	20
Butter | West 40s	22
Buttermilk Channel | Carroll Gard.	25
Cafe Clover | W. Vill.	19
Cafeteria | Chelsea	18
Cebu | Bay Ridge	18
Chadwick's | Bay Ridge	24

Charlie Bird | SoHo	25
Charlie Palmer | West 40s	23
Chefs Club | NoLita	25
Cherry Point | Greenpoint	22
Chez Ma Tante | Greenpoint	26
Clay | Harlem	25
Clinton St. Baking Co | LES	25
Clocktower | Flatiron	23
Colonie | B'lyn Hts.	24
Commodore | W'burg	26
Community Food & Juice | M'side Hts.	22
Contra | LES	25
Cookshop | Chelsea	22
Cowgirl SeaHorse | South St. Seaport	19
Craft | Flatiron	25
NEW Crown Shy | FiDi	27
Dimes | LES	22
Diner | W'burg	25
Dutch | SoHo	21
E.A.T. | East 80s	21
Earl's | East 90s	23
East Pole | East 60s	21
Eastfield's | East 70s	19
Egg | W'burg	22
Egg Shop | multi.	19
Elephant & Castle | W. Vill.	20
Z Eleven Madison Park | Flatiron	28
Eli's Table | East 80s	22
Emily | multi.	26
Emmy Squared | multi.	26
Empire Diner | Chelsea	20
Esme | Greenpoint	23
Estela | NoLita	26
Extra Fancy | W'burg	18
Farm on Adderley | Ditmas Park	22
Fat Radish | LES	20
Fedora | W. Vill.	23
Ferris | NoMad	25
Finch | Clinton Hill	26
Five Leaves | Greenpoint	22
Flora Bar | East 70s	24
NEW Fly | Bed-Stuy	–
Foragers Table | Chelsea	22
44 & X | West 40s	22

Tribeca Grill | TriBeCa — 23
Tuome | E. Vill. — 26
Z 21 Club | West 50s — 23
21 Greenpoint | Greenpoint — 21
Z Union Square
   Cafe | Gramercy — 26
Z Upland | Murray Hill — 25
Vandal | LES — 18
Vinegar Hill House | Dumbo — 22
NEW Violet | E. Vill. — 19
Virginia's | E. Vill. — 23
Vitae | East 40s — 25
Walker's | TriBeCa — 18
Walter's | Ft. Greene — 22
Waverly Inn | W. Vill. — 21
West~Bourne | SoHo — 21
Westville | multi. — 21
Wildair | LES — 26
Writing Room | East 80s — 20
Yves | TriBeCa — 20
NEW Zodiac Room | West 30s — —

ARGENTINEAN

Chimichurri Grill | West 40s — 24

AUSTRALIAN

Burke & Wills | West 70s — 20
Ruby's Cafe | multi. — 22
Two Hands Cafe | multi. — 22

AUSTRIAN

Wallsé | W. Vill. — 27

BARBECUE

Blue Smoke | multi. — 21
Butcher Bar | Astoria — 23
Dinosaur | multi. — 22
Ducks Eatery | E. Vill. — 25
Fette Sau | W'burg — 25
Holy Ground | TriBeCa — 25
Z Hometown | Red Hook — 28
John Brown | LIC — 23
Mable's | W'burg — 23
Morgan's | Prospect Hts. — 23
Pig Beach | Gowanus — 20

BRITISH

Bluebird | West 50s — 16
Breslin | NoMad — 22
Clinton St. Baking Co. | — 25
   LES
Clocktower | Flatiron — 23
Jones Wood | East 70s — 18

NEW Queensyard | West 30s — —
Spotted Pig | W. Vill. — 22

BURGER JOINT

Burger Joint | multi. — 24
Corner Bistro | multi. — 23
Donovan's | multi. — 22
Z JG Melon | multi. — 23
P.J. Clarke's | multi. — 19
Shake Shack | Flatiron — 21

CAJUN/CREOLE

Bayou | Rosebank — 24
Sugar Freak | Astoria — 23

CARIBBEAN

Ali's Roti Shop | multi. — 25
Glady's | Crown Hts. — 26
Malecon | multi. — 23
Miss Lily's | multi. — 20

CHINESE

Amazing 66 | Chinatown — 22
Asian Jewels | Flushing — 23
Bao | E. Vill. — 24
Big Wong | Chinatown — 22
Z Birds of a Feather | — 26
   W'burg
Café China | Murray Hill — 25
China Blue | TriBeCa — 25
Congee Village | multi. — 21
Z Decoy | W. Vill. — 28
Dim Sum Go Go | — 21
   Chinatown
Dumpling Galaxy | Flushing — 24
East Harbor Seafood | — 26
   Sunset Park
88 Lan Zhou | Chinatown — 25
Excellent Dumpling — 22
   House | Chelsea
Flor De Mayo | multi. — 22
456 Shanghai | Chinatown — 23
Golden Unicorn | — 22
   Chinatown
Grand Sichuan | multi. — 22
Great NY Noodletown | — 23
   Chinatown
Guan Fu | Flushing — 26
Hakkasan | West 40s — 24
Han Dynasty | multi. — 23
Handpulled Noodle | — 26
   Harlem
Hao Noodle | multi. — 23

Hop Kee | Chinatown · 22
Hunan Slurp | E. Vill. · 22
Hwa Yuan Szechuan | · 24
Chinatown
NEW Jiang Diner | E. Vill. · —
Jing Fong | multi. · 21
Joe's Shanghai | multi. · 23
Joe's Ginger | Chinatown · 20
Jue Lan Club | Flatiron · 18
Kings Co. Imperial | multi. · 25
Kung Fu Little Steamed · 22
Buns | multi.
Little Alley | Murray Hill · 23
Little Pepper | College · 24
Point
MáLà Project | multi. · 24
Mimi Cheng's | multi. · 21
Mission Chinese | multi. · 21
Mr Chow | multi. · 23
99 Favor Taste | multi. · 21
Nom Wah | multi. · 23
Oriental Garden | Chinatown · 23
Pacific Palace | Sunset Park · 25
Peking Duck House | multi. · 24
Philippe | multi. · 22
Pig Heaven | East 80s · 20
Ping's Seafood | · 22
Chinatown
Radiance Tea | multi. · 19
Z RedFarm | multi. · 25
Shanghai You Garden | · 24
Flushing
Shun Lee Palace | East 50s · 23
Shun Lee West | West 60s · 21
Spicy Village | LES · 28
Szechuan House | Flushing · 26
Szechuan Mountain · 26
House | multi.
Tim Ho Wan | multi. · 22
NEW Uluh | E. Vill. · —
Vanessa's Dumpling | multi. · 20
Wa Jeal | East 80s · 24
White Bear | Flushing · 25
Wo Hop | Chinatown · 24
Wu Liang Ye | West 40s · 24
Wu's Wonton King | LES · 24
Xi'an Famous Foods | · 23
multi.
Yun Nan Flavour Garden | · 26
Sunset Park

CUBAN

Café Habana | multi. · 22
Coppelia | Chelsea · 22

DELI

Z Barney Greengrass | · 26
West 80s
Baz Bagel | Little Italy · 23
Brennan & Carr | · 24
Sheepshd Bay
David's Brisket House | · 26
Bed-Stuy
Eisenberg's | Flatiron · 21
Frankel's | Greenpoint · 24
Z Katz's | LES · 26
Mile End | Boerum Hill · 23
Mill Basin Deli | M. Basin · 24
Pastrami Queen | East 70s · 24
Roll-N-Roaster | · 22
Sheepshd Bay
Z Russ & Daughters · 26
Cafe | multi.
Sarge's | Murray Hill · 23
Z 2nd Ave Deli | multi. · 24

DINER

B & H Dairy | E. Vill. · 24
Court Square Diner | LIC · 19
NEW Golden Diner | LES · —
Joe Junior | Gramercy · 18
La Bonbonniere | W. Vill. · 19
MeMe's | Prospect Hts. · 23
Neil's | East 70s · 16
Neptune Diner | Astoria · 18
Z Russ & Daughters Cafe | · 26
multi.
Z Sadelle's | SoHo · 23

EASTERN EUROPEAN

Baba's Pierogies | Gowanus · 25

ETHIOPIAN

Awash Ethiopian | multi. · 23
Bunna Cafe | Bushwick · 26

EUROPEAN

NEW Madre | Greenpoint · —

FILIPINO

Jeepney | E. Vill. · 20
Pig and Khao | LES · 23

FRENCH

A.O.C. | W. Vill. · 21
Augustine | FiDi · 23
Bacchus | Downtown Bklyn. · 23

Bagatelle	MePa	18
☒ Balthazar	SoHo	25
☒ Bar Boulud	West 60s	24
Bar Tabac	Cobble Hill	20
Bâtard	TriBeCa	26
Beaubourg	Battery Pk.	18
Benno	NoMad	26
Benoit	West 50s	22
Boucherie	multi.	20
☒ Bouley at Home	Flatiron	29
☒ Brasserie 8 1/2	West 50s	24
Brasserie Ruhlmann	West 50s	19
Buvette	W. Vill.	26
☒ Cafe Boulud	East 70s	28
Cafe Cluny	W. Vill.	22
Cafe D'Alsace	East 80s	22
Cafe Gitane	multi.	22
Café Henri	LIC	20
Cafe Luluc	Cobble Hill	22
☒ Cafe Luxembourg	West 70s	22
Carlyle	East 70s	24
Caviar Russe	East 50s	26
Chez Moi	B'lyn Hts.	22
Claudette	G'wich Vill.	21
☒ Daniel	East 60s	29
db Bistro	West 40s	25
Dirty French	LES	24
French Louie	Boerum Hill	23
☒ Frenchette	TriBeCa	24
☒ Gabriel Kreuther	West 40s	28
Indochine	G'wich Vill.	23
☒ Jean-Georges	West 60s	28
JoJo	East 60s	25
King	Hudson Sq.	26
L'Atelier de Joël Robuchon	Chelsea	28
L'Express	Gramercy	18
La Goulue	East 60s	22
☒ La Grenouille	East 50s	28
La Mercerie	SoHo	23
La Mirabelle	West 80s	24
La Sirène	multi.	22
Lafayette	NoHo	22
☒ Le Bernardin	West 50s	29
Le Bilboquet	East 60s	22
Le Colonial	East 50s	23
Le Coq Rico	Flatiron	24
☒ Le Coucou	SoHo	27
Le French Diner	LES	28
Le Gigot	W. Vill.	25
Le Parisien	Murray Hill	25
Le Relais de Venise	East 50s	22
Le Veau d'Or	East 60s	21
Lucien	E. Vill.	24
Lucky Strike	SoHo	18
M. Wells Steakhouse	LIC	26
Maison Harlem	Harlem	22
NEW Maison Yaki	Prospect Hts.	—
☒ Majorelle	East 60s	27
☒ Manhatta	FiDi	24
Mark Restaurant	East 70s	23
Mercer Kitchen	SoHo	22
MIMI	G'wich Vill.	24
☒ Minetta Tavern	G'wich Vill.	25
Mountain Bird	East Harlem	28
Nice Matin	West 70s	19
☒ Nougatine	West 60s	27
Odeon	TriBeCa	22
Orsay	East 70s	20
NEW Oxalis	Prospect Hts.	26
Pascalou	East 90s	23
NEW Pastis	MePa	—
☒ Per Se	West 50s	28
Racines NY	TriBeCa	21
Raoul's	SoHo	26
Rotisserie Georgette	East 60s	23
☒ Simone	East 80s	27
Table d'Hôte	East 90s	24
☒ Tocqueville	Flatiron	28
Tournesol	LIC	24
☒ Vaucluse	East 60s	25

GASTROPUB

Boulton & Watt	E. Vill.	18
Breslin	NoMad	22
Brooklyn Cider	Bushwick	18
Fraunces Tavern	FiDi	19
Jeffrey Craft Beer	East 60s	23
Jones Wood	East 70s	18
Lee's Tavern	Dongan Hills	24
Molly's	Gramercy	20
Penrose	East 80s	20
Pete's Tavern	Gramercy	16
Pier A Harbor House	FiDi	15
2nd Floor Bar & Essen	East 70s	22
Spotted Pig	W. Vill.	22
Tørst	Greenpoint	24

GEORGIAN

Old Tbilisi Garden | 23
  G'wich Vill.

GERMAN

Heidelberg | East 80s 21
Rolf's | Gramercy 15
Standard Biergarten | 15
  MePa
Zum Schneider | E. Vill. 20
Zum Stammtisch | 27
  Glendale

GREEK

Agnanti | Astoria 25
Ammos | East 40s 23
Anassa | East 60s 21
Z Avra | multi. 26
Z Bahari | Astoria 28
Elea | West 80s 24
Elia | Bay Ridge 26
Z Estiatorio Milos | multi. 27
Ethos Gallery 51 | East 50s 23
Gregory's 26 | Astoria 25
Kefi | West 70s 21
Kellari | West 40s 25
Z Kiki's | LES 25
Kyma | Flatiron 25
Loukoumi | Astoria 25
Molyvos | West 50s 23
Nerai | East 50s 25
Periyali | Flatiron 25
Pylos | E. Vill. 26
Snack Taverna | W. Vill. 20
Souvlaki GR | multi. 21
Z Taverna Kyclades | 25
  multi.
Telly's | Astoria 25
Thalassa | TriBeCa 24
Yefsi Estiatorio | East 70s 22

HAWAIIAN

Noreetuh | E. Vill. 23

INDIAN

Z Adda | LIC 28
Z Amma | East 50s 27
Awadh | West 90s 24
Baar Baar | E. Vill. 24
Babu Ji | G'wich Vill. 24
BK Jani | Bushwick 25
Brick Lane | E. Vill. 22
Bukhara Grill | East 40s 21

Chola | East 50s 22
Darbar | multi. 22
Dawat | East 50s 24
Dhaba | Murray Hill 23
GupShup | Gramercy 23
Z Indian Accent | West 50s 27
Junoon | Flatiron 25
Moti Mahal | East 60s 23
Pondicheri | NoMad 19
Rahi | W. Vill. 26
Saravanaa Bhavan | multi. 23
Z Tamarind | TriBeCa 27
Utsav | West 40s 22
Vatan | Murray Hill 26

INDONESIAN

NEW Wayan | NoLita 27

ITALIAN

Acqua | South St. Seaport 24
Adrienne's Pizzabar | FiDi 23
Z Ai Fiori | West 30s 26
Aita | multi. 22
Al Di La | Park Slope 27
Alberto | Forest Hills 24
Altesi | multi. 23
Ammazzacaffe | W'burg 24
Angelina's | Tottenville 23
Antica Pesa | W'burg 23
Antonio's | Arthur Ave. 24
Antonucci | East 80s 25
Aria | multi. 21
Armani | East 50s 23
Arturo's | G'wich Vill. 22
Aurora | multi. 23
Babbo | G'wich Vill. 26
Bamonte's | W'burg 21
Bar Pitti | G'wich Vill. 24
Bar Primi | E. Vill. 22
Barbetta | West 40s 22
Barboncino | Crown Hts. 25
Basso56 | West 50s 23
Basta Pasta | Flatiron 23
Z Becco | West 40s 22
Beccofino | Riverdale 24
Bella Blu | East 70s 22
Bocca | Flatiron 23
Bocelli | Old Town 26
Brioso | New Dorp 24
Brunetti | W. Vill. 24
Cacio e Pepe | E. Vill. 21
Café Altro Paradiso | 24
  Hudson Sq.
Cafe Fiorello | West 60s 22

Campagnola | East 70s	23
Caravaggio | East 70s	26
Z Carbone | G'wich Vill.	26
Carmine's | multi.	21
Casa Apicii | G'wich Vill.	21
Casa Lever | East 50s	23
Cecconi's | Dumbo	20
Celeste | West 80s	24
Cesca | West 70s	22
Cipriani | multi.	24
Charlie Bird | SoHo	25
Coco Pazzo | SoHo	27
Convivium | Park Slope	27
Cotenna | W. Vill.	24
Crispo | W. Vill.	25
Da Andrea | G'wich Vill.	24
Da Nico | Little Italy	25
Da Noi | Travis-Chelsea	24
Da Tommaso | West 50s	21
Da Umberto | Chelsea	26
Dante NYC | G'wich Vill.	21
Dee's | Forest Hills	23
Z Del Posto | Chelsea	27
Denino's Pizzeria | multi.	25
Dominick's | Arthur Ave.	24
Z Don Angie | W. Vill.	28
Don Antonio | West 50s	25
Don Peppe | South Ozone Park	26
Elio's | East 80s	25
Emilio's Ballato | NoLita	25
Enoteca Maria | St. George	25
Enzo's | multi.	26
Epistrophy | NoLita	17
Erminia | East 80s	26
Faro | Bushwick	28
Fausto | Park Slope	23
Felice | multi.	20
Z Felidia | East 50s	26
NEW Feroce | Chelsea	–
Fiaschetteria Pistoia | multi.	26
Firenze | East 80s	22
Follia | Gramercy	21
Fragole | Carroll Gard.	26
Frank | E. Vill.	26
Frankies 457 | Carroll Gard.	25
Frankies 570 | W. Vill.	23
Fresco by Scotto | East 50s	23
Gaia Italian Cafe | LES	26
Galli | SoHo	17
Gargiulo's | Coney Island	22
Gemma | E. Vill.	21
Gennaro | West 90s	25
Gigino | multi.	23
Gino's | Bay Ridge	25
Gnocco | E. Vill.	21
Gradisca | W. Vill.	23
NEW Gran Tivoli | NoLita	–
Z I Sodi | W. Vill.	28
I Trulli | Murray Hill	22
Il Bambino | Astoria	24
Il Brigante | South St. Seaport	22
il Buco | NoHo	27
il Buco Alimentari | NoHo	25
Il Cantinori | G'wich Vill.	25
Il Cortile | Little Italy	24
Il Falco | LIC	25
Il Gattopardo | West 50s	25
Il Mulino | multi.	26
Il Riccio | East 70s	20
John's of 12th | E. Vill.	22
Kesté | multi.	24
King | Hudson Sq.	26
L'Amico | West 30s	21
Z L'Artusi | W. Vill.	28
L&B Spumoni | Gravesend	25
La Masseria/Masseria dei Vini | multi.	24
La Mela | Little Italy	21
La Pecora Bianca | multi.	21
La Vigna | Forest Hills	22
La Villa | multi.	23
LaRina | Ft. Greene	25
Lattanzi | West 40s	22
Lavagna | E. Vill.	24
Lavo | East 50s	17
Leonti | West 70s	25
Leopard | West 60s	23
Leuca | W'burg	25
Lido | Harlem	24
Lil' Frankie's | E. Vill.	25
Z Lilia | W'burg	27
Z Lincoln | West 60s	25
Locanda Verde | TriBeCa	25
Locanda Vini & Olii | Clinton Hill	26
Luigi's | Glen Oaks	23
Lupa | G'wich Vill.	26
Z Lusardi's | East 70s	24
Z Maialino | Gramercy	26
Maiella | LIC	24
Malaparte | W. Vill.	22
Malatesta | W. Vill.	25
Manducatis | multi.	25
Manetta's | LIC	26
Manzo | Flatiron	26
Z Marea | West 50s	28
Maria Pia | West 50s	21

288

JAPANESE (*INDICATES SUSHI SPECIALIST)

Aburiya Kinnosuke | East 40s	—‖
*Blue Ribbon | multi.	25‖
Bohemian | NoHo	26‖
*BondST | NoHo	26‖
Chuko Ramen | Prospect Hts.	25‖
Cocoron | multi.	25‖
Davelle | LES	24‖
*Domodomo | G'wich Vill.	24‖
EN Japanese | W. Vill.	24‖
*15 East | Union Square	26‖
*Fushimi | multi.	22‖
NEW Hanon | W'burg	—‖
*Haru | multi.	20‖
*Hatsuhana | East 40s	26‖
*Hibino | multi.	24‖
Hide-Chan | multi.	24‖
Ichiran | multi.	23‖
Ikinari Steak | multi.	19‖
Inakaya NY | West 40s	20‖
Ippudo | multi.	25‖
Ivan Ramen | multi.	23‖
*Japonica | G'wich Vill.	24‖
*Jewel Bako | E. Vill.	25‖
Jin Ramen | multi.	24‖
Kajitsu | Murray Hill	27‖
*Kanoyama | E. Vill.	24‖
*Kappo Masa | East 70s	29‖
Z *KazuNori | NoMad	28‖
*Ki Sushi | multi.	26‖
*Koi | West 40s	24‖
*Kurumazushi | East 40s	26‖
Kyo Ya | E. Vill.	28‖
*Lobster Club | East 50s	22‖
NEW Maison Yaki | Prospect Hts.	—‖
*Masa | West 50s	27‖
Meijin | East 80s	28‖
Momosan | Murray Hill	25‖
*Momoya | multi.	24‖
*Morimoto | Chelsea	26‖
Mu Ramen | LIC	25‖
*Natsumi | West 50s	20‖
NEW Niche | LES	—‖
Z *Nobu | multi.	27‖
Nonono | NoMad	25‖
*O Ya | Murray Hill	27‖
NEW Odo | Flatiron	—‖
Okonomi / Yuji Ramen | W'burg	26‖
*1 OR 8 | W'burg	21‖
*Restaurant Nippon | East 50s	25‖
Sakagura | multi.	26‖
*Sasabune | East 70s	27‖
Sen Sakana | West 40s	21‖
Shabushabu Macoron | LES	28‖
NEW Shabushabu Mayumon | LES	—‖
Shalom Japan | W'burg	25‖
*Shuko | G'wich Vill.	28‖
*Silver Rice | multi.	26‖
Sobaya | E. Vill.	25‖
*Sugarfish | multi.	25‖
*Sushi Azabu | TriBeCa	28‖
*Sushi By Bou | multi.	26‖
NEW *Sushi By M | E. Vill.	27‖
*Sushi Dojo | E. Vill.	26‖
*Sushi Ginza Onodera | East 40s	29‖
*Sushi Ishikawa | East 70s	27‖
*Sushi Kaito | West 70s	27‖
*Sushi Katsuei | multi.	26‖
Z *Sushi Nakazawa | W. Vill.	29‖
*Sushi of Gari | multi.	26‖
*Sushi Seki | multi.	26‖
*Sushi Yasaka | West 70s	26‖
Z *Sushi Yasuda | East 40s	28‖
*Sushi Zo | G'wich Vill.	29‖
Suzume | W'burg	24‖
NEW TabeTomo | E. Vill.	—‖
*Takahachi | multi.	24‖
Takashi | W. Vill.	26‖
NEW *Takeshi | SoHo	—‖
*Tanoshi Sushi | East 70s	29‖
Tempura Matsui | Murray Hill	29‖
Tokyo Record Bar | G'wich Vill.	21‖
*Tomoe | G'wich Vill.	25‖
Torishin | West 50s	27‖
Totto Ramen | multi.	23‖
TsuruTonTan | multi.	23‖
Wokuni | Murray Hill	23‖
Yakitori Totto | West 50s	24‖
*Yama | multi.	24‖
Zuma | Murray Hill	24‖

KOREAN

Z Atoboy | NoMad	27‖
Z Atomix | NoMad	29‖
Barn Joo | multi.	21‖
BCD Tofu House | multi.	23‖
Cho Dang Gol | West 30s	24‖
Z Cote | Flatiron	26‖

Danji | West 50s — 25
Dons Bogam | Murray Hill — 24
Gaonnuri | West 30s — 22
🆕 Golden Diner | LES — —
🆕 Haenyeo | Park Slope — 27
🅩 Hangawi | Murray Hill — 28
Hanjan | Flatiron — 23
Her Name is Han | East 30s — 25
Hwaban | Flatiron — 23
Insa | Gowanus — 24
Jeju Noodle Bar | W. Vill. — 27
Jongro BBQ | West 30s — 22
Jungsik | TriBeCa — 29
Kang Ho Dong Baekjeong | — 26
  East 30s
🆕 Kāwi | West 30s — —
🆕 Kichin | Bushwick — —
KumGangSan | Flushing — 21
Kunjip | West 30s — 19
Mapo | Flushing — 26
Miss Korea BBQ | West 30s — 20
New Wonjo | West 30s — 20
🆕 O:n | East 30s — —
Oiji | E. Vill. — 26
Thursday Kitchen | E. Vill. — 25

LAOTIAN

Khe-Yo | TriBeCa — 24

LATIN AMERICAN

🅩 ABC Cocina | Flatiron — 25
🅩 Arepa Lady | Jackson — 26
  Hts.
Arepas Café/Grill | multi. — 24
Bogota | Park Slope — 21
Cabana | Forest Hills — 24
Caracas Arepa | multi. — 24
Churrascaria Plataforma | — 22
  West 40s
Empanada Mama | multi. — 23
Flor De Mayo | multi. — 22

MALAYSIAN

Kopitiam | LES — 20
Laut | Union Square — 23
Nyonya | multi. — 24

MEDITERRANEAN

Amali | East 60s — 22
Amaranth | East 60s — 21
Balaboosta | W. Vill. — 24
Barbounia | Flatiron — 23
Blue | Randall Manor — 22

Bodrum | West 80s — 20
🅩 Boulud Sud | West 60s — 26
Bustan | West 80s — 23
Celestine | Dumbo — 22
Covina | Murray Hill — 22
Extra Virgin | W. Vill. — 18
Fig & Olive | multi. — 22
Gato | NoHo — 24
Glasserie | Greenpoint — 24
Ilili | NoMad — 25
Jack's Wife Freda | multi. — 21
Kashkaval Garden | — 22
  West 50s
🆕 Leyla | West 70s — —
Limani | West 50s — 25
Little Owl | W. Vill. — 24
Pera | multi. — 21
🆕 Savida | TriBeCa — —
Shuka | SoHo — 23
Smile | NoHo — 18
Taboon | West 50s — 25
Tessa | West 70s — 22

MEXICAN

Alma | Carroll Gard. — 22
Atla | NoHo — 24
Barrio Chino | LES — 24
Black Ant | E. Vill. — 15
Bodega Negra | Chelsea — 21
🅩 Casa Enrique | LIC — 27
Cascabel Taqueria | multi. — 17
Chavela's | Crown Hts. — 24
Claro | Gowanus — 26
🅩 Cosme | Flatiron — 26
Cowgirl SeaHorse | South — 19
  St. Seaport
El Parador | Murray Hill — 24
El Toro Blanco | W. Vill. — 16
El Vez | Battery Pk. — 20
Empellon | East 50s — 22
Empellon Taqueria | W. Vill. — 23
5 Burro Cafe | Forest Hills — 23
Fonda | multi. — 22
Gran Electrica | Dumbo — 21
Hell's Kitchen | West 50s — 19
🅩 La Contenta | LES — 27
La Contenta Oeste | — 22
  G'wich Vill.
La Esquina | multi. — 21
La Morada | Mott Haven — 27
Los Mariscos | Chelsea — 25
🅩 Los Tacos No.1 | multi. — 27
Maya | East 60s — 22
Mexico Lindo | Murray Hill — 23

Z Oxomoco | Greenpoint 27
Pampano | East 40s 21
Playa Betty's | West 70s 17
Rosa Mexicano | multi. 21
Rosie's | E. Vill. 19
Tacombi | multi. 20
Tacos El Bronco | multi. 25
Tacuba | multi. 22
Taqueria St. Marks | E. Vill. 21
Taqueria Tlaxcalli | 27
Parkchester
Toloache | multi. 23
Xixa | W'burg 28

MIDDLE EASTERN

Almayass | Flatiron 25
Au Za'atar | E. Vill. 20
Balade | E. Vill. 23
Beyoglu | East 80s 23
Cafe Mogador | multi. 24
Gazala's Place | multi. 21
NEW HaSalon | West 50s —
Kubeh | G'wich Vill. 22
NEW Lamalo | East 30s —
Mimi's | Ditmas Park 23
Miriam | Park Slope 24
Z Miss Ada | Ft. Greene 27
Miznon | multi. 25
Moustache | W. Vill. 26
Naya | East 50s 25
Nur | Flatiron 24
Taci's Beyti | Midwood 23
Z Tanoreen | Bay Ridge 27
12 Chairs Cafe | multi. 23
Yemen Café | multi. 24

NEW ZEALAND

Musket Room | NoLita 25

PAKISTANI

BK Jani | Bushwick 25

PAN-ASIAN

Buddakan | Chelsea 25
Z Momofuku Ssäm | E. Vill. 26
Tao | multi. 23
NEW Wild Ink | West 30s —

PERSIAN

Persepolis | East 70s 22
Z Ravagh | multi. 26
Sofreh | Prospect Hts. 26

PERUVIAN

Z Llama Inn | W'burg 26
Pio Pio | multi. 23
Sen Sakana | West 40s 21

PIZZA

Adrienne's | FiDi 23
Artichoke | E. Vill. 22
Barboncino | Crown Hts. 25
Bella Blu | East 70s 22
Best Pizza | W'burg 25
Brioso | New Dorp 24
Brunetti | W. Vill. 24
Cafe Fiorello | West 60s 22
Cecconi's | Dumbo 20
Celeste | West 80s 24
Da Nico | Little Italy 25
Dee's | Forest Hills 23
Denino's | multi. 25
Di Fara | Midwood 26
Don Antonio | West 50s 25
Emily | multi. 26
Emmy Squared | multi. 26
Follia | Gramercy 21
Fornino | multi. 23
Gino's | Bay Ridge 25
Gnocco | E. Vill. 21
Grimaldi's | multi. 23
Industry Kitchen | South 16
St. Seaport
Joe & Pat's | multi. 26
Z Joe's | multi. 25
John's | multi. 24
Juliana's | Dumbo 27
Kesté | multi. 24
L&B Spumoni | Gravesend 25
La Villa | multi. 23
Lee's Tavern | Dongan Hills 24
Lil' Frankie's | E. Vill. 25
Lombardi's | multi. 23
Z Lucali | Carroll Gard. 28
Luzzo's | multi. 24
Malaparte | W. Vill. 22
Mama's Too | West 100s 25
Manetta's | LIC 26
Marta | NoMad 23
Milkflower | Astoria 25
Motorino | multi. 23
New Park | Howard Beach 25
Nucci's | Tottenville 23
Ops | Bushwick 28
Otto Enoteca | G'wich Vill. 22
Z Pasquale Jones | NoLita 25

Patricia's | Morris Park	25
Patsy's Pizzeria | multi.	22
Paulie Gee's | Greenpoint	26
PizzArte | West 50s	21
Pizzeria Sirenetta | West 80s	23
Posto | Gramercy	23
Z Prince Street | NoLita	27
Ribalta | G'wich Vill.	22
Z Roberta's | Bushwick	27
Z Rubirosa | NoLita	26
Sal and Carmine | West 100s	25
San Matteo | East 80s	26
Scarr's Pizza | LES	26
Serafina | multi.	19
Sorbillo | NoHo	22
Sottocasa | multi.	26
Speedy Romeo | multi.	23
Stella 34 | West 30s	24
Tavola | West 30s	21
Tiella | East 60s	25
Totonno's | Coney Island	26
Trattoria Romana | Dongan Hills	25
Una Pizza | LES	25
Vesta | Astoria	27
Vesuvio | Bay Ridge	23
Vezzo | Murray Hill	24
NEW Violet | E. Vill.	19
Wheated | Ditmas Park	27
Zero Otto Nove | multi.	24

PORTUGUESE

Aldea | Flatiron	26

RAMEN

Chuko | Prospect Hts.	25
Hide-Chan Ramen | multi.	24
Ichiran | multi.	23
Ippudo | multi.	25
Ivan Ramen | multi.	23
Jeju Noodle Bar | W. Vill.	27
Jin Ramen | multi.	24
Kung Fu Little Steamed Buns Ramen | multi.	22
Meijin Ramen | East 80s	28
Z Momofuku Noodle Bar | multi.	24
Momosan | Murray Hill	25
Mu Ramen | LIC	25
NEW Niche | LES	–
Okonomi / Yuji Ramen | W'burg	26

NEW TabeTomo | E. Vill.	–
Totto Ramen | multi.	23

RUSSIAN

Mari Vanna | Flatiron	24
Russian Tea Room | West 50s	19

SCANDINAVIAN

Agern | East 40s	26
Z Aquavit | East 50s	27

SEAFOOD

AbuQir | Astoria	28
Z Aquagrill | SoHo	26
Artie's | City Island	24
Astoria Seafood | LIC	27
Atlantic Grill | West 60s	23
Blue Fin | West 40s	22
Brooklyn Crab | Red Hook	19
Catch NYC | MePa	23
Cervo's | LES	27
Chef's Table | West 30s	28
City Island Lobster House | City Island	21
Clam | W. Vill.	23
Crave Fishbar | multi.	23
Cull & Pistol | Chelsea	24
Desnuda | multi.	26
Docks | East 40s	22
Elias Corner | Astoria	25
Fish | W. Vill.	23
Flex Mussels | multi.	24
Flora Bar | East 70s	24
NEW Fulton | South St. Seaport	–
Grand Army | Boerum Hill	20
Grand Banks | TriBeCa	17
Z Grand Central Oyster Bar | East 40s	23
Greenpoint Fish & Lobster Co. | Greenpoint	23
Gregory's 26 | Astoria	25
Johnny's Reef | City Island	18
Littleneck | multi.	21
Lolo's | Harlem	22
Lure | SoHo	24
Maison Premiere | W'burg	26
NEW Mar | West 30s	–
Mary's Fish Camp | W. Vill.	24
Z Mermaid Inn | multi.	23
Ocean Prime | West 50s	25
Oceana | West 40s	25

Original Crab Shanty | City Island	24
Z Pearl Oyster | W. Vill.	27
Randazzo's | Sheepshd Bay	24
Sea Fire Grill | East 40s	26
Sea Grill | West 40s	24
Seamore's | multi.	19
Upstate | E. Vill.	25
ZZ's Clam Bar | G'wich Vill.	25

SOUTHERN

Amy Ruth's | Harlem	23
Bobwhite Counter | E. Vill.	25
Jacob's Pickles | West 80s	23
Melba's | Harlem	26
Miss Mamie's | M'side Hts.	22
Peaches HotHouse | multi.	25
Pies 'n' Thighs | W'burg	23
Queens Comfort | Astoria	24
Red Rooster | Harlem	22
Root & Bone | E. Vill.	24
Sweet Chick | multi.	23
Sylvia's | Harlem	21

SPANISH

Alta | G'wich Vill.	23
Bar Jamon | Gramercy	25
Beso | St. George	24
Boqueria | multi.	23
Casa Mono | Gramercy	26
El Porrón | East 60s	24
El Pote | Murray Hill	24
El Quinto Pino | Chelsea	25
Huertas | E. Vill.	22
La Fonda | East 40s	20
La Vara | Cobble Hill	27
NEW Leña | West 30s	–
NEW Mar | West 30s	–
Salinas | Chelsea	27
Sevilla | W. Vill.	24
Socarrat Paella | multi.	20
Tía Pol | Chelsea	23
Txikito | Chelsea	26
Vinateria | Harlem	25

SRI LANKAN

Lakruwana | Stapleton	26

STEAKHOUSE

American Cut | multi.	25
Beatrice Inn | W. Vill.	24
NEW Belcampo | West 30s	–

Ben & Jack's | East 40s	25
Z Benjamin | multi.	27
NEW BLT Prime | East 70s	–
BLT Steak | East 50s	25
Bobby Van's | multi.	23
Bowery Meat Co. | E. Vill.	24
Capital Grille | multi.	25
Chimichurri Grill | West 40s	24
Christos | Astoria	26
Club A | East 50s	26
Z Cote | Flatiron	26
Del Frisco's | multi.	25
Delmonico's | multi.	25
Famous Sammy's Roumanian | LES	19
Z 4 Charles | W. Vill.	28
Frankie & Johnnie's | multi.	22
Gallaghers | West 50s	25
Harry's NYC | FiDi	23
Hunt & Fish Club | West 40s	21
Ikinari Steak | multi.	19
Z Keens | West 30s	27
Le Marais | West 40s	22
Lincoln Square Steak | West 70s	19
Maloney & Porcelli | East 50s	25
Mastro's | West 50s	25
Morton's | multi.	24
Nick & Stef's | West 30s	23
Old Homestead | Chelsea	24
Palm | multi.	24
Z Peter Luger | W'burg	28
Z Porter House | West 50s	27
Quality Eats | multi.	22
Quality Meats | West 50s	25
St. Anselm | W'burg	27
Z Smith & Wollensky | East 40s	25
Z Sparks | East 40s	26
STK | multi.	22
Strip House | multi.	23
TBar | East 70s	22
212 Steakhouse | East 50s	21
Z Wolfgang's | multi.	26
Wollensky's | East 40s	26

TAIWANESE

886 | E. Vill.	23
Ho Foods | E. Vill.	23
Win Son | W'burg	27

THAI

Ayada Thai | multi.	26
Erawan | Bayside	21
Fish Cheeks | NoHo	23
Joya | Cobble Hill	23
Khao Kang | Elmhurst	28
NEW **Krok** | Carroll Gard.	–
Land Thai | West 80s	22
Laut | Union Square	23
Obao | multi.	20
Pig and Khao | LES	23
Pure | West 50s	26
Room Service | West 40s	19
Sea | W'burg	16
Somtum Der | E. Vill.	24
SriPraPhai | Woodside	27
NEW **Taladwat** | West 40s	–
Thai Market | West 100s	23
Ugly Baby | Carroll Gard.	26
Z **Uncle Boons** | NoLita	27
Up Thai | East 70s	24
NEW **Wayla** | LES	–
Wondee Siam | West 50s	21

TIBETAN

Lhasa | Jackson Hts.	28
A La Turka | East 70s	21
NEW **Lokanta** | Astoria	–
NEW **Turk's Inn** | Bushwick	–
Turkish Kitchen | Murray Hill	23

UKRAINIAN

Veselka | E. Vill.	22

UZBEK

Nargis | Sheepshd Bay	23

VEGAN/VEGETARIAN

Z **abcV** | Flatiron	26
Avant Garden | E. Vill.	26
Blossom | multi.	22
Butcher's Daughter | multi.	19
Candle Café | multi.	22
Dirt Candy | LES	24
Modern Love | W'burg	23
Nix | G'wich Vill.	24
Peacefood | multi.	21
Superiority Burger | E. Vill.	25

VIETNAMESE

Banh Mi Saigon | Little Italy	24
Bricolage | Park Slope	23
Bunker | Bushwick	22
Di An Di | Greenpoint	24
Hanoi House | E. Vill.	25
Indochine | NoHo	23
Madame Vo | E. Vill.	23
NEW **Madame Vo BBQ** | E. Vill.	–
Nha Trang | Chinatown	23
Obao | multi.	20
Vietnaam | East 80s	23

Locations

Includes restaurant names, cuisines, and Food ratings.

MANHATTAN

BATTERY PARK CITY

Beaubourg | French — 18
Blue Smoke | Barbecue — 21
Del Frisco's | Steakhouse — 25
El Vez | Mexican — 20
Gigino | Italian — 23
Parm | Italian — 19
P.J. Clarke's | American — 19

CENTRAL PARK

Loeb Boathouse | American — 19
Tavern on the Green | — 18
   American

CHELSEA

Ayada Thai | Thai — 26
Blossom | Vegan — 22
Bodega Negra | Mexican — 21
Buddakan | Pan-Asian — 25
Cafeteria | American — 18
Cookshop | American — 22
Coppelia | Cuban — 22
Corkbuzz | Wine Bar — 21
Cull & Pistol | Seafood — 24
Da Umberto | Italian — 26
Z Del Posto | Italian — 27
El Quinto Pino | Spanish — 25
Empire Diner | American — 20
Excellent Dumpling | — 22
   Chinese
NEW Feroce | Italian — −
Fonda | Mexican — 22
Foragers Table | American — 22
Freds | American — 22
Friedman's Lunch | — 21
   American
Grand Sichuan | Chinese — 22
Grand Sichuan Eastern | — 22
   Chinese
Hao Noodle Chelsea | — 23
   Chinese
Jack's Wife Freda | — 21
   Mediterranean
L'Atelier de Joël — 28
   Robuchon | French
Lombardi's | Pizza — 23
Los Mariscos | Mexican — 25

Z Los Tacos No.1 | Mexican — 27
Meatball Shop | Italian — 20
Miznon | Middle Eastern — 25
Momofuku Nishi | Italian — 22
Momoya | Japanese/Sushi — 24
Morimoto | Japanese — 26
   /Sushi
Motel Morris | American — 19
Old Homestead | — 24
   Steakhouse
Salinas | Spanish — 27
Seamore's | Seafood — 19
Socarrat Paella Bar | — 20
   Spanish
Sushi Seki | Japanese — 26
Tao Downtown | Pan-Asian — 23
Tía Pol | Spanish — 23
Txikito | Spanish — 26
Westville | American — 21

CHINATOWN

Amazing 66 | Chinese — 22
Big Wong | Chinese — 22
Dim Sum Go Go | Chinese — 21
88 Lan Zhou | Chinese — 25
456 Shanghai | Chinese — 23
Golden Unicorn | Chinese — 22
Great NY Noodletown | — 23
   Chinese
Hop Kee | Chinese — 22
Hwa Yuan Szechuan | — 24
   Chinese
Jing Fong | Chinese — 21
Joe's Shanghai | Chinese — 23
Joe's Ginger | Chinese — 20
Nha Trang | Vietnamese — 23
Nom Wah | Chinese — 23
Oriental Garden | Chinese — 23
Peking Duck House | — 24
   Chinese
Ping's Seafood | Chinese — 22
Wo Hop | Chinese — 24
Xi'an Famous Foods | — 23
   Chinese

EAST 30S

Her Name Is Han | Korean — 25
Kang Ho Baekjeong | — 26
   Korean
NEW Lamalo | Middle Eastern — −

O:n | Korean	—|
Sushi By Bou | Japanese	26|

EAST 40S

Aburiya Kinnosuke | Japanese	—|
Agern | Scandinavian	26|
Ammos Estiatorio | Greek	23|
Aretsky's Patroon | American	25|
Z Avra Estiatorio | Greek	26|
Ben & Jack's | Steakhouse	25|
Z Benjamin | Steakhouse	27|
Z Benjamin Prime | Steakhouse	27|
Bobby Van's | Steakhouse	23|
Bukhara Grill | Indian	21|
Capital Grille | Steakhouse	25|
Darbar | Indian	22|
Docks Oyster | Seafood	22|
Z Grand Central Oyster Bar & Restaurant | Seafood	23|
Cipriani Dolci | Italian	24|
Hatsuhana | Sushi	26|
Kurumazushi | Sushi	26|
La Fonda Del Sol | Spanish	20|
Morton's | Steakhouse	24|
Osteria Laguna | Italian	22|
Palm Too | Steakhouse	24|
Pampano | Mexican	21|
Patsy's Pizzeria | Pizza	22|
Pera | Mediterranean	21|
Pietro's | Italian	25|
Sakagura | Japanese	26|
Sea Fire Grill | Seafood	26|
Z Smith & Wollensky | Steakhouse	25|
Z Sparks | Steakhouse	26|
Sushi Ginza Onodera | Sushi	29|
Z Sushi Yasuda | Sushi	28|
Vitae | American	25|
Z Wolfgang's | Steakhouse	26|
Wollensky's | Steakhouse	26|
Yama 49 | Japanese/Sushi	24|

EAST 50S

American Cut | Steakhouse	25|
Z Amma | Indian	27|
Z Aquavit | Scandinavian	27|
Armani | Italian	23|
BLT Steak | Steakhouse	25|
Bobby Van's | Steakhouse	23|

Casa Lever | Italian	23|
Caviar Russe | French	26|
Chola | Indian	22|
Club A | Steakhouse	26|
Crave Fishbar | Seafood	23|
Darbar Grill | Indian	22|
Dawat | Indian	24|
Empellon | Mexican	22|
Ethos Gallery 51 | Greek	23|
Z Felidia | Italian	26|
Fig & Olive | Mediterranean	22|
Fresco by Scotto | Italian	23|
Grand Sichuan Eastern | Chinese	22|
Z Grill | American	25|
Harry Cipriani | Italian	24|
Hide-Chan | Ramen	24|
Hillstone | American	23|
Kung Fu Little Steamed Buns | Chinese/Ramen	22|
Z La Grenouille | French	28|
La Pecora Bianca | Italian	21|
Lavo | Italian	17|
Le Colonial | French	23|
Le Relais de Venise | French	22|
Lobster Club | Japanese	22|
Maloney & Porcelli | Steakhouse	25|
Monkey Bar | American	21|
Montebello | Italian	24|
Morso | Italian	25|
Mr Chow | Chinese	23|
National | American	17|
Naya | Middle Eastern	25|
Nerai | Greek	25|
Obao | Thai/Vietnamese	20|
Peking Duck House | Chinese	24|
P.J. Clarke's | American	19|
Polo Bar | American	23|
Radiance | Chinese	19|
Restaurant Nippon | Japanese/Sushi	25|
Rosa Mexicano | Mexican	21|
San Pietro | Italian	24|
Shun Lee Palace | Chinese	23|
The Smith | American	19|
Socarrat | Spanish	20|
Souvlaki GR | Greek	21|
Tao Uptown | Pan-Asian	23|
Totto Ramen | Ramen	23|
212 | Steakhouse	21|
Valbella | Italian	26|
Z Wolfgang's | Steakhouse	26|

EAST 60S

Altesi | Italian — 23
Amali | Mediterranean — 22
Amaranth | Mediterranean — 21
Anassa Taverna | Greek — 21
Z Avra Madison | Greek — 26
Z Daniel | French — 29
East Pole | American — 21
El Porrón | Spanish — 24
Felice 64 | Italian — 20
Fig & Olive | Mediterranean — 22
Freds | American — 22
Il Mulino | Italian — 26
Jeffrey | Gastropub — 23
JoJo | French — 25
La Goulue | French — 22
Le Bilboquet | French — 22
Le Veau d'Or | French — 21
Z Majorelle | French — 27
Maya | Mexican — 22
Moti Mahal | Indian — 23
Philippe | Chinese — 22
Z Ravagh | Persian — 26
Regency | American — 19
Rotisserie Georgette | — 23
    French
Scalinatella | Italian — 21
Sushi Seki | Sushi — 26
Tiella | Italian/Pizza — 25
Tony's Di Napoli | Italian — 21
Z Vaucluse | French — 25

EAST 70S

A La Turka | Turkish — 21
Bar Pleiades | American — 22
Bella Blu | Italian/Pizza — 22
NEW BLT Prime | Steakhouse — –
Boqueria | Spanish — 23
Z Cafe Boulud | French — 28
Campagnola | Italian — 23
Candle 79 | Vegan — 22
Candle Cafe | Vegan — 22
Caravaggio | Italian — 26
Carlyle Restaurant | French — 24
Eastfield's | American — 19
Flora Bar | American — 24
Il Riccio | Italian — 20
Z JG Melon | Burger Joint — 23
Jones Wood | — 18
    British/Gastropub
Kappo Masa | Japanese — 29
    /Sushi
La Esquina | Mexican — 21

Z Lusardi's | Italian — 24
Mark Restaurant | French — 23
Meatball Shop | Italian — 20
Mezzaluna | Italian — 21
Neil's Coffee Shop | Diner — 16
Orsay | French — 20
Parma | Italian — 22
Pastrami Queen | Deli — 24
Persepolis | Persian — 22
Quality Eats | Steakhouse — 22
Sant Ambroeus | Italian — 23
Sasabune | Sushi — 27
Z 2nd Ave Deli | Deli — 24
2nd Floor | Gastropub — 22
Serafina | Italian/Pizza — 19
Sette Mezzo | Italian — 24
Sojourn | American — 19
Sushi Ishikawa | Sushi — 27
Sushi of Gari | Sushi — 26
Tanoshi Sushi | Sushi — 29
TBar | Steakhouse — 22
Up Thai | Thai — 24
Uva | Italian — 22
Via Quadronno | Italian — 22
Yefsi Estiatorio | Greek — 22

EAST 80S

Antonucci Cafe | Italian — 25
Beyoglu | Middle Eastern — 23
Cafe D'Alsace | French — 22
Cascabel | Mexican — 17
E.A.T. | American — 21
Eli's Table | American — 22
Elio's | Italian — 25
Erminia | Italian — 26
Felice 83 | Italian — 20
Firenze | Italian — 22
Flex Mussels | Seafood — 24
Heidelberg | German — 21
Meijin | Ramen — 28
Nicola's Restaurant | Italian — 24
Penrose | Gastropub — 20
Pig Heaven | Chinese — 20
San Matteo | Italian/Pizza — 26
Sandro's | Italian — 24
Z Simone | French — 27
Sistina | Italian — 25
Toloache | Mexican — 23
Vietnaam | Vietnamese — 23
Wa Jeal | Chinese — 24
Writing Room | American — 20

EAST 90S

Earl's	American	23
Paola's	Italian	26
Pascalou	French	23
Pio Pio	Peruvian	23
Ⓩ Russ & Daughters Cafe	Deli/Diner	26
Sarabeth's	American	20
Sfoglia	Italian	24
Table d'Hôte	French	24

EAST HARLEM

Mountain Bird	French	28
Patsy's Pizzeria	Pizza	22
Rao's	Italian	23

EAST VILLAGE

Artichoke	Pizza	22
Au Za'atar	Middle Eastern	20
Avant Garden	Vegan	26
Awash	Ethiopian	23
B & H Dairy	Diner	24
Baar Baar	Indian	24
Balade	Middle Eastern	23
Bao	Chinese	24
Bar Primi	Italian	22
Black Ant	Mexican	15
Bobwhite	Southern	25
Boulton & Watt	Gastropub	18
Bowery Meat Co.	Steakhouse	24
Brick Lane	Indian	22
Cacio e Pepe	Italian	21
Cafe Mogador	Middle Eastern	24
Caracas	Latin American	24
Desnuda	Seafood	26
Ducks Eatery	Barbecue	25
886	Taiwanese	23
Emmy	American/Pizza	26
Fiaschetteria Pistoia	Italian	26
Fonda	Mexican	22
Frank	Italian	26
Gemma	Italian	21
Gnocco	Italian/Pizza	21
Han Dynasty	Chinese	23
Hanoi House	Vietnamese	25
Hearth	American	25
Ho Foods	Taiwanese	23
Huertas	Spanish	22
Hunan Slurp	Chinese	22
Jeepney	Filipino	20

Jewel Bako	Japanese /Sushi	25
🆕 Jiang Diner	Chinese	–
Joe & Pat's	Pizza	26
John's of 12th	Italian	22
Kanoyama	Sushi	24
Kyo Ya	Japanese	28
Lavagna	Italian	24
Lil' Frankie's	Italian/Pizza	25
Lucien	French	24
Luzzo's	Pizza	24
Madame Vo	Vietnamese	23
🆕 Madame Vo BBQ	Vietnamese	–
MáLà Project	Chinese	24
Ⓩ Mermaid Inn	Seafood	23
Mimi Cheng's	Chinese	21
Miss Lily's 7A Cafe	Caribbean	20
Ⓩ Momofuku Ko	American	28
Ⓩ Momofuku Noodle Bar	Ramen	24
Ⓩ Momofuku Ssäm Bar	Pan-Asian	26
Motorino	Pizza	23
Narcissa	American	21
99 Favor Taste	Chinese	21
Noreetuh	Hawaiian	23
Oiji	Korean	26
Porsena	Italian	25
Prune	American	25
Pylos	Greek	26
Ⓩ Ravagh	Persian	26
Root & Bone	Southern	24
Rosie's	Mexican	19
Ruffian	Wine Bar	25
Sakagura	Japanese	26
Smith	American	19
Sobaya	Japanese	25
Somtum Der	Thai	24
Superiority Burger	Vegetarian	25
Supper	Italian	24
🆕 Sushi By M	Sushi	27
Sushi Dojo	Sushi	26
Szechuan Mountain House	Chinese	26
🆕 TabeTomo	Japanese /Ramen	–
Takahachi	Japanese	24
Taqueria St. Marks	Mexican	21
Ⓩ Taverna Kyclades	Greek	25

Thursday Kitchen | Korean 25
Tuome | American 26
🆕 Uluh | Chinese –
Upstate | Seafood 25
Vanessa's Dumpling | 20
Chinese
Veselka | Ukrainian 22
🆕 Violet | American/Pizza 19
Virginia's | American 23
Westville | American 21
Zum Schneider | German 20

FINANCIAL DISTRICT

Adrienne's | Italian/Pizza 23
Augustine | French 23
Blue Ribbon Federal Grill | 21
American
Bobby Van's | Steakhouse 23
Capital Grille | Steakhouse 25
🆕 Crown Shy | American 27
Delmonico's | Steakhouse 25
Felice | Italian 20
Fraunces | Gastropub 19
Cipriani Club 55 | Italian 24
Harry's NYC | American/ 23
Steakhouse
Haru Sushi | Japanese 20
Kesté Fulton | Italian/Pizza 24
🅩 Manhatta | French 24
Morton's | Steakhouse 24
🅩 Nobu | Japanese 27
Obao | Thai/Vietnamese 20
Pier A | Gastropub 15
Seamore's | Seafood 19
Westville | American 21

FLATIRON

🅩 ABC Cocina | Latin 25
American
🅩 ABC Kitchen | American 25
🅩 abcV | Vegan/Vegetarian 26
Aldea | Portuguese 26
Almayass | Middle Eastern 25
Barbounia | Mediterranean 23
Basta Pasta | Italian 23
Blue Smoke | Barbecue 21
Bocca | Italian 23
Boqueria | Spanish 23
🅩 Bouley at Home | French 29
Burger & Lobster | 19
American
Clocktower | American 23
/British
🅩 Cosme | Mexican 26

🅩 Cote | Korean/ 26
Steakhouse
Craft | American 25
Eisenberg's | Deli 21
🅩 Eleven Madison Park | 28
American
Giorgio's | American 23
🅩 Gramercy Tavern | 28
American
Grimaldi's | Pizza 23
Hanjan | Korean 23
Hwaban | Korean 23
Jue Lan Club | Chinese 18
Junoon | Indian 25
Kyma | Greek 25
La Pecora Bianca | Italian 21
Le Coq Rico | French 24
Manzo | Italian 26
Mari Vanna | Russian 24
Nur | Middle Eastern 24
🆕 Odo | Japanese –
🅩 Park Avenue | American 25
Periyali | Greek 25
🆕 Rezdôra | Italian –
Rosa Mexicano | Mexican 21
Scampi | Italian 21
Serra by Birreria | Italian 16
Shake Shack | Burger Joint 21
Sugarfish | Sushi 25
Sushi By Bou | Sushi 26
Tacombi | Mexican 20
🅩 Tocqueville | French 28
Zero Otto Nove | Italian 24
/Pizza

GRAMERCY

Bar Jamon | Spanish 25
Boucherie | French 20
Casa Mono | Spanish 26
Follia | Italian/Pizza 21
GupShup | Indian 23
House | American 21
Joe Junior | Diner 18
L'Express | French 18
🅩 Maialino | Italian 26
Molly's | Gastropub 20
Novitá | Italian 25
Pete's Tavern | Gastropub 16
Posto | Italian/Pizza 23
Rolf's | German 15
🅩 Union Square Cafe | 26
American
Yama 17 | Japanese/Sushi 24

GREENWICH VILLAGE

Alta | Spanish 23
Arturo's | Italian 22
NEW Babs | American —
Babbo | Italian 26
Babu Ji | Indian 24
Bar Pitti | Italian 24
Z Blue Hill | American 28
Z Carbone | Italian 26
Casa Apicii | Italian 21
Claudette | French 21
Corkbuzz | Wine Bar 21
Da Andrea | Italian 24
Dante NYC | Italian 21
Denino's | Pizza 25
Domodomo | Sushi 24
Gotham Bar and Grill | —
    American
Ikinari Steak | Japanese 19
    /Steakhouse
Il Cantinori | Italian 25
Il Mulino | Italian 26
Ippudo | Japanese/Ramen 25
Jane | American 19
Japonica | Japanese/Sushi 24
Z JG Melon | Burger Joint 23
Z Joe's Pizza | Pizza 25
Kubeh | Middle Eastern 22
La Contenta Oeste | 22
    Mexican
Z Loring Place | American 25
Lupa | Italian 26
Z Mermaid Oyster Bar | 23
    Seafood
MIMI | French 24
Z Minetta Tavern | French 25
Miss Lily's | Caribbean 20
Nix | Vegan/Vegetarian 24
North Square | American 23
Old Tbilisi Garden | 23
    Georgian
Otto Enoteca | Italian/Pizza 22
Peacefood | Vegan 21
Ribalta | Italian/Pizza 22
Shuko | Japanese/Sushi 28
Strip House | Steakhouse 23
Sushi Zo | Sushi 29
Tim Ho Wan | Chinese 22
Tokyo Record Bar | 21
    Japanese
Toloache | Mexican 23
Tomoe Sushi | Sushi 25
Villa Mosconi | Italian 25
ZZ's Clam Bar | Seafood 25

HARLEM

Amy Ruth's | Southern 23
Clay | American 25
Grange | American 22
Handpulled Noodle | 26
    Chinese
Harlem Shake | American 20
Lido | Italian 24
Lolo's Seafood Shack | 22
    Seafood
Maison Harlem | French 22
Melba's | Southern 26
Red Rooster | Southern 22
NEW Reverence | American —
Safari | African 26
Sottocasa | Italian/Pizza 26
Sylvia's | Southern 21
NEW Teranga | African —
Vinateria | Spanish 25

HUDSON SQUARE

Café Altro Paradiso | Italian 24
Houseman | American 23
King | French/Italian 26
La Sirène | French 22
Westville | American 21

LITTLE ITALY

Banh Mi Saigon | 24
    Vietnamese
Baz Bagel | Deli 23
Da Nico | Italian 25
Il Cortile | Italian 24
La Mela | Italian 21
Nyonya | Malaysian 24
Two Hands | Australian 22
Umbertos | Italian 21

LOWER EAST SIDE

Barrio Chino | Mexican 24
Beauty & Essex | American 22
Blue Ribbon Sushi 25
    Izakaya | Japanese/Sushi
Cervo's | Seafood 27
Clinton St. Baking 25
    Company | American
Cocoron | Japanese 25
Congee Village | Chinese 21
Contra | American 25
Davelle | Japanese 24
Dimes | American 22
Dirt Candy | Vegetarian 24
Dirty French | French 24

Empanada Mama | Latin   23
  American
Famous Sammy's   18
  Roumanian | Steakhouse
Fat Radish | American   20
Freemans | American   21
Gaia Italian Cafe | Italian   26
🆕 Golden Diner | Diner   —
  /Korean
Ivan Ramen | Ramen   23
🅩 Katz's | Deli   26
🅩 Kiki's | Greek   25
Kings Co. Imperial | 25
  Chinese
Kopitiam | Malaysian   20
🅩 La Contenta | Mexican   27
Le French Diner | French   28
Meatball Shop | Italian   20
Mission Chinese | Chinese   21
🆕 Niche | Japanese/Ramen   —
99 Favor Taste | Chinese   21
Pig and Khao | Filipino   23
  /Thai
🅩 Russ & Daughters   26
  Cafe | Deli/Diner
Scarr's Pizza | Pizza   26
Shabushabu Macoron | 28
  Japanese
🆕 Shabushabu Mayumon | —
  Japanese
Souvlaki GR | Greek   21
Speedy Romeo | Italian   23
  /Pizza
Spicy Village | Chinese   28
Sweet Chick | Southern   23
Una Pizza | Pizza   25
Vandal | American   18
Vanessa's Dumpling | 20
  Chinese
🆕 Wayla | Thai   —
Wildair | American   26
Wu's Wonton King | 24
  Chinese

MEATPACKING DISTRICT

Bagatelle | French   18
Bubby's | American   21
Catch NYC | Seafood   23
Fig & Olive | Mediterranean   22
High Street on Hudson | 22
  American
🆕 Pastis | French   —
Philippe | Chinese   22

RH Rooftop | American   20
Santina | Italian   20
Serafina | Italian/Pizza   19
Standard Biergarten | 15
  German
Standard Grill | American   22
STK | Steakhouse   22

MORNINGSIDE HEIGHTS

Community Food & Juice | 22
  American
Dinosaur Bar-B-Que | 22
  Barbecue
Friedman's | American   21
Jin Ramen | Japanese   24
  /Ramen
Miss Mamie's | Southern   22
Pisticci | Italian   25

MURRAY HILL

Café China | Chinese   25
Covina | Mediterranean   22
Dhaba | Indian   23
Dons Bogam | Korean   24
El Parador Cafe | Mexican   24
El Pote Español | Spanish   24
🅩 Hangawi | Korean   28
I Trulli | Italian   22
Kajitsu | Japanese   27
Le Parisien Bistrot | French   25
Little Alley | Chinese   23
Mexico Lindo | Mexican   23
Momosan | Ramen   25
O Ya | Japanese/Sushi   27
Pio Pio | Peruvian   23
🅩 Riverpark | American   25
Rossini's | Italian   23
Ruby's Cafe | Australian   22
Sarabeth's | American   20
Saravanaa Bhavan | Indian   23
Sarge's | Deli   23
🅩 2nd Ave Deli | Deli   24
Simon & The Whale | 20
  American
Tempura Matsui | Japanese   29
Turkish Kitchen | Turkish   23
🅩 Upland | American   25
Vatan | Indian   26
Vezzo | Italian/Pizza   24
Wokuni | Japanese   23
🅩 Wolfgang's | Steakhouse   26
Zuma | Japanese   24

NOHO

Acme	American	19
Atla	Mexican	24
Bohemian	Japanese	26
BondST	Japanese/Sushi	26
Fish Cheeks	Thai	23
Gato	Mediterranean	24
il Buco	Italian	27
il Buco Alimentari	Italian	25
Indochine	French /Vietnamese	23
Lafayette	French	22
Saxon + Parole	American	19
Smile	Mediterranean	18
Sorbillo	Pizza	22
Vic's	Italian	22

NOLITA

Butcher's Daughter	Vegan/Vegetarian	19
Cafe Gitane	French	22
Habana To Go	Cuban	22
Café Habana	Cuban	22
Chefs Club	American	25
Cocoron	Japanese	25
Egg Shop	American	19
Emilio's Ballato	Italian	25
Epistrophy	Italian	17
Estela	American	26
🆕 Gran Tivoli	Italian	–
La Esquina	Mexican	21
Lombardi's	Pizza	23
Mimi Cheng's	Chinese	21
Musket Room	New Zealand	25
Nom Wah	Chinese	23
Parm	Italian	19
Ⓩ Pasquale Jones	Italian/Pizza	25
Peasant	Italian	23
Ⓩ Prince Street	Pizza	27
Ⓩ Rubirosa	Italian/Pizza	26
Ruby's Cafe	Australian	22
Sant Ambroeus	Italian	23
Seamore's	Seafood	19
Socarrat	Spanish	20
Tacombi	Mexican	20
Ⓩ Uncle Boons	Thai	27
🆕 Wayan	Indonesian	27

NOMAD

Ⓩ Atoboy	Korean	27
Ⓩ Atomix	Korean	29
Benno	French	26
Black Barn	American	21
Breslin	British/Gastropub	22
Ferris	American	25
Hillstone	American	23
Ilili	Mediterranean	25
Ⓩ KazuNori	Sushi	28
Marta	Italian/Pizza	23
NoMad Bar	American	25
Ⓩ The NoMad	American	26
Nonono	Japanese	25
Pondicheri	Indian	19
Quality Eats	Steakhouse	22
Ⓩ Ravagh	Persian	26
Scarpetta	Italian	23
The Smith	American	19
Vini e Fritti	Italian	24

SOHO

Altesi Downtown	Italian	23
Ⓩ Aquagrill	Seafood	26
Aurora	Italian	23
Ⓩ Balthazar	French	25
Blue Ribbon Brasserie	American	25
Blue Ribbon Sushi	Sushi	25
Boqueria	Spanish	23
Burger & Barrel	American	21
Charlie Bird	American /Italian	25
Coco Pazzo	Italian	27
Dutch	American	21
Galli	Italian	17
Cipriani Downtown	Italian	24
Jack's Wife Freda	Mediterranean	21
La Mercerie	French	23
Ⓩ Le Coucou	French	27
Lucky Strike	French	18
Lure Fishbar	Seafood	24
Mercer Kitchen	French	22
🆕 Niche Niche	Wine Bar	–
Osteria Morini	Italian	25
Pera	Mediterranean	21
Raoul's	French	26
Ⓩ Sadelle's	Diner	23
St Tropez	Wine Bar	20
Shuka	Mediterranean	23
Sugarfish	Sushi	25
🆕 Takeshi	Japanese /Sushi	–
12 Chairs	Middle Eastern	23
West-Bourne	American	21

SOUTH STREET SEAPORT

Acqua | Italian	24
Cowgirl SeaHorse |	19
American/Mexican	
NEW Fulton | Seafood	–
Il Brigante | Italian	22
Industry Kitchen |	16
American/Pizza	
10 Corso Como | Italian	24

TRIBECA

A Summer Day Cafe |	17
American	
American Cut | Steakhouse	25
Atera | American	28
NEW Au Cheval | American	26
Bâtard | French	26
Bubby's | American	21
China Blue | Chinese	25
Z Frenchette | French	24
Gigino Trattoria | Italian	23
Grand Banks | Seafood	17
Holy Ground | Barbecue	25
Il Mulino New York | Italian	26
Jungsik | Korean	29
Khe-Yo | Laotian	24
Little Park | American	23
Locanda Verde | Italian	25
Marc Forgione | American	26
Mr Chow | Chinese	23
Odeon | French	22
Palm Tribeca | Steakhouse	24
Pepolino | Italian	25
Racines NY | French	21
Rosa Mexicano | Mexican	21
Sarabeth's | American	20
NEW Savida | Mediterranean	–
Z Scalini Fedeli | Italian	27
Sushi Azabu | Sushi	28
Sushi of Gari | Sushi	26
Takahachi | Sushi	24
Z Tamarind | Indian	27
Terroir | Italian	19
Thalassa | Greek	24
Tiny's | American	20
Tribeca Grill | American	23
Tutto il Giorno | Italian	21
Two Hands | Australian	22
Walker's | American	18
Z Wolfgang's |	26
Steakhouse	
Yves | American	20

UNION SQUARE

Barn Joo | Korean	21
15 East | Japanese/Sushi	26
Z Joe's Pizza | Pizza	25
Laut | Malaysian/Thai	23
Sushi By Bou | Sushi	26
TsuruTonTan | Japanese	23

WASHINGTON HEIGHTS

Malecon | Caribbean	23

WEST 30S

Abigael's | American	19
Z Ai Fiori | Italian	26
Barn Joo 35 | Korean	21
BCD Tofu House | Korean	23
NEW Belcampo | American	–
/Steakhouse	
Chef's Table at Brooklyn	28
Fare | Seafood	
Cho Dang Gol | Korean	24
Delmonico's | Steakhouse	25
Z Estiatorio Milos | Greek	27
Frankie & Johnnie's |	22
Steakhouse	
Friedman's | American	21
Gaonnuri | Korean	22
NEW Hudson Yards Grill |	–
American	
Ichiran | Japanese/Ramen	23
Jongro BBQ | Korean	22
NEW Kāwi | Korean	–
Z Keens | Steakhouse	27
Kung Fu Little Steamed	22
Buns | Chinese/Ramen	
Kunjip | Korean	19
L'Amico | Italian	21
Legacy Records |	23
American	
NEW Leña | Spanish	–
NEW Mar | Spanish/Seafood	–
Mercato | Italian	24
Miss Korea BBQ | Korean	20
New Wonjo | Korean	20
Nick & Stef's | Steakhouse	23
Parker & Quinn | American	20
NEW Queensyard | British	–
Stella 34 | Italian	24
Tacombi | Mexican	20
NEW TAK Room | American	–
Tavola | Italian/Pizza	21
NEW Wild Ink | Pan-Asian	–
NEW Zodiac Room | American	–

WEST 40S

Z Aureole	American	26
Bar Centrale	American	17
Barbetta	Italian	22
Z Becco	Italian	22
Blue Fin	Seafood	22
Bobby Van's	Steakhouse	23
Boqueria	Spanish	23
Bryant Park Grill	American	20
Burger & Lobster	American	19
Butter	American	22
Carmine's	Italian	21
Charlie Palmer	American	23
Chimichurri Grill	Steakhouse/Argentinean	24
Churrascaria Plataforma	Latin American	22
db Bistro	French	25
Del Frisco's	Steakhouse	25
44 & X	American	22
Frankie & Johnnie's	Steakhouse	22
Friedman's	American	21
Z Gabriel Kreuther	French	28
Gazala's Place	Middle Eastern	21
Hakkasan	Chinese	24
Haru Sushi	Japanese	20
Hunt & Fish Club	Steakhouse	21
Ichiran	Japanese/Ramen	23
Ikinari Steak	Japanese/Steakhouse	19
Inakaya NY	Japanese	20
Ippudo	Japanese/Ramen	25
Ivan Ramen	Ramen	23
Joe Allen	American	20
Z Joe's Pizza	Pizza	25
John's	Pizza	24
Kellari Taverna	Greek	23
Koi	Japanese/Sushi	24
Kung Fu Little Steamed Buns	Chinese/Ramen	22
La Masseria	Italian	24
Lambs Club	American	23
Lattanzi	Italian	22
Le Marais	Steakhouse	22
Z Los Tacos	Mexican	27
MáLà Project	Chinese	24
Marshal	American	22
Obao	Thai/Vietnamese	20

Oceana	Seafood	25
Osteria al Doge	Italian	21
Pio Pio	Peruvian	23
Ribbon	American	20
Room Service	Thai	19
Sardi's	Italian	17
Sea Grill	Seafood	24
Sen Sakana	Japanese/Peruvian	21
STK Midtown	Steakhouse	22
Strip House	Steakhouse	23
Sushi By Bou	Sushi	26
Sushi of Gari 46	Sushi	26
Sushi Seki	Sushi	26
NEW Taladwat	Thai	—
Thalia	American	20
Tim Ho Wan	Chinese	22
Tony's Di Napoli	Italian	21
Trattoria Trecolori	Italian	22
TsuruTonTan	Japanese	23
Utsav	Indian	22
Z Wolfgang's	Steakhouse	26
Wu Liang Ye	Chinese	24
Xi'an Famous Foods	Chinese	23

WEST 50S

Aldo Sohm	Wine Bar	22
Aria	Italian/Wine Bar	21
Asiate	American	25
Basso56	Italian	23
Benoit New York	French	22
Blue Ribbon Sushi	Japanese/Sushi	25
Bluebird London	British	16
Bobby Van's	Steakhouse	23
Z Brasserie 8 1/2	French	24
Brasserie Ruhlmann	French	19
Burger Joint	Burger Joint	24
Capital Grille	Steakhouse	25
Casellula	Wine Bar	24
Da Tommaso	Italian	21
Danji	Korean	25
Del Frisco's	Steakhouse	25
Don Antonio	Italian/Pizza	25
Empanada Mama	Latin American	23
Z Estiatorio Milos	Greek	27
Gallaghers	Steakhouse	25
Haru Sushi	Japanese	20
NEW HaSalon	Middle Eastern	—
Hell's Kitchen	Mexican	19

Hide-Chan | Ramen — 24
Il Gattopardo | Italian — 25
Z Indian Accent | Indian — 27
Ippudo | Japanese/Ramen — 25
Jams | American — 19
Kashkaval Garden | — 22
  Mediterranean
La Esquina | Mexican — 21
Masseria dei Vini | Italian — 24
Z Le Bernardin | French — 29
Limani | Mediterranean — 25
Z Marea | Italian — 28
Maria Pia | Italian — 21
Masa | Japanese/Sushi — 27
Mastro's | Steakhouse — 25
Meatball Shop | Italian — 20
Michael's | American — 23
Z Modern | American — 28
Molyvos | Greek — 23
Z Momofuku Noodle Bar | — 24
  Ramen
Natsumi | Japanese/Sushi — 20
Z Nobu | Japanese/Sushi — 27
Norma's | American — 24
Ocean Prime | Seafood — 25
Palm | Steakhouse — 24
Palm Court | American — 22
Patsy's | Italian — 23
Z Per Se | French — 28
PizzArte | Italian/Pizza — 21
Z Porter House | — 27
  Steakhouse
Pure | Thai — 26
Quality Italian | Italian — 24
Quality Meats | Steakhouse — 25
Radiance | Chinese — 19
Redeye Grill | American — –
Remi | Italian — 24
Robert | American — 23
Russian Tea Room | — 19
  Russian
Sarabeth's | American — 20
Souvlaki GR | Greek — 21
Taboon | Mediterranean — 25
Tacuba | Mexican — 22
Toloache | Mexican — 23
Torishin | Japanese — 27
Totto Ramen | Ramen — 23
Trattoria Dell'Arte | Italian — 23
Z 21 Club | American — 23
ViceVersa | Italian — 23
Westville | American — 21
Wondee Siam | Thai — 21
Yakitori Totto | Japanese — 24

WEST 60S

Atlantic Grill | Seafood — 23
Aviary NYC | American — 20
Z Bar Boulud | French — 24
Z Boulud Sud | — 26
  Mediterranean
Cafe Fiorello | Italian/Pizza — 22
Z Jean-Georges | French — 28
Leopard | Italian — 23
Z Lincoln Ristorante | — 25
  Italian
Z Nougatine | French — 27
P.J. Clarke's | American — 19
Rosa Mexicano | Mexican — 21
Shun Lee West | Chinese — 21
Smith | American — 19

WEST 70S

Boat Basin Cafe | American — 15
Burke & Wills | American — 20
  /Australian
Z Cafe Luxembourg | — 22
  French
Cesca | Italian — 22
Friedman's | American — 21
Jing Fong | Chinese — 21
Kefi | Greek — 21
Leonti | Italian — 25
NEW Leyla | Mediterranean — –
Lincoln Square Steak | — 19
  Steakhouse
NEW Miznon | Middle Eastern — –
Nice Matin | French — 19
Pappardella | Italian — 20
Parm | Italian — 19
Patsy's Pizzeria | Pizza — 22
Playa Betty's | Mexican — 17
Z RedFarm | Chinese — 25
Ribbon | American — 20
Salumeria Rosi | Italian — 24
Saravanaa Bhavan | Indian — 23
Serafina | Italian/Pizza — 19
Storico | Italian — 18
Sushi Kaito | Sushi — 27
Gari | Sushi — 26
Sushi Yasaka | Sushi — 26
Tessa | Mediterranean — 22

WEST 80S

Z Barney Greengrass | Deli — 26
Blossom | Vegan — 22
Bodrum | Mediterranean — 20
Bustan | Mediterranean — 23
Celeste | Italian/Pizza — 24

Crave Fishbar | Seafood	23
Elea | Greek	24
Flor De Mayo | Chinese /Latin American	22
Gazala's | Middle Eastern	21
Good Enough to Eat | American	19
Han Dynasty | Chinese	23
Haru Sushi | Japanese	20
Jacob's Pickles | Southern	23
☒ JG Melon | Burger Joint	23
Jin Ramen | Ramen	24
La Mirabelle | French	24
La Sirène | French	22
Land Thai Kitchen | Thai	22
Maison Pickle | American	22
☒ Mermaid Inn | Seafood	23
Milling Room | American	23
Momoya | Japanese/Sushi	24
Motorino | Pizza	23
Peacefood Cafe | Vegan	21
Pizzeria Sirenetta | Pizza	23
Sarabeth's | American	20

WEST 90S

Awadh | Indian	24
Carmine's | Italian	21
Gennaro | Italian	25
Malecon | Caribbean	23
Pio Pio | Peruvian	23

WEST 100S

Awash | Ethiopian	23
Cascabel Taqueria | Mexican	17
Flor De Mayo | Chinese /Latin American	22
Mama's Too | Pizza	25
Sal and Carmine | Pizza	25
Thai Market | Thai	23

WEST VILLAGE

A.O.C. | French	21
Aria | Wine Bar/Italian	21
Balaboosta | Mediterranean	24
Bar Sardine | American	23
Beatrice Inn | Steakhouse	24
Blenheim | American	21
Boucherie | French	20
Brunetti | Italian/Pizza	24
Butcher's Daughter | Vegan/Vegetarian	19
Buvette | French	26
Cafe Clover | American	19

Cafe Cluny | French	22
Clam | Seafood	23
Corner Bistro | Burger Joint	23
Cotenna | Italian	24
Crispo | Italian	25
☒ Decoy | Chinese	28
☒ Don Angie | Italian	28
El Toro Blanco | Mexican	16
Elephant & Castle | American	20
Emily | American/Pizza	26
Empellon | Mexican	23
EN | Japanese	24
Extra Virgin | Mediterranean	18
Fedora | American	23
Fiaschetteria Pistoia | Italian	26
Fish | Seafood	23
Flex Mussels | Seafood	24
☒ 4 Charles | Steakhouse	28
Frankies 570 | Italian	23
Gradisca | Italian	23
Hao Noodle | Chinese	23
Happiest Hour | American	19
Hudson Clearwater | American	19
☒ I Sodi | Italian	28
Jack's Wife Freda | Mediterranean	21
Jeffrey's Grocery | American	22
Jeju Noodle Bar | Korean	27
John's | Pizza	24
Joseph Leonard | American	23
Kesté | Italian/Pizza	24
☒ L'Artusi | Italian	28
La Bonbonniere | Diner	19
Le Gigot | French	25
Left Bank | American	20
Little Owl | Mediterranean	24
Loyal | American	21
Malaparte | Italian/Pizza	22
Malatesta Trattoria | Italian	25
Market Table | American	22
Mary's Fish Camp | Seafood	24
Meatball Shop | Italian	20
Morandi | Italian	21
Moustache | Middle Eastern	26
🆕 North Fork | American	—
One If by Land | American	25
Palma | Italian	23

Z Pearl Oyster Bar | 27
Seafood
Perry St | American 25
Piccolo Angolo | Italian 25
Quality Eats | Steakhouse 22
Rafele | Italian 24
Rahi | Indian 26
Z RedFarm | Chinese 25
Rosemary's | Italian 21
St Tropez | Wine Bar 20
Sant Ambroeus | Italian 23
Sevilla | Spanish 24
Snack Taverna | Greek 20
Sotto 13 | Italian 17
Spotted Pig | Gastropub 22
Sushi Katsuei | Sushi 26
Z Sushi Nakazawa | Sushi 29
Tacombi | Mexican 20
Takashi | Japanese 26
Z Via Carota | Italian 28
Wallsé | Austrian 27
Waverly Inn | American 21
Westville | American 21

BROOKLYN

BATH BEACH

Nyonya | Malaysian 24

BAY RIDGE

Cebu Bar & Bistro | 18
American
Chadwick's | American 24
Elia | Greek 26
Fushimi | Japanese/Sushi 22
Gino's | Italian/Pizza 25
Z Tanoreen | Middle 27
Eastern
Tuscany Grill | Italian 23
Vesuvio | Italian/Pizza 23
Yemen Café | Middle 24
Eastern

BEDFORD-STUYVESANT

Ali's Trinidad Roti Shop | 25
Caribbean
David's Brisket House | 26
Deli
NEW Fly | American –
Hart's | American 26
Peaches | Southern 25

BOERUM HILL

French Louie | French 23
Grand Army | Seafood 20
Ki Sushi | Japanese/Sushi 26
Mile End | Deli 23
Rucola | Italian 25
Sottocasa | Italian/Pizza 26

BROOKLYN HEIGHTS

Chez Moi | French 22
Colonie | American 24
Fornino | Pizza 23
Henry's End | American 25
Jack the Horse Tavern | 23
American
Luzzo's BK | Pizza 24
Noodle Pudding | Italian 26
Queen | Italian 25

BUSHWICK

BK Jani | Indian/Pakistani 25
Z Blanca | American 29
Brooklyn Cider House | 18
Gastropub
Bunker | Vietnamese 22
Bunna Cafe | Ethiopian 26
Faro | Italian 28
Ichiran | Japanese/Ramen 23
NEW Kichin | Korean –
Mission Chinese | Chinese 21
Ops | Pizza 28
Z Roberta's | American 27
/Pizza
NEW Turk's Inn | Turkish –

CARROLL GARDENS

Alma | Mexican 22
Brooklyn Farmacy | 22
American
Buttermilk Channel | 25
American
Fragole | Italian 26
Frankies 457 | Italian 25
NEW Franks | Wine Bar –
NEW Krok | Thai –
Z Lucali | Pizza 28
Ugly Baby | Thai 26

CLINTON HILL

Aita | Italian 22
Emily | American/Pizza 26
Finch | American 26

Locanda Vini & Olii | Italian 26
Otway | American 24
Speedy Romeo | Italian 23
/Pizza

COBBLE HILL

Awash | Ethiopian 23
Bar Tabac | French 20
Cafe Luluc | French 22
Hibino | Japanese/Sushi 24
Joya | Thai 23
La Vara | Spanish 27
Yemen Café | Middle 24
Eastern

CONEY ISLAND

Gargiulo's | Italian 22
Grimaldi's | Pizza 23
Totonno's | Pizza 26

CROWN HEIGHTS

Aita Trattoria | Italian 22
Ali's Roti Shop | Caribbean 25
Barboncino | Italian/Pizza 25
Chavela's | Mexican 24
Glady's | Caribbean 26
NEW Hunky Dory | American –
Silver Rice | Sushi 26

DITMAS PARK

Farm on Adderley | 22
American
Mimi's | Middle Eastern 23
Wheated | Pizza 27

DOWNTOWN BROOKLYN

Bacchus | French 23
Han Dynasty | Chinese 23

DUMBO

Atrium Dumbo | American 20
Cafe Gitane | French 22
Cecconi's | Italian/Pizza 20
Celestine | Mediterranean 22
Gran Electrica | Mexican 21
Grimaldi's | Pizza 23
Juliana's | Pizza 27
Z River Café | American 26
Seamore's | Seafood 19
Sugarcane | American 22

Vinegar Hill House | 22
American
Westville | American 21

DYKER HEIGHTS

La Villa | Italian/Pizza 23

FORT GREENE

Habana Outpost | Cuban 22
LaRina | Italian 25
Z Miss Ada | Middle 27
Eastern
Peaches HotHouse | 25
Southern
Walter's | American 22

GOWANUS

Baba's Pierogies | Eastern 25
European
Claro | Mexican 26
Dinosaur Bar-B-Que | 22
Barbecue
Insa | Korean 24
Littleneck | Seafood 20
Pig Beach | Barbecue 20
Runner & Stone | American 22

GRAVESEND

L&B Spumoni | Pizza 25
Pio Pio | Peruvian 23

GREENPOINT

Bernie's | American 25
Cherry Point | American 22
Chez Ma Tante | American 26
Di An Di | Vietnamese 24
Esme | American 23
Five Leaves | American 22
Fornino | Pizza 23
Frankel's | Deli 24
Glasserie | Mediterranean 24
Greenpoint Fish & Lobster 23
Co. | Seafood
Littleneck Outpost | 20
Seafood
NEW Madre | American/ –
European
Z Oxomoco | Mexican 27
Paulie Gee's | Pizza 26
Tørst | Gastropub 24
21 Greenpoint | American 21

MIDWOOD

Di Fara Pizza | Pizza — 26
Taci's Beyti | Middle — 23
   Eastern

MILL BASIN

La Villa | Italian/Pizza — 23
Mill Basin Deli | Deli — 24

PARK SLOPE

Al Di La Trattoria | Italian — 27
Blue Ribbon Brasserie | — 25
   American
Bogota | Latin American — 21
Bricolage | Vietnamese — 23
Convivium | Italian — 27
Fausto | Italian — 23
Fonda | Mexican — 22
NEW Haenyeo | Korean — 27
Ki Sushi | Japanese/Sushi — 26
La Villa | Italian/Pizza — 23
Miriam | Middle Eastern — 24
Rose Water | American — 25
Sushi Katsuei | Sushi — 26

PROSPECT HEIGHTS

Chuko Ramen | Ramen — 25
James | American — 23
NEW LaLou | Wine Bar — –
NEW Maison Yaki | French — –
   /Japanese
MeMe's Diner | Diner — 23
Morgan's | Barbecue — 23
Z Olmsted | American — 27
NEW Oxalis | French — 26
Sofreh | Persian — 26
Sweet Chick | Southern — 23

PROSPECT LEFFERTS GARDENS

Ali's Roti Shop | Caribbean — 25
Silver Rice | Sushi — 26

RED HOOK

Brooklyn Crab | Seafood — 19
Good Fork | American — 25
Z Hometown | Barbecue — 28
NEW Red Hook Tavern | — –
   American

SHEEPSHEAD BAY

Brennan & Carr | Deli — 24
Nargis Cafe | Uzbek — 23
Randazzo's | Seafood — 24
Roll-N-Roaster | Deli — 22
Sushi By Bou | Sushi — 26

SUNSET PARK

Burger Joint | Burger Joint — 24
East Harbor Seafood — 26
   Palace | Chinese
99 Favor Taste | Chinese — 21
Pacific Palace | Chinese — 25
Tacos El Bronco | Mexican — 25
Yun Nan Flavour | Chinese — 26

WILLIAMSBURG

Allswell | American — 21
Ammazzacaffe | Italian — 24
Antica Pesa | Italian — 23
Aurora | Italian — 23
Bamonte's | Italian — 21
Best Pizza | Pizza — 25
Z Birds of a Feather | — 26
   Chinese
Butcher's Daughter | — 19
   Vegan/Vegetarian
Cafe Mogador | Middle — 24
   Eastern
Caracas Arepa Bar | Latin — 24
   American
Commodore | American — 26
Desnuda | Seafood — 26
Diner | American — 25
Egg | American — 22
Egg Shop | American — 19
Emmy | American/Pizza — 26
Extra Fancy | American — 18
Fette Sau | Barbecue — 25
Four Horsemen | Wine Bar — 26
Fushimi | Japanese/Sushi — 22
NEW Gertie | American — –
NEW Hanon | Japanese — –
Z Joe's Pizza | Pizza — 25
Kings County Imperial | — 25
   Chinese
Leuca | Italian — 25
Z Lilia | Italian — 27
Littleneck Outpost | — 20
   Seafood
Z Llama Inn | Peruvian — 26
Mable's | Barbecue — 23
Maison Premiere | Seafood — 26

Marlow & Sons | American	24
Ⓩ Meadowsweet | American	27
Meatball Shop | Italian	20
Misi | Italian	26
Modern Love | Vegan/Vegetarian	23
🆕 Montesacro Pinseria | Italian	—
Motorino | Pizza	23
Okonomi / Yuji Ramen | Japanese	26
1 OR 8 | Japanese/Sushi	21
Ⓩ Peter Luger | Steakhouse	28
Pies 'n' Thighs | Southern	23
St. Anselm | Steakhouse	27
Sea | Thai	16
Shalom Japan | Japanese	25
Sunday In Brooklyn | American	23
Suzume | Japanese	24
Sweet Chick | Southern	23
Traif | American	27
12 Chairs | Middle Eastern	23
Vanessa's | Chinese	20
Win Son | Taiwanese	27

BRONX

ARTHUR AVENUE/ BELMONT

Antonio's | Italian	24
Dominick's | Italian	24
Enzo's | Italian	26
Mario's | Italian	23
Roberto's | Italian	25
Tra Di Noi | Italian	26
Zero Otto Nove | Italian /Pizza	24

CITY ISLAND

Artie's | Seafood	24
City Island Lobster House | Seafood	21
Johnny's Reef | Seafood	18
Original Crab Shanty | Seafood	24

KINGSBRIDGE

Malecon | Caribbean	23

MORRIS PARK

Enzo's | Italian	26
Patricia's | Italian/Pizza	25

MOTT HAVEN

La Morada | Mexican	27
Pio Pio | Peruvian	23

PARKCHESTER

Taqueria Tlaxcalli | Mexican	27

RIVERDALE

Beccofino | Italian	24

WAKEFIELD

Ali's Roti Shop | Caribbean	25

QUEENS

ASTORIA

AbuQir | Seafood	28
Agnanti | Greek	25
Arepas Cafe | Latin	24
Arepas Grill | Latin	24
Bahari Estiatorio | Greek	28
Butcher Bar | Barbecue	23
Christos | Steakhouse	26
Elias Corner | Seafood	25
Gregory's 26 | Greek/Seafood	25
Il Bambino | Italian	24
Lokanta | Turkish	—
Loukoumi Taverna | Greek	25
Milkflower | Italian/Pizza	25
Neptune Diner | Diner	18
Piccola Venezia | Italian	25
Queens Comfort | Southern	24
Sanfords | American	22
Sugar Freak | Cajun/Creole	23
Tacuba | Mexican	22
Ⓩ Taverna Kyclades | Greek	25
Telly's Taverna | Greek	25
Ⓩ Trattoria L'incontro | Italian	28
Vesta Trattoria | Italian	27

BAYSIDE

BCD Tofu House | Korean — 23
Donovan's | Burger Joint — 22
Erawan | Thai — 21
🅉 Taverna Kyclades | — 25
  Greek

COLLEGE POINT

Little Pepper | Chinese — 24

CORONA

Park Side | Italian — 25

DOUGLASTON

Grimaldi's | Pizza — 23

ELMHURST

Ayada Thai | Thai — 26
Khao Kang | Thai — 28

FAR ROCKAWAY

Sayra's Wine Bar | — 25
  Wine Bar

FLUSHING

Asian Jewels | Chinese — 23
Congee Village | Chinese — 21
Dumpling Galaxy | Chinese — 24
Guan Fu | Chinese — 26
Joe's Shanghai | Chinese — 23
KumGangSan | Korean — 21
Mapo | Korean — 26
99 Favor Taste | Chinese — 21
Shanghai You Garden | — 24
  Chinese
Szechuan House | Chinese — 26
Szechuan Mountain — 26
  House | Chinese
Totto Ramen | Ramen — 23
White Bear | Chinese — 25
Xi'an Famous Foods | — 23
  Chinese

FOREST HILLS

Alberto | Italian — 24
Cabana | Latin American — 24
Dee's | Italian/Pizza — 23
5 Burro Cafe | Mexican — 23
Grand Sichuan | Chinese — 22
La Vigna | Italian — 22

Nick's Pizza | Italian — 24

GLEN OAKS

Luigi's | Italian — 23

GLENDALE

Zum Stammtisch | German — 27

HOWARD BEACH

La Villa | Italian/Pizza — 23
New Park Pizza | Pizza — 25

JACKSON HEIGHTS

🅉 Arepa Lady | Latin — 26
Lhasa Fast Food | Tibetan — 28
Pio Pio | Peruvian — 23

LONG ISLAND CITY

🅉 Adda | Indian — 28
Astoria Seafood | Seafood — 27
Café Henri | French — 20
🅉 Casa Enrique | Mexican — 27
Corner Bistro | Burger Joint — 23
Court Square Diner | Diner — 19
Hibino | Japanese/Sushi — 24
Il Falco Restaurant | Italian — 25
John Brown | Barbecue — 23
LIC Market | American — 21
M. Wells Steakhouse | — 26
  French
Maiella | Italian — 24
Manducatis | Italian — 25
Manetta's | Italian — 26
Mu Ramen | Ramen — 25
Sweet Chick | Southern — 23
Tournesol | French — 24

MIDDLE VILLAGE

Pio Pio | Peruvian — 23

ROCKAWAY PARK

Caracas Arepa Bar | Latin — 24
  American

SOUTH OZONE PARK

Don Peppe | Italian — 26

WOODSIDE

Donovan's | Burger Joint — 22
SriPraPhai | Thai — 27

STATEN ISLAND

CASTLETON CORNERS

Joe & Pat's | Pizza   **26**

DONGAN HILLS

Lee's | Gastropub/Pizza   **24**
Trattoria Romana | Italian   **25**
  /Pizza

ELM PARK

Denino's | Italian/Pizza   **25**

GRANT CITY

Fushimi | Japanese/Sushi   **22**

NEW DORP

Brioso | Italian/Pizza   **24**

OLD TOWN

Bocelli Ristorante | Italian   **26**

RANDALL MANOR

Blue | Mediterranean   **22**

ROSEBANK

Bayou | Cajun/Creole   **24**

ST. GEORGE

Beso | Spanish   **24**
Enoteca Maria | Italian   **25**

STAPLETON

Lakruwana | Sri Lankan   **26**
Vinum | Italian   **24**

TOTTENVILLE

Angelina's | Italian   **23**
Fushimi | Japanese/Sushi   **22**
Nucci's | Italian/Pizza   **23**

TRAVIS-CHELSEA

Da Noi | Italian   **24**

Special Features

Includes restaurant names, locations, and Food ratings.

BAR SCENES

Acme	NoHo	19
Anassa	East 60s	21
Bagatelle	MePa	18
Bar Centrale	West 40s	17
Bar Jamon	Gramercy	25
Bar Sardine	W. Vill.	23
Bar Tabac	Cobble Hill	20
Bayou	Rosebank	24
Beatrice Inn	W. Vill.	24
Beauty & Essex	LES	22
Bernie's	Greenpoint	25
Black Barn	NoMad	21
Boat Basin	West 70s	15
Bobby Van's	multi.	23
Bodega Negra	Chelsea	21
Bogota	Park Slope	21
Boqueria	multi.	23
Boulton & Watt	E. Vill.	18
Z Brasserie 8 1/2	West 50s	24
Brooklyn Cider House	Bushwick	18
Brooklyn Crab	Red Hook	19
Bryant Park Grill	West 40s	20
Burger & Barrel	SoHo	21
Café Altro Paradiso	Hudson Sq.	24
Cafe Clover	W. Vill.	19
Cafeteria	Chelsea	18
Casa Lever	East 50s	23
Catch NYC	MePa	23
Chavela's	Crown Hts.	24
Capital Grille	multi.	23
Commodore	W'burg	26
Corkbuzz	multi.	21
Corner Bistro	multi.	23
Cowgirl SeaHorse	South St. Seaport	19
Dante NYC	G'wich Vill.	21
Del Frisco's	multi.	25
Delmonico's	multi.	25
Dirty French	LES	24
Docks	East 40s	22
Donovan's	multi.	22
Earl's	East 90s	23
East Pole	East 60s	21
El Porrón	East 60s	24

El Toro Blanco	W. Vill.	16
Empellon Taqueria	W. Vill.	23
Estela	NoLita	26
Extra Fancy	W'burg	18
Fedora	W. Vill.	23
NEW Feroce	Chelsea	–
NEW Fly	Bed-Stuy	–
Fonda	multi.	22
Four Horsemen	W'burg	26
NEW Franks	Carroll Gard.	–
Freemans	LES	21
Gradisca	W. Vill.	23
Gran Electrica	Dumbo	21
NEW Gran Tivoli	NoLita	–
Grand Banks	TriBeCa	17
Z Grand Central Oyster	East 40s	23
Grange	Harlem	22
GupShup	Gramercy	23
Hakkasan	West 40s	24
Happiest Hour	W. Vill.	19
Harry's NYC	FiDi	23
Hell's Kitchen	West 50s	19
Hillstone	multi.	23
Z Hometown	Red Hook	28
Huertas	E. Vill.	22
NEW Hunky Dory	Crown Hts.	–
Hunt & Fish	West 40s	21
Industry Kitchen	South St. Seaport	16
Jeffrey Craft Beer	East 60s	23
Z JG Melon	multi.	23
Jones Wood	East 70s	18
Z Keens	West 30s	27
NEW Kichin	Bushwick	–
La Esquina	NoLita	21
Lavo	East 50s	17
Le Colonial	East 50s	23
Lee's Tavern	Dongan Hills	24
Legacy Records	West 30s	23
Z Llama Inn	W'burg	26
Locanda Verde	TriBeCa	25
Loyal	W. Vill.	21
Lucien	E. Vill.	24
Lucky Strike	SoHo	18
Lure Fishbar	SoHo	24
Maison Premiere	W'burg	26
Maloney & Porcelli	East 50s	25

BREAKFAST

Cookshop | Chelsea	22
Coppelia | Chelsea	22
Court Square Diner | LIC	19
Covina | Murray Hill	22
Davelle | LES	24
David's Brisket | Bed-Stuy	26
Dimes | LES	22
Dirty French | LES	24
E.A.T. | East 80s	21
East Harbour | Sunset Park	26
Egg | W'burg	22
Egg Shop | multi.	19
Eisenberg's | Flatiron	21
Elephant & Castle | W. Vill.	20
Empire Diner | Chelsea	20
Epistrophy | NoLita	17
Five Leaves | Greenpoint	22
Frankel's | Greenpoint	24
Friedman's | multi.	21
Gemma | E. Vill.	21
NEW Gertie | W'burg	—
NEW Golden Diner | LES	—
Good Enough to Eat | West 80s	19
Harlem Shake | Harlem	20
High Street | MePa	22
NEW Hunky Dory | Crown Hts.	—
Ichiran | multi.	23
Il Buco Alimentari | NoHo	25
Jack's Wife Freda | multi.	21
Jams | West 50s	19
Jeffrey's Grocery | W. Vill.	22
Joe Junior | Gramercy	18
Joseph Leonard | W. Vill.	23
Z Katz's | LES	26
Kopitiam | LES	20
Kubeh | G'wich Vill.	22
La Bonbonniere | W. Vill.	19
La Mercerie | SoHo	23
La Pecora Bianca | multi.	21
Lafayette | NoHo	22
NEW Lamalo | East 30s	—
Lambs Club | West 40s	23
Z Le Coucou | SoHo	27
Leuca | W'burg	25
Little Park | TriBeCa	23
Locanda Verde | TriBeCa	25
Z Maialino | Gramercy	26
The Mark | East 70s	23
Marlow & Sons | W'burg	24
Mercer Kitchen | SoHo	22
Michael's | West 50s	23
Mile End | Boerum Hill	23
Morandi | W. Vill.	21
National | East 50s	17

Neil's | East 60s	16
Neptune Diner | Astoria	18
Nice Matin | West 70s	19
Norma's | West 50s	24
North Square | G'wich Vill.	23
Z Nougatine | West 60s	27
Oceana | West 40s	25
Odeon | TriBeCa	22
Okonomi / Yuji Ramen | W'burg	26
Pacificana | Sunset Park	25
The Palm Court | West 50s	22
Parker & Quinn | West 30s	20
NEW Pastis | MePa	—
Pondicheri | NoMad	19
NEW Queensyard | West 30s	—
Regency | East 60s	19
Z River Café | Dumbo	26
Rosemary's | W. Vill.	21
Rucola | Boerum Hill	25
Z Russ & Daughters | multi.	26
Z Sadelle's | SoHo	23
Sarabeth's | multi.	20
Saravanaa Bhavan | multi.	23
Sarge's | Murray Hill	23
Scarpetta | NoMad	23
Z 2nd Ave Deli | multi.	24
Simon & The Whale | Murray Hill	20
Smile | NoHo	18
Smith | multi.	19
Sunday In Brooklyn | W'burg	23
Sylvia's | Harlem	21
NEW Teranga | Harlem	—
Thalia | West 40s	20
Tiny's | TriBeCa	20
12 Chairs | multi.	23
Two Hands | Little Italy	22
Veselka | E. Vill.	22
Via Quadronno | East 70s	22
West-Bourne | SoHo	21
Westville | multi.	21

BRUNCH

MANHATTAN

A Summer Day | TriBeCa	17
A.O.C. | W. Vill.	21
Z ABC Cocina | Flatiron	25
Z ABC Kitchen | Flatiron	25
abcV | Flatiron	26
Acqua | South St. Seaport	24
Altesi | multi.	23
Amali | East 60s	22

Amaranth | East 60s	21
Anassa | East 60s	21
⚡ Aquagrill | SoHo	26
Asiate | West 50s	25
Atlantic Grill | West 60s	23
▩ Au Cheval | TriBeCa	26
Au Za'atar | E. Vill.	20
Augustine | FiDi	23
Aurora | multi.	23
Baar Baar | E. Vill.	24
Babu Ji | G'wich Vill.	24
Bagatelle | MePa	18
Balaboosta | W. Vill.	24
⚡ Balthazar | SoHo	25
⚡ Bar Boulud | West 60s	24
Bar Pitti | G'wich Vill.	24
Bar Primi | E. Vill.	22
Bar Sardine | W. Vill.	23
Barbounia | Flatiron	23
⚡ Barney Greengrass | West 80s	26
Basta Pasta | Flatiron	23
Beaubourg | Battery Pk.	18
Beauty & Essex | LES	22
Bella Blu | East 70s	22
Benoit | West 50s	22
Black Barn | NoMad	21
Blenheim | W. Vill.	21
Blossom | multi.	22
Blue Fin | West 40s	22
Blue Ribbon Federal Grill | FiDi	21
Blue Smoke | multi.	21
Bluebird | West 50s	16
Bodrum | West 80s	20
Boqueria | multi.	23
Boucherie | multi.	20
Boulton & Watt | E. Vill.	18
⚡ Boulud Sud | West 60s	26
⚡ Brasserie 8 1/2 | West 50s	24
Brasserie Ruhlmann | West 50s	19
Breslin | NoMad	22
Bryant Park Grill | West 40s	20
Bubby's | multi.	21
Burger & Barrel | SoHo	21
Burke & Wills | West 70s	20
Butcher's Daughter | multi.	19
Butter | West 40s	22
Buvette | W. Vill.	26
Café Altro Paradiso | Hudson Sq.	24
⚡ Cafe Boulud | East 70s	28
Cafe Clover | W. Vill.	19
Cafe Cluny | W. Vill.	22
Cafe D'Alsace | East 80s	22
Cafe Fiorello | West 60s	22
Cafe Gitane | NoLita	22
Café Habana | multi.	22
⚡ Cafe Luxembourg | West 70s	22
Cafe Mogador | E. Vill.	24
Cafeteria | Chelsea	18
Candle Cafe | multi.	22
Capital Grille | Flatiron	23
Caracas Arepa | E. Vill.	24
Caravaggio | East 70s	26
Carlyle | East 70s	24
Casa Lever | East 50s	23
Cascabel Taqueria | multi.	17
Catch NYC | MePa	23
Caviar Russe | East 50s	26
Cesca | West 70s	22
Charlie Bird | SoHo	25
Charlie Palmer | West 40s	23
Chimichurri Grill | West 40s	24
Clam | W. Vill.	23
Claudette | G'wich Vill.	21
Clinton St. Baking Co. | LES	25
Commodore | W'burg	26
Community Food & Juice | M'side Hts.	22
Cookshop | Chelsea	22
Coppelia | Chelsea	22
Covina | Murray Hill	22
Cowgirl SeaHorse | South St. Seaport	19
Danji | West 50s	25
Dante NYC | G'wich Vill.	21
DB Bistro | West 40s	25
Dimes | LES	22
Dirt Candy | LES	24
Dirty French | LES	24
Ducks Eatery | E. Vill.	25
Commodore | SoHo	21
Earl's | East 90s	23
East Pole | East 60s	21
Eastfield's | East 70s	19
El Quinto Pino | Chelsea	25
El Toro Blanco | W. Vill.	16
El Vez | Battery Pk.	20
Elea | West 80s	24
Elephant & Castle | W. Vill.	20
Eli's Table | East 80s	22
Empanada Mama | multi.	23
Empellon Taqueria | W. Vill.	23
Empire Diner | Chelsea	20

EN Japanese	W. Vill.	24
Epistrophy	NoLita	17
Estela	NoLita	26
Extra Virgin	W. Vill.	18
Fat Radish	LES	20
Felice	multi.	20
Ferris	NoMad	25
Fig & Olive	multi.	22
Firenze	East 80s	22
Flex Mussels	multi.	24
Flora Bar	East 70s	24
Follia	Gramercy	21
Foragers Table	Chelsea	22
44 & X	West 40s	22
Frank	E. Vill.	26
Frankies 570	W. Vill.	23
Fraunces Tavern	FiDi	19
Freds	multi.	22
Freemans	LES	21
Z Frenchette	TriBeCa	24
Friedman's	multi.	21
Galli	SoHo	17
Gato	NoHo	24
Gazala's Place	West 40s	21
Gemma	E. Vill.	21
Glasserie	Greenpoint	24
Gnocco	E. Vill.	21
Good Enough to Eat	West 80s	19
NEW Gran Tivoli	NoLita	–
Grand Banks	TriBeCa	17
Grange	Harlem	22
GupShup	Gramercy	23
Hanoi House	E. Vill.	25
Harry's NYC	FiDi	23
Hearth	E. Vill.	25
Her Name is Han	East 30s	25
High Street	MePa	22
House	Gramercy	21
Houseman	Hudson Sq.	23
Hudson Clearwater	W. Vill.	19
Hwaban	Flatiron	23
Il Buco Alimentari	NoHo	25
Il Gattopardo	West 50s	25
Il Riccio	East 70s	20
Ilili	NoMad	25
Z Indian Accent	West 50s	27
Industry Kitchen	South St. Seaport	16
Jack's Wife Freda	multi.	21
Jacob's Pickles	West 80s	23
Jams	West 50s	19
Jane	G'wich Vill.	19
Japonica	G'wich Vill.	24
Jeepney	E. Vill.	20

Jeffrey	East 60s	23
Jeffrey's Grocery	W. Vill.	22
Joe Allen	West 40s	20
JoJo	East 60s	25
Jones Wood	East 70s	18
Joseph Leonard	W. Vill.	23
Jue Lan Club	Flatiron	18
Kashkaval Garden	West 50s	22
Kefi	West 80s	21
Kellari Taverna	West 40s	23
Khe-Yo	TriBeCa	24
Kubeh	G'wich Vill.	22
Kyma	Flatiron	25
L'Amico	West 30s	21
Z L'Artusi	W. Vill.	28
L'Express	Gramercy	18
La Bonbonniere	W. Vill.	19
Z La Contenta	LES	27
La Contenta Oeste	G'wich Vill.	22
La Goulue	East 60s	22
La Mercerie	SoHo	23
La Mirabelle	West 80s	24
La Pecora Bianca	multi.	21
La Sirène	multi.	22
Lafayette	NoHo	22
Lambs Club	West 40s	23
Lavagna	E. Vill.	24
Le Bilboquet	East 60s	22
Le Coq Rico	Flatiron	24
Le Gigot	W. Vill.	25
Le Marais	West 40s	22
Le Parisien	Murray Hill	25
Left Bank	W. Vill.	20
Legacy Records	West 30s	23
NEW Leyla	West 70s	–
Lido	Harlem	24
Lil' Frankie's	E. Vill.	25
Z Lincoln	West 60s	25
Little Owl	W. Vill.	24
Little Park	TriBeCa	23
Locanda Verde	TriBeCa	25
Loeb Boathouse	Central Park	19
Z Loring Place	G'wich Vill.	25
Loyal	W. Vill.	21
Lucky Strike	SoHo	18
Lure Fishbar	SoHo	24
Z Lusardi's	East 70s	24
Z Maialino	Gramercy	26
Maison Harlem	Harlem	22
Maison Pickle	West 80s	22
Malaparte	W. Vill.	22

Malatesta Trattoria | W. Vill.	25
Marea | West 50s	28
The Mark | East 70s	23
Market Table | W. Vill.	22
The Marshal | West 40s	22
Maya | East 60s	22
Melba's | Harlem	26
Mercer Kitchen | SoHo	22
☑ Mermaid Inn | multi.	23
Milling Room | West 80s	23
Mimi | G'wich Vill.	24
Minetta | G'wich Vill.	25
Miss Lily's | multi.	20
Miss Mamie's | West 100s	22
Molly's | Gramercy	20
Momofuku Nishi | Chelsea	22
☑ Momofuku Ssäm | E. Vill.	26
Morandi | W. Vill.	21
Morso | East 50s	25
Motel Morris | Chelsea	19
Moti Mahal | East 60s	23
Narcissa | E. Vill.	21
National | East 50s	17
Nice Matin | West 70s	19
Nix | G'wich Vill.	24
☑ The NoMad | NoMad	26
Nonono | NoMad	25
Norma's | West 50s	24
North Square | G'wich Vill.	23
☑ Nougatine | West 60s	27
Novitá | Gramercy	25
Nur | Flatiron	24
Nyonya | multi.	24
NEW O:n | East 30s	—
Odeon | TriBeCa	22
Old Tbilisi | G'wich Vill.	23
One If by Land | W. Vill.	25
P.J. Clarke's | multi.	19
The Palm Court | West 50s	22
Palma | W. Vill.	23
Pampano | East 40s	21
Paola's | East 90s	26
Pappardella | West 70s	20
☑ Park Avenue | Flatiron	25
Parker & Quinn | West 30s	20
Pascalou | East 90s	23
NEW Pastis | MePa	—
Penrose | East 80s	20
Perry St | W. Vill.	25
Pete's Tavern | Gramercy	16
Pig and Khao | LES	23
Pisticci | M'side Hts.	25
Pizzeria Sirenetta | West 80s	23

Playa Betty's | West 70s	17
Pondicheri | NoMad	19
Prune | E. Vill.	25
Pylos | E. Vill.	26
Quality Eats | multi.	22
NEW Queensyard | West 30s	—
Rafele | W. Vill.	24
Rahi | W. Vill.	26
Raoul's | SoHo	26
Red Rooster | Harlem	22
Redeye Grill | West 50s	—
☑ RedFarm | multi.	25
Regency | East 60s	19
RH Rooftop Rest. | MePa	20
Ribbon | multi.	20
☑ Riverpark | Murray Hill	25
Root & Bone | E. Vill.	24
Rosa Mexicano | multi.	21
Rosemary's | W. Vill.	21
Rotisserie Georgette | East 60s	23
☑ Rubirosa | NoLita	26
☑ Russ & Daughters | multi.	26
Russian Tea Room | West 50s	19
☑ Sadelle's | SoHo	23
Safari | Harlem	26
Salumeria Rosi | West 70s	24
San Pietro | East 50s	24
Sant Ambroeus | multi.	23
Santina | MePa	20
Sarabeth's | multi.	20
Sarge's | Murray Hill	23
Saxon + Parole | NoHo	19
Scampi | Flatiron	21
Scarpetta | NoMad	23
Seamore's | multi.	19
Serafina | multi.	19
Sevilla | W. Vill.	24
Shuka | SoHo	23
Simon & The Whale | Murray Hill	20
Smile | NoHo	18
Smith | multi.	19
Snack Taverna | W. Vill.	20
Socarrat Paella Bar | multi.	20
Sojourn | East 70s	19
Sotto 13 | W. Vill.	17
Speedy Romeo | multi.	23
Spotted Pig | W. Vill.	22
St Tropez | W. Vill.	20
Stella 34 | West 30s	24
Storico | West 70s	18
Supper | E. Vill.	24
Sweet Chick | multi.	23

Sylvia's | Harlem	21
Taboon | West 50s	25
Tacuba | multi.	22
Tavern On the Green |	18
Central Park	
Tavola | West 30s	21
TBar | East 70s	22
10 Corso Como | South	24
St. Seaport	
Tessa | West 70s	22
Thalia | West 40s	20
Tía Pol | Chelsea	23
Tiny's | TriBeCa	20
Toloache | multi.	23
Trattoria Dell'Arte |	23
West 50s	
Turkish Kitchen |	23
Murray Hill	
12 Chairs | multi.	23
Two Hands | Little Italy	22
☒ Union Square Cafe |	26
Gramercy	
☒ Upland | Murray Hill	25
Uva | East 70s	22
Veselka | E. Vill.	22
Vic's | NoHo	22
ViceVersa | West 70s	23
Vinateria | Harlem	25
☒ Violet | E. Vill.	19
Virginia's | E. Vill.	23
Waverly Inn | W. Vill.	21
☒ Wayan | NoLita	27
☒ Wayla | LES	–
West-Bourne | SoHo	21
Westville | multi.	21
Yefsi Estiatorio | East 70s	22
Yves | TriBeCa	20
Zum Schneider | E. Vill.	20

BROOKLYN

Aita | multi.	22
Allswell | W'burg	21
Atrium Dumbo | Dumbo	20
Bacchus | Downtown Bklyn.	23
Bar Tabac | Cobble Hill	20
Barboncino | Crown Hts.	25
Bogota | Park Slope	21
Bricolage | Park Slope	23
Brooklyn Cider House |	18
Bushwick	
Bunker | Bushwick	22
Bunna Cafe | Bushwick	26
Buttermilk Channel |	25
Carroll Gard.	

Cafe Gitane | Dumbo	22
Cafe Luluc | Cobble Hill	22
Cafe Mogador | W'burg	24
Cebu | Bay Ridge	18
Cecconi's | Dumbo	20
Celestine | Dumbo	22
Chavela's | Crown Hts.	24
Chez Ma Tante |	26
Greenpoint	
Chez Moi | Brooklyn Hts.	22
Colonie | Brooklyn Hts.	24
Diner | W'burg	25
Egg | W'burg	22
Emmy Squared | multi.	26
Esme | Greenpoint	23
Farm on Adderley |	22
Ditmas Park	
Fausto | Park Slope	23
Five Leaves | Greenpoint	22
Fornino | multi.	23
Fragole | Carroll Gard.	26
Frankies 457 |	25
Carroll Gard.	
French Louie | Boerum Hill	23
Fushimi | Bay Ridge	22
☒ Gertie | W'burg	–
Glady's | Crown Hts.	26
Good Fork | Red Hook	25
Gran Electrica | Dumbo	21
Greenpoint Fish &	23
Lobster | Greenpoint	
Hart's | Bed-Stuy	26
☒ Hunky Dory | Crown Hts.	–
Jack the Horse |	23
Brooklyn Hts.	
James | Prospect Hts.	23
La Vara | Cobble Hill	27
LaRina | Ft. Greene	25
Leuca | W'burg	25
Littleneck | multi.	20
☒ Llama Inn | W'burg	26
Mable's | W'burg	23
Maison Premiere | W'burg	26
☒ Meadowsweet | W'burg	27
MeMe's | Prospect Hts.	23 3
Mile End | Boerum Hill	23
Mimi's | multi.	23
Miriam | Park Slope	24
☒ Miss Ada | Ft. Greene	27
Modern Love | W'burg	23
☒ Olmsted | Prospect Hts.	27
Otway | Clinton Hill	24
☒ Oxomoco | Greenpoint	27
Peaches | Bed-Stuy	25

Pies 'n' Thighs | W'burg — 23
Z River Café | Dumbo — 26
Z Roberta's | Bushwick — 27
Rose Water | Park Slope — 25
Rucola | Boerum Hill — 25
Runner & Stone | Gowanus — 22
Shalom Japan | W'burg — 25
Sugarcane | Dumbo — 22
Sunday In Brooklyn | W'burg — 23
Suzume | W'burg — 24
Z Tanoreen | Bay Ridge — 27
12 Chairs | multi. — 23
21 Greenpoint | Greenpoint — 21
Vinegar Hill House | Dumbo — 22
Walter's | Ft. Greene — 22
Win Son | W'burg — 27

QUEENS

Butcher Bar | Astoria — 23
Café Henri | LIC — 20
Z Casa Enrique | LIC — 27
Court Square Diner | LIC — 19
5 Burro Cafe | Forest Hills — 23
Il Bambino | Astoria — 24
LIC Market | LIC — 21
Maiella | LIC — 24
Milkflower | Astoria — 25
Neptune Diner | Astoria — 18
Queens Comfort | Astoria — 24
Sanfords | Astoria — 22
Sugar Freak | Astoria — 23
Tournesol | LIC — 24
Vesta | Astoria — 27

STATEN ISLAND

Bayou | Rosebank — 24
Blue | Randall Manor — 22
Lakruwana | Stapleton — 26

BUSINESS DINING

Z abcV | Flatiron — 26
Agern | East 40s — 26
Ammos | East 40s — 23
Z Aquagrill | SoHo — 26
Z Aquavit | East 50s — 27
Asiate | West 50s — 25
Atlantic Grill | West 60s — 23
Augustine | FiDi — 23
Aureole | West 40s — 26
Z Avra | East 40s — 26
Ben & Jack's | East 40s — 25
Z Benjamin | East 40s — 27

BLT Steak | East 50s — 25
Blue Ribbon Federal Grill | FiDi — 21
Bluebird | West 50s — 16
Bobby Van's | multi. — 23
Brasserie Ruhlmann | West 50s — 19
Café Altro Paradiso | Hudson Sq. — 24
Z Cafe Boulud | East 70s — 28
Capital Grille | multi. — 25
Casa Lever | East 50s — 23
Chefs Club | NoLita — 25
Churrascaria Plataforma | West 40s — 22
Cipriani | multi. — 24
Covina | Murray Hill — 22
Crown Shy | FiDi — 27
Da Umberto | Chelsea — 26
Z Daniel | East 60s — 29
Del Frisco's | multi. — 25
Z Del Posto | Chelsea — 27
Delmonico's | multi. — 25
Docks | East 40s — 22
Empellon | East 50s — 22
Z Estiatorio Milos | multi. — 27
Fausto | Park Slope — 23
NEW Feroce | Chelsea — –
Finch | Clinton Hill — 26
Frankie & Johnnie's | multi. — 22
Fresco by Scotto | East 50s — 23
Gallaghers | West 50s — 25
Glasserie | Greenpoint — 24
Gino's | Bay Ridge — 25
Gotham Bar and Grill | G'wich Vill. — –
Z Gramercy Tavern | Flatiron — 28
Z Grand Central Oyster | East 40s — 23
Z Grill | East 50s — 25
Hakkasan | West 40s — 24
Harry's NYC | FiDi — 23
Hatsuhana | East 40s — 26
Houseman | Hudson Sq. — 23
Hunt & Fish | West 40s — 21
Hwaban | Flatiron — 23
Il Gattopardo | West 50s — 25
Z Jean-Georges | West 60s — 28
NEW Kāwi | West 30s — –
Z Keens | West 30s — 27
Z Le Bernardin | West 50s — 29

Molly's | Gramercy	20
☑ Momofuku Ko | E. Vill.	28
Morimoto | Chelsea	26
🆕 Niche Niche | SoHo	–
99 Favor Taste | multi.	21
☑ Nobu | multi.	27
O Ya | Murray Hill	27
Oceana | West 40s	25
🆕 Odo | Flatiron	–
Old Homestead | Chelsea	24
One If by Land | W. Vill.	25
Otto Enoteca | G'wich Vill.	22
Pacificana | Sunset Park	25
The Palm Court | West 50s	22
Palma | W. Vill.	23
☑ Park Avenue | Flatiron	25
☑ Pasquale Jones | NoLita	25
🆕 Pastis | MePa	–
Peking Duck House | multi.	24
☑ Per Se | West 50s	28
Perry St | W. Vill.	25
☑ Peter Luger | W'burg	28
Playa Betty's | West 70s	17
☑ Porter House | West 50s	27
Quality Eats | multi.	22
Quality Italian | West 50s	24
Quality Meats | West 50s	25
Rao's | East Harlem	23
Red Rooster | Harlem	22
RH Rooftop Rest. | MePa	20
☑ Riverpark | Murray Hill	25
Rolf's | Gramercy	15
Rosa Mexicano | multi.	21
Rosie's | E. Vill.	19
Russian Tea Room | West 50s	19
Salinas | Chelsea	27
San Pietro | East 50s	24
☑ Scalini Fedeli | TriBeCa	27
Scarpetta | NoMad	23
Serra By Birreria | Flatiron	16
Shuko | G'wich Vill.	28
Shun Lee Palace | East 50s	23
☑ The Simone | East 80s	27
Sistina | East 80s	25
Standard Biergarten | MePa	15
☑ Sushi Nakazawa | W. Vill.	29
Sushi Zo | G'wich Vill.	29
Sylvia's | Harlem	21
Takashi | W. Vill.	26
☑ Tamarind | TriBeCa	27
Tao | multi.	23
Tavern On the Green | Central Park	18

☑ Tocqueville | Flatiron	28
Tokyo Record Bar | G'wich Vill.	21
Toloache | multi.	23
Tony's Di Napoli | multi.	21
☑ Trattoria L'incontro | Astoria	28
Tribeca Grill | TriBeCa	23
🆕 Turk's Inn | Bushwick	–
21 Club | West 50s	23
☑ Union Square Cafe | Gramercy	26
Vandal | LES	18
Wallsé | W. Vill.	27
🆕 Wayan | NoLita	27
🆕 Wayla | LES	–
☑ Wolfgang's | multi.	26
Zum Schneider | E. Vill.	20
Zum Stammtisch | Glendale	27

CHILD-FRIENDLY

Baba's Pierogies | Gowanus	25
Bella Blu | East 70s	22
Blue Smoke | multi.	21
Brooklyn Crab | Red Hook	19
Brooklyn Farmacy | Carroll Gard.	22
Bubby's | multi.	21
Buttermilk Channel | Carroll Gard.	25
Carmine's | multi.	21
Celeste | West 80s	24
City Island Lobster | City Island	21
Court Square Diner | LIC	19
Dee's | Forest Hills	23
Don Antonio | West 50s	25
E.A.T. | East 80s	21
Egg Shop | multi.	19
Gigino | multi.	23
☑ Hometown | Red Hook	28
Il Brigante | South St. Seaport	22
Joe & Pat's | multi.	26
Joe Junior | Gramercy	18
Johnny's Reef | City Island	18
La Bonbonniere | W. Vill.	19
La Mela | Little Italy	21
La Villa | multi.	23
Lil' Frankie's | E. Vill.	25
Little Pepper | College Point	24

🆉 **Los Tacos No.1** | multi.	27
Luzzo's | multi.	24
Manducatis | multi.	25
Mapo | Flushing	26
Meatball Shop | multi.	20
MeMe's Diner | Prospect Hts.	23
Mile End | Boerum Hill	23
Milkflower | Astoria	25
Mill Basin Deli | Mill Basin	24
Miriam | Park Slope	24
Nick's Pizza | Forest Hills	24
99 Favor Taste | multi.	21
Nucci's | Tottenville	23
Oriental Garden | Chinatown	23
Original Crab Shanty | City Island	24
Otto Enoteca | G'wich Vill.	22
Pacificana | Sunset Park	25
Palm | multi.	24
Parm | multi.	19
Pastrami Queen | East 70s	24
Patricia's | Morris Park	25
Patsy's Italian | West 50s	23
Patsy's Pizzeria | multi.	22
Pig Beach | Gowanus	20
Playa Betty's | West 70s	17
Posto | Gramercy	23
Roll N Roaster | Sheepshd Bay	22
Sardi's | West 40s	17
Sarge's | Murray Hill	23
Seamore's | multi.	19
Serafina | multi.	19
Shake Shack | multi.	21
Shun Lee Palace | East 50s	23
Sottocasa | multi.	26
Sylvia's | Harlem	21
Tacos El Bronco | Sunset Park	25
Taqueria Tlaxcalli | Parkchester	27
Tony's Di Napoli | multi.	21
Vesuvio | Bay Ridge	23
Via Quadronno | East 70s	22
Westville | multi.	21

COMMUTER OASIS

GRAND CENTRAL

Agern | East 40s	26
Ammos Estiatorio | East 40s	23
Aretsky's Patroon | East 40s	25
🆉 **Aureole** | West 40s	26
🆉 **Avra** | East 40s	26
Ben & Jack's | East 40s	25
Capital Grille | East 40s	25
Cipriani | East 40s	25
Darbar | East 40s	22
Docks Oyster Bar | East 40s	22
Fonda | multi.	22
🆉 **Grand Central Oyster** | East 40s	23
Hatsuhana | East 40s	26
Ippudo | West 40s	25
Koi | West 40s	24
Little Alley | Murray Hill	23
MáLà Project | West 40s	24
Momosan | Murray Hill	25
Morton's | East 40s	24
Osteria Laguna | East 40s	22
Parker & Quinn | West 30s	20
Pietros | East 40s	25
Rossini's | Murray Hill	23
Sakagura | East 40s	26
Sea Fire Grill | East 40s	26
Seamore's | East 40s	19
🆉 **Sparks** | East 40s	26
Sushi Ginza Onodera | East 40s	29
Vitae | East 40s	25
Wokuni | Murray Hill	23
Wollensky's Grill | East 40s	26
Xi'an Famous Foods | West 40s	23
Zuma | Murray Hill	24

PENN STATION

Abigael's | West 30s	19
Barn Joo | West 30s	21
BCD Tofu House | West 30s	23
Cho Dang Gol | West 30s	24
Delmonico's | West 30s	25
Frankie & Johnnie's | West 30s	22
Friedman's | West 30s	21
Gaonnuri | West 30s	22
Gazala's Place | West 40s	21
Ichiran | West 30s	23
Jongro BBQ | West 30s	22
🆉 **Keens** | West 30s	27
Kunjip | West 30s	19

LIC Market | LIC — 21
Lido | Harlem — 24
Littleneck | multi. — 20
Lolo's | Harlem — 22
Los Mariscos | Chelsea — 25
🄩 Los Tacos No.1 | multi. — 27
Mama's Too | West 100s — 25
Meijin Ramen | East 80s — 28
Mile End | Boerum Hill — 23
Miznon | Chelsea — 25
🄩 Momofuku Noodle | — 24
  multi.
Momosan | Murray Hill — 25
Mu Ramen | LIC — 25
Neil's | East 60s — 16
New Park Pizza | Howard — 25
  Beach
Nha Trang One | — 23
  Chinatown
🆕 Niche | LES — —
Okonomi / Yuji Ramen | — 26
  W'burg
Parm | multi. — 19
Pastrami Queen | East 70s — 24
Peacefood | multi. — 21
Peaches | Bed-Stuy — 25
Pete's Tavern | Gramercy — 16
Porsena | E. Vill. — 25
🄩 Prince Street Pizza | — 27
  NoLita
Racines | TriBeCa — 21
Ruffian | E. Vill. — 25
Sakagura | multi. — 26
Sarge's | Murray Hill — 23
Sasabune | East 70s — 27
Sayra's | Far Rock. — 25
Silver Rice | multi. — 26
Sobaya | E. Vill. — 25
Somtum Der | E. Vill. — 24
Spicy Village | LES — 28
Sugarfish | multi. — 25
Superiority Burger | E. Vill. — 25
Sushi Azabu | TriBeCa — 28
Sushi By Bou | multi. — 26
🆕 Sushi By M | E. Vill. — 27
Sushi Dojo | E. Vill. — 26
Sushi Katsuei | multi. — 26
Sushi Seki | multi. — 26
🄩 Sushi Yasuda | East 40s — 28
Suzume | W'burg — 24
🆕 TabeTomo | E. Vill. — —
Tacos El Bronco | Sunset — 25
  Park
Takahachi | multi. — 24

🆕 Taladwat | West 40s — —
Tanoshi | East 70s — 29
Taqueria Tlaxcalli | — 27
  Parkchester
🆕 Teranga | Harlem — —
Tomoe Sushi | G'wich Vill. — 25
Torishin | West 50s — 27
Totto Ramen | multi. — 23
12 Chairs | multi. — 23
Two Hands | Little Italy — 22
Upstate | E. Vill. — 25
Veselka | E. Vill. — 22
Via Quadronno | East 70s — 22
Vini e Fritti | NoMad — 24
Walker's | TriBeCa — 18
West-Bourne | SoHo — 21
White Bear | Flushing — 25
Xi'an Famous Foods | multi. — 23

FINE DINING

Agern | East 40s — 26
🄩 Aquavit | East 50s — 27
Aretsky's Patroon | — 25
  East 40s
Asiate | West 50s — 25
Atera | TriBeCa — 28
Atomix | NoMad — 29
🄩 Aureole | West 40s — 26
Barbetta | West 40s — 22
Bâtard | TriBeCa — 26
Benno | NoMad — 26
Benoit | West 50s — 22
🄩 Blanca | Bushwick — 29
🄩 Blue Hill | G'wich Vill. — 28
🄩 Bouley at Home | — 29
  Flatiron
🄩 Boulud Sud | West 60s — 26
🄩 Cafe Boulud | East 70s — 28
Caravaggio | East 70s — 26
Carlyle | East 70s — 24
Casa Lever | East 50s — 23
Caviar Russe | East 50s — 26
Chef's Table | NoLita — 28
Cipriani | multi. — 24
Contra | LES — 25
Craft | Flatiron — 25
🄩 Daniel | East 60s — 29
🄩 Del Posto | Chelsea — 27
Delmonico's | multi. — 25
🄩 Eleven Madison Park | — 28
  Flatiron
🄩 Gabriel Kreuther | — 28
  West 40s

Restaurant	Score
Pacificana | Sunset Park	25
Z Park Avenue | Flatiron	25
Park Side | Corona	25
Patricia's | Morris Park	25
Patsy's Italian | West 50s	23
Patsy's Pizzeria | multi.	22
Pera | multi.	21
Z Peter Luger | W'burg	28
Philippe | multi.	22
Piccola Venezia | Astoria	25
Pier A Harbor House | FiDi	15
Pig Beach | Gowanus	20
Pig Heaven | East 80s	20
Ping's Seafood | Chinatown	22
Pisticci | M'side Hts.	25
Z Porter House | West 50s	27
NEW Queensyard | West 30s	–
Ravagh | multi.	26
Red Rooster | Harlem	22
Remi | West 50s	24
Ribbon | multi.	20
Z Riverpark | Murray Hill	25
Robert | West 50s	23
Roberto's | Arthur Ave.	25
Rolf's | Gramercy	15
Rosa Mexicano | multi.	21
Rosie's | E. Vill.	19
Z Rubirosa | NoLita	26
Russian Tea Room | West 50s	19
Santina | MePa	20
Sarabeth's | multi.	20
Sardi's | West 40s	17
NEW Savida | TriBeCa	–
Z Scalini Fedeli | TriBeCa	27
Sea Grill | West 40s	24
Serra By Birreria | Flatiron	16
Shake Shack | multi.	21
Shuka | SoHo	23
Shun Lee Palace | East 50s	23
Sotto 13 | W. Vill.	17
Z Sparks | East 40s	26
Speedy Romeo | multi.	23
Standard Biergarten | MePa	15
Standard Grill | MePa	22
STK | multi.	22
Strip House | multi.	23
Sugar Freak | Astoria	23
Sugarcane | Dumbo	22
Sunday In Brooklyn | W'burg	23
Sylvia's | Harlem	21
Szechuan House | Flushing	26
Taci's Beyti | Midwood	23

Restaurant	Score
Tacombi | multi.	20
NEW TAK Room | West 30s	–
Z Tanoreen | Bay Ridge	27
Tao | multi.	23
Taqueria St. Marks | E. Vill.	21
Tavern On the Green | Central Park	18
Taverna Kyclades | multi.	25
Telly's Taverna | Astoria	25
10 Corso Como | South St. Seaport	24
Tim Ho Wan | multi.	22
Z Tocqueville | Flatiron	28
Tony's Di Napoli | multi.	21
Z Trattoria L'incontro | Astoria	28
Trattoria Trecolori | West 40s	22
Tribeca Grill | TriBeCa	23
Tuscany Grill | Bay Ridge	23
Z 21 Club | West 50s	23
NEW Uluh | E. Vill.	–
Z Union Square Cafe | Gramercy	26
Z Upland | Murray Hill	25
Utsav | West 40s	22
Vandal | LES	18
Vesta | Astoria	27
Vic's | NoHo	22
Villa Mosconi | G'wich Vill.	25
Vinegar Hill House | Dumbo	22
Wa Jeal | East 80s	24
Wu's Wonton King | LES	24
Yun Nan Flavour Garden | Sunset Park	26
Zuma | Murray Hill	24

HEALTHY

Restaurant	Score
A Summer Day | TriBeCa	17
Z ABC Kitchen | Flatiron	25
Z abcV | Flatiron	26
Avant Garden | E. Vill.	26
BCD Tofu House | multi.	23
Blossom | multi.	22
Bunna Cafe | Bushwick	26
Butcher's Daughter | multi.	19
Cafe Clover | W. Vill.	19
Candle Cafe | multi.	22
Cho Dang Gol | West 30s	24
Community Food & Juice | M'side Hts.	22
Dimes | LES	22
Dirt Candy | LES	24
Fat Radish | LES	20
Foragers Table | Chelsea	22

Z **Hangawi** | Murray Hill	28
Hearth | E. Vill.	25
Kajitsu | Murray Hill	27
Kubeh | G'wich Vill.	22
LIC Market | LIC	21
Market Table | W. Vill.	22
Modern Love | W'burg	23
Narcissa | E. Vill.	21
Nix | G'wich Vill.	24
Peacefood | multi.	21
Ruby's | multi.	22
Seamore's | multi.	19
Two Hands | multi.	22
Vatan | Murray Hill	26
West~Bourne | SoHo	21
Westville | multi.	21

HOT SPOTS

Z **abcV** | Flatiron	26
Atla | NoHo	24
Z **Atoboy** | NoMad	27
Z **Atomix** | NoMad	29
NEW **Au Cheval** | TriBeCa	26
Z **Balthazar** | SoHo	25
Beatrice Inn | W. Vill.	24
Bernie's | Greenpoint	25
Z **Birds of a Feather** | W'burg	26
Buvette | W. Vill.	26
Café Altro Paradiso | Hudson Sq.	24
Z **Carbone** | G'wich Vill.	26
Cecconi's | Dumbo	20
Charlie Bird | SoHo	25
Chez Ma Tante | Greenpoint	26
Coco Pazzo | SoHo	27
Z **Cosme** | Flatiron	26
Z **Cote** | Flatiron	26
NEW **Crown Shy** | FiDi	27
Dirty French | LES	24
Z **Don Angie** | W. Vill.	28
886 | E. Vill.	23
Emily | multi.	26
Emmy Squared | multi.	26
Estela | NoLita	26
NEW **Franks Wine Bar** | Carroll Gard.	—
Z **Frenchette** | TriBeCa	24
NEW **HaSalon** | West 50s	—
NEW **Haenyeo** | Park Slope	—
Jack's Wife Freda | multi.	21
Jeffrey's Grocery | W. Vill.	22
JoJo | East 60s	25

NEW **Kāwi** | West 30s	—
Z **Kiki's** | LES	25
King | Hudson Square	26
Z **L'Artusi** | W. Vill.	28
La Esquina | NoLita	21
La Mercerie | SoHo	23
Z **Le Coucou** | SoHo	27
Legacy Records | West 30s	23
Z **Lilia** | W'burg	27
Locanda Verde | TriBeCa	25
Z **Loring Place** | G'wich Vill.	25
Z **Lucali** | Carroll Gard.	28
Lucien | E. Vill.	24
Z **Maialino** | Gramercy	26
Z **Majorelle** | East 60s	27
Misi | W'burg	26
Z **Olmsted** | Prospect Hts.	27
Ops | Bushwick	28
NEW **Pastis** | MePa	—
Z **Pasquale Jones** | NoLita	25
Polo Bar | East 50s	23
Red Rooster | Harlem	22
NEW **Rezdôra** | Flatiron	—
RH Rooftop | MePa	20
Z **Roberta's** | Bushwick	27
Z **Rubirosa** | NoLita	26
Z **Sadelle's** | SoHo	23
Shuko | G'wich Vill.	28
Simon & The Whale | Murray Hill	20
Standard Grill | MePa	22
Sugarfish | multi.	25
NEW **TAK Room** | West 30s	—
Tokyo Record Bar | G'wich Vill.	21
Ugly Baby | Carroll Gard.	26
Z **Union Square Cafe** | Gramercy	26
NEW **Wayan** | NoLita	27
NEW **Wayla** | LES	—
Wildair | LES	26

JURY DUTY

MANHATTAN

A Summer Day Cafe | TriBeCa	17
NEW **Au Cheval** | TriBeCa	26
Dim Sum Go Go | Chinatown	21
456 Shanghai | Chinatown	23
Golden Unicorn | Chinatown	22

Great NY Noodletown | Chinatown — 23

Hop Kee | Chinatown — 22

Joe's Ginger | Chinatown — 20

La Mercerie | SoHo — 23

Little Park | TriBeCa — 23

Nha Trang One | Chinatown — 23

Peking Duck House | Chinatown — 24

Pepolino | TriBeCa — 25

Spicy Village | LES — 28

Takahachi | TriBeCa — 24

Two Hands | multi. — 22

Vanessa's Dumpling | LES — 20

Wo Hop | Chinatown — 24

Xi'an Famous Foods | multi. — 23

BROOKLYN

Atrium Dumbo | Dumbo — 20

Awash | Cobble Hill — 23

Cecconi's | Dumbo — 20

Celestine | Dumbo — 22

Gran Electrica | Dumbo — 21

Han Dynasty | Downtown Bklyn. — 23

Luzzo's | Brooklyn Hts. — 24

Mile End | Boerum Hill — 23

Queen | Brooklyn Hts. — 25

Yemen Café | Cobble Hill — 24

LATE-NIGHT DINING

Artichoke | E. Vill. — 22

Bar Jamon | Gramercy — 25

Bar Tabac | Cobble Hill — 20

Barboncino | Crown Hts. — 25

Barrio Chino | LES — 24

Blue Ribbon Brasserie | SoHo — 25

Blue Ribbon Sushi | SoHo — 25

Blue Ribbon Sushi Bar & Grill | West 50s — 25

Blue Ribbon Sushi Izakaya | LES — 25

Boulton & Watt | E. Vill. — 18

Burke & Wills | West 70s — 20

Buvette | W. Vill. — 26

Cafeteria | Chelsea — 18

Casellula | West 50s — 24

Catch NYC | MePa — 23

Chez Moi | B'lyn Hts. — 22

City Island Lobster | City Island — 21

Commodore | W'burg — 26

Coppelia | Chelsea — 22

Corner Bistro | multi. — 23

Court Square Diner | LIC — 19

Empanada Mama | multi. — 23

Extra Fancy | W'burg — 18

5 Burro Cafe | Forest Hills — 23

Five Leaves | Greenpoint — 22

Z 4 Charles | W. Vill. — 28

Frank | E. Vill. — 26

Fraunces Tavern | FiDi — 19

Gemma | E. Vill. — 21

NEW Gran Tivoli | NoLita — –

Grand Banks | TriBeCa — 17

Grange | Harlem — 22

Great NY Noodletown | Chinatown — 23

Happiest Hour | W. Vill. — 19

Harry's NYC | FiDi — 23

Hop Kee | Chinatown — 22

Hudson Clearwater | W. Vill. — 19

Ichiran | West 30s — 23

Jacob's Pickles | West 80s — 23

Z JG Melon | East 70s — 23

Z Joe's Pizza | multi. — 25

Jongro BBQ | West 30s — 22

Kang Ho Dong Baekjeong | East 30s — 26

Kashkaval Garden | West 50s — 22

Z Katz's | LES — 26

The Kunjip | West 30s — 19

L'Express | Gramercy — 18

La Contenta Oeste | G'wich Vill. — 22

La Esquina | East 70s — 21

La Mela | Little Italy — 21

Lil' Frankie's | E. Vill. — 25

Lucky Strike | SoHo — 18

Mark Restaurant | East 70s — 23

Meatball Shop | LES — 20

Miss Korea BBQ | West 30s — 20

Molly's | Gramercy — 20

Neptune Diner | Astoria — 18

New Park Pizza | Howard Beach — 25

New Wonjo | West 30s — 20

99 Favor Taste | Sunset Pk. — 21

NoMad Bar | NoMad — 25

Original Crab Shanty | City Island — 24

The Penrose | East 80s — 20

Pete's Tavern | Gramercy — 16

P.J. Clarke's | East 50s — 19

Sarge's | Murray Hill — 23

Sayra's Wine Bar | Far Rockaway	25
The Spotted Pig | W. Vill.	22
Standard Biergarten | MePa	15
Sushi Seki | multi.	26
Sweet Chick | mutli.	23
Tacos El Bronco | Sunset Pk.	25
Terroir Tribeca | TriBeCa	19
Uva | East 70s	22
Vini e Fritti | NoMad	24
Wo Hop | Chinatown	24
Wollensky's Grill | East 40s	26

MUSIC / LIVE ENTERTAINMENT

Ammazzacaffe | W'burg	24
Aretsky's Patroon | East 40s	25
Arturo's | G'wich Vill.	22
Bar Tabac | Cobble Hill	20
Barn Joo | multi.	21
Bayou | Rosebank	24
Black Barn | NoMad	21
Blue Smoke | multi.	21
Bodega Negra | Chelsea	21
Docks | East 40s	22
Famous Sammy's Roumanian | LES	18
Happiest Hour | W. Vill.	19
Z Hometown | Red Hook	28
Il Gattopardo | West 50s	25
Ilili | NoMad	25
Insa | Gowanus	24
La Mela | Little Italy	21
Lambs Club | West 40s	23
Leopard | West 60s	23
Maison Harlem | Harlem	22
North Square | G'wich Vill.	23
One If by Land | W. Vill.	25
Penrose | East 80s	20
Pio Pio | Jackson Hts.	23
Pisticci | M'side Hts.	25
Red Rooster | Harlem	22
Rossini's | Murray Hill	23
Socarrat Paella Bar | multi.	20
Sylvia's | Harlem	21

NEWCOMERS

NEW Au Cheval | TriBeCa	26
NEW Babs | G'wich Vill.	26
NEW Belcampo | West 30s	–
NEW BLT Prime | East 70s	–
NEW Crown Shy | FiDi	27
NEW Feroce | Chelsea	–
NEW Fly | Bed-Stuy	–
NEW Franks | Carroll Gard.	–
NEW Fulton | South St. Seaport	–
NEW Gertie | W'burg	–
NEW Golden Diner | LES	–
NEW Gran Tivoli | NoLita	–
NEW Haenyeo | Park Slope	27
NEW Hanon | W'burg	–
NEW HaSalon | West 50s	–
NEW Hudson Yards Grill | West 30s	–
NEW Hunky Dory | Crown Hts.	–
NEW Jiang Diner | E. Vill.	–
NEW Kāwi | West 30s	–
NEW Kichin | Bushwick	–
NEW Krok | Carroll Gard.	–
NEW LaLou | Prospect Hts.	–
NEW Lamalo | East 30s	–
NEW Leña | West 30s	–
NEW Leyla | West 70s	–
NEW Lokanta | Astoria	–
NEW Madame Vo BBQ | E. Vill.	–
NEW Madre | Greenpoint	–
NEW Maison Yaki | Prospect Hts.	–
NEW Mar | West 30s	–
NEW Montesacro Pinseria | W'burg	–
NEW Niche | LES	–
NEW Niche Niche | SoHo	–
NEW North Fork | W. Vill.	–
NEW Odo | Flatiron	–
NEW O:n | East 30s	–
NEW Oxalis | Prospect Hts.	26
NEW Pastis | MePa	–
NEW Queensyard | West 30s	–
NEW Red Hook Tavern | Red Hook	–
NEW Reverence | Harlem	–
NEW Rezdôra | Flatiron	–
NEW Savida | Tribeca	–
NEW Shabushabu Mayumon | LES	–
NEW Sushi By M | E. Vill.	27
NEW TabeTomo | E. Vill.	–
NEW TAK Room | West 30s	–
NEW Takeshi | SoHo	–
NEW Taladwat | West 40s	–
NEW Teranga | Harlem	–
NEW Turk's Inn | Bushwick	–
NEW Uluh | E. Vill.	–

NEW Violet | E. Vill. `19`
NEW Wayan | NoLita `27`
NEW Wayla | LES `–`
NEW Wild Ink | LES `–`
NEW Zodiac Room | West 30s `–`

OLD NY VIBE

Arturo's | G'wich Vill. `22`
Bamonte's | W'burg `21`
Barbetta | West 40s `22`
Z Barney Greengrass | `26`
 West 80s
Brennan & Carr | `24`
 Sheepshd Bay
Brooklyn Farmacy | `22`
 Carroll Gard.
Carlyle | East 70s `24`
Chadwick's | Bay Ridge `24`
Corner Bistro | multi. `23`
Delmonico's | multi. `25`
Eisenberg's | Flatiron `21`
Elio's | East 80s `25`
Emilio's Ballato | NoLita `25`
Z 4 Charles | W. Vill. `28`
Fraunces Tavern | FiDi `19`
Gallaghers | West 50s `25`
Z Grand Central Oyster | `23`
 East 40s
Z Grill | East 50s `25`
Joe Junior | Gramercy `18`
John's of 12th Street | `22`
 E. Vill.
Z Katz's | LES `26`
Z Keens | West 30s `27`
La Bonbonniere | W. Vill. `19`
Leopard | West 60s `23`
Lombardi's | NoLita `23`
Molly's | Gramercy `20`
Monkey Bar | East 50s `21`
Neil's | East 60s `16`
Nom Wah | multi. `23`
Old Homestead | Chelsea `24`
One If by Land | W. Vill. `25`
P.J. Clarke's | multi. `19`
Palm | multi. `24`
Pete's Tavern | Gramercy `16`
Z Peter Luger | W'burg `28`
Rao's | East Harlem `23`
Raoul's | SoHo `26`
Rolf's | Gramercy `15`
Russian Tea Room | `19`
 West 50s
Sardi's | West 40s `17`
Z Sparks | East 40s `26`

Z 21 Club | West 50s `23`
Veselka | E. Vill. `22`
Wollensky's Grill | East 40s `26`

OUTDOOR DINING

Acqua | South St. Seaport `24`
Adrienne's Pizzabar | FiDi `23`
Agnanti | Astoria `25`
Alma | Carroll Gard. `22`
Altesi | multi. `23`
Amaranth | East 60s `21`
A.O.C. L'aile | W. Vill. `21`
Z Aquagrill | SoHo `26`
Aretsky's Patroon | `25`
 East 40s
Aurora | multi. `23`
Z Avra | East 40s `26`
Bacchus | Downtown Bklyn. `23`
Z Bar Boulud | West 60s `24`
Bar Pitti | G'wich Vill. `24`
Bar Primi | E. Vill. `22`
Bar Tabac | Cobble Hill `20`
Beaubourg | Battery Pk. `18`
Blenheim | W. Vill. `21`
Blue | Randall Manor `22`
Bodrum | West 80s `20`
Brasserie Ruhlmann | `19`
 West 50s
Bricolage | Park Slope `23`
Brooklyn Crab | Red Hook `19`
Brunetti | W. Vill. `24`
Bryant Park Grill | `20`
 West 40s
Bubby's | multi. `21`
Bustan | West 80s `23`
Buttermilk Channel | `25`
 Carroll Gard.
Cacio e Pepe | E. Vill. `21`
Cafe Clover | W. Vill. `19`
Cafe Fiorello | West 60s `22`
Cafe Gitane | multi. `22`
Cafe Luluc | Cobble Hill `22`
Cafe Mogador | multi. `24`
Cafeteria | Chelsea `18`
Casa Lever | East 50s `23`
Catch NYC | MePa `23`
Cebu Bar & Bistro | `18`
 Bay Ridge
Cecconi's | Dumbo `20`
Charlie Bird | SoHo `25`
City Island Lobster | `21`
 City Island
Claro | Gowanus `26`
Claudette | G'wich Vill. `21`

Community Food & Juice | M'side Hts.	22	Maison Harlem | Harlem	22
Cookshop | Chelsea	22	Maison Premiere | W'burg	26
Crispo | W. Vill.	25	Majorelle | East 60s	27
Da Nico Ristorante | Little Italy	25	Malatesta Trattoria | W. Vill.	25
		Marlow & Sons | W'burg	24
Dante NYC | G'wich Vill.	21	⚡ Meadowsweet | W'burg	27
El Vez | Battery Pk.	20	Milkflower | Astoria	25
Elias Corner | East 80s	25	Morandi | W. Vill.	21
Empire Diner | Chelsea	20	Narcissa | E. Vill.	21
Extra Fancy | W'burg	18	Nargis Cafe | Sheepshd Bay	23
Extra Virgin | W. Vill.	18		
Farm on Adderley | Ditmas Park	22	Nice Matin | West 70s	19
		Nouigatine | West 60s	27
Felice | multi.	20	Old Tbilisi Garden | G'wich Vill.	23
Firenze | East 80s	22		
Flora | East 70s	24	Paola's | East 90s	26
Fornino | multi.	23	⚡ Pasquale Jones | NoLita	25
44 & X | West 40s	22		
Frank | E. Vill.	26	Pig Beach | Gowanus	20
Frankies 457 Spuntino | Carroll Gard.	25	Pier A | FiDi	15
		RH Rooftop Rest. | MePa	20
French Louie | Boerum Hill	23	⚡ Roberta's | Bushwick	27
Gemma | E. Vill.	21	Rose Water | Park Slope	25
Gnocco | E. Vill.	21	Sant Ambroeus | multi.	23
Good Enough to Eat | West 80s	19	Sayra's Wine Bar | Far Rock.	25
Good Fork | Red Hook	25	Seamore's | FiDi	19
Gran Electrica | Dumbo	21	Serra By Birreria | Flatiron	16
Grand Banks | TriBeCa	17	Sorbillo Pizzeria | NoHo	22
Gregory's 26 | Astoria	25	Standard Grill | MePa	22
Harlem Shake | Harlem	20	Sugar Freak | Astoria	23
Hudson Clearwater | W. Vill.	19	Sugarcane | Dumbo	22
Il Bambino | Astoria	24	Sunday In Brooklyn | W'burg	23
Il Buco | NoHo	27		
Il Cortile | Little Italy	24	Tavern on the Green | Central Park	18
Jacob's Pickles | West 80s	23		
Jeffrey Craft Beer | East 60s	23	Telly's Taverna | Astoria	25
		Thai Market | West 100s	23
John Brown | LIC	23	Thalia | West 40s	20
Jones Wood | East 70s	18	ViceVersa | West 70s	23
Joya | Cobble Hill	23	Vinateria | Harlem	25
Jue Lan Club | Flatiron	18	Vinegar Hill House | Dumbo	22
🆕 Krok | Cobble Hill	–	🆕 Wayla | LES	–
Lafayette | NoHo	22	Westville | multi.	21
LaRina | Ft. Greene	25		

PRE-THEATER EATS

NEAR BAM

L&B Spumoni Gardens | Gravesend	25	Bar Tabac | Cobble Hill	20
		Cafe Luluc | Cobble Hill	22
LIC Market | LIC	21	Colonie | Brooklyn Hts.	24
Lido | Harlem	24	French Louie | Boerum Hill	23
Loeb Boathouse | Central Park	19	James | Prospect Hts.	23
		Joya | Cobble Hill	23
Loukoumi Taverna | Astoria	25	Littleneck | Gowanus	20
Maiella | LIC	24		

NEW **Maison Yaki** | Prospect Hts.	—
Miriam | Park Slope	24
Morgan's BBQ | Prospect Hts.	23
Peaches HotHouse | Ft. Greene	25
Rucola | Boerum Hill	25
Sofreh | Prospect Hts.	26
Sweet Chick | Prospect Hts.	23

NEAR BROADWAY

Abigael's | West 30s	19
Aldo Sohm | West 50s	22
Ammos Estiatorio | East 40s	23
Aria | West 50s	21
Z **Aureole** | West 40s	26
Bar Centrale | West 40s	17
Barbetta | West 40s	22
Basso56 | West 50s	23
Z **Becco** | West 40s	22
Benoit New York | West 50s	22
Blue Fin | West 40s	22
Blue Ribbon Sushi Bar & Grill | West 50s	25
Bluebird London | West 50s	16
Bobby Van's | multi.	23
Z **Brasserie 8 1/2** | West 50s	24
Burger Joint | West 50s	24
Butter | West 40s	22
Capital Grille | West 50s	25
Carmine's | West 40s	21
Casellula | West 50s	24
Charlie Palmer | West 40s	23
Chimichurri Grill | West 40s	24
Churrascaria Plataforma | West 40s	22
Da Tommaso | West 50s	21
Danji | West 50s	25
DB Bistro | West 40s	25
Del Frisco's | multi.	25
Don Antonio | West 50s	25
Z **Estiatorio Milos** | West 50s	27
44 & X | West 40s	22
Frankie & Johnnie's | West 40s	22
Friedman's | multi.	21
Gallaghers | West 50s	25

Gazala's Place | West 40s	21
Hakkasan | West 40s	24
Haru Sushi | West 40s	20
Hell's Kitchen | West 50s	19
Hunt & Fish Club | West 40s	21
Ikinari Steak | West 40s	19
Il Gattopardo | West 50s	25
Inakaya | West 40s	20
Z **Indian Accent** | West 50s	27
Ippudo | multi.	25
Z **Jean-Georges** | West 60s	28
Joe Allen | West 40s	20
Kung Fu | multi.	22
Z **La Grenouille** | East 50s	28
La Masseria | multi.	24
Lambs Club | West 40s	23
Lattanzi | West 40s	22
Le Marais | West 40s	22
Leopard | West 60s	23
MáLà Project | West 40s	24
Maria Pia | West 50s	21
The Marshal | West 40s	22
Mastro's | West 50s	25
Meatball Shop | West 50s	20
Mercato | West 30s	24
Natsumi | West 50s	20
Nerai | East 50s	25
Obao | West 40s	20
Ocean Prime | West 50s	25
Oceana | West 40s	25
Osteria al Doge | West 40s	21
Palm | West 50s	24
Patsy's Italian | West 50s	23
PizzArte | West 50s	21
Pure Thai | West 50s	26
Quality Italian | West 50s	24
Quality Meats | West 50s	25
Redeye Grill | West 50s	—
Remi | West 50s	24
Robert | West 50s	23
Room Service | West 40s	19
Rosa Mexicano | multi.	21
Russian Tea Room | West 50s	19
Sardi's | West 40s	17
Sen Sakana | West 40s	21
Souvlaki GR | West 50s	21
STK | West 40s	22
Strip House | West 40s	23
Sushi By Bou | West 40s	26
Sushi of Gari | West 40s	26
Taboon | West 50s	25

Tacuba | West 50s	22
NEW Taladwat | West 40s	–
Tavola | West 30s	21
Thalia | West 40s	20
Tim Ho Wan | West 40s	22
Tony's Di Napoli | West 40s	21
Torishin | West 50s	27
Trattoria Trecolori | West 40s	22
Z 21 Club | West 50s	23
Utsav | West 40s	22
Wu Liang Ye | West 40s	24

NEAR LINCOLN CENTER

Atlantic Grill | West 60s	23
Aviary | West 60s	20
Z Bar Boulud | West 60s	24
Z Boulud Sud | West 60s	26
Blue Ribbon Sushi Bar & Grill | West 50s	25
Cafe Fiorello | West 60s	22
Z Cafe Luxembourg | West 70s	22
Z Jean-Georges | West 60s	28
Leopard | West 60s	23
Z Lincoln | West 60s	25
Lincoln Square Steak | West 70s	19
Molyvos | West 50s	23
P.J. Clarke's | West 60s	19
Patsy's Italian | West 50s	23
Z Porter House | West 50s	27
Smith | West 60s	19
Rosa Mexicano | West 60s	21
Tavern on the Green | Central Park	18

PRIVATE ROOMS

Amali | East 60s	22
Ammos Estiatorio | East 40s	23
Aretsky's Patroon | East 40s	25
Asiate | West 50s	25
Aureole | West 40s	26
Awadh | West 90s	24
Bacchus | Downtown Bklyn.	23
Barbetta | West 40s	22
Bayou | Rosebank	24
Beauty & Essex | LES	22
Z Becco | West 40s	22
Benno | NoMad	26

Benoit | West 50s	22
Black Barn | NoMad	21
Blenheim | W. Vill.	21
BLT Steak | East 50s	25
Z Blue Hill | G'wich Vill.	28
Blue Ribbon Sushi Izakaya | LES	25
Bocelli Ristorante | Old Town	26
BondSt | NoHo	26
Z Brasserie 8 1/2 | West 50s	24
Brioso | New Dorp	24
Brooklyn Crab | Red Hook	19
Buddakan | Chelsea	25
Burger & Barrel | SoHo	21
Burger & Lobster | multi.	19
Burke & Wills | West 70s	20
Butter | West 40s	22
Z Cafe Boulud | East 70s	28
Cafe Mogador | E. Vill.	24
Capital Grille | multi.	25
Casa Apicii | G'wich Vill.	21
Casa Lever | East 50s	23
Cecconi's | Dumbo	20
Celestine | Dumbo	22
Charlie Bird | SoHo	25
China Blue | TriBeCa	25
Christos Steak House | Astoria	26
City Island Lobster | City Island	21
Club A | East 50s	26
Commodore | W'burg	26
Congee Village | multi.	21
Craft | Flatiron	25
Z Daniel | East 60s	29
Darbar | multi.	22
Dee's | Forest Hills	23
Z Del Posto | Chelsea	27
Delmonico's | multi.	25
Dirty French | LES	24
Dutch | SoHo	21
East Pole | East 60s	21
El Parador | Murray Hill	24
Z Eleven Madison Park | Flatiron	28
Emilio's Ballato | NoLita	25
Emily | W. Vill.	26
Esme | Greenpoint	23
Fat Radish | LES	20
Fedora | W. Vill.	23
NEW Feroce | Chelsea	–
Ferris | NoMad	25

Z 21 Club | West 50s _23_
Z Union Square
   Cafe | Gramercy _26_
Utsav | West 40s _22_
Uva | East 70s _22_
Vatan | Murray Hill _26_
Villa Mosconi | G'wich Vill. _25_
Vinegar Hill House |
   Dumbo _22_
Vinum | Stapleton _24_
Writing Room | East 80s _20_

QUIET CONVERSATIONS

Agern | East 40s _26_
Z Ai Fiori | West 30s _26_
Alberto | Forest Hills _24_
Z Amma | East 50s _27_
Armani | East 50s _23_
Asiate | West 50s _25_
Z Atomix | NoMad _29_
Z Bar Boulud | West 60s _24_
Benoit | West 50s _22_
Z Bouley at Home | _29_
   Flatiron
Z Boulud Sud | West 60s _26_
Z Brasserie 8 1/2 | _24_
   West 50s
Z Cafe Boulud | East 70s _28_
Caravaggio | East 70s _26_
Caviar Russe | East 50s _26_
Charlie Palmer | West 40s _23_
Z Daniel | East 60s _29_
Darbar | multi. _22_
El Parador Cafe | _24_
   Murray Hill
Elephant & Castle | W. Vill. _20_
Z Felidia | East 50s _26_
15 East | Union Square _26_
Firenze | East 70s _22_
Gotham Bar and Grill | _—_
   G'wich Vill.
Il Gattopardo | West 50s _25_
Z Jean-Georges | _28_
   West 60s
Jewel Bako | E. Vill. _25_
Jungsik | TriBeCa _29_
Junoon | Flatiron _25_
Kajitsu | Murray Hill _27_
La Mirabelle | West 80s _24_
La Vigna | Forest Hills _22_
Z Le Bernardin | West 50s _29_
Le Colonial | East 50s _23_
Le Gigot | W. Vill. _25_

Le Veau d'Or | East 60s _21_
Leopard | West 60s _23_
Z Lincoln | West 60s _25_
Lusardi | East 70s _24_
Majorelle | East 60s _27_
Mark | East 70s _23_
Z Modern | West 50s _28_
Morso | East 50s _25_
North Square | G'wich Vill. _23_
Novitá | Gramercy _25_
Z Per Se | West 50s _28_
Perry St | W. Vill. _25_
Radiance | East 50s _19_
Z Riverpark | Murray Hill _25_
Rotisserie Georgette | _23_
   East 60s
Z Scalini Fedeli | TriBeCa _27_
Z Simone | East 80s _27_
Table d'Hôte | East 90s _24_
Z Tocqueville | Flatiron _28_
Z Vaucluse | East 60s _25_

ROMANTIC PLACES

Al Di La | Park Slope _27_
Angelina's | Tottenville _23_
Asiate | West 50s _25_
Atera | TriBeCa _28_
Augustine | FiDi _23_
Bohemian | NoHo _26_
Z Carbone | G'wich Vill. _26_
Carlyle | East 70s _24_
Casa Apicii | G'wich Vill. _21_
Caviar Russe | East 50s _26_
Cipriani | multi. _24_
Convivium Osteria | _27_
   Park Slope
Z Daniel | East 60s _29_
Z Don Angie | W. Vill. _28_
Z Eleven Madison Park | _28_
   Flatiron
Erminia | East 80s _26_
Z 4 Charles | W. Vill. _28_
French Louie | Boerum Hill _23_
Giorgio's | Flatiron _23_
Z Gramercy Tavern | _28_
   Flatiron
Z I Sodi | W. Vill. _28_
I Trulli | Murray Hill _22_
Il Buco | NoHo _27_
Il Cantinori | G'wich Vill. _25_
Z Jean-Georges | _28_
   West 60s
Jungsik | TriBeCa _29_

King | Hudson Square	26
Z La Grenouille | East 50s	28
Lambs Club | West 40s	23
Z Le Bernardin | West 50s	29
Z Le Coucou | SoHo	27
Le Gigot | W. Vill.	25
Leopard | West 60s	23
Z Lincoln | West 60s	25
Little Owl | W. Vill.	24
Locanda Vini & Olii |	26
Clinton Hill	
Loeb Boathouse |	19
Central Park	
Lucien | E. Vill.	24
Maiella | LIC	24
Maison Premiere | W'burg	26
Malatesta Trattoria | W. Vill.	25
Mimi | G'wich Vill.	24
Z Momofuku Ko | E. Vill.	28
Monkey Bar | East 50s	21
Mountain Bird | East	28
Harlem	
Nerai | East 50s	25
Z The NoMad | NoMad	26
NEW Odo | Flatiron	–
One If by Land | W. Vill.	25
The Palm Court | West 50s	22
Palma | W. Vill.	23
Z Park Avenue | Flatiron	25
Pepolino | TriBeCa	25
Z Per Se | West 50s	28
Perry St | W. Vill.	25
Racines | TriBeCa	21
Z Riverpark | Murray Hill	25
Robert | West 50s	23
Russian Tea Room |	19
West 50s	
Salinas | Chelsea	27
San Pietro | East 50s	24
Santina | MePa	20
Z Scalini Fedeli | TriBeCa	27
Sea Grill | West 40s	24
Sette Mezzo | East 70s	24
Sfoglia | East 90s	24
Sistina | East 80s	25
St Tropez | W. Vill.	20
Strip House | multi.	23
Supper | E. Vill.	24
Sushi Zo | G'wich Vill.	29
Tavern on the Green |	18
Central Park	
Z Tocqueville | Flatiron	28
Tuscany Grill | Bay Ridge	23
Uva | East 70s	22

Wallsé | W. Vill.	27
ZZ's Clam Bar | G'wich Vill.	25

SMALL PLATES

Z ABC Cocina | Flatiron	25
abcV | Flatiron	26
Aldo Sohm | West 50s	22
Alta | G'wich Vill.	23
Aria | multi.	21
Atla | NoHo	24
Atoboy | NoMad	27
Au Za'atar | E. Vill.	20
Baar Baar | E. Vill.	24
Balaboosta | W. Vill.	24
Balade | E. Vill.	23
Bar Centrale | West 40s	17
Bar Jamon | Gramercy	25
Bar Pleiades | East 70s	22
Barbounia | Flatiron	23
Barn Joo | multi.	21
Beauty & Essex | LES	22
Beso | St. George	24
Beyoglu | East 80s	23
Bodrum | West 80s	20
Boqueria | multi.	23
Buvette | W. Vill.	26
Casa Mono | Gramercy	26
Casellula | West 50s	24
Cotenna | W. Vill.	24
Danji | West 50s	25
El Porrón | East 60s	24
El Quinto Pino | Chelsea	25
Empellon Taqueria | W. Vill.	23
Estela | NoLita	26
Felice | multi.	20
Four Horsemen | W'burg	26
NEW Franks Wine Bar |	–
Carroll Gard.	
Glasserie | Greenpoint	24
NEW Gran Tivoli | NoLita	–
GupShup | Gramercy	23
Hanjan | Flatiron	23
Huertas | E. Vill.	22
NEW Hunky Dory | Crown Hts.	–
Kashkaval Garden |	22
West 50s	
Khe-Yo | TriBeCa	24
NEW Kichin | Bushwick	–
La Vara | Cobble Hill	27
NEW LaLou | Prospect Hts.	–
NEW Leña | West 30s	–
NEW Leyla | West 70s	–
NEW Lokanta | Astoria	–

Ⓩ **Loring Place** | G'wich Vill. — 25
🆕 **Maison Yaki** | — —
  Prospect Hts
🆕 **Mar** | West 30s — —
Milkflower | Astoria — 25
Nonono | NoMad — 25
Noreetuh | E. Vill. — 23
Ruffian | E. Vill. — 25
Sakagura | multi. — 26
Salinas | Chelsea — 27
Sayra's Wine Bar | — 25
  Far Rock.
Socarrat Paella Bar | multi. — 20
St Tropez | multi. — 20
Thursday Kitchen | E. Vill. — 25
Tía Pol | Chelsea — 23
Tørst | Greenpoint — 24
Txikito | Chelsea — 26
Vini e Fritti | NoMad — 24
Vinum | Stapleton — 24
Wildair | LES — 26
Zuma | Murray Hill — 24

SPORTS ON TV

Blue Smoke | multi. — 21
Jeffrey Craft Beer | — 23
  East 60s
John Brown | LIC — 23
Jones Wood | East 70s — 18
Ⓩ **Hometown** | Red Hook — 28
Lee's Tavern | Dongan Hills — 24
Mable's | W'burg — 23
Morgan's | Prospect Hts. — 23
Nick & Stef's | West 30s — 23
Parker & Quinn | West 30s — 20
Parm | West 70s — 19
Pete's Tavern | Gramercy — 16
Ribalta | G'wich Vill. — 22
Ribbon | multi. — 20
Standard Biergarten | — 15
  MePa
Thalia | West 40s — 20
Walker's | TriBeCa — 18
Wollensky's Grill | East 40s — 26

TASTING MENUS

Ⓩ **ABC Cocina** | Flatiron — 25
Agern | East 40s — 26
Aldea | Flatiron — 26
Almayass | Flatiron — 25
Amma | East 50s — 27
Ⓩ **Aquavit** | East 50s — 27
Armani | East 50s — 23

Asiate | West 50s — 25
Atera | TriBeCa — 28
Ⓩ **Atomix** | NoMad — 29
Aureole | West 40s — 26
Aviary | West 60s — 20
Babbo | G'wich Vill. — 26
Babu Ji | G'wich Vill. — 24
Bâtard | TriBeCa — 26
Ⓩ **Blanca** | Bushwick — 29
Ⓩ **Blue Hill** | G'wich Vill. — 28
Bohemian | NoHo — 26
BondSt | NoHo — 26
Bouley at Home | Flatiron — 29
Boulud Sud | West 60s — 26
Chef's Table | NoLita — 28
Cherry Point | Greenpoint — 22
Contra | LES — 25
Ⓩ **Daniel** | East 60s — 29
Danji | West 50s — 25
Dirt Candy | LES — 24
Domodomo | G'wich Vill. — 24
Ⓩ **Eleven Madison Park** | — 28
  Flatiron
15 East | Union Square — 26
Ⓩ **Gramercy Tavern** | — 28
Ⓩ **Hangawi** | Murray Hill — 28
Hwaban | Flatiron — 23
Indian Accent | West 50s — 27
Jewel Bako | E. Vill. — 25
Jungsik | TriBeCa — 29
Junoon | Flatiron — 25
Kanoyama | E. Vill. — 24
Kurumazushi | East 40s — 26
L'Atelier de Joël — 28
  Robuchon | Chelsea
Le Bernardin | West 50s — 29
Lupa | G'wich Vill. — 26
🆕 **Mar** | West 30s — —
Marea | West 50s — 28
Masa | West 50s — 27
Ⓩ **Meadowsweet** | W'burg — 27
Ⓩ **Momofuku Ko** | E. Vill. — 28
Momofuku Nishi | Chelsea — 22
Morimoto | Chelsea — 26
Musket Room | NoLita — 25
Ⓩ **Nobu** | multi. — 27
O Ya | Murray Hill — 27
🆕 **Odo** | Flatiron — —
Okonomi / Yuji Ramen | — 26
  W'burg
One If by Land | W. Vill. — 25
1 or 8 | E. Vill. — 21
🆕 **Oxalis** | Prospect Hts. — 26

VIEWS

WINE BARS

WINNING WINE LISTS

Z Blue Hill | G'wich Vill.	28
Blue Ribbon Sushi | SoHo	25
Blue Ribbon Sushi Bar &	25
Grill | West 50s	
Z Boulud Sud | West 60s	26
Z Cafe Boulud | East 70s	28
Caravaggio | East 70s	26
Carlyle | East 70s	24
Casa Apicii | G'wich Vill.	21
Casa Mono | Gramercy	26
Charlie Bird | SoHo	25
Chez Ma Tante |	26
Greenpoint	
Cipriani | multi.	24
Clam | W. Vill.	23
Clay | Harlem	25
Colonie | Brooklyn Hts.	24
Contra | LES	25
Convivium Osteria |	27
Park Slope	
Corkbuzz | multi.	21
Z Cosme | Flatiron	26
Z Cote | Flatiron	26
Craft | Flatiron	25
Z Daniel | East 60s	29
Z Del Posto | Chelsea	27
Delmonico's | multi.	25
Dirty French | LES	24
Elea | West 80s	24
Z Eleven Madison Park |	28
Flatiron	
Estela | NoLita	26
Z Estiatorio Milos | multi.	27
Z Felidia | East 50s	26
Finch | Clinton Hill	26
Flora Bar | East 70s	24
NEW Fly | Bed-Stuy	—
Four Horsemen | W'burg	26
Frankies 457 Spuntino |	25
Carroll Gard.	
NEW Franks Wine Bar |	—
Carroll Gard.	
Z Frenchette | TriBeCa	24
Gallaghers | West 50s	25
Gotham Bar and Grill |	—
G'wich Vill.	
Gradisca | W. Vill.	23
Z Gramercy Tavern |	28
Flatiron	
Harry's NYC | FiDi	23
Hearth | E. Vill.	25
Il Buco | NoHo	27
Il Buco Alimentari &	25
Vineria | NoHo	
Ilili | NoMad	25
Z Indian Accent | West 50s	27
Z Jean-Georges |	28
West 60s	
Jeffrey's Grocery | W. Vill.	22
Kappo Masa | East 70s	29
King | Hudson Square	26
La Goulue | East 60s	22
Z La Grenouille | East 50s	28
Lafayette | NoHo	22
NEW LaLou | Prospect Hts.	—
Lavagna | E. Vill.	24
Z Le Bernardin | West 50s	29
Z Le Coucou | SoHo	27
Legacy Records | West 30s	23
Z Lincoln | West 60s	25
Little Park | TriBeCa	23
Locanda Verde | TriBeCa	25
Locanda Vini & Olii |	26
Clinton Hill	
Loyal | W. Vill.	21
Z Maialino | Gramercy	26
Z Marea | West 50s	28
The Mark | East 70s	23
The Marshal | West 40s	22
Marta | NoMad	23
Mastro's | West 50s	25
Z Momofuku Ko | E. Vill.	28
Momofuku Nishi | Chelsea	22
Morton's | multi.	24
Nerai | East 50s	25
Nice Matin | West 70s	19
NEW Niche Niche | SoHo	—
Z The NoMad | NoMad	26
Noreetuh | E. Vill.	23
Novitá | Gramercy	25
Nur | Flatiron	24
O Ya | Murray Hill	27
Ocean Prime | West 50s	25
Oceana | West 40s	25
1 or 8 | W'burg	21
Ops | Bushwick	28
Otway | Clinton Hill	24
Palm | multi.	24
Z Park Avenue | Flatiron	25
Z Pasquale Jones | NoLita	25
Z Per Se | West 50s	28
Z Porter House | West 50s	27
Prune | E. Vill.	25
Pylos | E. Vill.	26
Quality Meats | West 50s	25
Racines | TriBeCa	21
Roberto's | Arthur Ave.	25
Rotisserie Georgette |	23
East 60s	

Ruffian	E. Vill.	25	**ᴺᴱᵂ** TAK Room	West 30s	–
Salinas	Chelsea	27	Tía Pol	Chelsea	23
San Pietro	East 50s	24	**Z** Tocqueville	Flatiron	28
Santina	MePa	20	Tribeca Grill	TriBeCa	23
Sayra's	Far Rock.	25	**Z** 21 Club	West 50s	23
Scarpetta	NoMad	23	**Z** Union Square Cafe	Gramercy	26
Shalom Japan	W'burg	25		
Z The Simone	East 80s	27	Vini e Fritti	NoMad	24
Sojourn	East 70s	19	Waverly Inn	W. Vill.	21
Z Sparks	East 40s	26	Wildair	LES	26

Notes